The College
and the Student

The College
and the Student

AN ASSESSMENT OF RELATIONSHIPS AND RESPONSIBILITIES

IN UNDERGRADUATE EDUCATION

BY ADMINISTRATORS, FACULTY MEMBERS, AND PUBLIC OFFICIALS

EDITORS *Lawrence E. Dennis & Joseph F. Kauffman*

American Council on Education · Washington, D.C.

Contributing Authors

RALPH F. BERDIE, Professor of Psychology, and Director, Student Counseling Bureau, University of Minnesota

GRAHAM B. BLAINE, JR., M.D., Chief, Psychiatric Service, University Health Services, Harvard University

KINGMAN BREWSTER, JR., President, Yale University

LAURENCE V. BRITT, S.J., President, University of Detroit

FREDERICK H. BURKHARDT, President, American Council of Learned Societies

CLARK BYSE, Professor of Law, Law School of Harvard University

JOSEPH P. COSAND, President, Junior College District of St. Louis

JOHN L. COWAN, Technical Director, Commission VIII, National Association of Student Personnel Administrators

LAWRENCE E. DENNIS, Education Program Adviser (Venezuela), Ford Foundation

JAMES P. DIXON, President, Antioch College

EDWARD D. EDDY, JR., President, Chatham College

ALAN FRANK, M.D., Head, Psychiatric Division, Student Health Service, University of Colorado

CHARLES FRANKEL, Assistant Secretary of State for Educational and Cultural Affairs

BUELL G. GALLAGHER, President, City College of the City University of New York

HARRY D. GIDEONSE, President, Brooklyn College of the City University of New York

ROSE K. GOLDSEN, Associate Professor of Sociology, Cornell University

SISTER JACQUELINE GRENNAN, President, Webster College

FREDERICK L. GWYNN, Chairman, Department of English, Trinity College

NICHOLAS HOBBS, Chairman, Division of Human Development, George Peabody College for Teachers

v

JOSEPH KATZ, Research Coordinator, Institute for the Study of Human Problems, and Research Director, Student Development Study, Stanford University

NICHOLAS deB. KATZENBACH, Attorney General of the United States

JOSEPH F. KAUFFMAN, Dean of Student Affairs, University of Wisconsin, Madison

WILLIAM L. KOLB, Dean of the College, Beloit College

MELVIN KRANZBERG, Professor of History, Case Institute of Technology

MAX LERNER, Professor of American Civilization, Brandeis University

GREG LIPSCOMB, Student, University of Texas

JOSEPH D. McCLATCHY, Student, Georgetown University

EDMUND McILHENNY, Legal Counsel, Tulane University

WILBERT J. McKEACHIE, Chairman, Department of Psychology, University of Michigan

DAVID MALLERY, Consultant, College Student Personnel Institute

LEWIS B. MAYHEW, Professor of Education, Stanford University

PHILLIP MONYPENNY, Professor, Department of Political Science, University of Illinois

DONALD C. MUNDINGER, Dean, College of Arts and Sciences, Valparaiso University

THEODORE M. NEWCOMB, Professor of Social Psychology, University of Michigan

CHARLES E. ODEGAARD, President, University of Washington

C. ROBERT PACE, Professor of Higher Education, University of California, Los Angeles

FREDERICK RUDOLPH, Professor of History, Williams College

DENNIS SHAUL, Student, Law School of Harvard University

PHILIP SHERBURNE, National Affairs Vice-President, U.S. National Student Association

Foreword

THE GENERATION OF POSTWAR AMERICANS reaching adulthood in the mid-sixties confronted higher education anew with a moment of truth in its perception of undergraduate students. In a world torn by ideological and military conflict, they have joined the Peace Corps; in a society of freedom and plenty, they have enlisted in the war against poverty and injustice; in an academic community pulled in many directions, they have championed the cause of teaching.

Who are these young men and women? Why did they go to college? What do they believe? Where are they heading? How can higher education serve their needs and help them toward worthwhile goals? To assist colleges and universities in their search for answers to such questions, the Board of Directors of the Council, following a 1963 study by the A.C.E. Commission on Academic Affairs, decided early in 1964 to devote the Council's 1965 Annual Meeting to the theme "The Student in Higher Education."

This volume of essays is an outgrowth of that meeting. Its publication not only marks the culmination of one important phase of the activities of the Commission on Academic Affairs, but also signifies the continuing concern of the Council and its constituency for the welfare of college students and the improvement of their education.

In behalf of the Council, I should like to thank the members and staff of the Commission on Academic Affairs for their assistance in planning the 1965 Annual Meeting, and in particular the editors of *The College and the Student*, Lawrence E. Dennis and Joseph F. Kauffman, who formerly served, respectively, as director and staff associate of the commission. Also, Olive Mills and Laura Kent, of the Council staff, rendered valuable assistance in making possible the prompt publication of this volume.

LOGAN WILSON, *President*
American Council on Education

November 1965

Preface

MOST OF THE PAPERS included in this volume were first prepared for the Annual Meeting of the American Council on Education in Washington, on October 6–8, 1965, but the presentation here is not simply a set of proceedings. Six of the papers (those by Max Lerner, Frederick Rudolph, C. Robert Pace, Theodore M. Newcomb, Lewis B. Mayhew, and Charles Frankel) were published prior to the conference in a booklet entitled *The Student in Higher Education* and circulated to members of the Council as background material for the discussions to follow.

The study reported by E. G. Williamson and John L. Cowan first appeared in the *Educational Record*, Fall 1965, under the title "The Role of the President in the Desirable Enactment of Academic Freedom for Students." A background report for the A.C.E. Commission on Academic Affairs, "Student Personnel Services in Higher Education," prepared in 1963 and subsequently published in two issues of the *Educational Record* (Summer and Fall 1964), forms the basis for the essay on "The Student in Higher Education."

The two commentaries by Logan Wilson, "Is the Student Becoming the 'Forgotten Man' in Higher Education?" and "Freedom and Responsibility in Higher Education," are adaptations of addresses delivered, respectively, at Franklin and Marshall College (October 1964) and the University of Tennessee (June 1965). "The Time of the Student—Shall We Overcome?" by Joseph F. Kauffman is based on an address to the American Association of Collegiate Registrars and Admissions Officers (April 1965), later published in *College and University* (Summer 1965).

Although some of the papers presented at the Council's 1965 Annual Meeting were not entirely relevant to the reorganized treatment given the conference theme in this volume, thirty-four of them proved to be highly appropriate and have been edited for inclusion here. The authors are public officials, college or university students, faculty members, and administrators, all of whom have made recognized contributions to higher education.

xi

Personally and for the American Council on Education, we should like to express our appreciation to all of the authors whose essays appear in this book. We should also like to thank the members of the Commission on Academic Affairs and the A.C.E. Board of Directors and executive staff for their assistance in planning the conference from which *The College and the Student* took shape.

LAWRENCE E. DENNIS
JOSEPH F. KAUFFMAN

November 1965

Contents

xiv

PART 5   STRESS IN THE COLLEGE EXPERIENCE

PART 6   HIGHER EDUCATION AND THE MORAL
          REVOLUTION

On Discovering College Students

LAWRENCE E. DENNIS

To BE A COLLEGE STUDENT THESE DAYS is, almost by definition, to be one who has learned how to stay ahead of the game. The members of the new college generation, after all, have been discussing, dreaming about, and living with the idea of going to college for nearly as long as they can remember.

As far back as junior high school—perhaps earlier—today's college student found himself, whether by choice or chance, heading down the "academic track" at an accelerating pace with the risk of being derailed or rerouted at every turn. In addition to enduring the normal hazards of adolescence, he has been exposed in his unprecedented pre-college run to tremendous family pressures, a multiplicity of tests, enriched curricula, early entrance programs, science and mathematics courses that were college-level less than a decade ago, guidance counselors playing the odds on higher education admissions practices, and a social life increasingly patterned in the college mode. All this against the backdrop of a booming economy that puts its highest employment premium not always on how good you are at what you want to do, but often on how far you have progressed in the pursuit of higher learning.

It has been the new generation's lot to grow up in the era when Big Business, Big Labor, and Big Government have been joined by Big Education. Students didn't invent the college game, but they have had to play it long and hard—for the simple reason that, as yet, the adults who run things have not devised any socially acceptable options to college-going. One result of the race for higher education, therefore, is that most students have mastered the rules (though they don't always agree with them), learned to cope with the system (though a few of them are in active rebellion against it), and set themselves to negotiating all of the steep places (from College Boards through senior finals) right to the end of the line.

Another outcome is that many of today's students firmly believe they know as much about the educational process as those who teach in the colleges and those who administer them. This belief makes

1

some students sad, others restive, and still others confused. College isn't turning out to be the exciting summit they had hoped for, or the Camelot they had been told it would be by parents and teachers whose collegiate memories are rooted in an era long since ended. Students are finding that going to college is not always as it is glowingly depicted by some catalogues; nor do the realities of college, from the student viewpoint, correspond to the realities of higher education as seen by many faculty members and administrators.

How students view college differs, of course, from campus to campus. One man's Princeton is another man's Tech, and there is no *single* student "culture" in the United States any more than there are duplicates of Antioch scattered across the higher education landscape. As we begin to comprehend the meaning of Big Education in the Great Society, however, it may be safe to generalize at least to this extent about today's college students: they probably are more sophisticated about colleges than colleges are about them. Furthermore, they are going to keep on learning the values and folklore of education for as long as it counts, which means for all of their lives.

To catch up with and pace the new college generation will be no easy task for educators. For one thing, they are tired and overextended, their time and energies having been consumed in recent years by the problems connected with planning curricula, building facilities, climbing professional ladders, and raising funds. For another thing, they are, for the most part, conservative, ofttimes bland, in their outlook and attitudes; boat-rocking is anathema to them and if change must come, they feel, it comes best gradually (by means of the time-honored subcommittee, committee, and academic senate route). And, third, action—especially political and social action—has traditionally not been the academician's or educational administrator's dish; though he may be dedicated to the exploration and discussion of controversial issues in his classroom, he tends to shy away from the organizing and campaigning usually required to bring such issues into the public domain, where they can be fought out and resolved.

In contrast, the new college generation has energy to burn, years of time, a grim determination born of surmounting the precollege roadblocks, a penchant for activism, organizational skills perfected by summers in the Civil Rights Movement or on overseas service assignments, a deep sense of social justice, a healthy antipathy toward any Establishment, and—perhaps most important of all—an ability to adjust to change, whether it be technological, economic, political, or social.

But despite the possible handicaps of their age, outlook, and temperament, and the acknowledged fact that the hour for prolonged research and analysis comes dangerously late, educators know a few things about college students, as the essays in this volume will testify. Many educators are prepared to join college students in shaping the dialogue, which must now emerge—and swiftly—if higher education is to meet student needs in a truly constructive fashion.

As the college discovers its new student generation, and as the dialogue develops, the wise administrator and discerning faculty member will do well to keep in mind a few background facts, and to guard against a common habit of thought which could lead to a misreading of what makes college students tick.

First, as to background: What do we know about the world of the new generation?

We know a great deal, actually. (In higher education, the trick is to apply what general information we have to specific programs of study that mean something to students.) We know, for example, that the majority of today's college students grew up in an urban environment, and that even more of them will live out their lives in or near cities. Having lived in the shadow of nuclear weapons through childhood and adolescence, they have reached young adulthood at a time when the cold war has entered a new phase, with the Communist bloc torn by ideological strife and the Western alliance undergoing far-reaching changes.

We know, too, that the "revolution of rising expectations" that has held developing nations in its grip since World War II has suddenly, in the time of the student, fastened itself on the "forgotten fifth" of our own population who seek to climb above poverty, hunger, illiteracy, disease, and despair. Both overseas and at home, in the Peace Corps, the Civil Rights Movement, and the War on Poverty, the new generation has identified with that revolution, joined it, shaped it— and has every intention of staying with it all the way.

We also know that television has been an integral part of students' lives since early childhood, and although the curriculum in most colleges blithely ignores the *study* of mass media, the new generation has begun to adopt the movies as an art form and to pioneer in the production of experimental films.

We know that John F. Kennedy became a hero and a legend to college students. Always at his best on campuses, he had a special affinity for youth, and they, despite the two decades that separated their lives from his, seemed to look intuitively to him as their advocate. For him, the forties and fifties (which for the new generation had been the formative, uneven, frustrating years of Suburbia, Sputnik, and the Bomb) were the inquisitive, maturing years of political apprenticeship, intellectual probing, and personal ordeal—the turbulent postwar world of tension, change, and opportunity. His dramatic arrival at the center of the national political stage coincided with the coming-of-age of a generation of young men and women longing to strike out on their own, yearning for something to do above and beyond themselves. His murder moved them deeply; today his torch has become theirs to hold high in cause after cause.

The new college generation has its eyes and heart set, literally, on the moon. In science and mathematics most of them have had the benefit of a sound preparatory education. (Their younger brothers and sisters back home talk of space travel as though it were already commonplace.) Yet social science and humanities programs in the colleges still have not really come to terms with the meaning of science and technology for our time.

There is considerable speculation among pundits and scholars that the new generation may be concerned more with ends than with means, but we do not know yet that this is so. Certainly in their attitudes toward religion, morals, values—what may, for want of a better term, be called the "spiritual" side of life—college students today appear to be in a constant state of search, in quest of something sure, something to count on. And yet, one of their favorite phrases is "tough-minded" (JFK again?)—as though if one should disclose a softness of heart, he would somehow be left behind. Is it, once more, a task for the humanities?

So it goes. Educators can, if they try, compile a fairly lengthy list of what they know, or *think* they know about the new college generation. And, with the attention students are now getting, the list will surely grow. Within a relatively short period, in fact, the college student bids fair to become the most researched, analyzed, probed, charted, dissected, scrutinized, and catalogued species of our time, not even excluding the astronauts.

But such studies will not lead to a better understanding of college students if faculty members and administrators yield to the temptation (common in many "adult" circles these days) to dismiss student demonstrations, student interest in curricular reform, and student concern for the improvement of the state of society in general (and of higher education in particular) merely as a phenomenon peculiar to restive youth. "Just wait until they mature a little," so the line goes, "and they'll begin to see things differently. After all, they're still young. Give them time to grow up and they'll settle down."

No line of reasoning could be more fatal to the viability of higher education. Young people today are not "what they used to be" for the simple reason that theirs is a world of change, and they have learned to confront change far better than have adults. They may not have had the Great Depression and World War II to cut their eyeteeth on, but they have had Ghana, Bolivia, Selma, Pakistan, Mississippi, South Chicago, and Berkeley, to mention but a few of the testing grounds they themselves have chosen. Youthfulness is a relative quality: Two years from now over half the country's population will be under twenty-five years of age; will everyone else then be "old"? Charging the current student activism off to immaturity fights the problem: How can higher education be made more relevant to the lives and times of those it is designed to instruct?

Who is more of a stranger to the true meaning and purpose of college education in contemporary life—the student or the academician? Whose is the real world? Is not the basic question facing colleges and universities today, in essence, not what educators should do about students, but what they should do about themselves?

In short, as we contemplate "The College and the Student," we would do well to remember that it is *our* wisdom, *our* values, and *our* institutions that are on trial. Happily, this collection of essays by faculty members, administrators, students, and public officials gives heartening promise that the discovery of college students will be a rewarding experience for all.

PART 1 **Higher Education in Perspective**

The
Revolutionary
Frame
of Our
Time

MAX LERNER

I DON'T KNOW HOW the historians of the future will designate our era, but certainly the term will have to do with the shaking of the very foundations of our lives. When I speak of the revolutionary frame of our time, I have in mind two crucial meanings of the term *revolution*. First, as a *transfer of power*, usually from one class to another, as a result of direct action. In this sense the nationalist revolutions of Africa and Asia, which are in essence identity revolutions—efforts to discover and establish the identity of long-repressed peoples and cultures—make ours a revolutionary age. In this sense also the efforts (whether starting from Peking, Moscow, or Havana) to organize the overthrow of regimes which had already achieved their national identity by anticolonial revolts under non-Communist auspices, add to the revolutionary turmoil of our time.

In a second sense "revolution" means a *drastic, highly accelerated pace of change*—so accelerated as to effect a breakthrough representing a new level from which further cumulative changes go on. In that sense our American civilization is a deeply revolutionary one, despite the curious recoil of many Americans from this fact, and their fear of the term and idea of revolution. Our task is to locate these silent, often unnoted, revolutionary changes, to channel them, to tame them to humanist uses. Something of the same kind of revolution is taking place, at a later remove, throughout Western Europe and, at a still later remove, in Eastern Europe as well. It is in the frame of this kind of revolution, both in America and in the world outside, that we must carry out not only the planned and channeled social change I speak of, but also whatever insurrections of the mind and spirit we can manage within ourselves.

A university is the convergence point of the major revolutionary forces of our time. True, it is a subculture within itself, but a special

8

kind of subculture—the kind that must not simply mirror the changes in the civilization, but learn how to master them.

Emergence and Transcendence: Hopes for the Future

The idea of *emergence* I take to be one of the four or five key ideas to be reckoned with in our time. We speak of the emergent African and the emergent Asian societies: there is also the emergent American society.

The American civilization into which we are now moving—computer-geared, information-directed, leisure-oriented—promises to be an authentic revolutionary civilization. But we must make certain that it will not be simply a brave new world squeezed dry of human values, a world in which automation results in automated man.

I have a dream, and I dare to dream it when writing about the American college and its students. It is a dream of possibility, of a possible emergent man in the American civilization. He will be a revolutionary in the sense that he will meet the changes of his time with an unsurprised alertness. He will not recoil from the machine, from technology, from power, from change, from the reality principle, in a world which is neither a graceful nor a gracious world, but at the same time, along with that realism, he will not allow himself to become dehumanized. He will put out antennae of sensibility to pick up the new tremors that make themselves felt in the life of the mind and spirit. He will not succumb to the fanaticism of the true believer in an age of ideology; yet he will know the values he is committed to. He will be a unique individual in a society of diversity, but he will also know that man can become a monster unless he forges the nexus that ties him by a sure human connection with his fellow man.

I have given this as a dream of possibility, if not in the calculable future then in the distant future. One has a right to ask whether this type of personality structure is actually emerging in America today. The answer must be tentative in the extreme: it has some chances of emerging, and there are some signs, however slight and fragile, that it is emerging. Beyond that it would be foolhardy to go. What we do know is that the institutions of our society viewed as a going concern—the mélange of ways of doing things, ways of looking at things and comprehending things—do much to raise certain expectations about the college student and elicit certain responses from him. His behavior is not wholly conditioned by the institutions within which he is encased; if he has strength of mind and character and a bent for originality, he has an area of freedom within which he can shape his personality. Yet for most students, at most colleges, most of the time, the thrust of the institutional impact is more powerful than the ability to withstand it. A good deal of the future of American civilization is being hammered out at this point of convergence, where the culture-in-the-personality meets and shapes and is shaped by the personality-in-the-culture.

I have spoken of the idea of emergence. I must add the idea of transcendence. The difficult task that the creative student faces is to hold the institutions at arm's length without being hostile to them; at once to assimilate whatever in them is relevant to him, reject what is irrelevant, and transcend both. The students I am thinking of are, of course, not the run-of-the-mill students whom the society *trains* in order to transmit its traditions, but the carriers of promise whom we help *educate*—in the sense of eliciting their potentials for in-novating thought and art. I see the educational process as a tri-angular relationship between teacher, student, and society (including the intellectual and cultural tradition) in which each is transcended. The task of the carriers of promise is the task of transcendence: always to transmute the traditions within which they work, to go beyond them, to transform the society, to move it to the utmost limits of inner vision of which it is capable; finally, to transcend themselves, not an easy task in a world which is neither a graceful nor a gracious world.

The Nation-State in a World of Power Surplus

They must, moreover, carry on this task in a world frame so deeply in revolution that the expectations and claims of earlier generations of students have had to be drastically changed. The most obvious of these changes derives from the revolution of weapons technology which is part of the larger technological revolution of our time. I called a recent book of mine *The Age of Overkill* because the weapons now at the command of the Great Powers carry with them the overkill factor—the capacity to overdestroy their target many times. The Russians and we today, perhaps the French and the Chinese tomorrow, perhaps others the day after tomorrow, have weapons enough to overdestroy not only each other but also humanity itself. That we know, but we must explore some of the implications of what we know. If we reread Machiavelli, both *The Prince* and the *Discourses*, we will find that he gave us a grammar of power, that he traced out a system of classical politics in an era of nation-states.

Just as in classical economics the crucial concept was that of scarcity of wealth, so in the system of classical politics the crucial concept was that of scarcity of power. Each nation, each chief-of-state, could never get power enough. They had to pile power on power, and make alliances with others, until finally there came war as the test and showdown of power.

This is no longer possible. What these overkill weapons have done has been to transform a world of power scarcity into what is—at least for the nuclear Powers—a world of power surplus. They now have in their overkill weapons more power at their command than they can use, more than they dare use. Power has in that sense become powerless, and only the more limited forms of power are usable. The wars in the calculable future, like the war in Viet Nam, are likely to be wars not with nuclear weapons but with conventional weapons. Yet always there is the shadow of the possible use of nuclear weapons, for while their use is unthinkable, it is not impossible. For the American university student the not impossible use of these unthinkable weapons has darkened the future that he might otherwise claim. Hence we need to rethink the meaning of the nation-state and of absolute national sovereignty. Here too transcendence will be required.

I recall a conversation I had shortly before his death with the great Republican leader Wendell Willkie. We were talking about what these weapons meant and had done, and he said that "national sovereignty is no longer something to be hoarded, it is something to be spent." What I understood him to mean was that if we try to hoard sovereignty, if we cry, "Get the United States out of the United Nations, and the United Nations out of the United States," if we ask what concern it is of ours that there are peoples in the world who (in Sumner's unforgettable phrase) at the banquet of life have appetites without dinners while we have dinners without appetites, if we ask why we should take the trouble to link ourselves in a functional community with the peoples of Western Europe and with our neighbors to the south of us in Latin America, if we ask how what happens in Africa and Asia is any concern of ours, then we will find ourselves hugging our absolute sovereignty to our breasts while we all sit on a mound of radiated ashes. But if we are willing to surrender some of our absolute sovereignty and put it into a common decision-making pool with (let us say) our allies in Western Europe and Latin America and Asia and ultimately with others, then a new world of pooled sovereignty will become possible, and the student will feel that we can transcend the limits of the nation-state.

Along with the erosion of sovereignty there has been a considerable erosion of ideology in our contemporary world. In a very large part of the Communist world (although not yet in China or among the Viet Cong) there is a new skepticism of the ideology with which the Communists started. Within this frame of ideological erosion a polycentric revolution has taken place within the Communist camp, taking the form of a split between the Russians and the Chinese in their struggle for the mastery of world communism.

This gives us, luckily, a chance to practice the arts not so much of military as of political warfare, not so much of the arms race (important as that is for the present) but of the intelligence race. Given the revolution of polycentrism in the form of the split between the Russians and the Chinese, we may have a chance in the calculable future to develop something like a Concert of Powers, not an alliance but a meeting of minds between ourselves and the Great Powers of Western Europe, the Soviet Union, Japan, China itself if it will come into such a concert. This meeting of minds would be directed toward preventing that further diffusion of nuclear weapons which has become the great danger of our time. It could serve as a first step, with the second being perhaps a collective world authority, including a world policing force which would function under some form of world law. Until we have done that we will not have managed to assure ourselves in any tolerable way of a lasting peace.

I spoke of a world policing force, not of a world state nor of a homogenized world society. I call myself a cultural nationalist who cares deeply about American civilization, its achievements, its future creativeness. I say I do not want to see a homogenized world society, which blots out the cultural differences between nations any more than I want to see a homogenized American society that blots out the diversities of individuals and groups. The reason I care so deeply about a Concert of Powers which may lead to a world policing force, and the ultimate erosion of suicidal wars, is that I want America to remove the overkill shadow which hangs over our young people and their vision of the future.

Sometimes my students ask me whether I am an optimist or a pessimist about the future. I answer that in our collective affairs it is not in our stars but in ourselves that we shape our future, within our collective intelligence and our collective will. I say I am neither an optimist nor a pessimist: I am a *possibilist*. I believe that it will be possible to prevent both nuclear catastrophe and totalitarian tyranny—but that neither is guaranteed. When I write and teach history, I see not only the decisions that were made in the past and the consequences that followed, but also the decisions that were *not* made—in Robert Frost's phrase "the roads not taken," and what might have happened if they had been taken. As I look toward the future, I see the future as possibility, depending upon the decisions which the young people now in our universities make when they come to power as the commanding and creative elites.

We strike here one of the most difficult snags of our time: how to equate the need for a collective national intelligence and national will with the need for transcending the absolute sovereignty of the nation-state. At present, in the American frame, it takes the form of a conflict between the decision makers in Washington, who emphasize the need for decisive American action wherever non-Communist regimes are threatened, and a number of student leaders and organizations who seem to have lost their belief in the purposes and ethos of the nation. This is one of the acute forms which the generational struggle is taking at this moment of history. The whole intellectual community will have to find some solution for it. I have said that we must transcend the idea of absolute national sovereignty. But this does not mean that we can forget about the national will-to-survive and the collective will-to-create. If we neglect them, we shall do so at our peril. History is strewn with the wrecks of civilizations whose young people—following the lead of their elders—suffered a failure of nerve and a failure of will. In fact, if we are ever to transcend absolute national sovereignty and create a pool of shared sovereignty in order to set the conditions for world peace, we can do so only by putting the whole national will behind the necessary decisions.

The Revolution of Access

It will then be possible for our young people to claim the future. But we must first understand certain things about that future. It will not belong to democratic capitalism alone, nor to communism alone, to socialism alone, or any of the other varieties of social structure. The future belongs to various forms of welfarism. "In my Father's house are many mansions"—provided none of them is aggressive. But we must be ready to share the fruits of our technology inside our own society as equitably as possible, and with other societies as well.

It is within this frame that President Johnson has been talking of
the "Great Society," and has mapped out in a succession of state
messages an attack on poverty and the slums, a plan for urban re-
building, for increased educational opportunity, for meeting the tasks
of making medical skills available to more people. There are some
educators who believe that this is a controversial realm from which
they must steer clear. There are others who feel it is utopian. Some
of my own students have said to me that there have always been
poverty, slums, inequality and always will be. Life is tragic, they
say, but that is how it is. My answer is that, whatever they think,
they ought not to demean the tragic. Tragedy is part of the very
constitution of the universe. No man, no nation, is immune to it.
But there is a difference between the tragic and the pathetic. The
tragic is part of the constitution of the universe; the pathetic is not.
The pathetic is man-made, and because it is man-made it can be
man-resolved. Poverty is not tragic, it is pathetic; the slums are not
tragic, they are pathetic. Alcoholism, addiction, the breakdown of
the neighborhood and the family—these are not tragic, they are
pathetic. Racial discrimination, racial hatred on both sides, religious
bigotry—these are not tragic but pathetic. We will never eliminate
the tragic from life. But we can make sure at least of diminishing
the pathetic, if not eliminating it entirely.

Men are not equal, of course. I recall an evening I had with some
journalists and professors in Warsaw. The chairman of the evening
said, "Mr. Lerner, you have written a big book on American civilization. We haven't read it. But could you sum up in a single word
what is the essence of American civilization?" I thought very rapidly:
What is America? Is it freedom? Equality? Democracy? Tolerance?
Decency? Suddenly I heard myself say, "Access." The chairman
laughed. "We have heard of American success," he said, "but we
hadn't heard of American access." I said, "We have a Declaration of
Independence which says that all men are born free and equal. I
hope we are born free and will remain free. But we are not born
equal. We are born very unequal, with unequal abilities and potentials. Every employer knows it, every army commander, teacher,
parent. But we also have the notion that there ought to be equal
access to equal opportunities, so that every one of these unequally
born youngsters gets a chance to develop his unequal abilities to
the full."

To the idea of *emergence* and the idea of *transcendence*, with
which I started this paper, I add now the idea of *access*. One may
see the whole current struggle over civil rights as part of the revolu-

tion of access. It has not only its objective phases, in the struggle for equal legal rights in the Southern states, and the even more important struggle for equal *de facto* rights in the rest of the nation: it has also its subjective phases, in the sense of the image that whites and Negroes have of each other and of themselves. Thus in our elementary curricula we have not only the problem of remedial reading but the problem also of a remedial self-image for the children of groups that have lived in a context of social inferiority for generations. This does not mean giving them a crutch to lean on. It means building a floor below which their position in the society cannot fall. The rest will be up to them as individuals. A welfare society will not solve the problems of the individual life. It will only attempt to make sure that no person has to face those problems under a crippling social disadvantage, that the doors of opportunity, which are open to some, are not slammed shut in the face of others. Democracy does not mean equal abilities: it means only that each shall have an equal chance at a chance. A welfare society will not remove the tragic from life. It will mean only that each young American will not have to grapple hopelessly with the pathetic, and thus will have a chance to shape his abilities and personality so that he will be able to confront the inevitable tragedies of life.

Work, Play, and Cohesiveness in Our Civilization

Beyond welfarism there looms a spacious society which has to do not so much with achieving a consensus among Americans as with achieving a nexus between Americans. It has to do with the creativeness with which we work and play and live in our civilization.

It will be hard to achieve, because America is caught in an uprooting revolution which hobbles the effort to develop the whole person within a creative culture. We have become very aware of this recently because of the pervasive violence of our time, the breaking of internalized controls and standards, because of a certain anomie that has set in among portions of our community. We have become uprooted from the soil, from the farm, from the small town, from the neighborhood, from the city core, from our traditions, from the cohesive family. This is part of the price we have had to pay for the freedoms of a society of relatively free choices, and for the drastically accelerated changes in it.

I spoke, earlier in this paper, of the pressures from the culture on the individual student. I select from the large mass of these pressures three assaults on the identity of the individual. One comes from

the big media. I am not one of those who make the big media
responsible for every ill in our society. But I am concerned about the
obsession of the media with the big audience. In the case of TV,
for example, it is the big audience that is sold to a sponsor. What
counts is not quality but number. Every head is counted once, no
matter what's inside it. This is the principle of replaceable parts.
Which means that it is the principle of naked mechanism. "Be a
subject, not an object," said Kant. "Treat other human beings as
subjects, not as objects." But given the principle of replaceable
parts, we treat them as objects, not as subjects. This may be related
to the neutral technician of our time, who says in effect, "Give me
a job and I will do it, and I won't care about the *cui bono*." Technology carries no ethos with it. The ethos must be shaped, within
the culture, by the university.

The second assault is the assault from big organizations. The over-
organized is beginning to replace the organic. This is almost as true
of big universities as of big government, big corporations, big trade
unions, big churches, big law firms, big hospitals, and all the rest.
The university student knows he is going to have to live with big
organizations and work in them. But to live *with* them and to work
in them does not mean to live *by* them and their values. We have
a chance to insist that organization will not carry with it conformity,
that bureaucracy will not carry with it routineering. We have a
chance to care deeply about the individual as part of the small group,
to cultivate the small organic group as a life-core, even while we
are part of the big organization.

Finally there is the assault from the disintegrated, uprooted family.
A vacuum of authority has arisen in the family, and with it has
come a vacuum of identity and belief in the student. The problem
is how, in an uprooted society, one shapes adequately a sense of
selfhood. The pervasive violence of our time comes largely from
two groups. One is the rebels with a cause, who are willing to
challenge local ordinances, man-made laws, grapple with police.
The other kind of violence is that of rebels without a cause (to use
Lindner's old phrase)—the current "senseless" violence on the streets,
buses, and subways and in the tenements and dark alleys of the big
urban sprawls. While the individual acts of violence arise from individual situations, there is an over-all smoldering sense of grievance
against the society that informs most of them. The root of it does
not lie alone in poverty and the slums, since the conditions of life—
even in the depressed urban areas—are not deteriorating but improving. It lies rather in the residual gap between the actual and

potential conditions of life, a gap widened by the rising expectations of the young people in the minority groups and the depressed areas. It is part of the task of university study and teaching, as well as of government action, to keep the gap from becoming intolerable, and to make American civilization a credible civilization.

What is true in the ghettos of American Negroes and other minorities is, in another sense, true of the middle-class strata from which the American university students largely come. The American society subjects them to intense pressures of expectation. It is a competing society, that asks them constantly to test their skills, capacities, and resources against others, for prizes at once substantive and symbolic. It is an achieving society, that everywhere—in work, productivity, rewards, status—pushes its young people toward goals of achievement and judges its mature people by a hierarchy of achievement. It is a cornucopia society, that empties before them the horn of abundance as a glittering prize to strive for, and tells them that there is nothing in the whole array of accomplishment that the young American does not have within his reach, from bestsellerdom to the Pulitzer awards, from National Science scholarships to a Nobel laureate, from West Point selection to General of the Army, from off-Broadway success to Hollywood stardom, from corporation president to President of the United States. But at the same time it is a society in which those outside the success pyramid, the achievement hierarchy, and the power structure can get little social acceptance (if they are failures in conventional terms) for what they may in themselves *be*, as contrasted with what they have failed to *do*. It is a society, thus, with little tolerance for failure, and little feeling for the non-vendible qualities and talents.

It is, moreover, a society that slurs over the quality of integrity-in-action of what it teaches and preaches in rhetoric. In the economy there are the contrasting facets of affluence and hard-core poverty. In business, trade unionism, and politics there are rigging and corner-cutting. In the big media there is the cult of audience size and the resulting tendency toward a democratic aesthetic based on the principle of replaceable parts. In the universities there are maneuverings for position in the academic market place, and there are endowment drives which often overshadow the pursuit of excellence. In race relations there is a rhetoric of equality and a *de facto* structure of inequality. In foreign policy there is the absurdity of the race for nuclear weapons which cannot be used without collective suicide, and the steady pressure of the national military power along with the rhetoric which calls for the transcending of the nation-state. In family relations, within a frame that stresses togetherness, both the mother and the father are often too busy to serve as effective models for growing children, and all too often the father is simply *not there*, sometimes literally, more often as an effective authority-principle, both to follow and to rebel against. In a university community that stresses the face-to-face role of the teacher, he too is many times away from the classroom, bent on his own pursuit of advancement and achievement, and his chores are deputized to those less experienced and less adept at the necessary dialogue.

The Struggle between Generations

It is exactly in the adolescent years, of secondary school and college, that there is a craving for what Erik Erikson has called "fidelity"—the craving to find someone to trust, someone who will in turn trust you. One of the leaders in the Berkeley revolt admonished a campus rally with the warning slogan, "Don't trust anyone over thirty." One may take it as an unforgettable symbol of the generational struggle. It may seem a curious sentiment, but it is a sign that fidelity between the generations has eroded or that it never developed, and that walls of noncommunication have risen to make the campus not into a community but into a confronting of armed fortresses.

Some of the parents and teachers tend to attribute much of the mutiny of the young to a kind of diabolism, hugging the thought that a Devil has entered the young people and is working his will in them —a hypothesis that relieves them of a good deal of the burden of thought and action. I have never gone for any Devil theory, either of history or society. We can learn more about the sources of the mutiny of the young if we think of some of the contradictions they see in the society around them, and of the sense of emptiness and frustration in so many of them. Perhaps what they are saying —if we would only listen—is that they want teaching teachers, parents who live what they profess, effective models, mature people they can trust in a society they can believe in.

The crucial fact about them today is their effort to make themselves part of what is happening around them. "It is required of a man," said Justice Holmes, "that he should share the passion and action of his time at peril of being judged not to have lived." In the early 1930's the college generation was socially conscious; in the period that followed, largely in the forties, they went inward and become subjective and psyche-conscious; at some point then or later there was a period when many of them were largely *un*-conscious.

Today the wheel has swung, and again they have become socially conscious, far more perhaps than even in the thirties.

Many of them may be naïve, some may be dupes, and some may be manipulators; many are displacing their inner frustrations upon American society in a generalized negativism. Yet there is something about them that goes beyond any of these suggestions. It goes back to the early sit-ins, to the violence on the campus of the University of Alabama, to the sense of loss at the death of President Kennedy, and the sense of contagion from the activist example he set for young people in politics, to the Mississippi killings, to the struggle over Viet Nam and other foreign policy issues. They are, at least for the moment, irreverent, obstructive, exasperating. But many of the young people who keep marching about may ultimately find where they want to go. Out of their sitting they may develop, when their urgencies have dimmed a bit, a bent for the contemplative life. Out of their rebellious effort to dissociate themselves from their elders, they may start to discover who they are and develop a sense of selfhood. It is the road to *selfhood* that I stress here, and I add it to the ideas of *emergence, transcendence,* and *access* that I have already noted.

There are also, be it noted, a series of intellectual explosions taking place in American civilization, giving the student more resources than ever in history to draw upon. Things are happening which may bring within his reach a better chance to build a life with creative content, if he discovers how to make use of them. I speak of a paperback and reading explosion, an educational explosion, a cultural explosion, a communications explosion. But the meaning of these explosions must be defined by their impact on the American elites.

The Revolution of Elites, Leisure, and Work

There is a persistently antidemocratic overtone that attaches to the elite concept in American discussion of it. Yet the recognition, recruiting, education, and renewal of the elites are among the most important concerns of the American democracy. If America were only a mass culture, then whatever is easy, sleazy, vendible, nerveless, and homogenized about the mass culture would carry over by an infection to the whole of the society. But America is also (in Margaret Mead's term) a "spearhead culture," a culture of the elites. The elites in America have never been as tight and tidy as in the aristocratic societies of Europe, but the explosions I have cited have torn apart whatever tidiness they might have had. Students are invading high schools and colleges from population strata that had formerly not experienced secondary and higher education. As the university gates are stormed by a host of new students, and as the preparation track for technical and elite positions becomes longer, the nature and consciousness of class divisions are undergoing a major shift. The majorities were once outside the university system; they have now moved into it. This does not mean that they are all becoming members of the elites, but that they have a chance to. In Jefferson's exchange of letters with John Adams, he said that a democracy like the American would not survive unless it could develop "an aristocracy of virtue and talent." The Jefferson who said this was the radical, the Jacobin, the man who hated the aristocracies of birth and privilege, wealth and heredity, in a Europe encrusted in the blood-rust of centuries. It is striking that this Jefferson should have understood that America would need what we should today call a set of elites of character and ability.

I am not speaking now of a meritocracy, which is a too-mechanical approach to the problem of the elites in a democracy, but of what is potential within the young carriers of promise. The qualitative task of the university, as distinguished from its necessary quantitative tasks in doing what it can with the material at its command, must be concerned with them. There are two broad categories of elites in every society. One is the *commanding elites*, which have to do with power and authority. The other is the *intellectual elites*, that have to do with symbols, words, ideas and ideals, forms and reforms, colors, rhythms. In many cases they intersect in an individual, as with President Kennedy. One reason why he was so evocative a symbol for young Americans was that as he spoke to them he stood with one foot in the commanding elite and one in the intellectual elite. Thus he was able, for a time, to break down the hostility between the elites—a hostility that one finds through much of American and European history. The university has a triple task in shaping these elites: to recognize and elicit their best talent and character; to erode the hostility and develop some hospitality between the two main elite types; to make certain, as the student moves from the mass society into the elites, that he will not rip up the roots that nourished him in the soil of the people.

There have been leisure-class societies—those of Periclean Athens, Renaissance Florence and Venice, Elizabethan England, the Paris of Louis XIV—in which the leisure of the few was made possible by the toil and exploitation of the many. What I see ahead in America, with the revolution in automation, is not another *leisure-class* society but a *leisure* society, which will have added to the dimensions of freedom the new dimension of freedom from drudgery for the society as a whole, and which will have made more time available to more people than in any other culture in history.

But this will not mean much unless we can rid ourselves of our attitudes toward work and the job. There was a time when work meant something in the American ethos: a task in which a man could take pride because it gave him a chance to express himself and serve the community. Instead of that we now talk of "the job"—something that we put as little of ourselves into as we can, that we try to get as much for as we can, that we try to get away from as soon as we can. We shall not do much with the time revolution unless we recapture the idea of the dignity and creativeness of work, which the Protestant ethos once had in good measure. It may be work-on-the-job: a man who can find meaningful work on his job is one of the lucky of mankind. But it may also mean more time released for work, with or without remuneration, away from the job. We are becoming a nation of amateurs (I use the term in its original meaning of a "lover" of whatever his skill is). It includes those who love playing in a string quartet, or being a Civil War buff, or puttering with carpentry, or daubing away on canvas, or working within community organizations, or serving as a volunteer teacher. The time revolution is bound to help this kind of amateur put his stamp on a whole generation.

There is also the question of play, which is as important in the emergent American society as work. Paralleling the idea of the job is the idea of fun. We all have to have fun, even if it kills us: there is a fun imperative in American civilization. But it is a nervous, febrile, tension-filled, frenetic fun. Here again, more meaningful than the idea of fun is the idea of play—play as the full expressiveness of body, mind, and spirit, not in order to produce or achieve something or even master something (as with work), but for the joyousness of living.

I want to add a note on an ironic paradox of the time revolution. The leisure-class societies in the past gave leisure to a few which was made possible by the almost total lack of leisure for the many. In our society the groups who are least likely to have leisure, even in an automated economy, are the top elite groups: those in the high positions of government, corporation, trade union, church, university. Hence the rather elegant paradox: in the leisure-class society, the leisure of the few was provided by the work of the many; in our emerging society, the leisure of the many will largely be provided by the work of the work-driven few.

Commitment to the Future

In providing new opportunities for work and play, the time revolution may also provide a chance for a transvaluation of values. The traditional life goals in America have been those of power, money, success, prestige, security, happiness. But recent research on values has shown that these goals have been weakened, and that other values are taking their place. While this is not true of the majority of the young people, it is increasingly true of the creative margin of university students. The test of a society may, from one angle of vision, be the kind of questions that it asks—not the overt but the covert questions, not just those we teach and preach but those we live. I remember stopping at the window of a New York shop once, my attention caught by a sign on display: "If you're so smart, why aren't you rich?" That was one I couldn't answer, and after standing for a long time looking at it I walked away. But I was like a chicken fascinated by a snake, and I came back. Finally with a sigh of relief I had the answer: the answer was that it was the wrong question.

We ask a good many wrong questions in our society. Perhaps on university campuses here and there some of the right ones are beginning to be asked. There is the question of *emergence:* What kind of personality can I shape, in what kind of possible society? There is the question of *access:* Am I helping give others a chance at life chances equal to my own? There are questions of *selfhood:* Who am I? What are my threads of connection with my family, my community, my country, my fellow human beings? There are questions of *transcendence:* Do I dare make the journey into the interior which is the most dangerous journey of all? Do I dare confront what I find there and go beyond it? Do I dare face tragedy without being destroyed by it? There are questions of *commitment:* Do I have work I care about? Am I capable of play, of giving and receiving love, of taking risks for goals I value? Can I explore the depths and heights of joyousness? Finally, there is the question of *nexus:* Does my society have in it the stuff of cohesiveness? Do I have a sense of the human connection, in the sure knowledge that what happens to others happens thereby also to me?

If we ask some of these questions we shall be taking part in the values revolution which is the central aim of university education. We may also help make American civilization more credible to those who will be having to shape it.

The Purpose of Higher Education: A Re-examination

HARRY D. GIDEONSE

THE STRIKING EVENTS of the past year, ranging all the way from the Berkeley syndrome of frustrations to the phenomenal breakthrough in Federal fiscal support of education on all levels, make it clear that we are on the fringe of an age of unparalleled speed of change in education. I cite two statements as typical of the current climate. The first is the *New York Times'* summarizing caption over a recent report on our population statistics: "By 1966 one-half of the United States population will be under twenty-five." In other words: A twenty-five-year-old will be part of the older half of the American people. If we place that fact next to the Berkeley student slogan: Don't trust anyone over twenty-five (or thirty)!, we have the setting for a dramatic survey of predictable social, cultural, political, and educational trends.

My second statement is President Johnson's frequently repeated warning that in our social and economic life "ceaseless change is the one constant." It is probably true that decline begins when people ask "What is going to happen?" rather than "What shall *we* do?" In other words: In the forthcoming *aggiornamento* of American higher education, shall we just *undergo* the change? Or shall we organize our efforts and try to channel the direction of the flow? Are we prepared for such leadership intellectually? organizationally?

The Erosion of Social Cohesiveness

There is, of course, nothing new to the statement that the most significant characteristic of the modern world is the speed of social change. It is the predictable outcome of trends that have been visible for some two centuries. These trends are all related to the development of the scientific outlook, not merely in the scientists who see themselves as objective students of "truth" but in the forces that support their work because it creates *wealth*, it affords *comfort*, or it enhances *power*. In the world of today—and even more clearly in the

23

world of tomorrow—the social forces which have been strengthened by the progress of science raise searching questions about the continued viability of free institutions and even about the original commitment to the search for truth.

It is a commonplace that our enlarged physical power over the material environment has been accompanied by a continuous erosion of the traditional sources of moral authority which govern man's capacity for self-control. I do not have to remind educators of the historic movement which is characterized by Laplace's statement that there was no longer any need for "the hypothesis of God," by the Feuerbach phase in which God was redefined as man's projection of his own ideal self, and finally by the inevitable vulgarization that man himself is God. The movement is defined by Nietzsche's declaration, "God is dead," and Rilke's despairing words: "The world has fallen into the hands of men."

Today we are in the morally weary stages of completing the whole cycle: the free political and social institutions, which are the matrix in which free science and free scholarship have developed, depend for their viability upon sources of moral responsibility which have run dry. We have drawn checks upon the cultural deposits in our banks until the cashier has run out of funds, and now it is becoming apparent that the social cohesion which is required if free institutions are to endure will have to be created by rationally directed effort.

There are, of course, alternative methods of imposing cohesion: no one in this generation will overlook the totalitarian formula or the nostalgic efforts, of which French and some phases of current American politics supply many colorful examples, to impose order by a return to some romanticized picture of the past. There is an astonishing parallel—even in such incidentals as the preoccupation with sex, folk music, and choice of musical instruments—between the Beatnik phenomena in our youth culture and the dominant characteristics of the German middle class "youth movement" during the earlier part of this century. Walter Laqueur's *Young Germany: A History of the German Youth Movement* [1] makes it abundantly clear that the earlier apolitical phase of the movement, which was characterized by social criticism in the absence of clearly defined social goals, made the movement vulnerable to subsequent totalitarian exploitation.

Modern collectivism in its totalitarian and often in its nationalist form is a groping effort to hold together a society that has been ground to dust, to organize a community that has in the literal sense of the

[1] New York: Basic Books, 1962.

term been *dis*organized. In a remarkable recent book entitled *Insight and Responsibility*, Erik H. Erikson draws attention to man's tendency under the strain of indigestible change to restructure himself and the world by taking recourse to what we may call *totalism*:

> Where historical and technological developments severely encroach upon deeply rooted or strongly emerging identities (i.e., agrarian, feudal, patrician) on a large scale, youth feels endangered, individually and collectively, whereupon it becomes ready to support doctrines offering a total immersion in a synthetic identity (extreme nationalism, racism, or class consciousness) and a collective condemnation of a totally stereotyped enemy of the new identity.[2]

It is as if we were trying to install a prefabricated "community" in the place of the organic cohesion that was allowed to erode away. Such forms of social organization are not "social" in the sense of being rooted in community or shared values. They are simply "atomism packed tight." In the fashionable Western forms of the heresy, these "contemporary ancestors" weep about our glorious past, they long for a simpler and more innocent age, they deplore the "immorality" and the crime of our urban centers—all of these things Thomas Wolfe described a generation ago in *You Can't Go Home Again*. In the words of his leading character:

> You can't go back home to your family—
> to a young man's dream of fame and glory
> to the country cottage away from the strife and conflict
> to the father you have lost
> to the old forms and systems of things which seemed everlasting
> but are changing all the time.[3]

The prophets of the "new nostalgia" themselves are committed to accelerating the forces that make for intensified change. Their quarrel is not about the goal of material productivity; it is merely about the means of achieving it. They advocate increased productivity. The old stereotypes about "planning" and "free enterprise," about "socialism" and "capitalism" have become irrelevant in a period in which "conservatives" advocate collectivist fiscal and monetary controls as a method of achieving economic growth, while the same objective is sought by "collectivists" who now rely upon the price mechanism and market controls in Great Britain, Germany, and even the Soviet Union.

[2] New York: W. W. Norton & Co., 1964. P. 93.
[3] New York: Harper & Bros., 1940.

The symptoms of radical social unsettlement resulting from the indigestible pace of technical change are worldwide, and conservative preachment about the social byproducts is not "conservative" but simply irrelevant. Politically, there is no evidence that we understand the need for a therapy based on a realistic diagnosis, and this lack of understanding shows up most clearly in the behavior and the problems of the young.

The Sense of Uselessness

I said that the problem is worldwide—and it is independent of geography, culture, or ideology. We can think of juvenile behavior in the New York subways or on the campus in Berkeley. We can think of Soviet concern over the noninvolvement and the apolitical attitudes of their university youth. Or we can recall dramatic illustrations in old and culturally homogeneous countries such as Great Britain or the Netherlands.

One thing is certainly true of both contemporary America and the Soviet Union, of both the developed and the underdeveloped world, and that is that they will be radically different in 1970 and 1980. Productivity, scientific developments, and the related changes in the population structure have given us figures which indicate that in 1966 half of our people will be twenty-five years or under. In 1964 there were one million more seventeen-year-olds in the United States than in 1963. The old are retiring in constantly increasing numbers, and the "productive" are able to protect their interests in job rights and seniority through legislation and organization.

The unacknowledged god of the modern world—in developed and in underdeveloped countries, in Communist as well as in so-called capitalist countries—is productivity, higher standards of material living. This maximized rational exploitation of our productive potential gives us mobility, overly rapid growth of urban centers, and therefore urban slums. This is why we have automation and structural unemployment. It is better to have problems that result from progress than to have problems that result from stagnation, but at the same time the peculiar form of our American unemployment, which is disguised by a figure that includes a large number of young people and members of racial minorities and relatively few white adults, is a red-light warning.

Accelerated economic dislocation is the reason for the youth in our urban slums without "a sense of belonging." Thomas Huxley said a long time ago that "the sense of uselessness is the severest shock the human system can endure," or in James Baldwin's more recent words in *The Fire Next Time*: ". . . the most dangerous creation of any society is that man who has nothing to lose." [4] This is also why public opinion everywhere shows a feverish concern with "education," although it seems to be true that the concern frequently focuses on the problems that used to exist rather than on problems that exist now or that will exist in the near future.

There is nothing new about these facts or about their being inextricably interwoven with the progressive achievement of the central objective of increased productivity. More than twenty years ago the American Youth Commission, chaired by Owen D. Young, published its general report on *Youth and the Future*. Almost a year later, Dorothy Canfield Fisher published *Our Young Folks*, an account of her personal response to her service of seven years on the Commission.[5] These are shocking documents to anyone who thinks our present problems are new, or that they are the result of superficial causes such as automation or racial segregation. Owen D. Young and Dorothy Canfield Fisher were not radicals. They spoke for a culturally conservative tradition which can be distinguished from present conservativism by its respect for facts. They called for the recognition of the "harsh realities of the present," for a program of public and private planning in relation to the comprehensive needs of our youth, and they made specific predictions concerning the "poisonous mental confusion" about social usefulness and the presence of usefulness in the sense of availability for paid jobs.

Today we can read these reports only with a sense of dismay at the intellectual sclerosis which has beset us in the past twenty years. Very little has been done about the problem itself. Mild and patchy proposals to deal with social symptoms are discussed as if they were a reflection of Karl Marx's nineteenth-century theories rather than a response to America's twentieth-century experience. A generation of Americans, confronted with the accumulation of what James B. Conant called "social dynamite" in our cities, praises an educationally illiterate admiral as its leading educational philosopher and calls for the impeachment of a Chief Justice of the United States Supreme Court whose opinions are as socially innocuous as his original service as a Republican governor of California would lead one to expect.

Dorothy Canfield Fisher was a member of an American generation that had not yet been brainwashed. With a Vermont respect for

---

[4] New York: Dial Press, 1963. P. 90.
[5] New York: Harcourt Brace & Co., 1943.

Vermont wisdom she opens her book with a short program quotation
from John Dewey:

> What the best and wisest parent wants for his own child, that must
> the community want for all its children. Any other ideal for our
> schools is narrow and unlovely; acted upon, it destroys democracy.

They are simple words, but their radical implications in contemporary America are a measure of our failure to plan adequately for the
place of youth.

In an unpublicized spontaneous outburst in one of the panels at
the 1965 White House Conference on Education, a basic educational
insight emerged in an eloquent statement from the floor which can
be summarized in these words: Now that we have heard about the
radical educational rediscovery of the basic fact that our culturally
disadvantaged children need individual attention, that they need individual care, study, and—yes—"love," can we perhaps draw the startling conclusion that this new insight should be applied to the overwhelming majority of our normal students? The warm and rousing
endorsement in the applause of the rest of the panel was a comment
on the quality of the discussion concerning "innovations," many of
which are accelerating the trend toward impersonal handling and
computerized treatment of essentially human needs. I do not know
how many of the rest of the conference participants thought of it,
but my mind saw the picture of the Berkeley student picket carrying
the sign with the words: "I am a human being: do not fold, bend, or
mutilate."

Maintaining Equilibrium

For historical perspective let me cite also the two-volume report on
Recent Social Trends,[6] which was produced in 1933, as the result of
the initiative of President Hoover, by a distinguished group of American social scientists. On pages xii and xiii of the Committee Findings
(Volume I) one finds the following theme sentences:

> The outstanding problem might be stated as that of bringing about
> a realization of the interdependence of the factors of our complicated
> social structure. . . . It is the express purpose of this review of findings
> to unite such problems as those of economics, government, religion,

---

[6] *Recent Social Trends in the United States*, Report of the President's Research
Committee on Social Trends (New York: McGraw-Hill Book Co., 1933), 2 vols.
See also John Dewey's review in *International Journal of Ethics*, April 1933, pp.
339–45.

education . . . to direct attention to the importance of balance among the factors of change. A *nation advances not only by dynamic power, but by and through the maintenance of some degree of equilibrium* among the moving forces. [italics added]

For those who are concerned with the implications of Clark Kerr's statement that the "justification" of the modern American multiversity lies in its "consistency with the surrounding society," the key words in this summary are "the importance of *balance*" and "the maintenance of some degree of equilibrium." On page 122 of Volume I of this report it is stated that "science and technology are the most dynamic elements in our material culture," and a number of suggestive special studies of the social consequences of specified "inventions" are elaborated in great detail, with special emphasis on the cumulative character of modern inventions. The study of the social consequences of the automobile discusses the effects on cities, suburbs, railways, highway finance, hotels, on manners, morals, crime, on international trade (oil, rubber) and international politics (oil, rubber). The relationships between Ford's Model T and "communism" in the Malay States are traced as an example; European and Japanese readers might be distressed at the predictability from recorded American experience thirty years ago of their present experience with the automobile and the implication that cities and human life in general should be recast to fit the needs of a new means of transportation.

President Hoover's experts were not proposing a "moratorium on research." They were familiar with the most searching thought we can think—equally unfashionable in the Soviet Union, the United States, and Western Europe—which can be formulated quite simply in these words: Is it possible to reduce the impact of technical and scientific change to a pace more compatible with the psychological and moral tolerance of the average human being? They were not advising economic asceticism.They knew that poverty is tragically real and that productivity is the only source for its relief. In P. H. Wicksteed's words: "A man can be neither a saint, nor a lover, nor a poet, unless he has comparatively recently had something to eat." The report was quite clear about this:

> Effective coordination of the factors of our evolving society [may] mean, where possible and desirable, *slowing up* the changes which occur too rapidly and *speeding up* the changes which lag. The Committee does not believe in a moratorium upon research in physical science and invention, such as has sometimes been proposed. On the

contrary, it holds that social invention has to be stimulated to keep pace with mechanical invention. What seems a welter of confusion may thus be brought more closely into relationship with the other parts of our national structure, with whatever implications this may hold for ideals and institutions.[7]

And, to bring the topic quite clearly back into focus today: the Committee Findings stressed that it is possible to exaggerate personal aspects of moral problems, but there is little question that moral perplexities multiply when old institutions decay rapidly. In their words:

The spiritual values of life are among the most profound of those affected by developments in technology and organization. They are the slowest in changing to meet altered conditions. Moral guidance is peculiarly difficult when the future is markedly different from the past.[8]

It is an insight as old as Seneca that if a man does not know to what port he is sailing, no wind is favorable. If we are to build our youth *for* the future, and if we are to build our future *with* our youth, we need first of all a set of dependable blueprints. Building is a purposeful activity. No architect builds just for the fun of it. You must tell him what you are building for—and this is where our problem of building a future for our youth begins. Nostalgic prescriptions based upon beautiful rhetoric which usually begins with the words, "when I was young," are simply irrelevant. We are not dealing with people who *once* were young. We are dealing with people who are young *now*, and who will be young in the next ten or twenty years. There is only one thing that is certainly predictable about the circumstances of their lives. The pace of social and technical change, which is already difficult to digest today, will speed up and intensify. The competitive and conflicting pressures which beat about our heads will not diminish: they will grow in number and intensity.

The basic facts are brutal. We live in a society which is generous with part of its youth—if their aptitudes and values are in conformity with adult needs and concerns for productivity. We also live in a society which *excludes* part of its youth—in fact, whether by design or by drift. We all know that "youth needs to be needed," and we are compelled to deal with the predictable consequences of the development of a generation which is deprived of a sense of belonging.

[7] *Ibid.*, I, xv.
[8] *Ibid.*

Toward a Definition of Freedom

No one can foresee the face of tomorrow, but it is easy to predict that an adult generation that is as unsure of its basic values as ours is will not be able to pass on to its youth an ability to rearrange its conflicting priorities, unless we manage to clarify our own judgment on these matters. The most significant thing about a society is its ruling beliefs and values. The characteristic of our contemporary world which most confuses our youth is the total chaos in the rank order of our priorities that prevails in our discussion of, say, education in all its ramifications, or taxation, or the conservation of national resources, or in the semantic confusion that mars contemporary discussion of the nature of a free society. These are major problems to youth, but they are adult responsibilities. Adults make the world in which youth grows up. Adults determine the formative pattern in which youth develops. Every generation of adults gets the type of youth it deserves.

It is difficult to hit a target if you do not know where it is. This generation of adults will have a hard time restoring—or placing—freedom in a central position in its educational programs. Controversy about freedom is too often, in the language of Ecclesiastes, "vanity and a striving after wind."

Illiteracy concerning the meaning of freedom was glaringly illustrated in the Berkeley faculty resolution which stipulated that "the content of speech or advocacy should not be restricted by the university." The immediate and predictable consequence was the incident about the four-letter words which almost led to the resignation of the president and the chancellor of the university. How can a distinguished faculty take the position that "there is no such thing as more or less freedom," if it should think for one moment (for instance and to stay near the range of its immediate experience) of a student who would say that his examination results were influenced by bribing his teacher? Is this within the content of free speech, or is this a definition which makes freedom synonymous with anarchy? Would anyone familiar with the classical cycle described in Aristotle's *Politics* hesitate in classifying such a conception of "freedom" as the stage immediately preceding the resurgence of "despotism"?

There is quite a breeze now as our academic specialists focus their scholarship on ever-narrowing aspects of the broad ideal of freedom and free society, and as the ideal of freedom becomes a football in the arena of academic as well as world politics.

There is nothing new in semantic confusion about freedom. It is often defined in terms of the removal of the type of constraint that has been most recently experienced, just as order tends to be defined in terms of the type of insecurity that is currently remembered. Freedom was defined differently by the Greeks in Pericles' time, by the merchants of Adam Smith's time, by Karl Marx during the Industrial Revolution, and by the peasants in contemporary Russia. A continuous sifting of the literature is therefore necessary if we are to select the universal as against the contemporary and parochial elements in the tradition.

The semantic confusion that prevails in our discussion of freedom arises primarily from our specialization in scholarship, and secondarily from the identification in some quarters of freedom with total laissez faire in economic policy ("freedom from the state is freedom from law"), which is particularly common in the United States today but which had already led Tocqueville to tell his French materialistic contemporaries that "the man who asks of freedom anything other than itself is born to be a slave."

A physicist does not define his basic concepts by poetic imagination, by a dictionary definition, or by a Gallup poll. He defines his terms by reference to observed reality. Similarly, our discussions of freedom should be rooted in a realistic theory of human nature, social and historic experience, and a study of the social, political, and economic conditions under which human beings define their purposes, pursue them effectively, and reap the fruits of their labor. The concept of freedom should be defined in terms of the social context in which man as he *is*—and not as he *might* be—has achieved freedom and can extend his achievement by augmenting the freedoms that have historically been realized.

The primary cause of confusion lies in the varied types of freedom that together constitute our freedom as a whole. Our specialized scholars in their pursuit of separate splinters of the log are like the six blind men in the classical Indian story who describe an elephant in terms of his tail, his tusks, or his trunk. Liberty was not created by a philosopher's definition. It can be defined in a manner that will make it impossible to achieve, but we know that in varying degrees it *has* been achieved.

If freedom is the presence of responsible choice, the nature of the process through which the sources of responsibility are refreshed is crucial, and it is certainly not necessary to remind educators that choice implies commitment, and not "free-floating freedom" to follow whims or subjective aspiration.

Freedom is in its very nature always relative and never absolute. The nonconformist is never "on his own." He always draws his spiritual strength from a moral or philosophical tradition. In this sense a prisoner may be more free than the guardian at the gate of his cell. In an American setting we can think of Thoreau. In a Russian cultural context (and the Russian tradition of freedom is exceptionally rich in this respect, for obvious historical reasons) we can recall Dostoyevsky's rediscovery of the Biblical tradition during his period of Siberian exile, or Dudintsev's character, Lopatkin, who as a product of Soviet education had inevitably cultivated the questioning mind that was essential for good scientific and technical work and who tells about his prison experience in these sentences: "The words 'deprivation of liberty' are inaccurate. Whoever has learned to think cannot be completely deprived of liberty"; or, more recently, Boris Pasternak, who had "paid little attention to religious practice" until nonconformity made him seek for sources of moral support, which are described in the nineteenth poem attached to *Doctor Zhivago* as Biblical teachings which restored his "consciousness" and turned his "impotence into life."

Reforming the Curriculum: Faculty Responsibilities

While it is crucial to see freedom in the context of a culture as a whole, including its economic, its political, and its social institutions and "habits of thought," it would be a tragic misreading of the signs of our times to assume that the enormous expansion of enrollment in our baccalaureate colleges with their traditional stress on liberal and general education will automatically supply the essential balance and equilibrium. One of the most disturbing facts about current trends is that the sense of the relevance of liberal education is being lost precisely at the moment when in the words of one of the White House Conference's documents, a college education is becoming "an accepted norm" of American society.

Two-thirds of American baccalaureate education today has little or nothing to do with "liberal education"; and in the third that remains, frequently an empty shell of courses that reflect the curricular thought of a preceding generation is taught by an increasing multitude of recent graduates of specialized doctoral programs who have no training and little interest in teaching what they call "secondhand" subjects. If, in addition to this, the graduate faculty dominates the staffing of the undergraduate program and compels the colleges to use unqualified and uninterested graduate students to teach from 60 to 80 percent of the instructional hours in the freshman and sophomore years, it is clear that demoralization and lack of a sense of relevance are not due to "the conflict of generations" but are, rather, a predictable outcome of questionable educational practice.

There is, of course, a great variety of practice in American colleges, and the stress on inadequate and impersonal teaching can be overdone, but Jacques Barzun's address at Hofstra in December 1963,[9] with its deliberately selective stress on the critical aspects and its thesis that "the liberal arts tradition is dead or dying," was closer to the truth than is the euphoria induced by meditating on the free flow of Federal funds or the faith that all will be well since a college education is becoming the "accepted norm" of American society. The diploma is becoming the "norm" precisely at the moment when the unchecked trends toward specialization that govern the education of college teachers are destroying the educational significance of the traditional "degree."

The decline in the "relevance" of liberal education is intensified by the widening gap between the flexibility in institutional mechanism for change in elementary and secondary education on the one hand and in colleges on the other. While the graduate schools nibble away at the curricular autonomy of the colleges in the junior and senior years and erode the quality of college teaching in the freshman and sophomore years by imposing irrelevant methods of training on our teachers, a healthy and yeasty process of rethinking methods and content of instruction in the years below the college level is increasingly promoting the obsolescence of the college curriculum. If an effective "innovation" in the methods of teaching mathematics, science, or foreign language can be plausibly presented to a superintendent of schools or an able high school principal, the innovation will be given an experimental chance; this was the case in the past during the creative periods in American higher education that are recalled by the citation of names such as Eliot, Harper, Gilman, and Butler.

Today in our representative institutions the responsibility for the curriculum has practically everywhere shifted to the faculty. In a suggestive and forthright recent paper by Professor W. H. Cowley of Stanford on "Critical Decisions in American Higher Educa-

---

[9] Barzun, "College to University—And After," *American Scholar*, Spring 1964, pp. 212–19.

tion," [10] the full implications of our present rigidity are presented quite undramatically in a mild historical context, but the message is just as clear in the summarizing paragraphs in the seminal research report entitled *The American College: A Psychological and Social Interpretation of Higher Learning,* edited by Nevitt Sanford. Sanford, whose volume should be read by every college teacher and in my experience is typically read only by frustrated deans and college presidents, expects reform only when college teachers again assume "the professional identity of teachers of students rather than that of members of academic disciplines. . . ." [11] Sanford believes the faculty should have a major voice in determining educational policy and he stresses the inadequacy of the present method of implementing this professional objective. In a section on "Some Obstacles to Reform" one finds the following statements:

> There is no denying . . . that when there is a movement toward reform in a college it is the collective faculty who usually seem to be dragging their feet. There have been few fundamental innovations in higher education in the past twenty-five or thirty years, and in even fewer cases have innovations been initiated by college or university faculties . . .
>
> . . . college and university faculties, typically, have organized themselves in such a way as to make deliberate and concerted change of any kind exceedingly difficult. [12]

A perceptive student of the "multiversity" has recently summarized the trend in the following language:

> It is surely time that someone, perhaps one of the ever beneficent foundations, calculated the true cost (in terms of time and money) of, for example, making a vital *educational* decision in our larger institutions of "higher learning." Flexibility, outwardly so apparent in the vast array of special interests, is in reality incredible rigidity when it comes to such crucial educational decisions as curriculum development, student guidance, and so on. While we may have learned to move with the ease of a leopard technologically, educationally our bulk has reduced us to the state of a wooly mammoth. [13]

There is no willingness in the average contemporary faculty to deputize responsibility to selected spokesmen for the faculty. There is no willingness to relate change to research and evaluation. It is

[10] In *Current Issues in Higher Education, 1963,* ed. G. Kerry Smith (Washington: Association for Higher Education, N.E.A., 1963), pp. 13–21.

[11] New York: John Wiley & Sons, 1962. P. 24.

[12] *Ibid.,* pp. 19–20.

[13] Henry C. Johnson, "Are Our Universities Schools?" *Harvard Educational Review,* Spring 1965, p. 173.

probably no accident that in two of our largest Federal grant universities—one private, one public—recent proposals for curricular innovation in the *college* were defeated by an incoherent coalition of university and research professors—including what Clark Kerr calls "un-faculty"—in mass meetings composed of from one thousand to fourteen hundred "voting" colleagues.

Is the cloacal gathering of the staff of the multiversity, including a multitude of grant recipients chosen without any concern for their achievement as teachers, likely to result in educational wisdom in the formulation of a *college* curriculum? Would there be any loss in professional insight if the campus gardeners and the stenographers were also included? Shouldn't there be at least as much functional concern in the solicitation of relevant judgment in the determination of *educational objectives* as there normally is in the definition of a grant project?

Sanford correctly states that faculty-governed European universities have become extremely conservative institutions: "it has sometimes required acts of parliament to bring about changes in the curriculum." [14] Those of us who recall the juicy pages Adam Smith wrote in 1776 in *The Wealth of Nations* about Oxford will recognize hoary precedents for the professor whose status is measured by the disappearance of his "teaching schedule."

Today it is almost necessary to establish a new college with a hand-picked administration and faculty to ensure a willingness to venture curricularly on the basis of insight and experience, and even here sclerosis sets in rapidly as the vested interests organize and cohere on the basis of the preservation of established perquisites.

It will be futile to seek remedies "consistent with the culture" in this area, but it should be possible to work out patterns of reform that preserve and enhance faculty responsibility, that limit faculty participation to those who are involved in the process, and that are rooted in the academic acceptance of change related to research and development which academic consultants are so eager to see established in any activity "off campus" in which they are invited to play a creative role. It is possible that the large foundations which have played a crucial role in awakening public imagination to the nation's educational and social needs in recent decades may find a new creative function in the laggard and stagnant areas which I have stressed.

My eye has been focused on liberal education on the baccalaureate level, on the study of the type of education that makes men and

[14] Sanford (ed.), *The American College*, p. 21.

women fit for the intellectual and moral responsibilities of free society, and I have been deeply aware that this type of education has also been the principal baccalaureate source of our best scientific talent. Judging on the basis of the original competitive assumptions of rival teams for the Manhattan project, we need from four to six independent baccalaureate establishments, focused on the basic value of "freedom" in liberal education, and organized in a manner that relates faculty responsibility for the program to continuous research and evaluation—and one or two of these "models," which should be widely distributed, might be especially concerned with the general education program of the junior or community college. Such a program would be hard to sell to Congress. It is a "natural" for the venture capital in American culture, and it will meet a crucial need in satisfying the qualitative needs of our higher education.

The type of research which is illustrated by Sanford's volume and the type of concern for the "identity" of our youth which is reflected in the final paragraphs of Max Lerner's background paper will be directly relevant. The concepts of emergence, selfhood, commitment, and cohesion are basic to the problem. I do not know whether U.S. Commissioner of Education Francis Keppel's expressed interest in national testing to evaluate educational achievement is intended to apply to colleges, but I am certain that a test of the understanding of basic concepts such as freedom, equality, the rule of law, and the distinction between a Federal and a central government would reveal a total absence of the type of cultural foundations which could make a discussion of intercultural education realistic.

Enthusiasts for the introduction of "non-Western" cultures into the curriculum—and I have been one of them—sometimes forget that the "inter" in *intercultural* implies that the student understand his own culture. Today, with the disappearance of the study of the Bible as well as the inherited classical culture of Greece and Rome (and both of them represented *inter*cultural education), it is probable that our total educational impact has become *more* parochial rather than less—and primarily because the present programs do not supply an adequate basis for understanding the student's own culture, which is a prerequisite for comparative study. The "take-off" of our new pilot projects should be based on a study of our best existing practice in faculty and student participation,[15] in the evaluation of the faculty's

[15] See Sidney Hook's article on academic freedom and the rights of students (entitled "Freedom to Learn but Not to Riot") in *New York Times Magazine*, Jan. 3, 1965, pp. 89+. See also Dael Wolfle's editorial "The Great Teachers" in *Science*, Dec. 11, 1964, p. 1421.

teaching, in functional decentralization, and in continuous evaluation of effectiveness in relation to a carefully stated rank-order of objectives. It would also be rewarding if there could be some study of
the rich British and German literature concerning new academic
establishments as well as a systematic evaluation of many of our own
recently established "colleges within colleges." [16]

My stipulation that there should be four to six such experimental
foundations is rooted in the assumption that we need a diversity of
approach and that we should avoid the temptation to impose uniform patterns as a remedy to our problems, especially in view of the
fact that those groups who are the most deeply committed to "freedom" in the area of student life—such as the American Association
of University Professors and the American Civil Liberties Union—
are the most deeply tinged with the heresy that "freedom" and "uniformity" are somehow synonymous. Diversity will also afford opportunity to experiment with problems of size and functional decentralization, and with a variety of methods for developing a faculty who
will be committed to a career of teaching college students.

The need for diversity in the pattern of experimentation is also
indicated by some of the positive aspects of our current experience,
and they are more numerous than the selective publicity of the mass
media might suggest. Whatever we may think of details in the succeeding acts of the Berkeley drama, a great movement of creative and
critical innovation has developed on all levels at the University of
California, and any teacher would be impressed with the opportunity
held out in the following paragraph of a Berkeley faculty report:

> Studies already known to us show that a significant and growing
> minority of students are simply not propelled by what we have come
> to regard as conventional motivation. Rather than aiming to be
> successful men in an achievement-oriented society, they want to be
> moral men in a moral society. They want to lead lives less tied to
> financial return than to social awareness and responsibility. Our edu-
> cational plans should recognize these values. [17]

I was awestruck at finding this lovely spiritual rose blooming in
what is supposed to be the secular desert. It would not be good
pedagogy to confront the new Believers with the relevant citations

[16] There is nothing specifically American about most of our problems, as will be
clear from an evening spent with a collection of British articles edited by Marjorie
Reeves and entitled *Eighteen Plus: Unity and Diversity in Higher Education*
(London: Faber & Faber, 1965).

[17] *Preliminary Report of the Select Committee on Education*, Academic Senate
of the University of California (May 24, 1965).

from the old Gospel until they have clarified their new identity, but there may be a harvest coming in what will be a new tribute to youth's perennial ability to reject false idols and to expose sham. I do not know whether a publicly supported college can respond to this challenge, but if we are looking for polarity, balance, and, hopefully, equilibrium in the Great Society, "venture capital" in education might well be interested in this symptom of spiritual growth in the time of our troubles.

The New Condottieri

The strengthening of Federal fiscal involvement in meeting the country's educational needs—strengthening in the size of budgets and in the quality of leadership—raises one other large question that will be pressed with increasing urgency as we examine our current experience. Clark Kerr in his perceptive Godkin lectures poses the question in his forthright and realistic chapter on "The Realities of the Federal Grant University." A generation ago strong resistance "in principle" against Federal aid channeled the process through contracts negotiated by mission-oriented Federal agencies. It is not necessary to agree with all the implications of the use some of the student rebellion leaders are making of President Eisenhower's warning in his final speech as President of the United States against "the potential for the disastrous rise of misplaced power" in "the military-industrial complex," to become reflective when the current facts indicate that 15 percent of all expenditures in American institutions of higher learning and fully 75 percent of all research expenditures are now defrayed from those sources. The distinctions between private and public institutions are blurred, to put it mildly, when we note that Federal funds are responsible at the minimum for 32 percent of the total budget of one of our largest private universities and this percentage ranges to 85 percent of the total budgets elsewhere.

The impact of this fiscal dependence of our largest institutions on a project basis with grants rarely ranging beyond a two-year basis is, of course, emphatically clear throughout the country, including all the institutions that are not already directly involved, and an entrepreneurial spirit is rampant wherever administration has become dependent on such sources. It is literally true that administrations as well as faculties have lost control over their own fate—only one institution in this category is able to report that it would be able to honor all its commitments to permanent faculty members if Federal funds were to be cut off tomorrow. It may well be that Federal aid is indispensable if high-quality research operations are to be maintained, but the question is surely ripe to be faced openly and directly: If we are not to be destroyed by vulgar and entrepreneurial rivalry inappropriate to the preservation of the quality of higher education, should we not recognize the present grant system as a subterfuge for Federal aid and replace it with direct public subsidy allocated to the institutions at their professional discretion? How else can we restore academic control over our own operations?

Gerard Piel, publisher of the *Scientific American*, a sympathetic and friendly observer, has surveyed this whole field in a paper prepared for the American Philosophical Society under the title "The Treason of the Clerks." It is an astonishing and provocative challenge and it merits prayerful consideration throughout our academic community. The Federal panel disbursements have not only "made the rich richer and the poor poorer" but the "poor" as well as the "rich" have suffered the consequences in the impact on the quality of motivation of every applicant or candidate for a faculty appointment. The senior member of the faculty is chronically engaged in negotiations for the renewal of his project contracts and grants, and he "comes to think of the granting agencies as his alma mater, his 'true source of nourishment,' " identifying himself ever "more closely with his colleagues and competitors around the country than with his fellow faculty members." He even regards contributions to the overhead of his own university as deductions from "his" grant and he bargains them away in negotiations for the "transfer" of his grant to a less scrupulous administration elsewhere. In this connection I cite the following colorful paragraph from page 30 of the mimeographed version of the paper:

> With funds abounding for projects in every field of learning, the university campus has come to harbor a new kind of *condottieri*, mercenaries of science and scholarship hooded with doctorates and ready for hire on studies done to contract specification. Studies of this kind have been solemnly entered in the records of Congressional hearings, released as reports to Federal executive agencies and published by university presses.

The impact of the operations of the *condottieri* on the quality of faculty motivation and on the characteristics sought in candidates for high positions in academic administration is clear to any informed observer. It is also clear that the *condottieri* do not contribute to the clarification of academic educational objectives: their life interests and their personal values are subversive of the idea itself. The whole movement is clearly undermining the rich pluralism of the American academic establishment; impersonal competitive market forces are imposing a concrete-mixer uniformity, and in another decade the impact of the whole process on the quality of academic and faculty administration will make it almost impossible to reverse the trend. It is doubtful if the trend which has developed would have gone as far as it has if the successive stages proposed by individual members of the faculty had been submitted to collective faculty review and decision—the professor is sometimes right.[18]

Higher education is rightly proud of its contribution to material productivity and national power, but the country's colleges and universities cannot serve the end of building a Great Society by allowing themselves to be confused with the research and development department of a modern industry. We have other and more demanding values to serve, and the preservation of the pluralist variety of our heritage is an essential *end* as well as *means* in this process.

Freedom is the presence of choice and liberty is a blessing that must be earned before it can be enjoyed. Its vitality depends upon the clarification of the moral priorities in the exercise of choice. These are just modern ways of expressing the Biblical conception that freedom is service. "Where there is no vision, the people perish." If we restore the grip on our mind and on our will of what the prophet called the "vision," there will be no difficulty in bringing order to the present conflict in priorities. If the priorities are recognized as real we shall have commitment, and where there is commitment there is voluntarily accepted discipline—the discipline of shared values which Tocqueville and Lincoln have taught us to recognize as the healthy core of a free society.

The things we fear lose their power, if the things we really believe have clear priority. In this age in which the distinction between science fiction and national defense is becoming blurred, it will profit us nothing if we gain the moon and lose our own good earth. If we can recapture the "vision" for ourselves and for our youth, the rearrangement in individual and social priorities will see us through the

[18] See the perceptive treatment of these issues in Don K. Price's lectures at New York University, published by the New York University Press in 1954 under the title *Government and Science.* For a lucid comparison of university and multiversity, or university and publicly supported center for research and development, see Johnson, "Are Our Universities Schools?" See also Alvin M. Weinberg, "But Is the Teacher Also a Citizen?" *Science,* Aug. 6, 1965, pp. 601–6.

hazardous journey, like John Bunyan's pilgrim, "against wind and tide." [19]

Michael Polanyi, in a seminal book written some years ago, dealt with the problem in terms of the values taken for granted in the sciences themselves:

> We are living in the midst of a period requiring great readjustments. One of these is to learn once more to hold beliefs, our own beliefs. The task is formidable, for we have been taught for centuries to hold as a belief only the residue which no doubt can conceivably assail. There is no such residue left to-day, and that is why the ability to believe with open eyes must once more be systematically re-acquired.[20]

If we are to avoid what John Stuart Mill described as a conflict "between ignorant change on one hand and ignorant opposition to change on the other," the relation of science and society should not be studied in a panic of fear stimulated by recent dramatic examples in physics, or the even more radical social and political implications of the emerging molecular biology, but in the larger perspective of clarifying the moral presuppositions of free society, and of science as an aspect of free society.

The Compensatory Concept of Education

We are not born—as Woodrow Wilson was fond of saying—to sit still and merely know. We are put into this world to *act*. "Education," Woodrow Wilson said a long time ago, "is a branch of statesmanship." In other words, it is not just a matter of running a school or a college. It is a matter of channeling all the formative influences brought to bear on youth so that we shall develop men and women fit for the intellectual and moral responsibilities of free society, and this clearly calls for a program that will *offset* many of the cultural influences that are increasingly exercised by the society itself.

The call for a *compensatory* conception of education, in which our formative or educational agencies would deliberately develop an educational program designed to *offset* some of the lopsided educational consequences of the general drive for enhanced productivity,

[19] See Logan Wilson, "Setting Institutional Priorities," *Current Issues in Higher Education, 1965* (Washington: Association for Higher Education, N.E.A., 1965), pp. 33–39. When the latest eager beaver on the scent of a possible grant argues his case for space, time, staff, and nervous energy, how many of us remember the old rule: "How do we rate the *priorities* of the educational needs we now serve and those we are at present unable to meet? Is the lowest need now met more urgent than the highest need not met?"

[20] *The Logic of Liberty* (London: Routledge & Kegan Paul, 1951), p. 31.

should be carefully distinguished from the present concern throughout the world about the relation between educational policy and economic growth. It is true that economic growth depends upon investment in man as well as in physical and technical equipment, and it is clear from recent research into economic productivity that investment in education has been a major cause of economic development in the past; in fact, recent research points to American education outlay in the past as probably the largest single component of *all* investment.[21] In a rapidly changing economic order, educational development directly related to accelerated productivity is—although desirable in itself—simply an accelerating force in the promotion of the cultural by-products of productivity which I have traced here.

A "compensatory" conception of education would be strictly in accord with some of the healthiest and most enduring features of a free and democratic society. "Dispersed controls" in the form of checks and balances have been built into our political institutions, and in the development of contemporary economic and fiscal policy the compensatory or offsetting responsibility of the Federal or central government has become an easily recognizable economic feature of the American and the European landscape. If we are to achieve equilibrium and balance, the compensatory idea may have a constructive vitality in the educational future of free society. If education in all its ramifications restricts itself to analytical, intellectualistic, and vocational concerns, it will intensify the centrifugal forces now at work, but if its conception is broadened to include a major preoccupation with offsetting some of the unplanned and unintended cultural by-products of an increasingly specialized rational pursuit of material productivity, it may be the cornerstone of a social structure designed to ensure intellectual and moral fitness for the responsibilities of free society.[22]

Such fitness will not be found in exclusive pursuit of material security. The maturity of a free man is anchored in his moral and intellectual capacity to cope with the insecurity that is unavoidably interwoven with the pursuit of values which are all in some measure and to some degree in conflict with one another. The ability to cope with tension and with polar values has been recognized as the criterion of a free man by social philosophers as widely divergent as

---

[21] Gideonse, "Economic Growth and Educational Development," *College and University*, Summer 1963, pp. 421–33.

[22] See Gideonse, *On the Educational Statesmanship of a Free Society* (New York: Woodrow Wilson Foundation, 1959).

Alexis de Tocqueville and Martin Buber, and in walking "the narrow ridge," education can play a positive rather than a passive role.

We live in a time of danger and also in a time of great hope. Whoever offers us complacency blinds us to the danger and denies us the hope. Let me summarize and repeat: Every society gets the kind of youth it deserves. Young people do not make the world in which they grow up. Adults make the world in which young people grow up. These are simple words. They describe a terrifying characteristic of our present society.

The mission-oriented approach to our fiscal support and to the commitment of our talent threatens to convert our institutions to the role of *means* with which we pursue conventional *ends* defined by others, and in a time in which the fruits of affluence stimulated by the development of science are so abundantly available, nothing is more clearly urgent than the need for imagination and perspective in the redefinition of the ends themselves. The American Academy of Arts and Sciences has devoted a full issue of *Daedalus* to the study of "Utopia" and it affords a suggestive introduction to the study of the potentials of the Great Society. In a brilliant essay in this volume [23] Bertrand de Jouvenel reminds us that Utopian writers of the past paid scant attention to the material basis upon which the good life was to be reared, and one of the inexplicable characteristics of our generation of liberals and intellectuals is that we pay little or no attention to the nature of the Great Society and the good life which we might seek to establish on our unparalleled material basis.

It was characteristic of the World's Fairs of the past century that they were designed to display the *means* of material life; we need to prod our imagination by exhibitions of alternative and achievable *ends*, and these will be the expression of a progressive process of clarification of alternative *values*. French television programs, concerned with illustrating the basic problems of long-term economic and national planning, are seeking to bring this new philosophical approach to a mass audience. In our world of rapid technical progress, philosophy in the broadest possible sense of the term is the most practical subject in the curriculum. It is also the subject which is most sadly missing in our discussions of the problems of the multiversity. There is a staleness in our basic assumptions which recalls Whitehead's warning that a race makes progress only when it combines reverence for its symbols with courage in their revision.

[23] Jouvenel, "Utopia for Practical Purposes," *Daedalus*, Spring 1965, pp. 437–53.

The unchallenged primacy in the multiversity of the basic assumption that all fruitful intellectual inquiry must proceed in terms of precedents set in the study of inanimate nature has given an archaic flavor to the study of freedom and the responsible choices open to man, to the concern with man's moral and aesthetic values, as well as to William James', Alfred North Whitehead's, or Sir Richard Livingstone's insistence on the need for education "in the presence of greatness." Even the social sciences and the humanities suffer from this self-inflicted weakness, and any sensitive college administrator can contribute to the discussion of what I sometimes call the search for a "humanistic" professor of philosophy or of political economy. This is not new in the history of formal higher education, and in the past the essential correction in focus has sometimes come from responsible and creative *political* leadership in the community.

In one of John F. Kennedy's final speeches, delivered on October 26, 1963, at the Amherst ground-breaking exercises for the Robert Frost library, I find two paragraphs on "the great national purpose" and "the deepest sources of our national strength" as they are embodied in the study of the liberating arts. These statements are directly relevant to our concern here today. They were not the work of some script writer, and I am told the manuscript was covered with longhand insertions. They read as follows:

> When power leads man toward arrogance, poetry reminds him of his limitations. When power narrows the areas of man's concern, poetry reminds him of the richness and diversity of his existence. When power corrupts, poetry cleanses. For art establishes the basic human truths which must serve as the touchstone of our judgment.
>
> . . . .
>
> I look forward to . . . a future in which our country will match its military strength with our moral strength, its wealth with our wisdom, its power with our purpose. I look forward to an America which will not be afraid of grace and beauty . . . which commands respect throughout the world not only for its strength but for its civilization as well. And I look forward to a world which will be safe not only for democracy and diversity but also for personal distinction.

At the White House Conference on Education in the summer of 1965, I was deeply interested in a paragraph of President Johnson's address. It was not featured in the newspaper publicity that accompanied the conference. It certainly did not reflect a desire to restrict

American higher education to a program "consistent with the culture
of our society." It was closer to the old homiletical principle that we
should always preach to the culture but never preach the culture. I
quote from the President's address to the White House Conference
on July 21, 1965:

> Most of all we need an education which will create the educated
> mind. This is a mind—not simply a repository of information and
> skills—but a source of creative skepticism, characterized by a willing-
> ness to challenge old assumptions, and to be challenged—a spa-
> ciousness of outlook—and convictions deeply held, but which new
> facts and experience can modify. For we are a society which has
> staked its survival on the rejection of dogma—on the refusal to bend
> experience to belief, and in the determination to shape action to
> reality as reality reveals itself to us. This is the hardest course of all
> to take. And without education it is an impossible course.
>
> All of this means not merely more classrooms and more teachers
> —although we need them. . . . It means a fundamental improve-
> ment in the quality of American education. It means an educational
> system which does not simply equip the students to adjust to society,
> but which enables him to challenge and modify, and, at times, reject,
> if necessary, the received wisdom of his elders.

Every word in that statement deserves further thought and medita-
tion, but as a challenge in the definition of the purpose of higher
education it sets the stage for the critical and dangerous decade that
lies ahead of us, in which the academic community of the nation
which was established to be the custodian of a critically maintained
intellectual and moral tradition will either restore or lose its function
as an autonomous source and an independent critic of the values of
the Great Society.

On the second day of the White House Conference on Education
John W. Gardner pointed to the comparative placidity of the first
day's discussions and invited us "to snap at it with the bite of a
barracuda." In the Brooklyn fish tank—I hesitate to use the word
"pisciculture"—we are more gentle than the study of Washington's
competitive barracudas might suggest, but in this essay I have attempted some polite nibbling.

Neglect of Students as a Historical Tradition

FREDERICK RUDOLPH

COLLEGE STUDENTS constitute the most neglected, least understood element of the American academic community. Often in the past this neglect has been salutary, but more often it has required of students that they make some dramatic announcement of their presence. If their weapons of the 1960's are sit-ins, picket lines, and troublesome demonstrations, other weapons were appropriate at other times. The founding of the *Yale Literary Magazine* in 1837, the first intercollegiate baseball game between Amherst and Williams in 1859, the beginnings of an elaborate system of student government at the University of California early in the present century, the girls' smoking rooms set aside at Bryn Mawr in 1925—these are moments in American academic history that are pertinent to an understanding of the American student today.

But understanding requires something of a gigantic effort if we are to overcome the unrecognized bias of American academic tradition. That tradition acknowledges the rise and fall of presidents, professors, courses of study, and endowments. As for students, however, they flow rather aimlessly in and out of our picture of the past—wholesome and frolicsome young men and women of no very certain purpose, in the process of being rounded in mysterious ways, living on the whole rather safe and uninteresting lives, conforming to rather dull standards of undergraduate thought and behavior, capable of nothing more imaginative than such a stunt, say, as leading the village cow up the stairs of the chapel tower.

This picture is both unfair and inaccurate, for unquestionably the most creative and imaginative force in the shaping of the American college and university has been the students. Responding to the old admonition to "know thyself," they have made academic history quite as often as they have made personal history. In fact, the two have been inseparable. John Hersey, on accepting his appointment as master of Pierson College at Yale last spring, may really have been expressing an ancient truth when he observed: "It strikes me that the liveliest people in the United States at the present time are students." The truth may be ancient, but college administrators certainly are going to have difficulty believing it, so misled have they been by the mythology of higher education, particularly in the flattering notion that every college is the lengthened shadow of a man. And everyone knows who *that* man is.

I should like to offer in immediate evidence, however, an array of young men who revealed undergradute imagination at its best and whose exploits, traditionally regarded as pranks, might more properly be considered for the insights they provide to the collegiate experience and to shadows they cast across the history of higher education.

Let me begin in an Amherst classroom near the end of the nineteenth century. The professor of physics is explaining the action of a camera. He has darkened the room except for a small aperture in one shutter and he has shown the class that the image of trees outside appears inverted when thrown upon a sheet on the opposite side of the room. "Now, young gentlemen," he says, "if one of you should go out and walk across the field of vision, you would appear to us to be standing upon your head." Whereupon, in one of the great moments in the history of collegiate imagination, an Amherst athlete asks permission to try, leaves the classroom, and walks across the field of vision on his hands. The professor is dazed and the class, convulsed.

Earlier in the century a Bowdoin undergraduate seized an opportunity that opened before him when the great Lafayette suddenly changed his New England itinerary during an 1824 tour of the country. Lafayette had been expected in Brunswick, but he had sent hurried word that he could not make it, and the president of the college therefore rushed off to Portland to award Bowdoin's honorary degree to the eminent visitor. Communication being what it was in those simple days, word of Lafayette's change of plans had not got around—except, apparently, to one Bowdoin sophomore who, dressing himself as Lafayette, drove into Brunswick in a chaise, acknowledged the ringing bells and the marching townsmen, kissed the ladies, and finished the day in alcoholic bliss at a supper given in his honor.

For the want of recognizing the great imaginative qualities of such men as these, we have failed to see what goes on at an American college. One day in 1871 the town of Granville, Ohio, rocked with the news that oil had been struck in Granville. But did the faculty of Denison College thoroughly appreciate the qualities and the needs that had led several of their undergraduates to inspire the news in the first place—simply by pouring two gallons of oil in an abandoned well? I am not even sure that the faculty of Williams College read correctly the story we enjoyed a few years ago when one of our students successfully entertained two dates at a spring houseparty, neither girl suspecting during what must have been a very long week end for the boy that she was one of a pair.

College commons, so often the scene of disorder and rebellion, inspired one group of Princeton students in the late eighteenth century to an unusual display of imagination. They did not vent their ire against the steward by locking him out, refusing to eat, or demanding his dismissal. Instead, they hung by the neck in the dining room an image of the steward expertly carved from a huge block of rancid butter. I rather suspect that this expression of artistic talent was not appreciated, and there is little reason to believe that presidents, professors, and trustees anywhere understood what led students to practice ventriloquism on their tutors, and time after time bring the pompous disciplinarians among their elders to some appropriate embarrassment. I am reminded of the Dickinson College students who, in stage whispers, discussed outside the office of President Jesse Peck plans for helping themselves to oysters from a railroad car on a siding near the campus. They knew their victim, and before long *they* were locking him inside that railroad car.

But their feat was nothing when compared to the creative genius of a student at Oglethorpe in the 1850's, a young man for whom college was a whole set of challenges his elders did not even recognize. This young man rigged up a strong fishing line between the bell clapper in the chapel belfry, ran it down a lightning rod, over a grooved wheel and pulley to his dormitory room. And then he waited for a moonlit night when Professor Robert C. Smith was on patrol: The chapel bell rings. The professor quietly climbs the belfry. He finds no student, and the ringing has stopped. He descends. Again there is ringing. It stops. He sees a light in a dormitory room. He investigates, the student is studying Greek, and as the professor chides him for his late hours, the student swings his leg—to which is tied the fishing line—and the bell starts up again. For sure that was the longest night in the life of Professor Smith: the bells tolled for him, but he knew not why.

Collegians as Reformers of the College

Indeed, the bells tolled often, the bells tolled everywhere, but few knew what they were saying. To me, as I look back on the history of

American higher education and as I look around me today, those bells
were drawing attention to the students, to qualities about them that
were unappreciated, and to desires and needs that were going to be
left unfulfilled if the students waited for the colleges to do anything
about them. But the students did not make that mistake. Indeed,
when they talked about the college, they did not mean the president,
the professors, the tutors, the board of trustees, the alumni, or even
the curriculum. The students themselves—they were the college. In
a sense, these nineteenth-century collegians, in taking charge of themselves, took charge of the American college and shaped it according
to their wishes. They took what were pale imitations of English
residential colleges, given over to what was certainly more religion
than most students could bear, and they simply reformed them. And
what is remarkably instructive about what they did is how much
more effective they were than the would-be reformers in the ranks of
the presidents and the professors.

In the 1820's and 1830's a great many people knew that something
was wrong with the American college and that it did need reforming.
In Nashville, Philip Lindsley struggled heroically and unsuccessfully
to create a great university that would both serve the people and
develop standards of intellectual excellence. At Amherst, Jacob
Abbott and a faculty committee proposed a set of reforms and were
allowed by the board of trustees to carry some of them out. But the
reforms did not keep, any more than they did when George Ticknor
tampered with the structure of life at Harvard and James Marsh
overhauled the course of study at the University of Vermont. Nor
did Thomas Jefferson's bold departure at the University of Virginia
nor the hopeful launching at New York University of an institution
intended to be seriously dedicated to learning live up to their founders' expectations or seriously influence patterns of higher education
elsewhere. What these frustrated reformers had been hoping to do,
of course, was to make some vital connection with American life and
society and to make some vital connection between the curriculum
and their students as human beings.

This country is going to be a country of businessmen, George
Ticknor argued, and why should Harvard insist on adhering to a
course of study of no earthly use to businessmen? French and German are the useful languages of the future, Latin and Greek are the
dead languages of the past—so argued the Amherst faculty, as, indeed,
did a good many young men outside the colleges who simply could
not see much relationship between what went on in a college classroom or college chapel and what was going on where the roads and

canals and railroads were being built, where the forests were crashing down, and where the fascinating life of commerce and trade and manufacturing were being carried on. But the weight of tradition was against institutional reform. As the Yale faculty announced in 1828: "Our present course contains those subjects only which ought to be understood . . . by everyone who aims at a thorough education." Yale carried the day, and as far as the colleges were concerned, there was to be no reform. What had been was still to be. But they reckoned, as colleges so foolishly did and so often still do, without the students, who proceeded to take matters in their own hands and in the process to reshape completely the intellectual, social, and physical purposes of the American college.

When Greek letter fraternities were moving into the life of the colleges in the 1830's and after, Mark Hopkins of Williams was shaking his head and ineffectually corresponding with President Humphrey of Amherst on whether there was something they could do about them. Later, when he had decided that there was not, he had at least one word of praise: he thought that the fraternities had been responsible for improving undergraduate manners. Of course he was right, but because of his failure to direct any searching questions at the whole phenomenon of fraternities, he did not know why he was right. He missed entirely the symbolic relationship of manners to a whole set of values and preferences which fraternities were institutionalizing on the campus. This concern with manners may well have been a proper subject for congratulations, but more important, it was an indication that the college was being reformed, that students were institutionalizing in their fraternities new prestige values, the attributes of a successful man of the world, this world, at the expense of those various signs of Christian grace—humility, equality before God, and morality—which had long been the purpose of the college to foster. If Philip Lindsley and George Ticknor and Jacob Abbott and James Marsh could not bring the colleges to life, the students were prepared to prove that they could bring life to the colleges.

Another generation of college students forced the gymnasium movement on bewildered boards of trustees, and, still later, while faculties floundered in search of some rationale of control, students created the vast fabric of intercollegiate athletics. No one will argue that the American college was quite the same as it once had been after fraternities and intercollegiate athletics had carried out the reforms which their appearance portended. Conceivably, the colleges were better because of the change, but the instructive fact for anyone

connected with an American college or university today is the completely uninvited, uncontrolled, undirected nature of these revolutionary innovations. Colleges did not decide to have fraternities. They
did not ask to be split into bands of competing Greeks, cliques of
self-important little boys playing grown-up. No board of trustees met
and asked: What can we create as a diversion for the students, something to provide them with a time-consuming outlet for nonacademic
interests? No one asked: How can we best teach snobbery, prejudice,
and conformity, or, indeed, self-reliance, business management, and
good manners. Nothing of the sort. Nor did the rise of athletics
represent a conscious ordering of collegiate life by the governing
authorities. Fraternities and athletics essentially happened *to* the
colleges and they happened because students, left to their own
devices, decided that they would.

The agents of change were the students. The particular groups to
whom law and tradition had assigned the identity and purposes of
the colleges, the presidents and boards of trustees and the professors,
stood aside, indifferent or ineffectual observers, and failed to address
themselves to the questions which should always be raised on an
American college campus when any extracurricular development is
stirring. For if a college cannot keep ahead of its students, students
will surely get ahead of the college. Neglect demands response; the
young do not refuse to act merely because they are not understood.

Governing boards and faculties cannot be expected to turn the
tide of history, even if they are so inclined, and in the case of both
fraternities and intercollegiate athletics there is no question that
powerful and even healthy undergraduate needs and desires were
being expressed, needs that a backward-looking, unimaginative
official orientation insisted upon frustrating. These needs and desires
could not, and should not, have been throttled. It was quite another
matter, however, for collegiate corporations and faculties to be fundamentally unaware of what was going on and remarkably unprepared
to channel and direct such needs and desires within the context of
some conscious notion of what the college was doing and where it
should have been going.

The most sensitive barometer of what is going on in a college is
not its president, who is the victim of demands no six men could
handle ideally. Nor is a board of trustees any more reliable. They
trust the president to keep them informed, and they are both too
busy and generally too honest altogether to trust themselves in
matters that, after all, require some sense of continuing familiarity
with the nature of an academic community. A faculty cannot, either,

be counted on to record with clarity the prevailing climate. On the whole a faculty is likely to be too engrossed in its often rather narrow interests, too wedded to habit, or too accustomed to being ignored in matters of fundamental policy to be always dependable reporters of the academic weather.

The Extracurriculum as a Sensor

The most sensitive barometer of what is going on at a college is the extracurriculum. It is the instrument of change, the instrument with which generations of students, who possess the college for but a few years, register their values, often fleetingly, yet perhaps indelibly. It is the agency that identifies their enthusiasms, their understanding of what a college should be, their preferences. It reveals their attitude toward the course of study; it records the demands of the curriculum, or the lack thereof. It is a measure of their growth. And because it is the particular province of lively, imaginative young men and women not immobilized by tradition, rank, authority, and custom, the extracurriculum is likely to respond more quickly than any other agency of the college to the fundamental, perhaps not yet even clearly expressed, movements in the world beyond the campus and to the developing expectations of society. For this reason a whole range of what in time became respectable academic subjects received their first significant encouragement in the colleges from students, their clubs, their journals, their glee clubs, their dramatic groups, their libraries. For this reason a boys club or a student-run settlement house or an undergraduate branch of the Y.M.C.A. was an earlier manifestation of the Progressive Movement on the campuses than was the adoption of course programs in sociology.

A college president may be acutely aware of the delicate balance of power that he holds; a board of trustees may acknowledge the heavy weight which the past places upon them as successors to the founders; and a faculty may be conscious of and awed by the tremendous and awful knowledge that truth, after all, is still being discovered. But students are not inhibited by any comparable self-consciousness. For a few years the college is their oyster, and they will have it served up exactly as they wish it, unless there are those who help them to some other, perhaps even wiser, choice.

For these reasons an extracurriculum deserves the constant study of those whose business it is to care for the curriculum. Not because the extracurriculum is a repository of evil influence, but because it best tells the friends of a college or university what is going on, what requires attention, what may or may not happen unless conscious, responsible direction is asserted. I have sometimes wondered what passed through the minds of the Williams faculty in the 1840's when they learned that one of the undergraduates, as a purely extracurricular act, had shot and stuffed a set of forty birds of Williamstown, modeling his poses and arrangements after Audubon—whose folio of bird prints was available in the library of the student science club but not in the college library.

In the case of any particular extracurricular development, there are certain obvious questions, whether they are directed by a historian to the past or by any one of us to the present: What does it mean? What does it say about the process of growing up? What would the students be doing if they were not doing this? Why are they doing it? Is it a response to some stimulation or absence of stimulation in the curriculum? Is it a function of geographical isolation? an urban environment? the absence of women? or even the presence of women? Is this going on at other colleges and universities, perhaps suggesting some deeper explanation than that provided by purely local conditions? Has there been a change in the nature of the American family which helps to explain some new undergraduate practice? Is a change in child-rearing practices now reshaping some old collegiate institution? Are national goals undergoing any changes more likely to be asserted in the extracurriculum than in the curriculum? Is the fundamental nature of the college-going population changing?

Now, I do not contend that these questions have very often been asked in the past, but if they had been, it is conceivable that the shaping of the American college would not have been quite so much a matter of uninvited, uncontrolled, undirected student reform. College presidents and professors who did not ask these questions sometimes looked out on some extracurricular innovation and charged it off to excess student enthusiasm, whatever that may be, or to a healthy display of good old American self-reliance. There is something to the notion that students have been given salutary opportunities for testing their independence, their judgment, for trying themselves out in a country where trying oneself out has been something of a national purpose. But it seems to me that the opportunities for reform on the American campus have been embarrassingly, even excessively, plentiful and that the students have really been required to carry on a greater share of the reform than they should have been expected to.

In recognizing that we would not have fraternities and football teams if students had not introduced them to the campus, we sometimes forget that were it not for students, we would also have had to wait much longer for books. The student literary societies enshrined intellect at a time when the colleges' clear preference was for piety. They welcomed books to an environment so hostile that both Mark Hopkins of Williams and Eliphalet Nott of Union could unashamedly admit that they never read books. Not only did the literary societies often outstrip the college libraries in numbers of volumes, but the wide range of subject matter allowed far greater opportunity for the play of intellect than did the narrow religious fare of the usual college library.

By-products of Neglect

In a sense, the literary societies and their libraries, the clubs, journals, and organizations which compensated for the neglect of science, English literature, history, music, and art in the curriculum— this vast, developing extracurriculum was the student response to the classical course of study. It advanced the convincing argument that whereas the curriculum is dead, students are alive. It brought prestige to the life of the mind. It helped to liberate the intellect on the American campus, and it argued so persuasively that in time the colleges assumed responsibilities that they earlier had refused. If student reformers also introduced institutions of a nonintellectual, even anti-intellectual, character that would one day be of serious challenge to the intellectual life of the American college and university, it is also true that on the whole students first gave to American higher education any serious intellectual character at all. So . . . if the boys insist on playing ball and getting drunk, administrators and professors should remember that even before it occurred to us—they wanted to read books.

The day came when the professors also agreed, although several generations too late, that intellect required their attention. But the students had so reformed the colleges and brought them into line with much about the national culture that had no time for serious intellectual endeavor, by then the American college was on its way to two cultures—"theirs" and "ours," if I may speak of the classroom and the ascendancy of intellect from the point of view of the professional professor and call them "ours." As for "theirs"—their culture resided on fraternity row, rewarded the activities men on tap day or some equivalent, and consumed an inordinate amount of energy playing on the team or cheering it.

In the decades after the Civil War the American college and university were in the process of being redefined. During those years responding to a variety of forces, the professors took firm charge of the classroom and redefined it with such devices as the elective curriculum and the new courses of study that students had for so long wanted. But, while the professors took charge of the classroom, the students—who soon would be alumni—remained in charge of the college. The consequence of this somewhat paradoxical situation was to create among the professors the belief that the young men who passed through their classrooms became graduates of the curriculum, while among the young men themselves the belief developed that they would become graduates of their fraternities, their clubs, their teams—of all those aspects of college that really mattered.

In truth, graduates of both sorts were turned out, but it was among the graduates of the extracurriculum that alumni authority and power so often found its voice. The college alumnus who, as a student, had perhaps for the first time in his life taken stock of himself as a member of Alpha Delta Phi or as a member of the varsity football team developed an emotional investment in the preservation of institutions that one day might not be recognized by everyone as best serving an institution of learning. Thus, one consequence of the college student as college reformer has been the college alumnus as perpetual sophomore.

The twentieth-century legacy of these developments lurks in every undergraduate protest, every demonstration against authority, every effort to proclaim "We are here. Do not forget us." This sense of being forgotten derives in part from the extent to which earlier generations of students reformed too well: a world in which a student might play taxidermist after Audubon must have been, after all, rather comforting, a world peculiarly encouraging to individual growth and mastery. But the path of reform led from playing taxidermy to the demanding laboratory courses of today, and one consequence is that the opportunities for individual creativity and imagination have been circumscribed. The more the university takes charge, after all, the less in charge are the students—even of themselves.

When the colleges and universities decided to become intellectually serious and responsible, not only were they required to make a kind of innocent but deadly assault on much of the intellectual life of the extracurriculum, they also were required to change the nature of the professorial role and of the teaching and learning experience. The Mark Hopkins ideal cannot really be sustained by a coaxial cable, and probably no one seriously believes that it can, but the nature of the loss to students has not fully been appreciated. The *in loco parentis* tradition of the residential college, the college professor as friend and moral guide, the liberal arts as a passport to wisdom and self-knowledge—these dominant characteristics of the nineteenth-century college no longer define higher education for most American young men and women. Not yet is it possible to take an identity crisis to an IBM machine or to the great but distant professor who fills the lecture hall. Perhaps the *in loco parentis* tradition of the collegiate way required the colleges to "care" too much, but the outcome of institutional growth, an overwhelming intellectual purpose, and a professionally oriented faculty has been to create an academic environment insensitive to many of the human needs of growing adolescents. In every way the nineteenth century was probably a happier time for experiencing the mysterious needs and desires of growing up than is today, and probably no institution better served those needs and desires than did the colleges.

The Nurture of Student Academic Freedom

A glance back across American academic history suggests that students knew how to use a college as an instrument of their maturation. The university has become a less wieldy instrument for that purpose, often a most disappointing instrument. Students have strangely always had to insist that they are human beings. In the old days, when their insistence took the form of a most intricate extracurriculum or of a rebellion against some especially stringent application of the official code of discipline, they were encouraged either by a benevolent neglect or by some common-sense president or professor. Today neglect takes on new forms: neglect has become a function of size and of a shift in professorial commitment rather that of administrative absent-mindedness or blindness. And as a substitute for the concern and guidance of the collegiate tradition there is now the sensitivity to public relations and the assertion of power by academic governing boards, who in a simpler day assumed, certainly correctly, that presidents and professors knew more about students than they did. Even the debate over parietal rules at residential institutions depends far too much on official concern over what Mrs. Grundy will think than on why students think what they do.

Neglect of students as alive human beings is a venerable academic tradition, a tradition that deserves inspection and repudiation.

The absence of any rationale for student academic freedom in the old colleges rested in part on a carefully reasoned and consciously nurtured paternalism that was intended to help pave the way to freedom. The absence of any effective guidance and concern in the contemporary university rests on no rationale at all, but the consequence is to deliver over to students, in the form of neglect—even in the classroom—the kind of freedom that breeds license. There emerges from this reversal of emphasis the impression that perhaps like all the generations before them, today's students would actually prefer a happy blend of freedom and of guided concern. It was just such a blend that they achieved as nineteenth-century collegiate reformers and that they helped to carry into the early university movement. Whether the contemporary university can create that combination of freedom and concern is perhaps its greatest challenge. As usual, the challenge has been there for quite a while, but it has required students to draw it to our attention. And what is most distressing of all is how often in our history students have had to tell us of their presence—of their needs as young human beings, discovering the limits of their individual destinies.

Is the Student Becoming the "Forgotten Man"?

LOGAN WILSON

We ARE LIVING IN AN AGE in which our educational institutions are valued to an unprecedented extent. We hear daily—on spot radio and television announcements urging financial support for the "college of your choice"—that "college is America's best friend." The advertisements of insurance companies and banks enticingly describe the increased lifetime earnings of those who attend college. Such an expenditure of time, effort, and money, we are assured, is nothing less than a hardheaded "investment" with "practical dividends."

Local, state, and Federal governments place the hope of the nation on institutions of higher education, both in creating the knowledge to maintain our economic and defense superiority in the world and in ameliorating the social disorganization induced by rapid technological change.

From the goals of "expanding and expounding knowledge" we have moved to the goals encompassed by the term "knowledge industry." Not only from our major metropolitan areas, but also from hundreds of smaller communities across the land come the pressures to make colleges and universities mean all things to all people. The rest of the nation looks with envy at the economic growth of the San Francisco Bay region around Stanford and the University of California, or at the burgeoning electronics industry on Route 128 in Boston which leans on Harvard and M.I.T., and it is presumed that this is to be emulated everywhere, by everyone, for the good of all.

In short, the pendulum has swung from expecting too little of our colleges and universities to perhaps expecting too much—of straining the essential foundation of higher education on the assumption that it can support a structure which will give solutions to all our problems.

The spate of new demands and new expectations, without carefully selected priorities, contributes to an increasing danger that the individual student may be crowded out of the picture. For some of us, there is a recurrent need to recall that colleges were created primarily for students. The many pressures and diversions that beset us could create a deplorable condition where the student is the forgotten man.

The need to make higher education available to all qualified youth is being met by our unique American system of mass education, and in the process the notion is discarded that college is for only a small, elite group. Individual responses to the challenge by the two thousand or so junior colleges, colleges, and universities in our country have been laudable. Physical plant expansion, the growth of graduate education to provide the necessary faculty members, and creative fund raising for the support of all types of institutions have marked the past decade, and will, I trust, keep pace in the future.

One danger inherent in higher education's new-found success, however, is that created by a seller's market. With 40 percent, or more, of our youth seeking admission to college, it is all too easy for those of us engaged in teaching or administration to avoid confronting some of the issues involving students that should be at the heart of our concern. Because others are standing in line to take the places of the dropouts, there is a danger of our becoming indifferent, if not callous, to the sources of discontent and the causes of failure.

We know that the rate of expansion of enrollments in the next decade inevitably will have a heavy impact on student life. Increasingly, students may have less personal contact with professors and staff members of their institutions except as they find themselves in serious trouble and have to be dealt with in some official way. With the advent of programed instruction may also come the faceless anonymity that IBM cards, drop cards, seat numbers, and I.D. numbers represent. The depersonalization of the student, if allowed to go unchecked or unchallenged, represents a grave threat to the very purposes of higher education. We must not only sympathize with the student's desire to make a human or personal connection with his college, we must also vigorously assist him in making such a connection.

I believe we in higher education must confront and resolve at least three critical issues:

Implementing the Learning Goal

First, what factors obstruct or reinforce the learning goals of our colleges and universities?

Obviously, the first order of business in a college is learning. Yet we know that this cannot be truly fruitful if it takes place only—and grudgingly—in the classroom and laboratory. A student spends most of his time outside the periods of formal instruction. Therefore, what happens during this time may well be crucial in reinforcing or obstructing the goals of the college. The desire to learn, the cultivation of the mind and of individuality, the acquisition of literary judgment, aesthetic taste, and spiritual identity are goals for students that should pervade the atmosphere of the entire campus, not just the classroom. Several factors affect this issue: extracurricular activities, faculty and administration values, and the climate and environment of the campus.

We need to re-examine the extracurricular life of our colleges in light of present conditions. It may well be that certain of the adolescent preoccupations of nineteenth-century college life are no longer fitting. Let me be clear that I do not mean that any moment spent away from a book is a wasted or frivolous moment. Nor do I argue that entertainment has no place in institutions whose primary mission is edification. Everyone knows that leisure and diversion are necessary to keep our campuses from being grim, unsmiling, joyless places. But with the rising expectations about students and the higher standards demanded of them and, I hope, the increasing level of student maturity, we can afford to drop the enervating and time-consuming activities that (on some campuses) preoccupy the energies of students and obstruct realization of the true goals of education.

Extracurricular life can be both enjoyable and constructive and we should assist students in restructuring traditional student activities so that they have a more positive role in the campus environment. The pervading out-of-class values and climate of a campus are major factors in obstructing or reinforcing a student's acceptance of the intellectual mission of the college. In this sphere, too, the concepts of right and wrong, justice and injustice, truth or sham, are learned and reinforced.

Much has been said, but little done, about the "publish or perish" syndrome and the low value attributed by faculty and administration to the effective and committed teaching of students. Consultantships, outside research grants and contracts, and publications seem to score more points for faculty members. For this, faculty and administrators must accept responsibility.

Clark Kerr, in his book, *The Uses of the University*, summarizes it well in stating:

> the undergraduate students are restless. Recent changes in the American university have done them little good—lower teaching loads for the faculty, larger classes, the use of substitute teachers for the regular faculty, the choice of faculty members based on research accomplishments rather than instructional capacity, the fragmentation of knowledge into endless subdivisions. There is an incipient

revolt of undergraduate students against the faculty; the revolt that used to be against the faculty *in loco parentis* is now against the faculty *in absentia*.[1]

If the college does not reward faculty members for their devotion to teaching and relating to students, the student body can infer only that such activity is not considered terribly important. If the faculty itself regards *relief from teaching* as the chief reward for accomplish· ment, or as the highest status symbol, and relegates undergraduate teaching to inexperienced graduate assistants, we may be sure that the students perceive this situation too. Obviously, such matters can obstruct or reinforce whatever values a college seeks to attain.

In recent years, behavioral scientists have become interested in studying campus environments and climates as they affect student perceptions of college goals and values—a fascinating area of study, incidentally, which I urge colleges and universities to examine. In the book, *The American College*, edited by Nevitt Sanford, there is evidence enough to demonstrate that the environment in which learning takes place—or is supposed to take place—is of sufficient consequence to merit our efforts to do everything we can to improve it.

The work of Robert Pace of U.C.L.A. and George Stern of the University of Syracuse has a particular relevancy here. Using earlier research studies, Dr. Pace and the Educational Testing Service have developed College and University Environment Scales (CUES) wherein some 150 statements about college life are rated by students as generally "true" or "false" with reference to their college. A wide variety of aspects of the institutional environment are rated in this manner, and the results yield a highly interesting description of the college from the students themselves.[2] Because they are a part of the institution—live in it—they presumably are able to judge or describe best what that environment is.

Colleges are scored on five scales: *practicality, community, awareness, propriety,* and *scholarship.* I commend the significance of such research activities and hope that they will be helpful in re-examining the images we create, knowingly or unknowingly.

Guiding Student Conduct

A second issue that demands our attention is the student's personal conduct and behavior. Our newspapers and magazines are featuring,

---

[1] Cambridge, Mass.: Harvard University Press, 1963. P. 103.
[2] A summary of the study appears in the present volume; see "Perspectives on the Student and His College," by Pace, pp. 76–100.

with increasing frequency, popular articles on the subject of student morals, rebellion, drinking, and general strife.

Many self-styled experts are just discovering these problems, although those of us with long experience on campuses know that they are not of recent origin. Aristotle made a relevant comment when he said, long ago:

> [Youth] have exalted notions, because they have not yet been humbled by life or learnt its necessary limitations; moreover their hopeful disposition makes them think themselves equal to great things—and that means having exalted notions. They would always rather do noble deeds than useful ones: their lives are regulated more by moral feeling than by reasoning—all their mistakes are in the direction of doing things excessively and vehemently. They overdo everything—they love too much, hate too much, and the same with everything else.

A problem *does* exist in the area of student behavior. Colleges and universities cannot be indifferent to questions of honesty, integrity, and morality. But it is not easy to reach a consensus on expected standards of behavior and the means of enforcing them. In some of our "multiversities" the faculty has apparently disavowed any interest in student behavior outside the classroom or off the campus. Although individual faculty members may privately feel concern, the problems are so involved that they may adopt a "hands off" policy and leave the worries to the dean.

At the other extreme, there are colleges where the faculty take most seriously the *in loco parentis* concept; student life, both on and off campus, is regulated by a system of elaborate rules and regulations. Students need permission to leave campus, they must be in dormitories at specified hours, they are denied the use of automobiles, and their freedom of behavior is severely circumscribed.

For most of our colleges and universities, however, the situation lies between these two extremes. Many of them are groping for answers to cope with the changing values and mores of our society and particularly those of our youth.

We must acknowledge that the home milieu in which many of today's students were reared is different from that of their teachers and deans. The postwar period of general prosperity, mobility, and redefinition of values has witnessed a reduction in community and family restraints. Some parents do not support the restrictions which colleges have traditionally placed on students in matters of personal conduct. Other parents, however, expect colleges to police their sons and daughters in ways which they themselves did not, or could not, do. Our colleges, of course, cannot reasonably be expected to accept responsibilities which really belong to mothers and fathers. Given all this, it is no wonder that the present tension exists between students and institutions regarding rules, discipline, morals, rights, freedoms, and responsibilities.

The overburdened college president, possessing the ultimate responsibility, more often than not delegates matters affecting student life to other administrative officers, such as the dean of students; thus, the function of dealing with students in this crucial area becomes a segregated and negative one. The dean may readily become a scapegoat, for, without full faculty cooperation, he may be forced to promulgate proscriptions which he alone cannot enforce. This state of affairs is an open invitation to some students to protest, of course, but legitimate modes of protest and ground rules for settling grievances, both alleged and real, are unclear on many campuses.

The student newspaper is often a symbol of the tension that exists between undergraduates and local authority. Editors frequently want to be considered immune from responsibility or accountability—as though the campus or the principle of academic freedom provided a sanctuary from community standards of good taste, propriety, or responsibility. College officials may counter this situation, however, with a plea to the alumni and the community to recognize that the student newspaper is not an official spokesman for the institution and that one learns by doing and having to defend one's actions and words.

What are the answers to these and numerous other problems? Shall we do away with all rules and regulations? Do students really want to be left completely alone in nonacademic areas, as they are in some European countries? Do they want enough control over operations to be able to shut them down, as is the case in some Latin American countries?

There are no pat answers to these questions, and so we come back to the difficult job that each college or university must define for itself —the eternal question posed by freedom and responsibility. And the confrontation of this issue begins anew with each generation of students.

I believe that every college or university has a responsibility for what happens to a student outside the classroom, and this is especially true for the residential college. That obligation cannot be side-stepped, no matter how much we may wish to avoid it. Qualities of character, conscience, and citizenship are part of the educational development of our students. All of us, faculty as well as students, make a tragic mistake if we proclaim that this is not the proper business of the college.

Reducing Attrition

The third issue is of special concern to educators because it represents a waste of human potential. That is the continuing high rate of student attrition in higher education.

Nationally, various studies show, only about four out of every ten entering freshmen are graduated from college in four years. Although one or two more may finish sometime later, or somewhere else, the total picture is one of waste, inefficiency, and probably considerable personal unhappiness.

Some of these students are outright academic failures, but we have made real progress recently in our selection and prediction instruments that should soon reflect itself in a rapid decrease in attrition rate for academic reasons. Still other students find themselves out of step with institutional requirements, schedules, and unrealistic faculty expectations. The fact that they do not "fit" a preconceived mold or are repelled by the pressures and irrelevancies put upon them should give us pause for reflection. There is, in many instances, a real basis for complaints about the pedantic sterility of the curriculum and its lack of connection with the real world.

In the race for "excellence," too many students who would have been successes a decade ago are found in the tally of casualties. A great many colleges and universities have tended to denigrate academic adequacy in student capability and performance and to overemphasize a stringent definition of academic excellence.

A substantial portion of youth seek and can profit from higher education. We can demand adequacy for all students, but excellence can be expected only from a few. The danger is that we will eliminate those whose motivation and capabilities are only average or slightly above. We do so at the peril of the nation, for by definition such young people make up the foundation on which our society rests.

In dealing with this problem of attrition, institutions should not pose a dichotomy between unrealistically high expectations and no standards at all. We should demand the best from each student. Despite that best effort, however, there will still be a bottom quarter in each class. In many cases that category should not be regarded arbitrarily as failures. We can be flexible without being lax, and we can treat students as individuals without having academic chaos.

I have attempted to pose three critical issues which should engage the attention of faculties and students in our institutions of higher education: (1) the factors which obstruct or reinforce the learning goals of our colleges; (2) the problems of student personal conduct and behavior out of class; and (3) the continuing high rates of student attrition that cause waste of human resources. Some of the nation's colleges are fortunate in being homogeneous enough in size and purpose to retain that sense of community so precious in collegiate life. Their students and faculty and administrators have the opportunity for face-to-face discussion of these important issues and the possibility of achieving a consensus within the institution so that the means of coping with its problems can be discovered.

What is discovered in such deliberations not only will aid such colleges in achieving their goals, but also will prove to be of value to those more complex institutions that may not have the same opportunities for such discovery. There is much to be done.

Changing the Collegiate Culture

WILLIAM L. KOLB

IN THE COLLEGES AND UNIVERSITIES of the recent past, there was a continuous confrontation between the intellectual and scholarly culture of the faculty and the collegiate and vocational culture of the student and his parents. While the latter—who were much smaller in number than today—felt that a college degree was desirable, they did not for the most part take academic work very seriously. College was where one went to learn to get along well with other people and to make the social contacts that would serve one well in later life. Against this view, the faculty upheld the worthwhileness of the intellectual, scholarly, and creative life.

For the most part this confrontation resulted in victory for the students and parents. Whether in a prestigious college or not, whatever the social class of the student, the gulf between what the faculty, until disillusioned, hoped for and what actually took place in the way of learning was tremendous. Miraculously, however, some students did, either during college or later, come to be absorbed by the scholarly, intellectual, or creative life. Where this did happen, the life that was led had within it elements of leisure and grace, as well as elements of hard thought and hard work. While the Puritan ethic lay behind some aspects of academic achievement, particularly in science, for many others there were different motivations. Faculty members and interested students worked at their own pace and for their own ends. Such work resulted in a scholarly, intellectual, and creative culture which, although widely separated from the dominant culture of America, was critical, serious, and high in quality.

Since World War II all this has changed. The collegiate culture has diminished in strength, even though the number of students has increased. In the prestigious institutions it exists only as a remnant, while in other institutions it has been replaced to a considerable degree by a serious and grim vocationalism. At all points on the educational continuum, college has become a much more serious matter. Behind academic work from grade school on, all the status insecurities and drives of the parents, reflected in their concern for the future oc-

67

cupational status of their offspring, have been mustered. So also have the search for absolute national security through technical knowledge and the demand for specialized personnel in the increasingly intricate division of labor at the top levels of society.

Without question the faculty's expectations, so far as the student is concerned, are higher than they have ever been, although these expectations are blunted at the lower end of the continuum by the rather simple vocational demands of the student and the parents. These faculty expectations, however, are different from those of the past. They tend to be focused, even at the undergraduate level, on the specialized demands of particular disciplines and the subfields of those disciplines. While at the highest levels of academic life, interdisciplinary work is becoming more common, it is tending to disappear at the undergraduate level. All elements of leisure and grace have been removed from academic work, so that although the faculty's level of expectation is higher, its vocationalism is as serious and as grim as that of the student. This tendency is strengthened by the fact that most colleges on the make have been cultivating an image of toughness.

Although we certainly do not wish to return to the old collegiate culture, it appears to be legitimate to ask whether we wish to continue to identify intellectual excellence with this syndrome of the achievement drive and the demands of the knowledge industry. Although we do not necessarily pass negative judgment on the successful outcome of this orientation in the person of the highly motivated, highly trained, specialized intellectual who may also have some dimension of breadth in relating himself to his discipline, himself, and the world, the fact remains that we know empirically that the societal expectations described above can produce docile guilt-ridden individuals; aggressive and uncompassionate people interested primarily in external incentives like grades, money, and prestige, or in internal incentives like abstract knowledge totally unrelated to the human complex in which meaningful knowledge must be rooted; and, in more recent years, alienated students who respond either with a paralyzing apathy or with destructive rebellion to parental and societal goals and drives. We also know that for all these people the academic pressure cooker no longer provides the opportunity for a search for the self or for the making of a commitment. In light of this, should we not be asking whether there are possibilities open to us other than domination by either the collegiate culture of the past or the high-pressure knowledge industry of the present?

In asking such a question, a stance of total alienation from American culture makes very little sense. The knowledge explosion is here to stay. We are not going to surrender our urban-technical culture. The demands for high performance in specialized and administrative roles will continue. Yet at the same time we cannot remain complacent in the face of the strains and the actual destruction of personality which are resulting from these social expectations, and it is highly dubious that psychotherapy is the answer. Rather we must search for institutional means to place the present expectations within a broader and controlling framework. Can we create—at least during the undergraduate years—a nonthreatening environment for the student in which he can search out his identity, grapple with the problems of commitment, and become attracted to and involved with the intellectual life? Can we open up possibilities of a variety of modes of the intellectual life, some of which may contain elements of grace and leisure, elements of social responsibility and criticism? Can we, at the undergraduate level, make the specialty of the discipline or the occupation a liberal art in which the philosophical, religious, aesthetic, historical, and scientific dimensions of each specialty become so integral a part of the student's mind and self that they are never lost?

Are the only motivations toward excellence we can offer to the bright but unactivated student those of academic dismissal and consequent occupational failure? Is it impossible to build on the campus an intellectual culture which the rebel will find relevant to his own interests and concerns? Is it futile to hope that we can relate the constructive elements of student criticism and rebellion to a renewed concern for the uncoerced and uncoercive life of the mind that remains responsible to the world?

All these are the questions which face us if we take seriously the difficulties created by societal expectations in higher education today. As I indicated earlier neither the stance of total alienation nor that of complacency is relevant. Rather we must discover the possibilities open to us within the present structure of our society and culture.

Let me conclude with examples of situations where new developments seem possible to me. First, have we really yet taken the knowledge explosion seriously in the sense of recognizing that the appropriate response is being discriminating in what we teach, rather than simply pouring more and more materials into courses, much of which may be obsolete in a few years? Second, have we really examined seriously the elements of youth culture—mass-based though it may be —to discover the genuine as well as the spurious elements in it in order to relate the former to serious intellectual and aesthetic concern? There are those who believe that there is a genuine concern for form and substance relevant to the modern world embodied in much of the music, dance, motion pictures, and the like to which our youth attend. Third, have we really taken seriously the noncourse environment of the college as a place where serious intellectual concern may develop? Fourth, have we paid enough attention to the task of bringing the world into the campus and the campus into the world, so that knowledge may reveal its relevance to life beyond status and occupation? Fifth, have we been true to the ambivalent image of the college and the university as critic of the society of which it is a part?

Last, and perhaps most important, have we really made an effort to bring student, parent, and faculty member into our concerns for the whole of education? In my tenure as an administrator I have attended many meetings. They have been attended mostly by other administrators or by faculty who are not truly at the center of the intellectual life of their campuses. The best faculty seem to me for the most part to be relatively untouched by the ferment of ideas and concern for the whole of higher education. Administrators can talk forever about social expectations and other aspects of the educational scene, but it can only be talk until we get the faculty talking too. I frequently have the impression that beneath all the talk the trends in higher education proceed down the path toward intellectual barbarism without hindrance. If this is true, it is not because these trends are inevitable, but because administrators have not really involved the people who in their daily lives make the decisions—minute though they may be— which in their totality constitute the trends of which we have spoken.

New Responsibilities for an Old Generation

KINGMAN BREWSTER, JR.

BOREDOM IS NOT A NEWCOMER in the halls of academe. But there is a mounting impatience and, if we admit it, a new and unpleasant aroma of scorn among some student groups—impatience with education, scorn for educators.

Of course faculties are, and always should be, heavily populated by people who are dedicated to the proposition that the search for truth is an end in itself. I am not one of those who buy the notion that the only worthy end of thought is action. Thought and learning, like experience and beauty, can be ends in themselves. Not the least part of our job is to awaken a capacity for this enjoyment in the oncoming generations so that theirs may be delight in living as well as doing.

But the tragedy of the highly motivated impatient young activist is that he runs the serious risk of disqualifying himself from true usefulness by being too impatient to arm himself with the intellectual equipment required for the solution of the problems of war and poverty and indignity. I have seen too many among our students who show high promise of talent for a lifetime of constructive work at a high level squander that talent for the cheaper and transient satisfaction of throwing themselves on some immediate barricade in the name of "involvement." Posturing in the name of a good cause is too often the substitute for thorough thought or for the patient doggedness it takes to build something.

Because educators assume their own faith in education, perhaps they have not preached it well enough. We have left it to the economists and the politicians to translate the value of education into earning power and let it go at that. A generation whose brightest minds are dissatisfied with the dollar as the measure of success cannot be expected to find relevance in such appeals.

The first of the new responsibilities for the old generation of educators is to remind the most highly motivated among the oncoming
generation that there is no shortcut to the intellectual capacity which
is now required if one is to be useful in this ever-shrinking, ever-com-
plicating world. The chance to make a constructive difference in the
lives of others, not the full dinner pail, is the highest reward of a
higher education. If the impatient anti-intellectualism of the radical
left is not to seduce many of our best brains away from true usefulness,
college administrators and their faculties have to reassert again and
again that emotional oversimplification of the world's problems is not
the path to their solution.

But what of the ends? If they don't justify the means, what does?
Far more fundamental, far more pervasive, than the impatience of the
anti-intellectual activist is the uneasy feeling that society is a structure
of power without purpose, education's capacities have no convincing
objective, life serves no end larger than itself. "Fat City" is an image
that carries more meaning than does the "Great Society."

Disengagement bordering on indifference is a far greater threat to a
world on the verge of nuclear anarchy and riddled with urban inde-
cency than is the shrill cry of protest sometimes bent more on exhibi-
tionism and destruction than on construction. The pressures which
flatten a capacity for both moral outrage and a constructive conscience
are awfully great in our time. Some of these pressures are old, some are
intensified, some are new.

Privilege, including the privilege of the best in education, has always
run the dual risk of courting smugness on the one hand and defensive-
ness on the other. Neither self-satisfaction nor sheepishness is very
rich soil for morally motivated action.

Insensitivity is not a peculiarly modern trait. However, to the ranks
of the philistine is now joined that intellect whose critical and analytical capacity is so refined that he becomes paralyzed by doubt. Doubt
is rarely consciously cruel, but it can be just as callous as cruelty if it
paralyzes moral purpose.

The new allies of moral indifference are specialization and organization, which tend to mean that most people are responsible for only a
part of the life around them; very, very few see or feel responsibility
whole. And too many of those who do, feel so beholden to so many
constituencies that the value of achieving consensus receives preced-
ence over the value of expressing conviction.

So I come to the second responsibility of the old generation of educators, faculty and administrators alike. It is not new, it is simply harder to shoulder in an increasingly specialized, organized, "dependentized" world. We all have the responsibility to hold the scales of conflicting opinion evenly, so that neither the classroom nor the administrative office is used to suppress or prejudice the free thought and expression of teachers or students. We also have a responsibility not to let the sword of our own conviction fall to the ground—not because we are wiser or less fallible than those who have no audience, but because our preceptorial position puts the responsibility on us not to become faceless men incapable of expressing personal conscientious conviction. Not to please the activists, but to stem the tendencies to moral disengagement, teacher and dean and president must cure the misimpression that we approve of all we would permit or oppose all we would not espouse. To cultivate a weasel-worded tolerance in the name of objectivity is to fail the duty as preceptor to set an example of moral and intellectual courage. It can only confirm the allegation that ours is an apparatus of means without ends.

But the quest of the young for a more satisfactory purpose is our quest too. Our world and our country as well as all of us individually are in quest of ourselves. For survival the world must find a pattern of order which permits revolutionary change, and yet forbids resort to the weapons of total frightfulness. For survival, the nation must find a pattern for society which promises dignity and decency in urban work and life. For survival each of us individually must find a pattern for life which gives purpose to effort and satisfaction deeper than animal existence.

So to a final injunction to the old generation of educators: Let us never forget that the university is the last best hope for the discovery and articulation of ends which will justify the means—not only the means of education but the means of society and of life itself. Imparting information, deepening knowledge, training skill, enlarging intellectual capacity generally are our clearly visible tasks. Because it is at the core, perhaps it is less visible; it is the struggle for a system of values which will renew purpose.

I can do no better than to draw upon the articulate faith of my predecessor at Yale, the late Whitney Griswold, who once said:

> If we cannot say we know that liberal education is the surest educational source of the qualities of mind and spirit of which we now, at this moment in our history, stand most in need, you can say you believe that it is, and I shall say I agree with you. Never has the

future of our civilization depended as much as it does now upon our capacity to grow in intellectual and moral stature, and therefore upon the kind of education most conducive to that growth. The times call for boldness and innovation. Might not the boldest thing we could do, the greatest educational innovation of all, be to lift the bushel under which we have been hiding the light of liberal education and reveal its true power to its possessors? [1]

[1] *Williams Alumni Review*, November 1961, p. 25.

PART 2   The Campus
          Environment:
          Focus on
          the Student

Perspectives
on the
Student
and
His College

C. ROBERT PACE

ONE OF THE popular freedom ballads is "Blowin' in the Wind,"
with the refrain:

> The answer, my friend,
> is blowin' in the wind—
> The answer is blowin'
> in the wind.

From the daily news one would think that in higher education, as
in civil rights, "The answer is blowin' in the wind." But the history
of higher education has often been breezy—sudden gusts between
town and gown, hot winds of heresy, chill winds of loyalty, swirling
eddies of curriculum reform, trade winds of academic freedom. So
what's new about a little wind? Is it a gust or a gathering storm?
Is the answer blowin' in the wind—powerful, inevitable? Indeed,
what answer and to what question?

The apprehension and irritation among some members of the
Regents of the University of California, the state legislature, and
California citizens generally over the Berkeley rebellion, and particularly over the style of the student protest, are reflected in a belief
that the critical problems now are to contain such outbreaks in the
future, to enforce discipline, and to demand respect for law and
order. There may occasionally be some local validity to such beliefs,
but there is little validity to them so far as higher education in the
United States is concerned.

It would be unfortunate if college presidents and faculty members
across the country now believed that their job is to batten down the
hatches against a rising wind of student rebellion. In the national
perspective, the needs and the problems of higher education are just
the opposite. The national need is not to suppress student protest
but to stimulate it, not to get students back to their books but to get
them into a larger society in which books are one among many

76

sources of knowledge and wisdom, not to fortify the castle of learning against a barbarian invasion but to open the gates wider to the fresh winds of innovation and change.

In the national perspective, some of the major problems in higher education have little to do with students or with undergraduate life on the campus. These are problems of finance, manpower, and management, deriving in part from population growth, technology, poverty, affluence, and other familiar phenomena of modern society. Other problems, of course, bear down more intimately upon the students: access to higher education, competition for grades, faculty neglect of teaching for research, institutional impersonality, and assorted regulations governing personal freedom and social protest. But even these problems have a different urgency at different institutions for the simple and obvious reason that the institutions themselves are different from one another. A perspective on the student and his college cannot be drawn from any fixed point. If higher education itself is characterized by diversity rather than similarity, and by complexity rather than consistency, then it can be seen in perspective only by looking at it from many different vantage points.

There are more than two thousand institutions of higher education—universities, state colleges, teachers colleges, liberal arts colleges, technical schools, and junior colleges. A majority of them are private, not public. A majority of the private ones are church related, not nonsectarian. My impression, from reading the daily editions of the two largest newspapers at both ends of the country during the past year, the *New York Times* and the *Los Angeles Times*, is that stories of student protests—at Berkeley, Stanford, Yale, Princeton, etc.—which, by their publication, have attained national visibility, have come from no more than twenty or so institutions; but even if this impression is grossly incorrect and there have been two hundred (ten times as many), the number of institutions involved would be no more than 10 percent of the total.

A very different perspective, however, is equally correct. Although there are more than two thousand institutions, half of all the college students in the country are concentrated in fewer than two hundred of these institutions; and two-thirds of all the students are in public institutions, not private ones. If one looks at where the students are, one sees that what is characteristic of a relatively small number of institutions is of relatively great significance in the national perspective.

Large-scale organized research, which nearly everyone agrees is now a major contribution of higher education to society, is often blamed for lowering the prestige of college teaching and for drawing professors away from the classroom. But research of this magnitude exists only in a very small number of institutions. About a fourth of all the Federal money spent on research activities in colleges and universities goes to just ten universities, and nearly all of it is spent in not more than one hundred or so colleges and universities. From this perspective, research is not taking professors away from their students except in a few places; but again, these few places include most of the largest universities so that the number of students affected is proportionately much greater than the number of institutions would suggest.

The distribution of institutions, the distribution of students, and the distribution of Federal research money illustrate three vantage points from which to view higher education, each providing a different perspective and suggesting different conclusions, no one of which is adequate to the complexity of the scene.

Perspectives from a Study of College Environments

With these complexities in mind let us look first at some of the characteristics of college environments today as they relate to various targets of student protest: teaching, impersonality and research, and freedom or constraint—stimulation or suppression of personal, social, and political activities. The perspective for this exploration comes from the responses of students at one hundred or so colleges and universities to an instrument called College and University Environment Scales, or CUES for short. The instrument consists of 150 statements about college life—rules and regulations, features and facilities, faculty, curriculum, instruction, extracurricular programs, informal student activities, and so forth. Students act as reporters about the environment of their college indicating whether, in their experience and judgment, the various statements in the test describe a condition that exists, an event that occurs or might occur, the way people feel or behave, or, in short, something that is generally true or characteristic of the college. When there is a high level of consensus among the reporters—an agreement of two to one, or better —the statement is regarded as characteristic of the college; that is, it represents something about which most students are aware, a collective and widely shared perception.

On teaching and faculty-student relationships

Among the items in the test, there are several which relate to aspects of teaching, faculty-student relationships, and research. To what extent is it generally true and at what types of institutions, that, in the perception of students, professors:

> are thorough teachers
> are dedicated scholars in their field
> set high standards for students to attain
> clearly explain the goals and purposes of their courses
> have vigorous classroom discussions
> don't expect students to wait to be called on before speaking in class
> give exams that are a genuine measure of students' understanding
> frequently revise their courses, examinations, and readings
> call students by their first names
> go out of their way to be helpful
> are interested in students' personal problems
> are not embarrassed by a display of emotion
> do not react to criticisms personally
> and, are actively engaged in research?

This inventory of virtues defines pretty well what most people would regard as the ideal professor: a scholar and a researcher, a thorough teacher, constantly keeping his materials up to date, making his goals clear to the students, demanding high standards of performance, provoking lively class discussions, and giving examinations that provide a genuine measure of students' understanding; at the same time, a friendly and mature individual, knowing his students by their first names, interested in their personal problems, going out of his way to be helpful, and reacting to hysteria or criticism with calm objectivity.

The paragon suggested by these virtues is not a mythical creature. He is seen most clearly on the campuses of high prestige, highly selective, nonsectarian liberal arts colleges—places like Antioch, Swarthmore, Bennington, Bryn Mawr, Oberlin, Reed. At such colleges, almost without exception, there is high agreement among the students that the professors are scholars, thorough teachers, set high standards, frequently revise their materials, encourage students to ask questions in class, know students by their first names, are interested in students' personal problems, go out of their way to be helpful, react to criticism objectively, and, on top of all this, are actively engaged in research. In at least a majority of these colleges, students also agree that the goals and purposes of courses are clear, that examinations are very good, and that professors are not upset by some display of emotion.

Most of these virtues are found less frequently in other types of colleges and universities. In the studies from which these data were obtained, over the past three years, the following categories have been examined:

Category	No. of Schools Studied
High prestige, nonsectarian, highly selective liberal arts colleges	10–15
Other liberal arts colleges, both nonsectarian and denominational	10–15
Strongly denominational colleges	10–15
Universities, public and private	15–20
State colleges, including teachers colleges	10–15
Junior colleges, public	25–30

In the total group, which includes institutions throughout the country, there are roughly 80 to 110 colleges and universities. The number varies somewhat because not all information was readily available from all institutions. The data for this discussion are shown in Table 1.

Characteristically, in almost all of these institutions, and in all types, the professors are described as dedicated scholars and as keeping their materials up to date; but this is the extent of across-the-board agreement.

The group of other liberal arts colleges and the group of strongly denominational colleges resemble the high prestige colleges described above in the following respects: the professors are thorough teachers, they explain the goals of their courses, they call students by their first names, go out of their way to be helpful, and are interested in students' personal problems.

In the group of universities, professors are described as being thorough teachers in about half of the institutions studied; in nearly all cases their examinations are described as providing a genuine measure of students' understanding; but in only one or two of the 15–20 universities was it said, by as much as a two-to-one majority of the students, that professors called students by their first names, that they were interested in students' personal problems, or that they went out of their way to be helpful. These latter aspects of friendly faculty-student relationships are conspicuously not characteristic of the universities. This is not to say that friendly faculty-student relationships are totally absent. Indeed, there may well be many individual examples of very stimulating and rewarding personal relationships on many large university campuses. It is to say, however, and quite clearly, that these are not common to the point of being regarded as a characteristic of the institutional atmosphere.

It is characteristic of most junior college environments that the

TABLE 1. *Quality of Teaching and Faculty-Student Relationships*

Students agree, by a margin of 2 to 1 or greater, that:	High Prestige Liberal Arts Colleges	Other Liberal Arts Colleges	Strongly Denominational Colleges	Universities	State Colleges	Junior Colleges
Professors						
are thorough teachers	all	nearly all	nearly all	half	half	most
dedicated scholars	all	nearly all	all	nearly all	nearly all	nearly all
set high standards	nearly all	less than half	a few	a few	none	a few
clearly explain goals of their courses	most	half	nearly all	a few	less than half	nearly all
give exams that are a genuine measure of students' understanding	about half	a few	about half	nearly all	none	most
frequently revise course materials	nearly all	most	most	most	most	about half
have vigorous class discussions	a few	a few	a few	a few	none	a few
don't expect students to wait to be called on before speaking in class	most	a few	a few	none	none	none
Moreover, in their relationships with students, they						
call students by first names	nearly all	all	all	a few	about half	most
are interested in students' personal problems	nearly all	all	all	a few	about half	most
go out of their way to be helpful	nearly all	all	all	a few	about half	most
would not be embarrassed by a display of emotion	about half	a few	a few	a few	a few	a few
and do not react to criticism personally	all	a few	most	a few	a few	most
And, they						
are actively engaged in research	nearly all	about half	none	nearly all	a few	none

81

professors are thorough teachers, that they clearly explain the purposes and goals of their courses, that they give good examinations, that they are interested in students' personal problems, and go out of their way to be helpful. Professors are not characterized, however, as being actively engaged in research.

In almost none of the colleges and universities was it said by the bulk of the students that class discussions were typically vigorous and intense.

If we were to give grades for the quality of teaching and faculty-student relationships to each of the categories of institutions we have described, we would clearly give an A to the high prestige liberal arts colleges, a B to the other liberal arts colleges, the strongly denominational colleges, and the junior colleges, and we would give a C to the universities and state colleges. Considering how students are distributed among the various types of colleges and universities across the country, we can put these ratings in some national perspective. As a rough estimate, about 5 percent of all college students are in prestige liberal arts colleges, perhaps another 5 percent in strongly denominational colleges, about 10 percent are in other liberal arts colleges, and 20 percent in junior colleges—with all these adding to about 40 percent. We would estimate that about 45–50 percent of all the students are in universities and state colleges, leaving about 10–15 percent distributed among other categories which we have not considered in this analysis.

What we have defined as indications of good teaching and faculty-student relationships are found most consistently and amply in institutions which enroll about 40 percent of the students—the liberal arts colleges and the junior colleges. For these students, the encounter with good teaching and friendly relationships with faculty members is a characteristic of their environment. For the majority of students in higher education, however, such an encounter is not characteristic of their college-level experience. It may occur and almost surely does occur in many individual instances in all kinds of institutions, but for most students the occurrence is not sufficiently common to be regarded as a characteristic of the college environment in which they live.

On politics, protest, and related activities

In the social and political arena, and the confrontation of ideas and actions, it is again in the high prestige liberal arts colleges where the greatest encouragement and the greatest response are characteristic. Again, if we were to give grades for the stimulation and interest which both the college and its students exemplify in these political and cultural aspects of campus life, we would give an A to the high prestige liberal arts colleges, a B to the universities, and a grade of C or below to all other categories of colleges and universities.

From the pool of items in College and University Environment Scales, we have selected a set which bears rather directly on these questions of social, political, and cultural stimulation and response. Does the college encourage students to criticize its administrative policies and teaching practices? Does it provide readily accessible channels for expressing student complaints? Are students encouraged to be active in social and political reforms? Are there prominent faculty members who are active in local or national politics? Are the students concerned about national and international affairs? Do they develop a sense of responsibility about their role in contemporary social and political life? Does a controversial speaker stir up a lot of student discussion? Are there frequent public debates on the campus? Does the college bring many famous people to the campus for lectures, discussion, and concerts? Does it provide good facilities for individual creative activity and many opportunities for students to understand and criticize important works of art, music, drama, etc.? Would there be a good crowd of students attending a lecture by an outstanding scientist, or literary critic, or philosopher or theologian? Do art exhibits and concerts draw good crowds of students? Are serious intellectual discussions common among the students? And is there a lot of interest in such things as poetry, painting, architecture, or the analysis of value systems and other cultures?

How frequently the bulk of students in various types of institutions gave "yes" answers to these questions is shown in Table 2. In all or most of the high prestige liberal arts colleges a "yes" answer to most of the questions is characteristic. By way of contrast, a "yes" answer is characteristic of few, none, or at best no more than half of the junior colleges. Nor are the results much different for any of the other categories of institutions.

Frequent public debates were not characteristic of any of the one hundred or so colleges and universities. And except in a few high prestige liberal arts colleges and a few universities, most students were not aware of any prominent faculty members active in local or national politics. Moreover, in only a few of the colleges and universities do the students agree, by a two-to-one margin or greater, that the college encourages them to be active in social and political reforms.

In one sense, it cannot be said that either the students or the col-

TABLE 2. Criticism and Politics, Stimulation and Response

Students agree, by a margin of 2 to 1 or greater, that:	High Prestige Liberal Arts Colleges	Other Liberal Arts Colleges	Strongly Denominational Colleges	Universities	State Colleges	Junior Colleges
The college						
encourages students to criticize administrative policies and teaching practices	most	a few	a few	a few	none	a few
has readily accessible channels for expressing student complaints	all	most	most	less than half	a few	a few
Politically						
students are encouraged to be active in social and political reforms	about half	a few	a few	a few	a few	a few
and there are prominent faculty members who are active in local or national politics	a few	none	none	a few	none	none
Moreover, the students						
are concerned about national and international affairs	all	a few	a few	all	most	a few
develop a sense of responsibility about their role in contemporary social and political life	all	a few	about half	about half	about half	about half
and engage in a lot of discussion after hearing a controversial speaker	all	most	most	about half	about half	about half
On a broader plain of stimulation in the college						
there are frequent public debates	none	none	none	none	none	none
many famous people are brought to the campus for lectures, discussions, and concerts	nearly all	about half	a few	nearly all	about half	a few
there are good facilities for individual creative activity	nearly all	most	a few	most	about half	a few
and many opportunities to understand and criticize art, music, drama, etc.	nearly all	a few	a few	most	about half	a few

Moreover, in terms of student response

	nearly all	a few	less than half	about half	less than half	less than half
a lecture by an outstanding scientist would be well attended	nearly all	a few	a few	half	a few	none
a lecture by an outstanding literary critic would be well attended	all	a few	a few	a few	none	none
a lecture by an outstanding philosopher or theologian would be well attended	nearly all	a few	a few	a few	none	none
concerts and art exhibits draw big crowds of students	about half	a few	a few	a few	none	a few
serious intellectual discussions are common	nearly all	less than half	a few	less than half	a few	none
and there is a lot of interest in poetry, painting, sculpture, architecture, etc.	nearly all	a few	a few	none	none	none
and in the analysis of values and cultures	nearly all	less than half	about half			

leges are uninterested. In most places, students say that being concerned about national and international affairs, developing a sense of responsibility about their social and political role in contemporary society, and getting involved in a lot of discussion after hearing a controversial speaker are characteristic of the campus environment. Moreover, except in the strongly denominational colleges and the junior colleges, students in most places say that the institution brings many famous people to the campus and provides good facilities for creative expression and for encountering art, music, drama, and similar cultural activities.

On the other hand there is an apparent discrepancy on many campuses between professing an interest, providing opportunities for expression, and taking advantage of the opportunities. For example, although students profess considerable interest in national and international affairs and in their roles in social and political life, the institution is not seen as encouraging them to be active in social and political reforms. At the same time, although it is seen as providing many opportunities to hear famous people and to encounter important works in art, music, and drama, the students do not say that a lecture by a famous scientist, or literary critic, or philosopher or theologian would be well attended, or that concerts and art exhibits draw big crowds of students, or that long, serious intellectual discussions are common on their campus, or that there is a lot of interest in poetry, or the analysis of value systems and other cultures. These discrepancies are most evident at the universities and state colleges. To some extent they may be a function of size. The large institutions are seen as providing many stimuli, but not as generating a large response to those stimuli. Perhaps on many large campuses the response is in fact quite ample and active but does not stand out with enough clarity amid the magnitude, complexity, and diversity of the total environment to be identified as characteristic of the environment. In a small college, as in a small town, people probably know more about one another and about the community in which they live than could possibly be true in a larger and more complex environment. So it may be that the larger campuses are not as lacking in student response as our data indicate them to be. Indeed, the events at Berkeley, Cornell, Yale, Columbia, and Princeton, to name five examples not included in our sample of institutions, would suggest that this may be the case.

The need to open more widely the lines of communication between the students and the faculty and the administration is clearly indicated by the fact that in the types of institutions enrolling the largest number of students—universities, state colleges, and junior colleges—few are characterized as having readily accessible channels for expressing student complaints. When one combines this perceived condition with the even more widely held belief that students are not encouraged to criticize administrative policies or teaching practices, one gets a potentially explosive mixture. Some analysts of the Berkeley rebellion have suggested that the sequence of events was from idealism to frustration to massive protest. The conditions that prevail on many campuses could lead to re-enactment of this same sequence.

On restrictiveness and supervision

It would be an error to conclude from the above discussion that college students are overly restricted or constrained. We have selected another set of items from College and University Environment Scales dealing with indications of close supervision and constraint. Must students have a written excuse when they are absent from class? Do they sit in assigned seats in many of their classes? Do the professors usually take attendance? And regularly check up on the students to make sure that assignments are being carried out properly and on time? Are student organizations closely supervised to guard against mistakes? Do the student publications never lampoon dignified people or institutions? In the high prestige liberal arts colleges the answer to all these questions is a resounding "no." There are a few such colleges in which the bulk of students said that professors usually took attendance in class; but none of the other questions was answered "yes" by a two-to-one majority of students in any college. The results for all the types of colleges are listed in Table 3.

Although students in about half of the universities say that it is characteristic to have assigned seats in class, none of the other items suggestive of restrictiveness was regarded as characteristic of more than a very few universities. The same was true for the state colleges. Taking class attendance was characteristic of all the junior colleges, all the strongly denominational colleges, and most of the other liberal arts colleges. An apparent reluctance to lampoon dignified people and institutions was characteristic of most of the strongly denominational colleges and about half of the junior colleges. Except in about half of the strongly denominational colleges, student organizations are not closely supervised.

For the most part, student organizations and student newspapers are relatively free from supervision and restraints and professors are not regularly checking up on the students. Although in large

TABLE 3. *Supervision and Constraints*

Students agree, by a margin of 2 to 1 or greater, that:	High Prestige Liberal Arts Colleges	Other Liberal Arts Colleges	Strongly Denominational Colleges	Universities	State Colleges	Junior Colleges
Students						
need a written excuse for absence from class	none	less than half	less than half	a few	none	less than half
have assigned seats in many classes	none	less than half	less than half	about half	about half	most
Professors						
usually take attendance in class	a few	most	all	a few	a few	all
regularly check up on the students to make sure that assignments are being carried out properly and on time	none	none	about half	a few	none	less than half
Student organizations						
are closely supervised to guard against mistakes	none	a few	about half	a few	none	less than half
And student publications						
never lampoon dignified people or institutions	none	a few	most	none	none	about half

institutions students may have assigned seats, they do not have to explain absence from class nor do professors usually take attendance.

In assigning grades to these characteristics which indicate a lack of restrictiveness and close supervision, I would give an A+ to the high prestige liberal arts colleges, an A to the universities and state colleges, a B to the other liberal arts colleges, a C+ to the junior colleges, and a C— to the strongly denominational colleges.

It would be interesting if we could make some direct comparisons between the data we have reported from the College and University Environment Scales and the data gathered by E. G. Williamson and John Cowan from their massive study of students and academic freedom.[1] On the subject of restrictiveness and permissiveness on college campuses today, theirs is the definitive study. They sent inquiries to the presidents, deans of students, chairmen of the student affairs committee, student body presidents, and editors of the student newspapers, in all of the four-year accredited institutions of the country, receiving answers from more than three-fourths of these individuals. In one type of analysis they developed "restrictiveness scores" for three freedoms of current interest—freedom to discuss a wide range of controversial topics, freedom to invite a wide range of controversial speakers, and freedom to act in a variety of controversial situations (such as picketing, sit-ins, writing editorials, sending petitions, passing resolutions, etc.). From these scores one can see what types of institutions are most permissive. Although the classifications used by Williamson and Cowan differ from those I have used in reporting the data on college environments, it is possible to make some approximate comparisons. In assigning the ranks shown in Table 4, I have used from Tables 2 and 3 selected CUES items that are most relevant to political activity; and, for the Williamson and Cowan data, I have made a composite judgment from the separate restrictiveness scores for controversial speakers, controversial topics, and controversial situations, as shown in Table 4.

The resulting rank orders are almost identical. In the Williamson and Cowan study, the large public and private nonsectarian universities emerge as the most permissive environments. From the CUES data, the high prestige, highly selective, liberal arts colleges emerge

---

[1] A study sponsored by Commission VIII of the National Association of Student Personnel Administrators and supported by the Edward W. Hazen Foundation. A summary of findings by Williamson and Cowan appeared under the title "The Role of the President in the Desirable Enactment of Academic Freedom for Students," *Educational Record*, Fall 1965, pp. 351–72, and also appears, in abridged form, in the present volume, pp. 252–83.

TABLE 4. *Institutional Permissiveness on Controversial Matters as Measured on Two Scales*

Composite Rank from Relevant Items in Tables 2 and 3	Approximately Corresponding Categories		Composite Permissiveness Rank
	CUES	Williamson & Cowan	
2	Universities (public and private, nonsectarian and denominational)	Large public universities, and private nonsectarian universities	1
1	High prestige liberal arts colleges	Private nonsectarian liberal arts colleges (not necessarily high prestige)	2
3.5	Other liberal arts colleges (some denominational and some nonsectarian)	Protestant liberal arts colleges	3.5
5	Strongly denominational liberal arts colleges (both Protestant and Catholic)	Catholic liberal arts colleges	5
3.5	State colleges (including teachers colleges)	Small public universities, teachers colleges	3.5

as the most permissive; but there is no exactly comparable category for such institutions in the Williamson and Cowan study. It is clear, however, that the large universities and the private nonsectarian liberal arts colleges are the most permissive and active environments in respect to political interest and social protest, and that strongly denominational colleges, including Catholic colleges, are the least permissive. The smaller universities, state colleges, and teachers colleges are at approximately the same middle position as the Protestant liberal arts colleges and other liberal arts colleges, including some nonsectarian ones. Williamson and Cowan did not study any junior colleges. From the CUES data, on items most directly concerned with political interests and restrictiveness, the junior colleges emerge as the least permissive category of institutions. We would guess that about a third of all college students are enrolled in types of institutions which rank high on these estimated indexes of permissiveness and political activity and that about a fourth of the students are enrolled in places which rank low in permissiveness and political activity. That there is room for a greater measure of freedom on many campuses is apparent from these results.

Perspectives from the Behavioral Sciences

Here we shall consider some problems of organization, administration, and the process of change; and we do this from the perspective of various research studies in the behavioral sciences. We conclude, from the data previously reported, that changes are needed. Are there generalizations from the behavioral sciences that throw any light on the process of change in organizations? If so, can we relate these generalizations to practices and conditions in colleges and universities in order to see what is likely to facilitate change and what is likely to be an obstacle in the way of change?

Consider the following set of generalizations from various studies of attitudes and group behavior: (1) attitudes of individuals tend to reflect the most common beliefs of the members of the groups they belong to; (2) the greater the clarity of the group situation, the more will the individual be directed to the group goal-related task; (3) pressures toward uniformity are stronger in a cohesive group; (4) the more cohesive a group is, the more difficult it is for the group to adapt to changes in external conditions.

Next, consider these generalizations about productivity, competition, and cooperation: (1) individual competition for rewards lowers the productivity of the group to which the individuals belong; (2)

greater group productivity occurs in a cooperative situation than in a competitive one; (3) competition also produces greater personal insecurity.

Third, consider these generalizations about group problem solving: (1) group problem solving, in tasks for which no one solution is necessarily correct, results in fewer poor solutions but also in a more restricted range of solutions than does individual problem solving; (2) a group whose task is problem solving often produces two divergent and incompatible lines of behavior among its members—a leadership role which, for the sake of getting the problem solved, may be destructive of the group, and a group-preserving role which is negatively related to solving the problem.

And finally, consider these two generalizations about supervision, productivity, and morale: (1) close supervision is associated with low productivity; (2) participation is associated with high morale.

In large universities, where the problems of undergraduate teaching and close faculty-student relationships are most acute, the organizational structure for decision making is often ill-adapted to change and innovation. It is common in the California university system, and in many other large universities, to have all-university committees reviewing and passing on proposals for change that come from the various departments, schools, and colleges, and reviewing and passing on recommendations for faculty appointments and promotion. The rationale for this device is that it assures some coherence and consistency in the total structure and maintains uniform standards. Typically, the members of the committee, although they may individually recognize differences in the functions and needs and desires of different parts of the institution, must, in order to operate as an effective group, find some common denominator of values to guide their judgment. Consequently, they tend to reflect whatever they regard as the dominant value system of the institution, and then to apply this dominant value to individual cases. In most large universities the dominant values, rewards, and prestige are associated with research and scholarly productivity; and the Ph.D. in well-established academic disciplines is the model for academic excellence. Thus, a proposal for a graduate degree in theater arts may not be approved; but a degree in theater history would be acceptable. Or, a professor of English may have written two novels but not any scholarly articles in a journal affiliated with the Modern Language Association and hence may be passed over for promotion. Or—a more common stimulus for student protest today—the excellent teacher who spends a great deal of time with his students may not be granted tenure because he has not published enough.

Precisely the same inappropriate pressure for conformity would result if the dominant value system were changed. Suppose, because of the recognition that more reward needs to be given to good undergraduate teaching, the dominant criterion became good undergraduate teaching. We would then find that some professor was not promoted because he had spent too much time contributing to the advancement of knowledge. In this case, the essential role of the university in producing new knowledge would be ill-served.

If complex institutions have multiple purposes and if each of these purposes is to be well served, then no common denominator of judgment can be applied to all of the purposes. We are concerned, presumably, with excellence in undergraduate teaching, with excellence in training for the professions, with excellence in research and the advancement of knowledge, with excellence in public service, with excellence in graduate and postgraduate study, with excellence in the arts, and so on. It may well be that multiple purposes require multiple structures and differential criteria of judgment if each major purpose is to be served with equal excellence. This suggests that the likelihood of change and of adapting to new demands would be increased to the extent that each major group in the organization had enough autonomy and enough authority to do what it believed would best serve its purposes. The greater the clarity of the group situation, the more will the individual be directed to group goal-related tasks. But the group must not be isolated, or become a tight little enclave, for under those conditions it may find itself even more resistant and less able to adapt to changes in external conditions.

It is no simple task to manage any large enterprise—to keep it responsive to new needs, adaptive, to encourage innovation and diversity in its several parts, and at the same time maintain some sense of a larger community. Arrangements which foster and reward varieties of excellence would seem to be better suited to the task than arrangements which tend to produce a common denominator of judgment.

In regard to cooperation and competition, as behavioral scientists have studied the consequences, the research data seem to have special relevance to the faculty practice, not uncommon in large undergraduate classes, of "grading on the curve." If, by policy or by custom, some students are destined to get a grade below C (no matter how hard they worked or how much they learned, but just because some other students in their class performed better than they did), what are the students learning about themselves and, indeed, about the reasons for learning? Morton Deutsch, in commenting on one of his own studies of cooperation and competition, added this note, "One may well question whether a competitive grading system produces the kinds of interrelationships among students, the task-directedness, and personal security that are in keeping with sound educational objectives." [2]

Tabulations at Berkeley a year or so ago indicated that about 30 percent of the freshmen had grade-point averages below C at the end of the first semester; yet presumably all the students at Berkeley come from the top levels of their high school classes and the top levels of academic aptitude. What accounts for this curious condition? It is conceivable that many students, despite evidence of top academic performance in twelve years of previous schooling, still have not learned to perform adequately by Berkeley standards. It is also conceivable that the results imply a failure in teaching, that many faculty members apparently have been unable to teach bright students successfully. More likely, however, it is an artifact of a grading system that is poorly related to the students being taught and to a national perspective on academic talent and performance.

One consequence of such competitive grading practices was highlighted in a recent nationwide study conducted by the National Opinion Research Center under the direction of James Davis.[3] Davis was concerned, among other things, with influences on students' decisions to choose science as a career and to continue the study of science in graduate school. He found that many of the high prestige, intellectually elite colleges and universities were serious underproducers of future scientists in relation to their talent supply and the initial interests of their students. One influential factor on the students' choice was encouragement from a faculty member; but faculty members rarely gave such encouragement to any but their A students. Since faculty members tended to distribute their grades along a more or less normal curve, many students got B's and C's even though all students in the college were in the top 10 percent or higher on any national measure of scientific aptitude and achievement. The consequence of this artifact in competitive grading was a lowering of the students' self-esteem and a lowering of their career aspirations.

The research data on supervision, morale, and productivity can be

[2] Dorwin Cartwright and Alvin Zander (eds.), *Group Dynamics* (New York: Harper & Row, 1960), p. 447.

[3] Davis, *Great Aspirations: The Graduate School Plans of America's College Seniors* (Chicago: Aldine Publishing Co., 1964).

related to policies about student government and campus life generally. If, as the data indicate, close supervision is related to low productivity, and participation is related to high morale, one might suggest that participation in the development and conduct of student government and other student organizations should be broader and more active than it now is on many campuses, and that, given this broad participation, the organizations should proceed in their business with a minimum of supervision.

One might suggest, further, that a similar inference is relevant to certain activities of the faculty and the administration. Surely, wide and active participation in the discussion of purposes can be acknowledged as of great importance, even essential. In fulfilling the institution's varied purposes, faculty members require, and in fact have, great freedom of personal decision with regard to their teaching and research, for they are, in the bureaucratic sense, unsupervisable and subject only to the judgment of their peers. A similar freedom, however, is needed by the administrators: freedom to develop the structures, the procedures, and the other mechanisms intended to serve best the shared purposes which emerge from broad-based discussion. A faculty would rise in massive protest if administrators told them what to teach, what to write, how to teach, or how to conduct research. But there are numerous examples of faculty committees and faculty groups that have assumed the prerogative of telling administrators how to administer, defining procedures, and in other ways circumscribing the freedom of judgment of those whose responsibility is management. Just as the attractiveness of teaching is based partly on the opportunities for independence, creativity, and scholarship which the professorial role affords, so also the attractiveness of management is based partly on the opportunities for analysis, invention, and judgment which the managerial role affords. There is no administrative tenure. Management decisions are subject to post-audit and evaluation—by the faculty, the students, and the board of trustees. But close supervision—of students, of faculty, or of administration—is unlikely to generate high productivity or high morale.

At a time when higher education is under scrutiny and facing complex problems and decisions, the capacity of institutions to innovate and adapt, to develop and strengthen, is of crucial importance.

Some Perspectives on Current Trends and Needed Change

There are a number of current trends in higher education that may be headed for trouble. Here are some of them:
• The increased selectivity of many colleges and universities

- The emphasis on high school grades and measured scholastic aptitude in college admission; and on college grades in graduate school admission
- The pressure on students to earn high grades
- The increased emphasis on abstract verbal learning
- The demands upon speed of reading and speed of writing
- In short, what Paul Woodring in the *Saturday Review* has called the "academic pressure cooker"

Among the reasons these trends may be headed for trouble are the following:
- Going to college is an increasing expectation on the part of young people and their parents
- As higher education becomes a more universal experience, the notion of increased selectivity becomes less tenable
- Academic potential and performance have little relationship to other kinds of socially important potential and performance
- The pressure for grades is not unrelated to the prevalence of cheating

Higher education is concerned with personal and social development as well as with the acquisition of knowledge and intellectual skills. The development of character and the development of intellect cannot really be separated, for we teach a person, not an abstraction called "intellect." We deal in reality with an accumulation of experience and feeling, of attitudes and appreciations, interests and values, skills and abilities, all wrapped up in one individual who differs in various ways from every other individual.

If we define higher education, and access to higher education, and success in higher education in such a way that only one type of human attribute is recognized and rewarded (abstract verbal learning) and the pay-off is only in one currency (grades), we find ourselves in a narrowing circle of academic inbreeding. We cannot on the one hand narrow our definition of academic performance and raise our standards of this performance, and on the other hand meet the demand for more higher education for a larger and larger segment of the population. As higher education becomes more universal, it must also become more diversified, rewarding and enhancing a greater variety of human talents and attainments, and offering wider avenues for the development of expression, insight, and knowledge.

The counterpart to individual differences in the student body is flexibility in the curriculum, in the modes of teaching and learning, and in the system of rewards. Are we now flexible enough?

Academic grades predict academic grades; and scholastic aptitude tests predict scholastic performance. But neither has much relationship to anything else—not creativity, not inventiveness, not leadership, not good citizenship, not compassion, not aesthetic sensitivity, not expressive talent in any of the performing arts, not personal and social maturity, not mental health, not vocational success, not family happiness, not honest workmanship. Yet are we not concerned with these things too? And do they not have profound implication for the selection of students and for the very process of education itself?

A college is a culture, with all the meaning that anthropologists would attach to that word. It is more than books and lectures and term papers and examinations. Fuller understanding of the subtle dependencies between all the components of this culture is greatly needed. There have, of course, been countless studies of higher education. In the 1920's and 1930's hundreds of colleges were surveyed by teams of educational experts. In the 1930's and 1940's many colleges established evaluation and testing offices and institutional research bureaus, and many more are establishing them today. In the 1950's self-studies were conducted on scores of college campuses. There are thousands of journal articles, monographs, and other reports about student characteristics, learning, and the evaluation of courses and curricula and other programs—by individual researchers and by national organizations. Scores of colleges have employed management consulting firms. Every year scores of colleges are visited and examined by accrediting agencies. In recent years sociologists and clinical psychologists have been taking a close look at the campus culture and the personality development of students. And opinion polling agencies and journalists have been looking too. There is no dearth of data or answers. And it cannot be said that higher education has been resistant to self-examination or to external appraisal. Moreover, the knowledge and understanding produced by all these inquiries have influenced educational practices in many ways that can be amply documented.

We have many answers, but we also have new questions. It is to the new questions and the more complex problems that new answers and new solutions must be found.

A year or so ago I attended a conference at which various new solutions were described and discussed. As I listened to the descriptions of experimental colleges and experimental programs, I came to feel that what was being presented, with obvious enthusiasm and hope for salvation, was curiously unreal, was somehow like the other side of the looking glass instead of the directly mirrored outline of what the current problems really were. All that was described was potentially good and obviously intended to overcome some current or local inadequacy in higher education. But it was not enough. Let us look at some of these new solutions.

One current trend appears to have several related facets, all intended to make learning more independent, more congenial, and more continuous. Greater independence in learning is fostered by honors programs, independent study programs, undergraduate theses, free periods in the school calendar with no classes scheduled, the availability of programed learning materials and taped lectures for individual use, open-stack libraries, and similar devices. Along with these devices, often in the same experimental programs or in other programs in the same universities, there appears to be a group emphasis. This is exemplified by some of the newer buildings in which faculty offices, classrooms, small reference libraries, living quarters for faculty members, and living quarters for students are all concentrated in one structure. The intent is to fuse living and learning. On a lesser scale, in many other colleges, there are systematic efforts to facilitate faculty-student association through informal evening seminars in the dormitories or in faculty homes. On a larger scale the benefits of close association and congenial relationships are intended to be preserved by campus development plans such as the Associated Claremont Colleges, Wesleyan University, and the new Santa Cruz campus of the University of California. The idea is to maintain small units—colleges or houses. Institutional growth is achieved by adding more units rather than by enlarging the units.

Between the emphasis on independent study and the emphasis on closer and more constant faculty-student association, there is of course at least one conflict. Certainly closer faculty-student relationships are needed in the universities; but independent study means working alone, and the faculty members need time for independent study just as the students do. The dilemma is unresolved.

The living-learning dormitory plans are applicable only in residential institutions. From the national perspective on higher education, we know that most students do not live at the college they attend. Public junior colleges and large urban universities enroll an increasing number of all college students today, and few of their students live in dormitories. The urbanization of the larger society has its counterpart in the urbanization of higher education. The trend toward denser concentration continues. Although the living-learning emphasis deals with a major problem, it is relevant to only a minor segment of higher education.

Another current trend involves a cluster of emphases around the library, reading and writing, and languages. Innovations in library development are numerous. The coding and retrieval of information electronically, the greater emphasis on individual study carrels, the incorporation of television tapes and listening and viewing facilities, the easier accessibility of microfilm materials—all these are developing rapidly. Language laboratories and similar devices have greatly facilitated the study of foreign languages. Voluntary courses and programed materials are available for students to increase their speed of reading. Perhaps not unrelated to this is the impression that reading lists and assignments in most courses are longer today than they were a few years ago. And perhaps essay examinations are not really meant to teach students how to write rapidly, but they at least enforce the practice of writing in a hurry.

Desirable as these emphases may be, I should like to suggest some countervailing needs. There is a need to teach students how to read slowly—how to spend two hours, for example, reading a twelve-line poem, or a twelve-page essay or short story. There is also a need to teach students how to write slowly—how to spend two hours on two paragraphs, and another two hours rewriting them, and another two hours rewriting them again.

Countering the current emphasis on verbal facility and verbal learning, there is a need for richer acquaintance with more of the great and universal nonverbal languages of man: the languages of movement and form, of color, and sequence, and sound, the languages of direct expression and feeling. Throughout history these have been powerful and significant avenues by which man has expressed his knowledge, his aspirations, his beliefs, his insights, and his wisdom. Are these still foreign languages to many of our students? Is the capacity to translate them, to understand their meaning, and to communicate through them teachable? If we must require competence in two languages for graduation from college, why not the languages of painting and sculpture, of drama and dance, or of music!

If higher education is to serve a diversity of students, it must reward a diversity of talents, and provide a diversity of methods by which knowledge and understanding may be acquired and expressed.

In this last section of the essay, I have suggested that some of the current emphases and trends and innovations in higher education need to be reappraised—the emphasis on academic talent and performance, the experiments with independent study and residential living-learning units, the preoccupation with books and libraries and languages. Let academic talent and academic performance be rewarded, but not to the exclusion of other talents and performances. Let independent study flourish, but not to the exclusion of group study, and vice versa. Let languages and libraries flourish, but not to the exclusion of other modes of learning.

For many restless students today the college environment deals too exclusively with abstractions and theories, and too little with morality and action and the direct confrontation of man with his society and his environment. They acknowledge the size and complexity of the world. The symbols of our age are General Motors, the Pentagon, Metropolitan government, and the Multiversity; not the country store, the town meeting, and the one-room school. They know that in large-scale activities many people are spectators rather than participants; that participation is limited to those with special talents and that the others are not allowed to play. But they do not like this. They want to participate. That is our problem, and that is the way the wind is blowing. But it is the problem, not the answer, that is blowin' in the wind.

Research

on

Student

Characteristics:

Current Approaches

THEODORE M. NEWCOMB

THERE ARE MANY sources of concern about what students are like, and, for that matter, what colleges are like. To express such concern is to imply that colleges have effects and, presumably, that some kinds of effects are preferable to others. In any case, the chief concern of this paper is with changes on the part of students rather than with their "static" characteristics. Further, the emphasis is on problems, and on researchers' approaches to them, rather than on research findings in themselves, though findings are noted when they illustrate a problem or an approach.

The stage can be set by citing two very inclusive, general reports about students. The first, by Thomas P. Wilson,[1] reflects a "shift in public concern." He analyzed the content of titles of articles on students published in "periodicals with general circulation, as indexed in the *Readers' Guide*," during two fourteen-month periods—in 1953–54 and again in 1963–64. Though Wilson is careful to note the shortcomings of the method (including the fact that only thirty-six such articles were found in the earlier and fifty-nine in the latter period), substantial changes appeared. At the earlier time, no less than 86 percent of all articles were classified as portraying either "life on the campus" or "fraternities, riots, drinking" (with about equal frequencies), whereas ten years later only 24 percent were so classified. The predominant classifications in the 1960's were "sex and morals" (25 percent) and "political activities, freedoms, attitudes" (41 percent)—a total of 66 percent, as compared with only 3 percent ten years earlier. The percentages for "religion" remained at 11–12 percent across the decade. Thomas comments that "public attention is now directed to matters much more central to the col-

[1] Wilson, *Colleges and Student Values: An Overview of Educational and Research Concerns*, prepared for the Carnegie Foundation for the Advancement of Teaching (New York: The Foundation, 1964).

leges' own definition of their role in society. . . . Higher education can no longer so easily perform its experiments behind a screen of football pageantry and homecoming parties."

The second report is taken from a comprehensive study of college seniors' plans for graduate schooling, by James A. Davis.[2] In the spring of 1961 expectant graduates, 33,982 of them, in 135 American colleges and universities answered a detailed questionnaire. The students, but not the colleges, were representative of the total college population, and 85 percent of all questionnaires were returned. Davis' own summary, only slightly abbreviated, of what this population was like some four years ago is as follows:

> The modal graduate . . . was more likely to be a man than a woman, was in his early twenties, . . . was unmarried, and was a white, native-born American from a city of over 100,000. He was a member of the middle or upper middle class; his father and mother had graduated at least from high school and had an income of over $7,500. His father was a manager or professional. The graduate had held at least a part-time job during his final year at college and was still a member of the Protestant religion in which he had been reared.
>
> He had warm and positive feelings toward his school and professors, planned to continue his education in graduate school (at least eventually), planned to be a professional of some kind . . ., did not particularly like businessmen, had at least a B minus average, thought of himself as being in the top one-fourth of his class and would look for intellectual and service values in his career . . . . he had lived in a dormitory or in off-campus housing; he was within four hours' driving time from his family.
>
> He thought of himself as conventional, religious, and politically liberal, and was inclined to describe himself as co-operative, ambitious, happy, fun-loving, easy-going, idealistic, athletic, and cautious.

These two pictures—of what recent graduates are typically like, and of the changing nature of public concern—can serve as a background for an examination of more specialized problems and of research approaches to them. This paper will consider, first, the individual student as the locus of change, and then go on to consider institutions, rather than persons, as units of study.

[2] Davis, *Great Aspirations: The Graduate School Plans of America's College Seniors* (Chicago: Aldine Publishing Co., 1964).

Individual Changes in Values and Attitudes

Philip Jacob, in his *Changing Values in College*,[3] reviewed much of the work in this area up to a decade ago. His conclusions, though not adequately taking into account the enormous range of sophistication shown in the several studies, are worth serious consideration. They may be summarized, for present purposes, under four headings included in his chapter "Value Outcomes of a College Education," as follows:

1. From diversity to uniformity: acquiring the college outlook
2. Toward flexibility and sociability
3. The myth of college liberalism
4. The constancy of basic values

Somewhat less succinctly, Jacob is saying that students tend to take on the prevalent norms of their own colleges; that they become less dogmatic, less prejudiced, and more critical-minded; but also tend not to become more "liberal," except superficially in the sense of taking on "a random collection of opinions in vogue during a particular generation"; and tend not to change in "basic values." Regarding the last of these, he concludes that upperclassmen have "achieved a synthesis of their values which reinforces . . . firms up their [pre-existing] attitudes on most issues. . . . They have simply worked out a greater internal consistency within their value system" (p. 56). Jacob's concluding statement is that "college has a socializing rather than a liberalizing impact on values. It softens an individual's extremist views . . . increases the tolerance potential. It strengthens respect for the prevailing social order."

More recent research has been less concerned with such global questions and answers. It has inquired into conditions, mechanisms, and dynamics—both of change and of resistance to change. It has looked *behind* the college scene itself, at the larger social-cultural environment. It has looked *at* the individual college as a social organization in its own right, and also as having a relationship of its own to that larger environment. It has looked *within* colleges, inquiring particularly into the kinds of experiences that students typically have in colleges that are affected in special ways by all of these considerations. And it has also looked within the individual *student*—his family background, for example, his personal aspirations, or his personality make-up. I now turn to some of these more specialized approaches.

[3] New Haven, Conn.: Edward W. Hazen Foundation, 1957.

"Maturing" versus college experience as basis of changes

Let us assume that Jacob's least pessimistic conclusions are pretty well justified—that college students typically become less dogmatic, less prejudiced, and more critical-minded; data subsequent to his would appear to support the general finding. Even so, the question immediately arises whether comparable changes are not also occurring on the part of young people of the same age who do not go to college. After all, they too have opportunities for extending their horizons, for becoming less naïve as a result of an increased range of experience, and they also live in a society in which intolerance is becoming less tolerable. How can we be sure that such changes, as reported among college students, are anything more than endemic changes that result from normal processes of growing up in American society?

A clear answer to this question presupposes the availability of research data that have been obtained in ways designed to answer it. One such approach is to compare different colleges: if significant differences are found, it is at least possible that the differential effects spring from distinctive kinds of college experiences, and not merely from growing up in the same society. But the issue is clouded by the fact that different colleges may select or attract different kinds of students; how can we be sure that College A, whose students show conspicuous change of a given kind, does not attract students who in one way or another are more open to change than those in College B, whose students show little change of the same kind?

My own now-ancient study of changes in attitudes toward public issues in Bennington College [4] illustrates, though imperfectly, one way of getting an answer to this kind of question in one particular setting. While (during the late 1930's) the older Bennington students were showing marked changes away from their initial political conservatism, juniors and seniors at two other, nearby colleges failed to show comparable changes. At both of them (Williams, whose men students came from families much like those of the Bennington women students, and Skidmore, also a small, liberal arts college for women), freshmen attitudes were indistinguishable from those at Bennington. This fact shows that differences in attitude change could not be accounted for by initial attitudes *of the particular kinds observed in this study.* The three sets of freshmen may, of course, have differed in unknown ways that differentially predis-

[4] Newcomb, *Personality and Social Change* (New York: Holt, Rinehart & Winston, 1943).

posed them toward or against change toward public issues of their time, though it is hard to escape the conclusion that very different college environments had a good deal to do with it.

A series of studies by W. T. Plant and his associates [5] raises a more basic question and yields some provocative findings. Plant began by summarizing a set of studies dealing with dogmatism, a characteristic that, according to Jacob's report, is rather likely to decline during college years. Drawing upon others' work as well as his own during the early 1960's, he was able to report that "without exception" post-senior averages of dogmatism scores [6] "were not only significantly lower than the post-freshmen means, but also significantly lower than the post-sophomore means *for the same subjects.*" (The italics are mine; the use of the same subjects is important, since it demonstrates that the differences do not result from the loss of more dogmatic students, through dropping out of college.) Furthermore, these findings apply to every one of the following institutions: a Western Roman Catholic university for men, a Southern Protestant college, a Midwestern public university, a Western public college, and six public junior colleges. Can it remain in doubt that colleges do reduce dogmatism—in contemporary America, at least?

But wait: this is only the beginning. Plant's real problem was to compare, not different colleges, but college versus no college at all. He therefore administered not only the dogmatism scale but also scales of ethnocentrism and of authoritarianism [7] to all acceptable applicants to the freshman class at San Jose State College in 1958. Two years later, and again four years later, the same three scales were administered to as many of the original subjects as could be located (1,448 in 1960, of whom 1,177 had attended no college; and 1,058 in 1962, of whom 974 had attended no college). The significant finding is that *all* groups—whether male or female, whether attending San Jose State College for eight semesters, for four, for two, or for none at all—showed significant declines in dogmatism, in ethnocentrism, and in authoritarianism. Beginning two years later, more-

[5] For example, J. C. McCullers and W. T. Plant, "Personality and Social Development: Cultural Influences," *Review of Educational Research*, December 1964, pp. 599–610.

[6] See M. Rokeach, *The Open and Closed Mind: Investigations into the Nature of Belief Systems and Personality Systems* (New York: Basic Books, 1960).

[7] Authoritarianism, commonly measured by the "F-scale," refers to a complex personality syndrome in which acquiescence before the strong (or the "right," or the in-group) and contempt for the weak (or the "wrong," or the out-group) is prominent. See T. W. Adorno, Else Frenkel-Brunswik, D. J. Levinson, and R. N. Sanford, *The Authoritarian Personality* (New York: Harper & Row, 1950).

over, a still larger number of applicants for admission to the same college in 1960 were followed for two years; using partially different personality scales, exactly the same results were obtained: college attendants for four, three, or two semesters as well as those not going to college at all showed significant changes in the same direction.

These findings are sobering, but they hardly justify the conclusion that the impact of all colleges with respect to these characteristics is the same as that of all extracollege environments. Problems stemming from varying admissions policies and differential attraction of colleges for certain kinds of student populations, to which I now turn, render this issue a very complicated one. Meanwhile, we have something to learn not only about precautions in research procedures, but also about humility.

The selective power of colleges

If there are colleges that attract or select freshmen most of whom already achieve very low scores of dogmatism, prejudice, or authoritarianism, we would hardly expect their freshmen to show much decrease in those scores. If, on the other hand, there are colleges whose freshmen are exceedingly high in those characteristics, their students are more likely to show decreases in those ways.

Bennington College, as of the early 1960's, was apparently of the former kind. Judging from responses by nearly all of its student population, neither in political liberalism nor in authoritarianism did more than slight average changes occur between freshman-to-junior or sophomore-to-senior years.[8] Although there is no necessary correlation between these two characteristics, it happened that this college at this time was receiving freshmen who were predominantly liberal in political attitudes and nonauthoritarian. What influence the college experience exerted on them was, on the average, to increase those tendencies slightly, but the changes were not statistically significant. Something, obviously, had happened since the study of the same college some twenty-five years earlier—perhaps a shift in that part of the spectrum where the college "image" fell.

Any college for which a clearly focused image exists will, in similar ways, tend to attract a homogeneous student body. By the same token, any college that boasts no particular image or that, for whatever reasons, is not highly selective, is likely to find its freshman class characterized by heterogeneity.

Returning now to the several institutions described by Plant, it

[8] The full data will appear in a forthcoming monograph by T. M. Newcomb, Kathryn Koenig, Richard Flacks, and D. P. Warwick.

appears that each of them may have selected primarily a set of freshmen who were either initially high in dogmatism and authoritarianism or were heterogeneous in these respects. In the former case they had, so to speak, nowhere to go but down; in the latter case (the relatively nonselective, public colleges), the college experience was such that it exerted more change on those initially higher in dogmatism and authoritarianism. Such an explanation would account for the contrasting findings reported by Plant and by the authors of the recent Bennington study.

In other words, interpretations of college students' changes in attitudes and values must take account of two kinds of background facts: like their noncollege peers, students are alive and young in a society that is changing in certain ways; and there is a mutual pulling power that certain colleges and certain students have upon one another, so that the likelihood of any particular kind of change varies among colleges and their student populations. These considerations, however, do not take into account the personal and interpersonal processes by which individual changes occur within colleges. Let us take a look at them.

Interpersonal experiences

Changes, whether in chemical properties or in student characteristics, do not automatically occur simply because of potentialities for change, nor merely because of "favorable" environments. In an immediate sense, things change as a result of events, the occurrence of which is facilitated or impeded by environment and the consequences of which are guided by potentialities. I shall refer to such events on the part of students as *experiences,* and, since I cannot deal with every conceivable kind of student experience, I shall concentrate on those of interpersonal nature.

During the past decade researchers have shown an increasing interest in a family of student characteristics that, from the point of view of most contemporary educators, are desirable outcomes of higher education. Relative freedom from dogmatism and authoritarianism are good examples; others include the development of theoretical and aesthetic interests, and tolerance for ambiguity and novelty.[9] Several of these scales differentiate rather dramatically among

---

[9] Scales for measuring these three characteristics, respectively labeled "Theoretical Orientation," "Estheticism," and "Complexity," have been developed and very widely applied by the Center for the Study of Higher Education of the University of California, Berkeley. See *Omnibus Personality Inventory—Research Manual* (Berkeley: University of California, 1962).

different colleges and, within a single college, among different sub-populations in ways that not only make good sense but also give promise of considerable validity as measures of intellectual development. And so my next special problem deals with such kinds of outcomes of college experience, as affected by students' interpersonal relationships.

In this context one inevitably thinks first, I suppose, of student-faculty relationships. Let me, therefore, begin by describing an experiment designed to show the differential effects of differing degrees of students' contact with their teachers, as reported in a study of two colleges, by E. K. Wilson of Antioch College.[10] He describes one of several experimental "manipulations" as follows. For each of eight different courses (including History of Art, Earth Sciences, American Government and Politics, for example), a research design was developed that allowed extent of contact with teachers to vary. Some courses were taught to different students (who had been matched for ability) in these three different ways: (1) conventional lecture-discussion, under continuous surveillance of the teacher; (2) small discussion groups having sporadic contact with the instructor; and (3) lone-wolf students, working independently, with the guidance only of a syllabus. In other courses, some students met the professor only in a large weekly lecture, and met more frequently with a laboratory assistant who conducted smaller groups; at the same time the professor met other enrollees in the same course in both lecture and discussion.

The outcomes of these different treatments included everything that the faculty thought that students should be learning in the courses, including knowledge, skills, and attitudes. They were measured in many different ways—for example, by essay examinations, short-answer tests, attitude scales, outside reading records, assigned papers, and teachers' grades. The interesting finding is that by not even one of these criteria, in any course in either college, were there any significant differences between students who had much contact, limited contact, or none at all with their instructors.

Before you conclude that college teachers have no influence on their students, let me suggest another possible interpretation of these findings. Both of these colleges are small (and, I might add, relatively isolated), with the consequence that students on each campus tend to know one another and to meet often and informally. Pre-

[10] In "The Study of College Peer Groups," a forthcoming monograph edited by T. M. Newcomb and E. K. Wilson.

sumably, therefore, the students in different thirds of the same course were not isolated from one another—indeed, they may have found time in their encounters to compare notes about whatever courses they had in common. Further, each of these colleges has a rather special public image, which facilitates the development and continuity of a community culture that includes student norms according to which one is responsible for one's academic work. According to this interpretation, in short, faculty influence was not absent but was modified by student culture. If I may inject an opinion, parenthetically, the values of "independent study" are typically dependent, in just such ways, upon student modification of faculty influence. Otherwise correspondence courses would be quite as effective as college experience, which I suspect is simply not the case for most American students.

Assuming that something is to be learned from students' own reports, I should like to quote further from Professor Wilson's paper. A content analysis was made of a systematic sample of Antioch seniors' autobiographies, and of responses to questionnaires and interviews—none of which was particularly directed at the present problem. Altogether, students mentioned, with sufficient frequency to be coded, seven different kinds of change that they felt they had undergone in college. Most of these kinds of changes were thought to be influenced both by teachers and by fellow students, but with some provocative differences. The only kinds of changes attributed more frequently to teachers than to students were those labeled "intellectual" and "career plans and choices." Four of the remaining five were attributed at least twice as frequently to peers as to teachers: "interest in new fields," "personality development," "social development," and "attitude toward Antioch College." And these differences appeared in spite of the fact that academic courses were mentioned as sources of influence much more frequently than either teachers or fellow students. From such data I conclude, again, that courses and teachers are necessary but not sufficient inducers of change: peer influence is also essential.

In a general way, probably no one has ever doubted this, but the supporting evidence has usually been impressionistic rather than systematic, and there has been exceedingly little attempt to investigate the specific interpersonal mechanisms by which peer-group influence is effected. Student "culture" or "norms" have often, quite properly, been called upon. The power of such normative influence has more than once been demonstrated. An example is Bennington College of the late 1930's,[11] where it was shown that students who were personally most influential were, almost uniformly, rather conspicuously nonconservative, and where individual changes toward nonconservatism varied, not with the student's college major, but with her degree of involvement with the college community. Similar effects have been shown in the setting of a medical school, where the power of student culture is mobilized in part against the medical faculty, in ways suggested by the title of one of the investigators' reports: "The Fate of Idealism in Medical School." [12] As clearly shown in both of these studies, faculty influence—whether resisted or embraced—is an essential ingredient in the student culture.

At a somewhat less inclusive level, formal organizations within colleges often serve as loci of peer-group influence. A recent study of the Harvard College Houses [13] shows that syndromes of attitudes and values labeled "individual-oriented" and "collectivity-oriented" varied rather consistently with membership in certain houses. The authors' conclusions are as follows:

> The Houses do affect student values and attitudes . . . . the affective climate of the House [apparently provides] the central mechanisms of . . . change. Student involvement with peers accounts heavily for extent of change, and in two of the Houses the moral climate formed by the student membership seems to account principally for the direction of these effects.

College fraternities and sororities have usually been thought to be creators or at least supporters of certain kinds of values on the part of their members, but objective studies are sorely wanting. One set of data from the University of Michigan [14] indicates that sophomores who were or who wanted to be fraternity members had, as prefreshman nearly two years earlier, described themselves in terms quite different from those of their other male peers. The following prefreshman self-descriptions from (among others) sophomore Greeks appeared significantly more frequently than from non-Greeks: nonintellectual, happy-go-lucky, rely on others' opinions, conventional, do not want a deep grasp of a specific field of study. If such characteristics represent a pattern, it appears to be typical, though by no

[11] Newcomb, *Personality and Social Change.*

[12] H. S. Becker and Blanche Geer, in *American Sociological Review,* XXIII (1958), 50–56.

[13] Rebecca S. Vreeland and C. E. Bidwell, "Organizational Effects of Student Attitudes: A Study of the Harvard Houses" (Mimeographed; 1964).

[14] Obtained as part of an ongoing study under the direction of Gerald Gurin and T. M. Newcomb, with support from the U.S. Office of Education.

means universal, among men at one university who offer themselves for Greekship.

A much more comprehensive study of fraternities and sororities at the University of Colorado,[15] by Professor W. A. Scott, just published, provides general support for these findings, and goes considerably beyond them. Freshman pledges, as compared with non-pledges, are significantly lower in valuing independence but higher in social skills and in loyalty, for both men and women; men only are relatively low in intellectual and creative values; women, only, value kindness less but academic achievement and social status more. (Each of these summary statements is based on self-ratings on several different items.) Scott was also able to show, by longitudinal studies, that little change in values occurred during the year following membership in the Greek houses: "The several houses made no distinctive impacts on their entire pledge groups." Considering the total twelve values as a total pattern, however, he did find that "pledging and non-pledging freshmen moved in different directions throughout the year." Perhaps we may conclude that although fraternities and sororities may reinforce and solidify their members' existing values, their net effect is rather by way of selection than by value change.

It has often been surmised that informal student peer groups exert more influence on their members, by and large, than the formally organized ones, though the proposition has rarely been put to an adequate test. There is plenty of evidence that, given opportunity for adequate acquaintance, students who form intimate cliques tend to share certain values that they regard as important. But there are two quite different processes by which this may occur: value-sharers may seek each other out, or influence processes within existing friendship groups may change members' values toward homogeneity. Researchers have rarely sorted out the two processes, perhaps because it cannot be done convincingly except through longitudinal studies. In one of my own studies [16] it proved possible to predict from attitudes expressed by total strangers, weeks before they were to meet as residents of the same student house, the subpopulations within which closely knit cliques would be formed after several months of acquaintance. Members of at least one of these cliques influenced one another rather profoundly, toward common vocational aspirations of "intellectual" nature.

[15] Scott, *Values and Organizations: A Study of Fraternities and Sororities* (Chicago: Rand McNally & Co., 1965).
[16] Newcomb, *The Acquaintance Process* (New York: Holt, Rinehart & Winston, 1961).

I am now engaged in an ambitious and systematic attempt to study these phenomena among undergraduates at the University of Michigan. Because we have obtained voluminous information from all entering freshmen in two successive classes concerning their interests and values, aspirations, and life histories, we are able at later times to select special samples for intensive interviewing and questionnairing, knowing that we have full information about them as prefreshmen. One of our procedures is labeled "snowball sociometrics." That is, we begin by interviewing a rather small sample, say of sophomores, concerning both their closest friendships, their own present attitudes and values, and the perceived attitudes of their selected friends. The persons whom they name are then interviewed in the same manner, and so on through series of expanding circles until our patience (if not the computer's) is exhausted. One or two years later the same process will be repeated, with the same students.

As of now it is too early to indicate what we have found, but I shall make bold to mention some hypotheses for which we hope to find support. We already know that a good many freshmen quickly team up with others very much like themselves, and we do not expect to find much value change within persisting peer groups initially formed in such ways, our assumption being that their members will tend to reinforce one another's existing values. If so, we shall be able to demonstrate a general phenomenon, of which fraternities and sororities (as shown by Scott, for example) are merely a special case, in that they tend to select homogeneous recruits and, relatively speaking, to insulate them from influences that might induce significant attitude change.

Another hypothesis deals with "openness to novelty" (including people different from oneself) on the part of freshmen. If, as we expect, freshmen who are high in this characteristic show more subsequent change than others, we think we shall be able to show that this outcome stems not simply from abstract "openness to new ideas" but also from experience in peer groups whose members either have different values to begin with, or who suffer value changes together.

Considerations of this kind raise a troublesome question, about which I know of no research findings. Suppose we do find, in fact, that freshmen who already have a good deal of "openness" are likely to profit more from college experience than others. Even so, it would hardly be justifiable to conclude that applicants for admission to college should be chosen on that basis; rather, I believe, we must assume that this characteristic is itself educable. There is an analogy here with tests of academic capacity, and we now know that applicants who have been culturally or educationally handicapped are often capable of improving their scores on such tests, given adequate opportunity. Just so, there are family and community backgrounds that are "crippling" with respect to the development of openness to new experience. The fact that an applicant does not already resemble the ideal "educated man" is a poor reason for rejecting him. Thus, such presumably desirable characteristics as openness and nonauthoritarianism, as possible criteria for admission to college, need to be assessed in light of previous opportunity for learning.

This section of the paper has dealt with a few research problems centered on students' interpersonal experiences and how they affect changes in values. I now turn to a set of problems that, even within this context, I have not been able to avoid entirely; they deal with the organization of the institutions within which students' experiences occur.

Academic Anonymity and Its Organizational Sources

There is a student characteristic that is so prevalent and potentially so contra-educational that I cannot ignore it, even though little research has been directed to it. For want of a better term, it may be labeled "academic anonymity." Broadly, anonymity is the opposite of identity, which refers to an individual's clear sense of who he is, in some specified context. Psychologically, anonymity derives either from uncertainty about others' expectations of oneself or from indifferences to the expectations of others—or, commonly, from both. I am not referring to uncertainty whether one can meet others' expectations, which is common enough among students, but to uncertainty or indifference about what the expectations are.

All forms of anonymity are apt to have environmental as well as psychological sources. And when, as is often the case with academic anonymity, it seems to be endemic on certain kinds of campuses, we must look to the nature of institutional organization if we are to understand it. These institutional sources include arrangements having the consequence that a person does not regularly interact with others with whom he has a personal identity and with whom he shares important academic and intellectual concerns. Not surprisingly, it turns out that it is the larger, and necessarily more bureaucratic, colleges and universities in which such arrangements are most prevalent. It also happens that an enormous proportion of American college students are to be found in just such institutions. Both common sense and research evidence suggest that the organizational features of an institution pretty much determine who will interact with whom, how frequently, and under what conditions of motivation. The research evidence comes mainly from studies of industrial, rather than educational, organizations, but at least one such study—by Professor Robert Kahn and his associates of the University of Michigan [17]—approaches the problem in ways that are directly relevant to higher education.

Kahn and his associates begin with the concept of personal identity, which develops and takes on meaning within the context of expectations of role associates. The conditions that they found regularly associated with stressful problems of identity were *role conflict* (facing incompatible sets of expectations) and *role ambiguity* (uncertainty about expectations). These, in turn, are associated with such organizational features as size of working units, formal relationships among units, and interpersonal "bonds" both within and between the units. Because these matters have been rather well studied within industrial organizations, and because they seem to me to have direct relevance to colleges and universities, I want to point to some more or less close parallels.

While Kahn *et al.* conclude, from their extensive research program, that role conflict and ambiguity increase more or less directly with the size of organizations (up to several thousand, at least), their remedial proposals have to do with structural changes rather than reductions in over-all size. The implications that they draw for builders and leaders of organizations are these:

> Minimize the requirements for coordination between positions and groups. . . . For each functional unit of the organization, ask how independent it can be. . . . For each position, ask how autonomous it can be made. . . . For each coordinative bond between positions and units, seek the minimum number of activities which must be coordinated. The basic justification for coordination becomes functional interdependence [p. 394].

Within certain limits, and with a caveat that I shall later add, I believe that higher education should take this advice to heart. If, as in my own university, undergraduate enrollment in a single liberal arts college moves into five figures, then its problems of formal coordination are inevitably solved in ways that contribute to academic anonymity. The curricular apparatus, for example, develops a mono-

---

[17] With D. M. Wolfe, R. P. Quinn, J. D. Snoek, and R. A. Rosenthal, *Organizational Stress: Studies in Role Conflict and Ambiguity* (New York: John Wiley & Sons, 1964).

lithic autonomy of its own. In another set of offices, perhaps in a separate building, a residential apparatus burgeons. Both are necessary, and each may be a marvel of efficiency. The organizational plan is neat, and (paraphrasing Kahn *et al.*) it minimizes the requirements for coordination between groups. But the question "How independent can each functional unit afford to be?" has either been ignored or has been answered only for staffing rather than for students, for whom the criterion of "functional interdependence" is not met.

What kinds of institutional organization could satisfy this criterion, given the situation that in America huge colleges and universities are here to stay? One important answer is now taking form: reduce the size, not of the total institution, but of its functional units within which students interact with each other and with their teachers. In at least two new institutions (the University of California at Santa Cruz and at San Diego) and one established institution (the University of Michigan) multiple small undergraduate colleges are being planned in such ways that the student's personal-social life is not automatically divorced from his academic life. Each of these campuses will include many thousands of undergraduates, each of them in a college of his own that is large enough to include most of the curricular spectrum but still small enough so that the same students will meet each other not just in residences and dining halls but also in classrooms and laboratories. The nature of this reorganization might be styled "decentralization," or, more fully, a shift to units each of which includes not only the diverse disciplines that in large colleges tend to become self-sufficient, but also both instructional and residential functions. The aim—which, relatively speaking, can hardly fail—is to make more probable the student's sense of a personal-institutional identity that includes academic as well as social expectations, by creating full-spectrum, semiautonomous communities within the larger community.

Such ideas are of course not new, but the sense of necessity for community within metropolis has only recently forced itself upon us. If the increasing size of universities has had the effect that, while the social-psychological motors of student life are racing, they are too often disengaged from the wheels of intellectual development, then the kind of repair work that is indicated consists, not of reducing the size of universities, but of reorganizing them. If my own experience is at all typical, the process of reorganization provides many opportunities for discarding educational atavisms of all kinds. If you take seriously the task of removing the conditions underlying academic anonymity, you may end up with an educational system that belongs in the last third of the twentieth century.

In pleading for an organizational solution to problems of academic anonymity, I hinted at a warning, and here it is. I hope the day has passed when the advantages of educational procedures, whether innovative or hallowed by long use, are accepted merely on faith. Even the most crassly commercial organizations devote part of their budgets to assessment of their products, especially new ones. I find it somewhat ironic that research-proud universities are, with few exceptions, devoting so little of their research sophistication to examination of their own procedures. If I have seemed to be proposing that universities consider radical changes, I now wish to go still further. Any plan for institutional change should include research on its effects, and this, to be at all convincing, will usually have to be interinstitutional in nature. If a change is important enough to institute, it is important enough to be examined with all the relevant research tools at our disposal. This, I think, is higher education's challenge of today. Experiment? Of course, but don't bother unless you are serious enough about it to be prepared to examine what you have done.

High
Hopes
and
Campus
Realities

ROSE K. GOLDSEN

MOST COLLEGE STUDENTS are pretty complacent about the value and meaningfulness of their undergraduate education. But many are nevertheless critical of their own student governments, their administrations, and their faculty—in that order. The best students feel they are not being taken seriously, that they are being relegated to busywork and drudgery whose relevance to any serious educational purpose is by no means clear to them. The best students are talking about how they are alienated from the real intellectual life of the university. They say they want small seminars in their freshman and sophomore years, more personal intellectual interchange with their professors, more participation in curriculum planning and allocation of academic budgets. The best students, especially student leaders, are balking at what they say is irrelevant nonsense in the curriculum.

This is not the first time universities have been accused of being preoccupied with nonsense. Lots of what goes on at a university is defined by laymen—and this includes students—as nonsense. The university as an institution protects the right of faculty to engage in such nonsense, for we have learned that some, at least, of the nonsense of today is the major breakthrough of tomorrow.

How does the community protect itself against the danger that the "nonsense" that goes on at a university may really *be* nonsense? Professional and scientific bodies offer that protection. A faculty member at a university must be defined as a serious professional by his own peers who vote for his appointment and grant him tenure. They are the only men and women qualified to make the judgment that what he is saying or doing is not likely to be crackpot foolishness or a waste of time, even when it seems that way to laymen outside the professional and scientific bodies of the disciplines. This is feasible only when these bodies are the repository of a certain kind of trust—trust that their judgments are being made responsibly and disinterestedly,

117

guided by dispassionate rules of logic and judicious weighing of what is, after all, very qualitative evidence.

Ultimately, therefore, the vigor of the university depends on the vigor of the professional associations to which faculty members belong. And faculty members orient themselves at least as much, if not more, to their own professional community—an international one— as to their local campuses, their local community. The ingredient that makes the special nature of the university community feasible is trust that the faculty are bona fide intellectual leaders in their fields. When this trust is lacking, something goes haywire.

For example: in Latin American universities, customarily a third of the governing body is made up of undergraduate students, who have equal voice with professors in deciding on educational policy, even staffing. The undergraduate students, in short, are the professor's peers when it comes to decisions on academic policy. This reflects not only a special historical tradition, but also a lack of trust that faculty members have any special capacity to make especially trained judgments that students and neophytes cannot make. And note that in many universities with this arrangement the faculty members are, in fact, part-time amateurs, appointed on the basis of extraprofessional considerations. It is under these conditions that their students reject their claim to intellectual leadership.

How Trust Fluctuates: Outcomes and Relevance

American college students by no means reject the intellectual leadership of their faculty. They acknowledge it. Indeed, part of the unrest among the articulate students comes from their desire for more of it. Again, it is the best students who are getting restless.

College students are asked to go through a great deal of drudgery. Their motivation to endure the drudgery is complex, to be sure. But one element in that motivation is the conviction that the drudgery they are asked to go through is relevant to a desired outcome. The outcome may not always be an intellectual one, in their eyes: but it often is. And since one of our tasks as university professors and administrators is to upgrade the value of the intellectual payoff in the students' value systems. I am going to discuss only that intellectual payoff. Thus, let me rephrase my previous comment: they must be convinced that the drudgery they are asked to go through is relevant to some desired intellectual outcome—that it is not nonsense.

Right now, what we call the "hard sciences" are not on the defensive in this regard. Students are willing to accept on faith that the drudgery they are asked to go through in these fields is not likely to be nonsense, that it will have a relevant intellectual outcome. Students do not really expect a Hans Bethe to supervise their laboratory work in Physics 101.

It is the social sciences and humanities that are on the defensive. Students look to these disciplines to help them approach answers to the explosive questions that trouble all of us. World peace. Distributive justice. The nature of thought. Control of atomic weapons. We tell them at least two things that cause them a lot of misgivings. First, we tell them they must learn some ABC's before they can intelligently examine such problems in any serious way. They must go through some paces that they see as drudgery, get themselves backgrounds and skills.

They don't always believe us. Undergraduate students are more convinced than their professors are that they can already read a document critically, analyze an argument, think independently, marshal and evaluate evidence, clearly engage in constructive exposition and clarifying dialogue about a problem. We tell them they are mistaken—and turn them over to graduate assistants to help them develop the skills and background. But these skills are not so concrete as those involved in, say, solving an equation or analyzing a chemical element. They are sharpened by bringing to bear informed judgment and judicious evaluation which the graduate assistant often doesn't have.

We tell students they are mistaken in another regard—that their explosive questions are really unaskable. They want to examine the dynamics of international tensions? Let's look at games theory, with statistics and calculus as prerequisities. Distributive justice interests them? It's a normative question and should be rephrased. What about the discrepancies between American ideals and the workings of our social system? Likewise. How did fascism come about? They must begin with an earlier historical period and a seminar on how to evaluate the authenticity of documents. The best students get restless. This is not what they meant at all.

I shall interrupt here to defend this procedure. The questions that society feels an urgent need to answer are not necessarily the questions that get you to the answer you yearn for. They are the questions an administrator puts, not necessarily a scientist or scholar. The alchemic question—how to turn base into precious metals—was such an administrative question, and it did not lead to an understanding of the transmutation of matter. The professional bodies can and should reject pressures to ask administrative questions rather than the questions that their professional judgment tells them are relevant at this stage of development in their fields.

Yet this is no justification for *not* exploring and examining with students the explosive questions of the day. It is not an either-or choice. There is no evidence that analyzing gaming models will yield new knowledge more relevant to understanding international negotiations than will an examination of the international negotiations themselves. The one does not foreclose the other as the only fruitful way to proceed or the best way. But any academic hesitancy to plunge into these questions is encouraged by trustees, legislatures, and administrations, who do not exactly relish questioning the wisdom of the establishment. And professors may simply be more comfortable in these environments if they question the outcomes of gaming models rather than the outcomes of international negotiations.

The Rewards of Drudgery

In either case—whether students are asked to look at the society-convulsing question or the rephrased question—much of what we demand of the students they define as drudgery. Is the game worth the candle? They wonder. Is it maybe all nonsense after all? In the social sciences and the humanities they are not bulwarked by the same faith they have in the "hard sciences" that the drudgery will have the kind of intellectual payoff they want and seek.

We are back to the special nature of the university community again. Only the professional can say if it is nonsense. We say it isn't. But we do not still their doubts. I shall touch upon only one of the many reasons why I think students' troubled doubts are not stilled; that reason has to do with the local versus the cosmopolitan institutions to which the professor refers himself. Joy or pleasure in drudgery seems a contradiction, but it need not be. When an enthusiastic professional shares with the student his own experience of the task, the student catches on. He sees that one man's drudgery is another man's intellectual tool. Yet, the professional scholar in the social sciences or the humanities does not maintain his position vis-à-vis his colleagues by initiating undergraduates into the excitement of sharpening intellectual tools. He does it by using these tools himself in his own scholarly work or research.

The students talk a lot these days about their own alienation. I want to point to the professor's alienation. In our best universities, the professor's commitment to his discipline alienates him from his undergraduate students. He gets no professional payoff from his undergraduate contacts, in the sense of renewing with them knowledge in his own field, sharpening his wits, or testing his ideas against them as a critical audience. This he gets from his graduate students, not his undergraduates.

And why should it be any other way? It requires a great deal of extra investment of himself for a professor to train his undergraduates up to this level. Why should he be motivated to do so, if there is no professional payoff to him if he does. The rewards in the coin of a college professor—rank, prestige, respect, and recognition from his colleagues in the international bodies of scholars—do not go to the people who meet large undergradute classes. (Our computer at Cornell recently ground out for us the information that the people who meet the biggest classes on the freshman and sophomore levels are typically twenty-six years old or under, do not have a Ph.D., are the lowest paid, and have the heaviest teaching obligations.)

The students are asking for seminars, face-to-face contact with professors, personal attention. It is by no means clear that this is the best way to "train them up." (Some professors are at their best in such small seminars, responding to give-and-take; but others are much better delivering a prepared lecture, following an outline, talking clear up to the end of the hour without brooking contradictions or questions from the students.) What *is* significant about the students' demands, and what *must* be taken seriously, is that they *want* to be "trained up." They want to be engaged in the professor's serious work, to have his serious attention. They want to be used by him as an academic resource, they want to be put to *work!*

Again, I repeat: not all students; not most students; but the articulate minority, the best students, the ones that graduate departments will be competing for.

I do not see professors devoting their serious and creative attention to "training up" freshmen and sophomores until two things happen. University administrations (on the professor's local level) and the professional associations in the disciplines (on the cosmopolitan level) must reward good and creative undergraduate teaching—creative *use* of undergraduate resources in the professor's scholarly and scientific work—in the coin that is meaningful to professors: Named chairs. Good equipment. Budgets, secretaries, assistants, leaves, local recognition by the university administrations. And, oh yes—coin. These are some of the rewards meaningful to the professor on his own campus. Specific recognition that the problem exists and deserves professional attention, serious examination of it, experimentation with alternative procedures of involving undergraduates in professional work, published papers on the subject—these are some of the rewards the professional associations can hold out to us.

Until I see at least some beginnings on these two institutional fronts, I shall doubt our seriousness of purpose in our efforts to engage undergraduate students in meaningful educational experiences.

Institutional
Expectations
and
Influences

STEPHEN J. WRIGHT

THE EVALUATION OF A COLLEGE'S INFLUENCE and expectations rests on four assumptions. They are:

1. That the learning environment is a major factor in motivating students to learn and to educate themselves, and perhaps *the* major factor in the educative process.

2. That the richer and more stimulating the learning environment, the greater the student motivation and, therefore, the greater the learning.

3. That the institutional expectations and certain special influences either determine, or go a very long way toward determining, the character and the atmosphere of the learning environment.

4. That there are effective ways by which the learning environment can be developed or maintained.

There is, I think, sufficient evidence to suggest the validity of these assumptions, even though the several elements that constitute a learning environment are intangible and therefore difficult to quantify and measure—except, perhaps, as they influence student behavior.

From the viewpoint of a college president, the crucial question is: How can the efforts of a college be organized and administered so as to achieve a rich, stimulating, educative, relevant learning environment by means of the expectations it holds for its students and by means of those influences over which it has some control? There is, unfortunately, no simple answer or formula, for college students, it must be remembered, live in several "worlds" of expectations and influences—their families and the larger real world, among others. It is these worlds that shape and develop the attitudes, the values, and the aspirations that students bring to college. In some instances, perhaps too many, what they bring to college from these other worlds has influenced them so deeply that they are either immune or antagonistic to the college's expectations and influences. When this happens in too many instances, a college should re-examine its aims, policies, or expectations, or all three.

Depending upon its objectives and the composition of its student body, a college may have a variety of expectations that contribute to or become a part of a stimulating learning environment. For instance, a college may expect a student to see an assigned academic counselor a specified number of times in a given period; to become deeply involved in culturally enriching programs; to live up to his academic potential; to observe the rules of an honors system, or to become a "second mile student" to compensate for a disadvantaged background. But if the expectations a college holds for its students are to be a meaningful part of the learning environment, they must be clearly understood by the students; they must be challenging to the students; and they must be acceptable to the majority of the students and the faculty. The chances of the institution's expectations becoming a part of the learning environment are increased, I think, to the extent that students participate in their development and to the extent that they are kept conspicuously and constantly before the students.

Colleges with sufficient financial resources have a tendency to provide a plethora of programs, activities, facilities, and gimmicks for the laudable purpose of stimulating and enriching the learning environment. And they do so without thought, I suspect, as to where the point of diminishing returns begins: there is too little definitive research on this point to be a great deal of help. But I am convinced that the really essential elements for such a stimulating environment are able, intellectually curious students and an able, student-oriented faculty, working together with a curriculum characterized by its intellectual challenge.

If for any reason an institution is unable to secure or afford either such students or such faculty, there are scarcely any compensatory approaches, programs, or activities that will prevent intellectual suffocation. The key factor that breathes life into a learning environment is *student involvement*. Without a student-oriented faculty—the key to student involvement—even bright students may leave an extensive library largely unexplored; may fail to see the relevance of special programs and lectures; and may not make effective use of facilities.

To suggest that some of the less potent elements in the learning environment may, under given circumstances, go unused is not to deprecate them, for if Mark Van Doren is correct in asserting that liberal education bestows upon a person "the power to multiply and explore choices so that the world ceases to be a little place, trimmed to one's private experiences," then the learning environment must include a wide range of opportunities to provide experiences, empirical and vicarious, to develop this power.

A college president may play an important, even a determining, role in developing the expectations and the special influences that will contribute to the mix of the learning environment on his campus. In a sense, he can play the role of a chief educational chemist, responsible for knowing whether the environment is stimulating and relevant to the purposes of the institution he leads, and helping to determine from a long list of possibilities what the environment needs and in what amounts.

Some of the obvious symptoms of a sterile learning environment include limited use of the library, poor attendance at educational programs of quality, the absence of requests and demands to improve aspects of the educational program, poor performance by graduates on standard tests for admission to graduate and professional schools, and a low percentage of students who go on to graduate and professional study.

In helping to determine what the environment needs, the president can initiate a number of approaches, among them being (1) the examination of institutions known to have stimulating learning environments (the actual work to be done by faculty and students); and (2) the internal auditing of the existing environment by faculty and students, with the understanding that the hypotheses arrived at and instituted will be tested.

In determining the particular influences in which the college will invest its resources, funds, and talent, the critical test to be applied is the effect on student behavior, and not all of the influences to be developed need be purely academic in character. At Fisk University, for example, we believe that a good liberal arts college should be a kind of microcosm of the world as it ought to be. For this reason, we make certain that our faculty is interracial, intercultural, and international; and so far as we are able, we see that the same is true of our student body. We believe that this influence speaks more loudly and clearly to our students than all the textbooks.

However competent an educational chemist a president may be, he must remember that the learning environment is infinitely complex, and that the mix that will stimulate the maximum growth requires the wisdom of faculty and of students—perhaps in equal amounts.

Some
Lessons
from
Berkeley

MARTIN TROW

WHAT ARE THE PRESSING PROBLEMS faced by large state universities stemming from their size and the heterogeneity of the student bodies? Why do teachers and administrators have difficulties in recognizing and assessing the many different kinds of students on their campuses? To answer these questions, I must refer to the recent events at Berkeley, both because I witnessed some of them, and because I think we all still have much to learn from those events and what lay behind them.

Berkeley has 27,500 students, of whom about 17,000 are undergraduates. We currently admit over 5,000 freshmen every year. One percent of 27,500 is 275; 3 percent is 825 students, roughly the number arrested during the sit-in demonstrations in the university's administration building last December.

The Berkeley student body is not only very large; it is also very heterogeneous. The great variety of students is visible immediately to a casual observer; young boys and girls just out of high school, many still living with their parents, mingle on the campus with men and women in their late twenties and early thirties, well along in their graduate careers, enough of them with school-age children of their own to overcrowd nearby elementary school systems. The differences are not only of age and maturity, but of basic attitudes and life styles: we have in the same classrooms well-to-do young sorority and fraternity members, sober commuters attending the equivalent of the local city college with eyes firmly fixed on a degree and a job, political activists with a summer or two in Mississippi behind them, bohemians and explorers in search of an identity, young scientists and scholars deep in research and study.

Differences in breadth of knowledge and sophistication are equally striking: at a world-renowned center of study and research on politics and government, a quarter of the entering freshmen class recently could not name the Secretary of State; half had never read a book of poetry for pleasure. Variations among the students in academic po-

126

tential are even more dramatic. If we take the Scholastic Aptitude Test Verbal Profile as a crude measure of readiness for college work, and compare the entering classes of 1960 at Berkeley with those at Harvard, Stanford, California Institute of Technology, and Massachusetts Institute of Technology—major private universities with whom we compete for faculty, graduate students, and research grants—the contrast in the quality of the entering classes is startling. At the four private universities, between 70 and 90 percent of their entering freshmen had SAT Verbal scores of over 600. At Berkeley the comparable figure was 30 percent. At the other end of the scale, none of the private universities had more than 2 percent of their entering students with Verbal scores of under 500; Berkeley admitted nearly a third of its freshmen with scores of 500 or below—this despite the fact that Berkeley is one of the more selective of state universities, admitting students who have been in the top 12 or 13 percent of their high school graduating classes. But these distributions, interesting as they are, conceal the fact that the large size of Berkeley's entering classes ensure that we have as many highly able students as these other selective private universities have. In 1960 Berkeley admitted "only" 4,200 freshmen, as compared with the more than 5,000 today. Yet even then we admitted 420 students with SAT Verbal scores of over 650, and almost 1,000 with SAT scores of over 600, more than entered M.I.T. and Amherst combined. On the other hand, in that same year we admitted over 500 students with SAT (V) scores of under 450 and over a thousand with scores of under 500, three times as many with scores that low as entered Kutztown State College in Pennsylvania. In other words, on this or other measures of academic ability, we have in the same institution and within the same classrooms and lecture halls, groups that match the entering classes of some of our most distinguished colleges and universities side by side with replicas of the entering classes of far more modest institutions.

I do not want to lay too great a stress on SAT scores. We have good comparative figures on them, and they give us a sense of one kind of variation, and a not unimportant one, in the student body at Berkeley. But the equally wide variations in student attitudes, orientations, motivations, and cultural styles are perhaps more important for the character of the institution, and for the problems it faces. For example, I have referred elsewhere to a crude typology of student subcultures, to which I have given the names "collegiate," "vocational," "academic," and "nonconformist." Students having these different orientations to their education differ in other important respects as

well: in their life experience before entering college, in what they hope
to do and be after leaving, and in their current relation to the university in all its aspects. In liberal arts colleges and leading private universities, the enormous growth in demand for college places since
World War II and the increased selectivity that has resulted have led
to a decline in the old collegiate culture of college fun and games, and
a decline also in a narrow vocationalism. We find in those institutions
a predominance of able, academically oriented students, the great
majority of whom are going on to graduate and professional school;
even their "nonconformists" and political activists are more cautious,
more aware of what they have to lose.[1] But, at Berkeley, in contrast
with the selective colleges and universities, all these and other subcultures are present and strongly represented. It is not possible to think
of the Berkeley student body as a group with certain predominant
characteristics and to treat those who differ as exceptional cases merit-
ing special treatment or attention. I said it is not possible; of course it
is possible to think that way, but to do so is remote from reality and
leads to trouble. Berkeley is not an academic community, despite all
the rhetoric; it is a collection of communities and aggregates of students. At least some of our difficulties have arisen out of our indifference to the nature of the complex society that these constitute.

The combination of size and heterogeneity which characterizes the
student body at Berkeley, and also, I believe, at other great state universities, is the source of various educational and institutional problems, some of which have long been visible, some of which have become visible in the past year, and some of which are still obscure but
gradually emerging. I can point only to one or two of them.

First, with nearly 30,000 students, a significant number, even though
a tiny proportion, can be found to support almost any social, political,
or educational position. Under some circumstances a minority position
will find latent or potential support among much larger numbers of
students and faculty. In the past the very number and range of activities on a campus like Berkeley's served to dilute the passions of a
minority, and to muffle its voice. The civil rights movement and the
new radicalism associated with it have created new forms of organization, disseminated political skills, and initiated or adapted modes of
political action. These forms of organization and modes of tactics have
greatly increased the influence and force of political activists in the

---

[1] The fact that education at Berkeley, at least for Californians, is "free," coupled
with the very high turnover and attrition rates, makes suspension a much weaker
sanction.

student body, and of their demands on the university. I do not want to discuss the very complicated specific issues that arose at Berkeley last year. But those events both posed and illustrated the more general problems of large public universities that center on the relations of such universities to a politically militant and active minority of its students. For example, university administrators know how to deal with adolescent "misbehavior"—panty-raids, vandalism, cheating, and the like. They know much less about how to deal with systematic violations of university regulations by large numbers of students who justify these violations by reference to moral conviction and idealism. Moreover, administrators can cope with infractions of rules by individuals or small groups of the size, say, of a fraternity; they are singularly ill-prepared to deal with mass infractions of rules. A dean calls a student to his office; two hundred appear, all claiming to have committed the same offense, all demanding to be treated like the named offender as a matter of right and justice. Corridors become clogged, it is not possible to take names; the alternatives—the use of force on a large scale or retreat—are immediately posed. And apart from the new tactics, the traditional disciplinary machinery is oriented toward the old collegiate culture and infractions that arise out of an excess of youthful high spirits and the perennial pleasures of drink and sex. Deans of students typically have good relations and good communications with the communities which give rise to such infractions: student residence halls, sororities and fraternities. When the familiar forms of trouble arise, there is a network of people and institutions that the authorities can call on for information and assistance: house mothers, residence hall officers, student judicial committees, and so forth. But administrators typically have much less knowledge of or relation to political activists, or graduate students, or commuters, or students living off campus. And, as at Berkeley, when new forms of disputes arise, there is no community of people or institutions they can turn to for advice and help. As I have suggested, the university machinery for dealing with student indiscipline has been oriented primarily toward the institutions where the collegiate subculture dominates, where the traditional forms of trouble arise. But political activists in large numbers pose new problems which the old machinery is ill-equipped to deal with, and which we at Berkeley are still struggling to solve.

Quite apart from its lack of knowledge about or communication with large segments of the student body, the administration faces a problem in devising rules that are applicable to and appropriate for quite different kinds of students. Students who cheat on exams, or crawl in windows after hours, or get drunk on campus are breaking rules, but not challenging the legitimacy of the rules, their moral rightness, or the way they are made. In these cases, a conventional student government and judicial system, without too heavy an emphasis on formal legal procedures, may well be the way to enforce the university's rules or to encourage the student community to make and enforce its own rules. But this machinery does not work so well in the face of political activists who do not accept the legitimacy of that kind of "student government," and who place very heavy emphasis on due process, and the full panoply of the civil judicial process and an adversary system under which professional defense attorneys face defenseless deans of students. And American academics, especially those in public universities, have difficulty in denying the full range of legal protections implied in the term "due process" to students charged with infractions of university rules—although universities are not really prepared to conduct their relations with students on the model of a democratic state in relation to its citizens. It is clear that this stance of the new student activists sharply challenges the remaining authority of the university *in loco parentis*, as well as its authority as a community of scholars and students whose members share basic values and purposes to which they can refer in governing the relations among them. But while we struggle to devise new forms of relationship with student activists, we still have thousands of students for whom the old forms are workable and appropriate. Berkeley has moved toward the creation of a dual system of rules and procedures for governing student activities, a new system for political activists and activities, and the old system for the traditional student activities and problems. It remains to be seen how well this works; the distinction between political and other forms of student activity can be a cloudy one, as we saw in connection with the issue of obscenity on campus last year.

I have attempted to point toward new and very complicated questions. I have spoken of the problems they pose for administrators; the difficulties of teaching such a heterogeneous student body are equally great. These difficulties are among the forces, along with the competitive pulls of research and graduate instruction, that lead teachers on campuses like Berkeley to withdraw much of their interest and energies from undergraduate education. But to return to my theme: the character of the student bodies at our very large state universities is not clearly perceived or understood by many administrators and faculty members at those institutions. Seeing our students more clearly, in all their variety, is a necessary if not sufficient condition for transforming some of these problems into educational opportunities.

Society
and
the
Campus

DAVID MALLERY

THE "NEW FERMENT" WE ARE SEEING on the campuses has already been assaulted by the first wave of analyzers, generalizers, and specializers. My part in this has been as a visitor on eight Western campuses, talking with students, and sometimes with deans and professors, about the campus and political and social action. The College Student Personnel Institute, in Claremont, California, sponsored this venture, with the help of a grant from the Edward W. Hazen Foundation, and I reported to an august group of deans of students, who were generous enough to help educate me and not simply to impress me.

You can imagine that it would indeed be an education for a visitor to encounter, often in extended conversations, wild-eyed students from Left and Right, searching, dedicated activists, supposedly apathetic spectators, wary searchers for some responsibility or at least some understanding in the world beyond the campus, and—they still exist—busy and absorbed students devoting little of their peripheral vision to the society whose influence is reaching onto the campuses in such dramatic ways.

The book describing these conversations and experiences—they were fascinating and, I hope, not only to me—will be published in a few weeks by Harper and Row, under the title *Ferment on the Campus*. Rather than summarize hundreds of voices and faces in ten minutes, I will just note a few fragments of the education I began with my first campus conversation in this adventure.

It is surely not news to say that a crucial influence in the recent ferment on campus has been the new intensity about the civil rights of American Negroes. The identification of white students with the struggle of American Negroes for rights, for freedom, for individual identity, and for opportunity has been extraordinary in the experience of some students, including those with real influence on campus. The Negroes' cause seems to link up with some students' personal drives for individual rights, freedom, identity, and opportunity, although these drives may at first seem remote from the actual feelings, the

131

actual struggle, of American Negroes in the civil rights arena. Yet hearing students talk, I have often thought that their feelings of wanting to throw off the "oppression" of adults and test their own powers, of wanting to be themselves and not someone else's image of themselves, of needing to count in the world's eyes (and their own) as individuals who matter—these feelings have found a powerful fellowship in what students see and hear in today's events in the civil rights movement.

This identification has led to action, and this action has led those young people involved to take a whole new attitude toward campus life and toward student initiative and student power. We see on campuses today some young men and women who have had the experience of organizing themselves into effective groups to set up voter registration, who have designed and taken part in massive protests and demonstrations, who have established relationships between the races and between power groups in explosive communities, who have been beaten up by racists and "treated," as one young man put it, "to the experience of being a victim in a police state." Other students have returned from a first encounter with tutoring deprived children, often Negroes, in desperately underprivileged neighborhoods, or from other service projects in which they felt they counted for something, were important to somebody.

Summer programs in Africa had an especially powerful impact on students I talked with, and here again the identification was similar to the identification with American Negroes. In some of the new African countries the fact of an emerging race is joined in these students' feelings with the idea of an emerging nation, a new status, a new place in the sun, wrung from oppressors and heavily paid for. These are personal feelings to these students, and not simply current events. As one professor said, "It's a case of 'how ya going to keep 'em down on the farm after they've seen'—not Paree but Birmingham or Uganda or the Boston slums."

The "New Veterans"

Today's new veterans of Selma and Ghana, of the New York slums and the Mississippi cellars, after hearing and reading for years about the futility-of-the-individual-in-a-complex-and-impersonal-society, feel that they can be a part of the solution of the problem that has awakened them to action on the front lines. Unlike the World War II veterans, this kind of veteran is not returning with the feeling of entering the desperately won sanctuary of books, classes, ideas, and encounters with "education." He is looking around to see what can be

done to enlist this education—the experiences, the people, the organization of the institution itself—in the solution of the problem. For
him, the dramatic reality is off campus. For the "old" veterans, the
reality, precious if not dramatic, was on campus, no matter how vivid
the memories of wartime experiences. They rejoiced that the war was
over. The new veterans see themselves in a war that has just begun.

The old veterans delighted their elders by their zeal for studies. The
new veterans disconcert their elders by their zeal for demonstrations.
And many of them have shown more than zeal: they have learned
how to demonstrate, to protest, to rally a crowd, to organize a movement, sometimes even to put their opponents against the wall. These
techniques look a little different on a college campus than they looked
on the street before an Alabama courthouse. College administrators
have been quick to say that the situations are different, that the campus is not the place for this kind of organized pressure. Some have
argued with deep conviction that the very fact that the university is
committed to rational discourse is reason enough for students to seek
styles and approaches different from those used in the streets. Nevertheless, such college leaders often find themselves cast by their new
veteran students in the role of a Governor Wallace or a Bull Connor.
This may be infuriating as well as unfair, but it is happening, and
many a dean of students or college president is being cornered into
fighting his way out of such a role.

One final comparison between the two sets of veterans: the 1946–50
veterans were not rallying their classmates to the cause of studying.
They were simply studying themselves, and providing some competition and some example in the process. Today's veterans are vigorously
rallying *their* classmates to *their* cause of concern or protest, service or
demonstration. Their efforts can be exploited by the whole range of
noise-makers from self-styled revolutionaries to free-riding sports on an
antiauthority spree. They can also evoke the most intense and admi-
rable idealism. Just who will control the leadership and point the direction for the new ferment is a reverberating question on campuses
today. And with it comes the immediate action question to professors,
deans, administrators, and students themselves: How can the campus
community draw out the most constructive forces in the ferment to
make the campus education and its contribution to society the more
searching and relevant?

The Classroom and the World Beyond

Today's post-Sputnik colleges are not automatically stimulating desirable interests and attitudes on political and social matters simply

because courses require "better preparation" and college admissions officers are more impressed with the current level of test scores than they were a few years ago. I met students in this study who are giving so much of themselves to their own kinds of political and social action that they are having to drop courses, to plan an extra year to graduate, or to flunk out. For some of them, the academic side of college is getting more and more remote. Those who stay in college are trying to cope with their academic work with a few fingers of their left hands. The practical thing for them to do is to cope as well as they can with the academic demands necessary for the degree and for some next step after graduation, but the real drive, energy, and concern is, as one young woman put it, "not just in a different world from the campus world, but on what seems sometimes like a different planet." I suspect there are many, many students like these who have given up ever finding *anything* in the curriculum that relates to what they can care about personally. They are not just looking for ideas they can identify with. Some are looking for an understanding about the world they see beyond the campus. Others want a sense of actually "doing something" in the world even if this doing is a new kind of talk, a gesture, a burst of emotion, or a temporary escape from what seems to them the irrelevance of their campus education and the reality of their experience—in the summer or in vacation time or even in a few borrowed hours—of a direct encounter with issues and problems they take seriously. The world is influencing such students as these, and, perhaps equally strongly but quite differently, so is a college curriculum and a set of campus activities which seem to them pointless. This strikes me as the dominant negative factor in the new ferment.

How surprising it is then, to see some students who see the adventure of college as one total experience in which the classroom, the community, and the world are all somehow related, rooms to walk about in naturally, from one to the other, to learn and live and belong in. These students are almost always intellectually powerful, not just bright. But their power is not what makes them see and seek the relationship of classroom and world. No one who talked with some of the intellectually crackling students I met on this study could say that the most intelligent concerned ones found stimulation in their courses and the least intelligent concerned ones did not. Rather, these are students who somehow can manage the balance between concern and relative inaction. They can accept the role of the learner, the explorer in life, whether in class, library, picket line, meeting, conversation, or service. They may have participated enough in the causes that concern them to feel that they are doing something some of the time; but they do not feel that the rest of their time is simply a waste stretch in which they scrounge for grades.

I suppose these are the students who seem to have solved the problem of conflict of demands between the classroom and the world. They surely look better to their professors than the ones who see the classroom as an island of irrelevancy. And unless their deans are edgy about *any* student involvement in political and social action, these students present fewer administrative headaches than the other type. Yet from the point of view of the young man or woman who has "left college for a world he can live and act in," as one student said about his roommate, these students seem pathetically deceived. The college dropout, watching his campus friends from the viewpoint of the barricades in Selma, wonders how they can be so blind, so childish, and so unrelated to the driving issues of the day. And, for a bit of sobering perspective, it is not hard to find students who think the fellow on the barricade is an impractical nut, and that even the best of the campus activists is deluding himself about doing something that matters, even if they would not actually attack the quality and sincerity of his concern.

There remain what I think of as the crucial majority of the students already awakened or awakening-to-concern. They look at the world and they look at the experiences and activities and material of their college education and they are increasingly concerned about why the world and the campus seem to have no relation to each other at all. Irrelevance and frustration are possible on a campus of 400 as well as one of 40,000, if nothing that goes on seems to students to be about anything real that they see and care about in the exploding world beyond the Gothic and grass. On the giant campuses and on the supposedly individual-minded small ones, the world and education need to have something to do with each other, and conversation about this relationship needs to go on between the generations.

There will be more campus explosions that look—and may be— foolish and irrelevant to the issues they are supposed to be about. And there will be more explosions on issues that don't seem to be worth fighting for at all. Headlines and television screens, political slogans from Right, Left, and Center sing the word "freedom." The events which for many students make up the major drama of the nation have at their center a great mass of Americans whose freedom and whose rights have been denied. Add this to the usual and normal reaching-out for independence and selfhood in eighteen-to-twenty-two-year-olds and there *is* indeed something new—and something complicated, for good or ill, on college campuses. It may bring a new kind of responsibility or a new kind of chaos, but it is way beyond kids-will-be-kids.

It seemed to me as I talked with students who were thinking seriously about political and social problems that a real hope is that the most astute and mature of them who are suddenly aroused to the idea of freedom denied will tend more and more to focus on the problem in his own country, even his own community, rather than translating it into "my personal rights" having to do with a traffic violation, dorm hours, or the dean's handling of a drinking problem. But this is a hope, and one not to be counted on even from the most mature students. In a time when authorities to rebel against are so often shadowy, the colleges are being asked to discriminate between real issues and post-adolescent rebellions. Yet the colleges need to be asked just this. And from what I heard on these campuses, many students themselves are asking this, and are asking it with a vigor and idealism and dedication which could promise much for our colleges and our nation.

Societal
Expectations
and
Influences

JOSEPH KATZ

WHY IS THERE an increasingly higher rate of college attendance? First, there is the economic incentive. The popular image is, and objective studies have confirmed it, that going to college provides access to a better job and to a higher income. Then, there are social incentives. College is perceived as a prestigious club in which one acquires friends, connections, a mate, and in which one may have a good time. A minority of students view college as providing the opportunity for continuing to satisfy the intellectual curiosity aroused previously at school, at home, or in their own explorations.

Whatever the causes of going to college may be, our research on students at two large universities showed that almost all students took their going for granted. Going to college was no longer a matter of choice to them; it was almost as natural and as unavoidable as being born. (The situation, of course, is different for those high school students who do not continue to college. But many of them, too, may have "no choice" in a different sense.) Parents, peers, and society at large, especially the press and magazines, all have conditioned our students to believe that their lives will be failures unless they go to college. This pressure, it appears, makes them stay in college even at those times when they despair of the meaningfulness of that experience.

The first difficulty, then, is that parental and societal expectations do not give our adolescents sufficient leeway to consider alternatives to going to college. We found only a few people at our two institutions who quit college after deciding they could pursue their occupational or personal goals better by seeking out other experiences and opportunities for training. Perhaps this same acceptance of the *necessity* of going to college has prevented many students, parents, and faculty from considering radically different methods of college instruction.

Another difficulty is that societal and parental expectations are ambiguous. In our very first interviews our student subjects told us that their parents made no demands on them in the planning of their lives, but expected them to choose as they saw fit. Our subjects seemed themselves to believe this, but as we probed in our questioning it became clear that their parents had very definite expectations regarding the appropriate behavior, attitudes, and plans of their offspring. Over the four college years, in spite of clashes over secondary issues, most students' occupational and marital choices, even their fundamental ideologies, have stayed close to parental wishes and beliefs. The issue here is not whether such agreement or disagreement is desirable, but rather the manner in which beliefs and attitudes are arrived at. The unseen pressures, behind the appearance of encouraging independence and self-determination, help to create personalities too unaware of what is for their own good and too dependent on what others think.

The same ambiguity, implicit domination behind the apparent encouragement of independence, is also mirrored in the structure of collegiate arrangements. Officially the college is dedicated to training independence of mind and character; but in fact, it asks students to do as they are told and encourages passive receptivity in classroom and homework. Our subjects have voiced over and over again the complaint that they are not really being treated as independent people. (There are related ambiguities, such as the one pointed out by Harold A. Korn,[1] of encouraging students to get a general education while at the same time creating an early concern for finding a major and favoring specialization.)

This playing fast and loose with independence may well be the expression of society's unconscious uncertainty about how much individual freedom to allow without its becoming disturbing to the social order—and perhaps the tendency is to tip the scales in favor of order. This concern for order makes it more difficult for education to be successful at a time in life when favorable personality change depends on the chance of trying out freely and imaginatively a variety of behavior patterns and life styles.

The present college system is well designed to create docile citizens (people, it must be understood, who are at the same time solid and decent, even while their docility goes at the expense of a higher degree of individual happiness and a fuller realization of their emotional and intellectual potential). Because of this encouragement of docility and passivity the colleges have, in spite of the recent emphasis on higher academic performance, continued to be largely unintellectual, thus mirroring our society also. Evidence for this can be found in the grad-

[1] Korn, "Careers: Choice, Chance and Inertia" (MS in preparation).

ing system, where dominance and equivalence to the monetary system in providing incentives and rewards has recently been pointed out by Howard S. Becker.[2] The post-Sputnik "raising of academic standards" has primarily encouraged higher grade-getting capacities. It has secondarily encouraged the mentality of the technician whose forte is specialized competence. It has had small, and sometimes negative, effects on the cultivation of general intelligence and intellectuality.

Grading is a selecting device rather than an educating one. But its persistence is due to its having other social utility. It is a good democratic instrument for classifying people in an impersonal manner and allowing for upward mobility and reshuffling of the elites by giving high performers access to the more prestigious schools and, from there, to positions of leadership. The fact that colleges are more social than intellectual institutions is also mirrored in students' self-concepts. In a recent large-scale survey only 19 percent of nearly 13,000 entering freshmen gave "academic orientation" as the most accurate description of themselves.[3]

One might raise the question: Is all this compulsivity necessary? Do we need our students to be that docile, that passive and conforming, in order to maintain the stability of our social order? So many of our subjects remind me of Marquand's heroes. When we asked these students what they expected to be doing ten years from now, they often replied with a description of a suburban existence that they considered rather routine. They thought it undesirable but at the same time expected that after some kind of fling and some travel, they would have to accept it as their lot. To them it was regrettable but unavoidable. Our questionnaire and interview data confirm that most students have a strongly "privatist" orientation. They rank highest their own individual careers and future family life. Involvement in international, national, or civic affairs and in service to other people are ranked astonishingly low and there is little change from the freshman to the senior year.[4] In spite of the recent student activism, *the primary need still is to wake up students, not to constrain them.*

The last year has brought to the surface the existence of a group of students who are actively challenging our conventional notions of

[2] Becker, "Student Culture and the Dynamics of Change in the Modern University," Paper presented at the Conference on the Dynamics of Change in the Modern University, Syracuse University, June 1965.
[3] Educational Testing Service, *Institutional Report* (Princeton, N.J.: E.T.S., January 1964).
[4] Joseph Katz et al., "Report of the Student Development Study" (MS in preparation).

society. The avenues for change taken by these students are diverse. One might, very roughly, divide them into those who seek change by modifying the external world and those who seek to do so through heightened individual experiences; often these two are combined. Seeking significant individual experiences can run the gamut from working toward more significant intellectual activity in the classroom to experimenting with various consciousness-altering drugs. The desire for external change can express itself in highly competent work with the underprivileged or in a protest against sexual conventions by the flaunting of one's own unconventionality—and anxieties.

It is of particular interest to observe the nonpolitical nature of the current student movement. Most of the students we have studied have not associated their protest with any of the existing political parties. Their protest seems at times a new version of anarchism, one that is closely related to the old-fashioned nineteenth century American virtue of individualism. It is an individualism coupled with the search for affectionate community and for the opportunity of expressing the aesthetic and feeling parts of human nature more freely.

In the university as in the society at large, the three qualities of relatedness, individual autonomy, and expression of impulse are underdeveloped. The current student "unrest" is a symptom and a signal. If we heed it, the university can be more than a mirror of society; it can assume its more lively function of being one of the primary agencies for the renewal of society and for constructive change. One avenue is to transform the large society of the university into series of overlapping smaller groups. Another is for the university to make learning more meaningful by taking up with renewed vigor the Deweyan challenge of relating the work in the classroom both to the student's phase of psychological development and to the many unsolved social tasks in his environment. Third, the university can give students more recognition for their efforts and considerably more opportunity for exercising responsibility and individuality in their work.

The
Student
in
Higher
Education

JOSEPH F. KAUFFMAN

ONE HAS BUT TO SCAN a drugstore magazine rack, the paperback books on display almost everywhere, or even the daily newspaper, to note with what concern our country views college and college students. How to get into college, how to finance college, how to stay in college—these are subjects neatly balanced against such concerns as morals on campus, the mood of the students, and their search for identity.

The substantial increase in the size of the college-age population and the increasing awareness of the necessity of higher education for one's economic survival, have made colleges and universities highly visible operations. No longer regarded as a "luxury," post-high-school education has become a standard part of life in America. This results in pressures not only on institutions but on individual students as well.

Student Personnel Services

In the first section of this report we shall deal with the following major topics: entry into the higher education process; the changing nature of the student's personal relationship to his institution; the new climate of student freedom and rights; and the "unsuccessful" student.

Entry into the higher education process

Some years ago, one would have described this topic as "college admission." For the present, and certainly for the future, it is necessary to appreciate the true complexity of this vital problem. As most parents are aware, concern with entry into higher education begins no later than the ninth grade—and sometimes earlier. But it does not end in the twelfth grade.

With the rapid expansion of community colleges, public and private junior colleges, and with the growing proportion of vocations and occupations which require graduate or professional school training,

141

there is a need to look at higher education as a *continuum*. The student can enter at more than one point on the continuum and, if he is to take full advantage of its opportunities, he needs information, advice, and counsel about a host of realities.

There are four categories of institutions involved in the higher education process, each of which must relate to the others. These are the secondary schools, the junior colleges, the colleges, and the graduate or professional schools of the university. Although some decry the power which graduate and professional education seem to hold over the college curriculum (and thus the junior college and high school), nevertheless the reality is such that few students, even in high school, can rule out, a priori, the possibility of some day having to meet the requirements of a graduate or professional school.

Along with the expansion of postcollege education and training we are witnessing a tremendous growth of postsecondary education and training in the type of institution termed "junior college." Most public junior colleges tend to be comprehensive in nature, offering terminal occupational curricula as well as college-parallel curricula. Thus, students are permitted, if not encouraged, to enter the junior college as a steppingstone, or entry port, for transfer to a college or university. Edmund J. Gleazer, Jr., executive director of the American Association of Junior Colleges, estimates that approximately 1 million students will attend junior colleges in 1963–64 and that by 1970, 50 percent of all beginning college students will start their college education in public junior colleges.

If these estimates are correct, we may assume that, by 1975, a majority of all first-year college students will be enrolled in junior colleges. To these facts could be added the possibility for extending public education two years beyond high school.

All these factors suggest that the question "Shall I go to college?" may well be out of date. It may be more appropriate to concern ourselves with the most effective means of entering the higher education process and making the wisest possible decisions about entry points along the continuum, to allow maximum flexibility and opportunity for the individual student.

QUESTIONS

1. What is the quality of information that students (and parents) receive from high schools about entry into junior college, college, or university; about student financial aid programs; about curriculum requirements, advanced placement, early admission, early decision plans; telescoped liberal arts/professional degree programs; about transfer

opportunities from junior college to senior institutions, admission to graduate and professional schools, and many more problems? Is it possible to remove some of the mystery, waste, and confusion about the higher education process in general?

2. School principals and counselors at the secondary school level are besieged by numerous "standardized" forms from various kinds of institutions of higher education, requiring evaluation of individual students both in highly quantified terms and in the most subjective terms of such characteristics as "sense of humor." Several national testing programs invade the secondary school, cost students a substantial sum of money and frenzy, and are not generally well interpreted to harassed school personnel.

Questions of professional standards, withholding confidential information, and the responsibility of the high school for "placing" its graduates in college are often expressed—at least covertly. How does one react to the entrepreneurlike college recruiter who visits the secondary schools? Does the high school have to take responsibility for protecting its students from misrepresentation by colleges? Should it show student records, test information, and interview material to college admissions staff? Just what is the role of the secondary school in college admissions?

Shouldn't we begin now to deal with these subjects on a national basis?

3. The junior college is obviously a reality on the higher education continuum. Pressures will mount for it to be all things to all people. One fact seems clear at this time: a large proportion of students, if not a majority, will utilize a junior college as the initial point of entry into the higher education process.

What testing and evaluation devices will become standard for admission to junior colleges? Will testing instruments and counseling be used to place students in terminal occupational curricula or college-parallel curricula? Will the testing program being developed by the American Association of Junior Colleges and the Educational Testing Service become a guidance device, or will it be used by colleges as the determining factor for transfer? If so, will the junior college find itself primarily preparing students to score well on such a standardized test? Will this be a way in which communities evaluate their public junior colleges?

Can we define the college and university transfer process sufficiently well to clarify it for junior college student personnel officers? Can we ask colleges and universities to re-examine their policies and procedures for transfer at the junior-year level for both admission and financial aid?

4. It is clear that the trend will be for an increasing proportion of college graduates to attend graduate and professional schools. The nature of our economy and manpower needs makes this trend understandable.

Except for a minority of students who attend graduate school because they do not know what else to do with themselves, graduate and professional study is decidedly a career decision. It is inevitably bound up with vocational counseling and career guidance. Yet in very few colleges and universities is significant effort given to career choice or eventual entry into the world of work. The placement office and corporation recruiters may play a significant role in the job-entry process, but students seeking information on graduate and professional study, financial aid, and concomitant opportunities face a no man's land.

Can we present to the student personnel worker on the college level more accurate, revelant, and helpful information on graduate and professional school admissions practices, testing programs, financial aid opportunities, and the like, so that he may communicate it to college students?

Student relationship

The writer is aware that one cannot generalize about "students" or even "higher education," for the diversity and pluralism inherent in postsecondary education in the United States are obvious to even the most casual observer. Nevertheless, there are broad trends, differing in speed of development, that are evident and that apply to the majority of students and institutions in higher education.

Increased pressure for university attendance, the rapid expansion of physical plant, the increasingly multiple and even conflicting commitments which the university has to government, industry, and research—all serve to diminish the once central role of the undergraduate student in the college and university. All too often we hear student complaints that informal, out-of-class contact with professors is impossible and that even in class the student is but one in a sea of unknown faces. Whether true or not, many feel that the administration considers them a number or a statistic, worthy of notice only when they "step out of line." This feeling of being inconsequential or expendable has implications that should concern us. For we know all too well that those students who are regarded (or regard themselves) as faceless, anonymous human beings are not the best hope for our society or for the future health and support of higher education.

There will probably always be small colleges, but the direction of expansion is clear. Lewis Mayhew predicts that by 1975 three-fourths of all students enrolled in institutions of higher education will be in five hundred institutions. Thus, we are talking about the majority of students.

We must add to the facts of immense campuses, large numbers of students, automated recording and teaching devices, centralization of services, and formality of student contact, an additional factor: the steady withdrawal of faculty from any out-of-class contact with students. As Clark Kerr points out in his *The Uses of the University*, students resent and protest against this withdrawal: "the revolt that used to be against the faculty *in loco parentis* is now against the faculty *in absentia*." [1]

It seems safe to assume that in the increasingly heterogeneous, impersonal, unconnected university, something has to give. Morale factors, counterproductive to the stated educational purposes of our institutions, demand attention.

There are some who would maintain that the increasing reliance of students on legalistic definitions of student rights is in direct proportion to their perception that they have been "rejected" by their teachers and institutions and that they will demand a relationship, even if it must be legally prescribed. When students, supported by civil liberties groups, demand precise definitions of relationships, responsibilities, obligations, and expectations, it seems evident that the student-teacher relationship is sorely tried—the *educational relationship* ruptured—and the governance of the institution defensive and harassed.

QUESTIONS

1. Is it possible to rationalize the implications of the trends described above so that some of the values and personal satisfactions that we assume rightfully belong to college attendance are seen as not our business at all? Are there myths about the undergraduate college or university experience that need to be dispelled so that the expectations of those outside the university will be properly altered?

If institutions of higher learning expand, must we necessarily expect some of the former values of the college experience to be lost? Should we seek new social institutions to meet the personal and develop-

[1] P. 103.

mental needs of the late adolescents who attend colleges and universities? Or is this problem not our proper concern?

2. If we accept at least part of the burden—as I believe we must—are there ways of organizing the teaching, the physical facilities, and the living arrangements of our expanding campuses so that anonymity and depersonalization are reduced to a minimum, so that identification and involvement are naturally facilitated? Can we organize the university with these problems firmly in mind? Are there things that university administrations might be able to do that we have not even begun to think about?

3. Is it possible to inject into our student personnel programs, in the ways in which we organize student services, something to compensate for this trend? Do we need to decentralize many student personnel functions—even deprofessionalize some of them—so that there can be more informal and less "official" contacts between students and adults in the campus community? Have we written off faculty involvement in our attempts to cope with this trend?

4. Is it possible that part of the solution lies in involving and utilizing the students themselves? Students now participate in off-campus tutoring of disadvantaged youth, social action programs, and the like. This same age group serves in the Peace Corps, in the Armed Forces, and in summer jobs that are often of a responsible nature. If we can create the machinery and the climate, is it not reasonable to assume that the older students might well perform functions and roles that would not only be personally satisfying but would also help create the reality of community and personal involvement in the "multiversity"?

The new climate of student freedom and rights

It should be obvious that there is a rapidly developing controversy over the question of "student rights." The writer believes that this controversy will increase in both tempo and intensity and that ways must be found to cope with it now. The new-found emphasis on student rights and freedoms stems from three main forces and their interaction.

The first of these is the gradual loss of personal contact and relationships between faculty and students outside the classroom. With the withdrawal of faculty from such contacts, the relations students have with university personnel outside the classroom are largely official and are characterized by the identification of the officials as "administration."

Second, there has been a recent growth and acceptance of non-violent social action as a legitimate and successful weapon against "bad" practices or "bad" laws. Many of the pioneers and participants in such social action have been students. The moral nature of the civil rights battle has put such participants "on the side of the angels," and there is no doubt that results have been obtained. This has not gone unnoticed by student leaders who wish to oppose administrative policies on our college campuses.

The third factor has to do with the family-social milieu in which many of today's college students were raised. The years following World War II have been marked by a general affluence, permissiveness in child rearing, mobility of families, and crucial changes in community life. Young people today are sophisticated in their social experiences far beyond their age group of two decades ago. This means that we need to change our definition of acceptable behavior, as well as our conception of effective restraints.

These three factors—and there may be others—have produced the present state of tension about rules, discipline, values, rights, and freedoms, and the colleges are finding it difficult to respond. I do not mean to imply that colleges and universities are innocent bystanders. We know all too well that arbitrary punishment, invasion of privacy, and noneducational pressures have provided students in some institutions with legitimate cause for complaint.

We can divide this matter into two parts: (1) *political and social action*—the rights of students to express themselves and participate in matters of controversy both on and off the campus; and (2) *personal behavior*—including questions involving sexual behavior, drinking, dress, and general conduct, both on and off campus.

POLITICAL AND SOCIAL ACTION

It would be instructive for all educators to read the revised (November 1963) edition of the American Civil Liberties Union statement on *Academic Freedom and Civil Liberties of Students in Colleges and Universities*. Several excerpts from the document are appropriate here.

[1] The college which wishes to set an example of open-minded inquiry in its classrooms will defeat its purpose if it denies the same right of inquiry to its students outside the classroom—or if it imposes rules which deny them the freedom to make their own choices, wise or unwise. Limitations on the freedom of students are not then to be seen as simple administrative decisions which adjust the school to the prevailing climate of public opinion. The college's policy vis-

à-vis its students goes to the heart of the condition necessary for adequate personal growth and thus determines whether an institution of higher education turns out merely graduates or the indispensable human material for a continuing democracy.

[2] *A. Freedom of Expression:* The student government, student organizations, and individual students should be free to discuss, pass resolutions, distribute leaflets, circulate petitions, and take other lawful action respecting any matter which directly or indirectly concerns or affects them.

Students should take responsibility for helping to maintain a free academic community. They should respect and defend not only their fellow students' freedoms; but also their teachers' right to the free expression of views based on their own pursuit of the truth and their right to function as citizens, independently of the college or university. . . .

[3] *D. Pamphlets, Petitions and Demonstrations:* Student organizations and individual students should be allowed, and no special permission should be required, to distribute pamphlets, except in classrooms and study halls, or collect names for petitions concerning either campus or off-campus issues. Orderly demonstrations on campus should not be prohibited.

[4] *E. Student Publications:* All student publications—college newspapers, literary and humor magazines, academic periodicals and yearbooks—should enjoy full freedom of the press. They are too often denied it by college administrations which fear public criticism. Except for the relatively few university dailies which are independent financially, college publications in general are dependent on the administration's favor in that they use campus facilities and are subsidized either directly by the college or indirectly by a tax on student funds.[a]

In the winter of 1964 a draft statement of the Association of American University Professors was circulated which took an almost identical position on the matters we are concerned with here.

On the basis of this, it seems clear that faculty voices, as well as civil liberties organizations, strongly support the proposition that students have a right to enter controversial political and social issues, petition, demonstrate, advocate, editorialize, and listen to controversial speakers. Some would argue that not only is this a fundamental right of students, but that the educational process is enriched and expanded by encouraging the use of such rights.

[a] New York: American Civil Liberties Union, 1963. Pp. 4, 7.

PERSONAL BEHAVIOR

Deans of students are well aware of the increasing problems caused by attempts to invoke rules, prohibitions, and controls for student behavior when the faculty, adult, and peer group populations seemingly do not support such rules. Curfew rules, drinking, coed visiting in dormitories—and, particularly, student behavior off campus—these seem to an increasing number of faculty members to be none of the business of higher education.

Public concern, particularly in the area of sexual behavior, is commonplace. Family magazines, if not the daily newspaper, comment on the "morals" problem on campus. Perhaps fortunately, it is difficult to quantify or be statistical about this matter, but the fantasies are bad enough.

But even if we acknowledge that a problem does exist, it is difficult for the college or university to find a solution to it. Just what *are* the institution's responsibilities in matters of student morality? What behaviors should they require of their students? An increasing proportion of faculty refuse to be concerned with nonacademic behavior matters. The principal sanction is expulsion, but the courts, along with civil liberties groups, are now raising serious questions concerning both the procedures used in expulsion and the substantive basis for expulsion. Meanwhile, with no new force moving into the fray, some fear a kind of moral anarchy or, worse, nihilism.

QUESTIONS

1. Must we acccept a legal or contractual definition of the relationship between a college and its students? Is there a way to define the relationship in educational terms, other than credits earned? Does the growth of the legal approach to the relationship imply that the gap between teacher and student, and college and student, must widen even further?

2. Can educational institutions make a case for protecting their "rights" and preserving their autonomy, or are faculty rights and student rights the only rights involved? Can we speak of the institution's unique position, apart from faculty and student rights?

3. Can the institution permit, and even encourage, partisan political and social activity—protecting those who are engaged in such controversy—and yet make clear its own refusal to be used for partisan political purposes? Is it now time for colleges and universities to remind legislatures and benefactors that the freedom it grants to its faculty and students is a part of the necessary climate of learning?

4. Shouldn't we re-examine, without delay, the *in loco parentis* concept on which most rules and regulations governing student behavior are based? Do we not require a new frame of reference, given the large number of nonresident students, students twenty-one years of age and older, and faculty refusal to act *in loco parentis?*

5. In light of the lifetime economic penalties implied by the act of expulsion, and the willingness of the courts to consider whether or not all of the rights of the expelled student have been protected, do we not have to re-examine the techniques, purposes, and degrees of discipline which colleges and universities invoke and, particularly, the procedures used in applying such discipline to the individual student?

6. Finally, can we assist institutions of higher education to define, at least in general terms, legitimate expectations regarding student behavior? Does the academic degree connote more than appropriate credits with appropriate grade-point averages? Is that what the faculty certifies when it recommends the awarding of the diploma? What do we expect (if anything) beyond this for the campus and off-campus student? Can we be explicit about this?

The "unsuccessful" student

While the writer knows of no definitive study of the college dropout problem or precise facts on student attrition, all studies that have been undertaken seem to agree on one generalization: approximately one-half of those who start college do not reach graduation.

Summerskill [3] reviewed 35 different studies on the college dropout, dating from 1913 to 1957. Median values were computed for the aggregate of these studies. The median loss in four years was 50 percent. The median percent graduated in four years was 37 percent. Variability in attrition rates among the colleges ranged from 12 percent to 82 percent in the 35 studies reviewed.

Summerskill's data led to this conclusion:

> Colleges lose, on the average, approximately half their students in the four years after matriculation. Some 40% of college students graduate on schedule and, in addition, approximately 20% graduate at some college, some day.[4]

One can posit that it is becoming increasingly important for students to "succeed" in college, since our economy and manpower re-

[3] John Summerskill, "Dropouts from College," *The American College,* ed. Nevitt Sanford (New York: John Wiley & Sons, 1962), pp. 629 ff.
[4] *Ibid.,* p. 631.

quirements make demands that only college training can fulfill. Thus, the extrinsic value of a college education has taken on an obvious economic dimension. Just as the courts have found denial of higher education to be a significant "injury," in that it denies the individual economic opportunity, so one may question whether inadequate conditions or attention to student needs may also lead to a similar injury. Certainly the question of the extent of responsibility a college or university has to the unsuccessful student or the would-be dropout is worthy of our consideration.

There are no data of a precise nature on the causes or reasons for student attrition. Among many factors one would have to include the following: motivation and expectation and their interaction with institutional environments and values; academic incompetence or unsuitability related to type of institution or major field of study; financial circumstances; personal or emotional adjustment problems.

It is interesting to note the problem of students in high-quality liberal arts institutions who drop out (many return later). Often good students, they are portrayed as nonvocational in orientation, constantly challenging the "unreality" of the college to the issues and tensions of the "real world."

An informal study of some dropouts in this category was reported in a recent issue of the student publication, *The Moderator*. They were described, in that brief report, in the following manner:

> Their common characteristic lies not so much in what kind of people they are, emotionally or intellectually, as it does in their common response to one of the most universal tensions of American college life: "College" versus "the real world." This is the vague but nonetheless emphatic assertion that there is a violent, almost ludicrous, disparity between the way you live, think, act and talk in a university dormitory and the way you do all these things—and anything else—"on the outside". . . . In a word, there is a feeling that college is something apart from reality.
>
> The Dropout is the person to whom this idea appears so blatantly obvious that he cannot put up with college anymore. He feels uncomfortable, thinks he is wasting his time in a fantastic shadowland of trivia and semantic gymnastics. So he quits, to try to find the real world.[5]

The above description, written by student editors, of fellow students at liberal arts colleges, may be contrasted with the observations of the attrition problems in schools of engineering. A report issued in

[5] "Must We Leave to Learn?" *The Moderator*, Spring 1964, pp. 3–5.

April 1963 from a committee of the Engineering Manpower Commission stated that the attrition rate in most engineering colleges is "far greater than that necessary to weed out the incompetent." Survival rates, from freshman enrollment to the bachelor's degree, were found to average 36 percent for state universities and 55 percent for private colleges, but as low as 20 percent at some state institutions.

The report points out that the problem is as much a human problem as an academic one and that high attrition "casts the spell of gloom" over the entire engineering program.

> The harsh, impersonal "sink or swim" theory seems inadequate to deal with all of the variable elements in student selection and survival. Some students who have all of the motivation and talents necessary for success are handicapped by inadequate educational backgrounds. On a rigid scale of selection, they are likely to sink. Then there is the shy, timid youngster who may feel all alone in a big machine. His outlook and his academic record are colored by his problems of social adaptation. Yet, in the long run, he may have all the qualities for success. In fact, it has not been unusual for such a person to rise to outstanding leadership in industry, government or society. There is also the youngster who is highly creative but perhaps doesn't fit too well into the academic mold. By academic standards he may be a poor risk, but his talents may place him far above his associates in ultimate promise.[6]

This is sufficient illustration that both liberal arts and professional schools face a problem of student failure, dropout, attrition, or unproductivity. Perhaps each institution must assess for itself the importance of this problem. Certainly no student personnel program can ignore such a matter.

QUESTIONS

1. What degree of responsibility, if any, does each institution have to its unsuccessful students? Is it possible to deal with this subject without, at the same time, implying that academic standards should be so flexible that we become all things to all people? Can large institutions really deal with those who are falling by the wayside? How much counseling, staff, and other university resources should be devoted to this problem?

2. Do we have sufficient data on the subject of attrition in general and academic failure in particular to plan programs for their alleviation? Do current surveys present an accurate picture of either the ex-

[6] *Engineering Student Attrition* (New York: Engineers' Joint Council, 1963).

tent of attrition or its causes? Is it possible to engage in substantial longitudinal studies, on a national basis, rather than draw inferences from the usual reports on a four-year span, which do not get at persistence and resumption of study?

3. To what extent is stress on students a factor of higher faculty expectations or our inability to relate the student's goals to the institution's goals? Is the stress of rising academic standards a result of our continuing to grade students on a curve, as though they represented a normal distribution—even though all may be carefully selected and accomplished students?

4. To what extent is the institutional environment related to attrition? Would an anthropological approach to the study of the campus cast more significant light on the conditions of learning?

Student Personnel Administration

The individual student is the subject of student personnel work, and concern with facilitating his complete development should be the goal of all student personnel services in education. In this section, I would like to call attention to some of the issues which should be on any agenda concerned with the future of student personnel services in higher education. Although they deal with the role and function of staff persons and their professional associations, these issues are, nevertheless, of significant relevance to the student. He, or she, will ultimately be affected by the quality and vision of those who develop the standards and expectations of this important area of service.

We shall deal with the following topics: student personnel administration and the faculty; student personnel administration and the president's office; selection and training of student personnel staff; and proliferation of student personnel associations and the need for greater unity of purpose and function.

Student personnel administration and the faculty

It is clear that conflicts exist between faculty and student personnel staff in most colleges and universities. They may differ in degree— from unwillingness to recognize such staff and their functions, all the way to vocal and vigorous opposition to the concept of student personnel work.

For the most part, however, there is little interaction, communication, or overt strife. The tragedy is that student personnel staff, on many campuses, know more about the reality of education on those campuses than does anyone else. Failure to communicate this awareness and knowledge not only frustrates the student personnel worker but also denies to the faculty those insights, perceptions, and facts which could be of invaluable assistance in shaping the total educational program of the institution.

Many persons would agree that there has been a steadily widening gap between administration and faculty in higher education. Some have termed the relationship one of "management and labor." Some academic romantics would like to think of the administration as functioning solely to facilitate the work of the faculty. In practice, in the larger, complex institutions of today, the administration must act in broad areas of finance, facilities, and community relations—often with rank-and-file faculty members unaware of the decisions, let alone participating in them. Paul Goodman to the contrary, the reality of the "knowledge industry" makes the administration an unequal partner of the faculty.

In its early days, student personnel staff—often faculty members serving part time—were in the middle between administration and faculty. In some ways they could provide a bridge between the two. However, as institutions and the student population grew, student personnel staff moved steadily toward the "administration" configuration and, in many ways, this sharpened the division between them and the faculty.

To make the writer's position clear, it may be advisable to state at the outset that the faculty's function is paramount in institutions of higher education. The role of the student personnel administrator is to assist in creating the conditions and opportunities for *reinforcing* the intellectual, cultural, and artistic purposes of the institution. But to place the faculty function at the apex is not to say that each individual faculty member is the "complete educator," who can speak with authority on the subject of the college student.

Joseph Katz, in writing of the general characteristics of the college teacher, summarized the variety of characteristics that are found:

> The classroom may provide the teacher with an opportunity to continue his own learning, with little regard for the effect on the students. Or it may provide an opportunity for the teacher to display his intellectual capacities or his powers of seductiveness. A teacher may use the classroom to satisfy his desire of being liked, or of being cruel, of manipulating people, or of preaching to them. Students of course are a particular variety of captive audience with only limited room for response or retaliation. . . . In sum, although ostensibly talking to the students in front of him, a teacher's principal attention can be focused on himself, his administrative

superiors, his local colleagues, his professional colleagues, his specialty heroes. The degrees to which this affects the task at hand vary considerably.[7]

It may also be said that the teacher is not always aware of how the student arrives in his classroom or of the student's view of what is going on. Dr. Katz, in commenting on the classroom and the teacher from the student's perspective, states:

Typically, [the student] arrives after having been shuffled through a rather soulless and bureaucratic process of registration, one concerned with credit points, prerequisites, corequisites, grade point averages. He is herded into a frequently uncomfortable classroom, often assigned a seat, his attendance is checked, regular assignments are given, as well as frequent quizzes, tests, exams, and papers. His written work may be read not by his teacher but by arrogant or timid graduate students on whose desks there is always a groaning pile of unfinished blue books through which they plod agonizingly. Objective tests may be a further step in making learning impersonal. The whole process is recorded and presided over by the IBM machine which is increasingly taking the place of the registrar, who in the past was often a friendly human being to whom students could turn in the process of grade-getting. A revealing caricature of the whole process is presented in the campus story of the instructor who, Europe-bound, mailed his grade sheet to the registrar, complete and properly curved. Only it turned out that he had filled out the grade sheet of a class he had not taught, the form having been sent to him by mistake.[8]

Student personnel staff, anxious about their status, want to improve their rapport with faculty. They also believe they have a contribution to make to the intellectual and developmental purposes of higher education. They certainly see the dangers of maintaining the *status quo*.

Faculty members are under pressure to distinguish themselves in their academic discipline; teaching students is only a part of the requirements they perceive in the expectations of their colleagues and of the academic dean. If students are to be educated, both teaching faculty and student personnel workers must find ways to communicate with one another.

QUESTIONS

1. How can the status which faculty ascribe to student personnel workers (and their functions) be improved? Granting that not all

[7] Katz, "Personality and Interpersonal Relations in the Classroom," *The American College*, ed. Nevitt Sanford, pp. 373–74.
[8] *Ibid.*, pp. 383–84.

student personnel administrators or staff are professionally prepared or effective, are there ways to improve relationships both on individual campuses and through the regional or national associations that exist?

2. How can we involve faculty in policy making and in the confrontation of students on vital institutional issues that lie outside the formal curriculum?

3. Can we establish a meaningful dialogue so that: (a) student personnel staff are reinforced in their need to keep central to their frame of reference the student *qua* student? and (b) faculty members are made aware of existing research and knowledge on student characteristics, values, attitudes, aspirations, and the like, so that this may be related to faculty teaching, freshman general education programs, honors programs, and academic policy?

Student personnel administration and the president's office

There is no one in higher education with a more demanding role than that of the university president. Clark Kerr's words in *The Uses of the University* are poignantly descriptive:

> [The president] is expected to be a friend of the students, a colleague of the faculty, a good fellow with the alumni, a sound administrator with the trustees, a good speaker with the public, an astute bargainer with the foundations and the federal agencies, a politician with the state legislature, a friend of industry, labor, and agriculture, a persuasive diplomat with donors, a champion of education generally, a supporter of the professions, a scholar in his own right . . . , a devotee equally of opera and football, a good husband and father . . . , firm, yet gentle.[*]

Kerr goes on to describe the moral virtues that the modern president must possess and says that "fortitude" is the most important. As for the roles he must play, the most important is that of "mediator."

Historically, presidents in many of the early colleges in the United States often taught a course in Moral Philosophy. They were concerned with the character of the institution and with the qualities of the students; in today's terms, they were concerned with the "climate" and environment of the institution.

But increasingly the energy and attention of the president have been turned outward, beyond the confines of the campus. The "audiences," or populations, with which he deals are often external to the campus—or at least to the students. Because of this, the dean of stu-

[*] Pp. 29–30.

dents has become the "twentieth-century moralist" of the campus. The student personnel staff, by commitment, orientation, and assigned responsibility, look inward—to the quality of the actions and interactions of the campus. Their audience is largely adolescent, rebellious, attention seeking, and often "unmanageable."

It is not unnatural for the president to become upset when there is disparity between the behavior of some students and the image of the institution. At such points he may find it necssary to order that there be at least the appearance of calm and tranquillity. And he may even evaluate the quality and success of a student personnel program on the basis of the dean's ability to "keep the lid on."

This unhappy state has led to many problems for student personnel administrators. They constantly fight the battle of being stereotyped, by both faculty and students, as disciplinarians and repressers of freedom. (Discipline is actually but a small part of the function of a student personnel program.) This, in turn, keeps many good people from entering a vital professional education field and may, conversely, result in the wrong kinds of people being attracted to the work.

The student personnel administrator should be viewed as an educator with a unique contribution to make. This contribution stems from his awareness of and involvement with the total student community. Presidents' decisions which will have any impact on the morale, climate, or life of the student community should be made with the help and participation of the personnel officer. If he has not earned the right to such participation, someone else should be hired who can meet the requirements.

QUESTIONS

1. How can we improve the relationships between complex student personnel structures and the president's office? Is there, despite his burdens, a way to communicate to the staff and students the president's awareness of feelings, problems, and issues on campus? Can concerns be channeled up as well as down?

2. How can student personnel administrators make a greater contribution to the solution of the problems that college and university presidents face? Can presidents, either individually or collectively, make known their expectations for student personnel administrators and their staffs? Are student personnel services tolerated, opposed, or encouraged? Are university presidents concerned about matters connected with these services? Would they prefer it if appropriate professional associations dealt with these matters?

Selection and training of student personnel staff

There need be no detailed analysis of developments in higher education to demonstrate that the expansion of present colleges and universities, as well as the founding of new ones, will result in a pressing need for new staff members. It is well known that student personnel services are now an integral part of most colleges and universities. In order to meet replacement needs, as well as the needs of newly created staff, some attention must be given to the manner of selecting and training student personnel staff. We know that, in the past, men and women entered student personnel work from other fields—with little or no training. Certain specialized services in the field are now staffed appropriately with counseling psychologists, psychiatric social workers, psychiatrists, physicians, nurses, and so on. To a large extent, residence halls are staffed by graduate students who may take on such assignments as a means of financial aid.

We are not concerned here with delineating all of the specialized staff requirements in admissions, financial aid, foreign student advising, and so on. Our foremost concern is the selection and training of the student personnel leader—the generalist who will serve as the senior student personnel officer of the institution. He must be sophisticated enough to coordinate testing, health, and counseling services. He must be able to administer substantial budgets and operations, yet be research-oriented and intellectually on a par with senior faculty members. Above all perhaps, he must be able to represent the office of the president on many delicate and difficult matters. Certainly he must be dedicated to the purposes for which institutions of higher learning stand.

Kate Mueller made an appropriate observation, when she said:

> It is easy enough to attract to the profession the non-intellectual student who perceives (or thinks he perceives) that college personnel offers a good life, free from the classroom reading and study (which he dislikes) and filled with human contacts, social activities and authority (all of which he enjoys). True, he cannot yet understand the intelligence and skill beneath the observable surface activities, but the danger to the profession is that he will never understand them even after he has entered it.[10]

The kinds of persons we seek to have enter the field, and the kind of training we recommend or require for such persons, should be based

[10] Mueller, "Some Problems of Recruiting in College Personnel," *Journal of College Student Personnel*, June 1963, p. 217.

on a greater consensus about the future and the changing role of student personnel work. Academic deans and presidents should assist in defining that role.

There is a growing development of graduate programs (many leading to the doctorate) in student personnel work for higher education. Some of these programs are receiving government or foundation support. Recent amendments to the NDEA extended training opportunities for guidance and student personnel staff to the college and university level. Some institutions prefer—and even require—such "professional" preparation. Others, unfortunately, look askance at such preparation and do not recognize that it is relevant or meaningful. (One of the real anomalies is that some institutions avoid hiring student personnel staff with this kind of training, even though they themselves offer master's and doctoral programs in the field!)

Several of the national student personnel associations have been studying and debating the question of appropriate training and credentials for years. There is also in existence a Joint Commission on Professional Development—an instrument of the Council of Student Personnel Associations in Higher Education. Recently this commission issued a report which, in my opinion, will find little or no consensus within the professional field. (The writer has been urging an emphasis on in-service training programs which will now be considered by the Joint Commission and will also be inplemented by the American College Personnel Association.)

QUESTIONS

1. Must we create a dichotomy between an interest in the student (and his environment) and an interest in an academic discipline? Can we get persons of outstanding academic performance to enter the field of student personnel administration without making it necessary for them to discard their intellectual interests? Is it desirable to recruit senior student personnel staff from the ranks of college teachers? What kinds of people do we want?

2. What are the crucial questions regarding the characteristics and effective preparation of the student personnel leader? Can we define the attributes he must bring to the assignment—the professional preparation or in-service training deemed essential? Can anybody fill this role?

3. Is there an essential unity to the major student personnel functions so that we can describe it as a field in functional terms? Is counseling, or a counseling orientation, the common factor in student personnel work?

4. Can we get some of the leaders in the behavioral sciences to help us define the training needs for student personnel staff? Can we leave the matter to the associations of student personnel workers? Will all formal academic programs in this field be in graduate schools of education?

5. Do college and university presidents and academic deans have an interest in who becomes the student personnel leader and the nature of his selection and preparation? Will failure to communicate opinions on this matter result in narrow criteria for entry and serious inbreeding of student personnel staff over the next decade?

Associations and the need for unity

Over the past twenty years there has been a significant increase in the number of student personnel associations formed on the basis of special functions. There now exist some thirty associations involving student personnel workers. This proliferation is a matter of concern not only because of its economic and manpower inefficiency, but for other reasons as well: (1) It tends to make "professions" out of certain tasks which fall between traditional job roles. (2) It tends to reduce the central focus of the whole student personnel enterprise—the individual, "whole" student, and the changing problems with which he must cope.

There are three major national associations which profess the broadest interest in the student and the entire gamut of student personnel work in higher education. These are:

National Association of Student Personnel Administrators (NASPA).—Founded in 1919 as the National Association of Deans and Advisers of Men, NASPA has some 400 institutional members. It has recently voted to admit individuals to associate membership on a nonvoting basis. It does not have a paid staff.

American College Personnel Association (ACPA).—Founded in 1924 as the National Association of Personnel and Placement Officers, ACPA is a division of the American Personnel and Guidance Association (membership 17,000). ACPA membership is on an individual basis and numbers some 3,500 at this time. It publishes the only professional journal exclusively devoted to college and university student personnel work—*The Journal of College Student Personnel*. It is served by the paid staff at APGA headquarters in Washington, D.C.

The National Association of Women Deans and Counselors (NAWDC).—Founded in 1916, and formerly named the National Association of Deans of Women, NAWDC is a department of the

National Education Association. It has approximately 2,000 members, on an individual basis, and has secondary school counselors in its membership, along with persons from colleges and universities. It is dominated by higher education personnel and interests, however. It publishes a quarterly journal.

There are at least two dozen other associations on the national scene, organized on the basis of special functional interests. These include associations concerned with admissions, registration and records, health, counseling center administration, college unions, housing, foreign student advising, and the like. Each of these associations has its own annual conference, committee activities, and newsletter or other means of communication. The leaders of each group are usually in attendance at the annual conference of one or more of the three general associations mentioned above—NASPA, ACPA, or NAWDC.

In the spring of 1958, a first attempt was made to bring together the leadership of several of these associations in order to explore ways of defining areas of common interest and means for cooperation. Those participating formed what was termed the Inter-Association Coordinating Committee (IACC). Strong leadership was given to the IACC idea by Dean J. C. Clevenger, past-president of NASPA.

In December 1963, with the support of the American Council on Education, a three-day meeting of the IACC leaders was held at Airlie House, Warrenton, Virginia. The business session was preceded by a two-day seminar on "crucial issues in higher education and their implications for student personnel work."

Representatives of the following associations attended: American College Personnel Association, American Association of Collegiate Registrars and Admissions Officers, Association of College Unions, Association of College and University Housing Officers, National Association of Women Deans and Counselors, National Association of Foreign Student Advisers, National Association of Student Personnel Administrators, Association of College Admission Counselors, American College Health Association, and the College Placement Council. There was remarkable agreement on the importance of working together "without attempting to inhibit the autonomy" of the member associations. The name of the group was changed to the Council of Student Personnel Associations in Higher Education (COSPA).

Some eight associations are now affiliated with COSPA. They are the major associations in the student personnel field. COSPA, as an idea, has potential significance. As of now, it is a concept which needs active encouragement from the academic community.

QUESTIONS

1. Is it possible to discourage further fragmentation of the student personnel field by consolidating some associations with others? Is proliferation a substantive danger? Is it possible that some needs, not now being met, will require still more new associations?

2. Does every function have to become a specialty, with "professionalization" the end result—with regional and national associations to be formed, and annual conventions to be conducted? Do we want to discourage such practices? Are there benefits from this?

3. What steps can be taken to get these associations to integrate their specialized concerns for an over-all focus on the "whole" student or the kinds of new problems that affect students?

4. What direction, support, or further encouragement can the Commission on Academic Affairs of the American Council give to the infant Council of Student Personnel Associations? Can we indicate what college and university presidents believe to be an "agenda for the future" concerning college students?

The questions raised in this discussion are not meant to provide a comprehensive coverage of the problems of student personnel administration. They do, however, suggest that this is an increasingly important area in the expansion of our system of higher education and that there is no longer any question whether the job needs to be done. The crucial question is, rather, how to do it to the best of our ability.

PART 3   The Campus
          Environment:
          Focus
          on Education

The Student's
Role in
Educational
Policy

JAMES P. DIXON

ALL EDUCATION IS EXPERIMENTAL. It is designed by trial and error. And while it may seem that the policy of higher education is largely determined by faculty, the concerns of students have been a historic force in shaping educational policy in American colleges and universities. At present the amount and openness of student criticism is greater than ever before. Criticism has extended beyond words to action. Many faculty members, administrators, and outside observers feel that, stridency aside, much of the students' criticism is valid. There is a search, then, for ways to determine whether the criticism is directed to transient or to deep-seated difficulties. For if it should be the latter, as I believe, then we are confronted with the prospect of arranging new ways for students to participate in the formulation of educational policy.

We should not feel too uneasy about this prospect. Overt institutional compliance with student demands is hardly new. It was in response to such demands, for example, that a sort of modified political democracy was established at Antioch a quarter century ago to enable student representatives to sit on college policy councils. It is in response to current student demands that one hears discussion among Berkeley faculty about a modification of curriculum that would permit the award of degree credit for student participation in civic affairs of the neighboring community.

These kinds of adjustment in educational policy occur because faculty and students *do* recognize that they must accommodate to their different but overlapping concepts of the meaning and purpose of the college or university.

Of crucial significance, one would suppose, is the faculty's concept that the college or university is indeed the social institution of the scholar-teacher, that it is within this setting that standards of scholarship and teaching and research and expert consultation are sustained, and that a principal function of the institution is to protect, in the

164

interests of the whole society, the autonomies we have come to call academic freedom.

Abler students may well identify closely with this concept of the scholar. The vast majority of students, however, seem to view the university and college as an experience that society has ordained as necessary both for achieving vocational success and for satisfying self-esteem. Most of them do not aspire to become scholars. And they care less than does the faculty about the necessity of preserving the authority of the teacher in the classroom or the authority of scholars to demand research. So one of the thrusts of student involvement in educational policy is likely to be a sharp questioning of faculty time spent away from teaching.

Nor do the political concepts of students and faculty entirely coincide. The scholar has traditionally opposed the propriety of any service role for the educational institution. For himself, he has seen his civic responsibility as the acquisition and transmission of knowledge, the use of this knowledge in expert consultation, and the training of the next generation of experts. With some remarkable exceptions, he has not ordinarily seen overt political activity as necessary to his central role, except when the traditional autonomy of the university is threatened.

Students, however, do conceive of themselves as agents of social change and are not entirely willing to participate in social change solely through reasoned inquiry. They have now learned from the civil rights movement the meaning of the force of their presence in social revolution, and they know that if the pattern of packing an increasing proportion of young people into our colleges continues, they will represent, within the next decade, a significant proportion of the American electorate. Students are, therefore, asking questions about the relevance of educational policy in training for social and civic behavior.

One may come at the question of student involvement in educational policy in other ways. If education is experimental, as in Theodore Newcomb's view, we might wisely begin to take into account the insights of research on student characteristics. Newcomb notes, for example, E. K. Wilson's findings on the importance of peer group influence.

Other new evidence about teaching and learning is coming from the curricular innovations in mathematics, physics, and biology at precollege levels. Their astonishing success suggests that desirable outcomes occur when the identities of student and teacher are blurred, or, as Jerrold Zacharias would put it, when the teacher learns through teaching and the student learns teaching through learning.

Students, then, have a proper interest, and are important as both resource and ingredient, in the determination of pedagogical and curricular arrangements. Their suggestions about curricular reform should be listened to. But far more threatening to the academic establishment than a sit-in in the president's office is the attack on prescribed curriculum. Already students know that, with the exception of the physical sciences, there need not be much relation between one's course of undergraduate study and one's graduate election. One beneficial consequence is that students are free to choose among many different routes within the curriculum. But this freedom disturbs many academicians, since it seems to leave to chance the recruitment of students into specialized fields and since it places less reliance on the faculty's wisdom in determining the choice of program.

The widening diversity of student bodies sets up a new quest for an intellectual democracy. What Horace Mann accomplished for the first twelve grades, Francis Keppel has now set in motion for the undergraduate years. It is ordained by public policy that there be opportunity for all citizens to participate in systematic, formal education beyond the high school. Increasingly, students feel that educational policy should define success not just in the terms prescribed by a given institution in its program for general education or by the conventions of the major academic fields, but by taking strongly into account the achievement of the student relative to his own capabilities.

They argue with cogency that this is not an unreasonable expectation in a democratic society. And while this need can be met in part by creating different kinds of colleges and universities, care should be taken to provide individuation within all institutions, else one verges on *de facto* segregation of intellectual elites.

John Gardner states the unique role of the university in these succinct terms: "[It] is not to apply present knowledge but to *advance the state of knowledge*, not only to supply experts today but to *train the next generation of experts*." [1]

How, then, can the university preserve this unique role and still be responsive to students' demands and other pressures for change in educational policy?

If the university is not to be blindly subverted by present pressures, the members of its faculty need to ask themselves whether the current

[1] *AID and the Universities*, A Report from Education and World Affairs in cooperation with the Agency for International Development [1964], p. 11.

notion of always regarding the student as less than equal in the community of scholars will really stand scrutiny. What do they make of the fact that the students who are abler in conventional intellectual terms are at the same time the leaders of the revolt against the establishment? If we could bring ourselves to accept the notion that in some ways all students and all teachers are members of a community of teaching and learning—of learning through teaching and teaching through learning—then we would soon find that it is important to hear what the student is saying, and to give him his say even in matters of curricular reform. Student opinion can be heeded in responding to the public criticism of courses and teaching. There is even isolated evidence that students can effectively participate in the recruitment and selection of faculty.

It is becoming increasingly important within all the parts of our educational system to recognize that teaching and learning are coterminous with life. One of the aims of the college and university is to open up this possibility for all students. In such a situation, it is crucial to know what students think is important to learning; otherwise, both teaching and learning suffer. And I think we need not fear that such knowledge will reduce the curriculum to the level of basket weaving. It is more likely to enlarge the fields of present inquiry so that students are able to think more intelligently and behave more wisely about the major questions of our times—the resolution of conflict, the arrangements of the environment, and the creation of a social order that challenges rather than demeans intelligence.

The arrangements that can be made to permit educational policy to evolve intelligently under the pressure of student concerns are likely to vary enormously. But perhaps some common elements may characterize them. Benson Snyder has pointed out that the language of dialogue as opposed to the language of negotiation is better suited to dealing with student demands. This suggests that it is not necessary to use the conventional model of political democracy. What is needed is a new model for an intellectual democracy—a democracy in which power and authority are ascribed to the person who knows and can communicate rather than to the representative of a constituency.

There needs to be recognition, as Theodore Newcomb points out in his background paper, that styles of organization in education sharply affect possibilities for change. In an intellectual democracy, arrangements would be such as to avoid overspecification of work, to distribute innovative functions to everyone—including students—in the organization, and to diminish the concentration of position and authority in individuals.

Arrangements need to take into account that students are calling to our attention the relevance of what is out there beyond the campus —that is to say, they are telling us that it is against racial inequality and poverty and war that they wish to apply the energies of their trained minds. In calling this to our attention they may not be asking the university as such to enter into a service role of applying present knowledge, but they are saying that in order to train the next generation of experts the faculty needs some knowledge of the context in which that generation will be performing.

Finally, we might admit that the questions asked by students are, as Max Lerner seems to suggest, less in the quest for the transfer of power than in the quest for educational leadership in a time of accelerating pace of change. How far will we be willing to go in organizing our educational policy of stating our curricular objectives in terms of student emergence, selfhood, transcendence, commitment, and nexus? If we were to look at the possibilities in these lights, we might even discover how easy it is to bring students into the nexus of the academic community.

Adlai Stevenson, in one of his last appearances before an academic community, took the opportunity to make the point that no proposal for reform was socially responsible if it did not include consideration of how that reform was to be accomplished. Mindful, then, of the futility of exhortation, I suggest the following: that students be invited to join faculty and administration in all their systematic endeavors, including research and experimentation, to refine and develop educational policy. To the extent that students accept this invitation, we are provided practical means to test the validity of our assumptions. I believe they will accept this invitation and will bring new, vital force into the now muddled process of modernization of higher education.

Some Suggestions
for Student
Involvement in
Educational Policy

EDWARD D. EDDY, JR.

I SUPPOSE THAT IT IS ALMOST unnecessary to state the obvious: the
once highly respected house of intellect has become a divided house,
beset by internal dissension and external doubting. American higher
education is currently suffering from an acute case of dyspepsia
brought on by our inability to acknowledge our own digestive problems, a condition that does little to enhance general public acceptance of colleges and universities as infallible social necessities. We
need to move fast to put the house of intellect in good order before
it becomes a slum.

The complaint is at least threefold: Faculty members are accused
of being devoid of any genuine sense of concern for the entire fabric
of education, including student responsibility and morality. Students
are said to be more interested in being heard than in hearing. And
administrators are labeled as being preoccupied with preserving form
rather than with extending substance.

One answer to this predicament is, I believe, simple and clear:
genuine student involvement in the formation of educational policy
offers the best hope of regaining the lost concept of an academic
community. The time is right and ripe for *all* American colleges and
universities to allow students a strongly contributing role in the shaping of educational policy. The "crazy colleges" of the past, such as
Antioch and Reed, may well become the sensible pattern of the future. Every college and university committee ought to include *voting*
student members. I would make an exception only of those committees which are engaged in personal discussion of individual faculty
members in matters of promotion and tenure. It is too much to ask
individual students in this case to pass on the qualifications of individual teachers.

I do not believe that students should have an *equal* role on all
committees. I do believe that this generation of students in particular
is deeply concerned with *meaningful* areas of human endeavor; functional trivia has no attraction for them. What, then, could or should

169

mean more to a student than educational policy as it is shaped by thousands of decisions which, when taken together, determine the posture and policy of an institution?

Students have already proved themselves capable of assisting substantially in their own education through independent study. We all know how much they help to educate other students also. They are full participants, not just receiving but continually giving. They can be encouraged to give in a much deeper dimension. Student participation, with the fresh point of view it brings, is highly desirable in such areas as curriculum planning, evaluation of teaching and teachers, and academic administration including degree requirements, grading systems, and calendars.

Our neglect of student opinion in faculty evaluation is one good example of our failure to make proper use of students' insights. Most of us are scared to death of such evaluation. In the great majority of colleges and universities, we have nervously laughed it off for years. And in the process we have lost valuable time which could have been used to fashion some fairly reliable ways of obtaining trustworthy student reaction.

Certain conditions and guidelines are important to the discussion of student involvement. Here are some which occur to me:

First, involving students is no simple, snap-of-the-finger activity. As Henry May observed, the student protest movements "express vague wishes for immediate and simple solutions to complex problems." [1] Student involvement *is* a complex problem. We are foolish to dismiss it as insoluble. We are equally foolish to attempt it by presidential decree.

Second, it is neither possible nor desirable for colleges to abdicate to the student the primary responsibility for policy. We cannot and we should not turn over our campuses to student rule. We would thereby negate the rationale for education: colleges exist because some people know more than other people. Nevertheless, we can take the cue from business and industry that it isn't reasonable to market what the consumer doesn't want to buy. Controlled consumer reaction never hurt any business and certainly won't destroy the integrity of any educational institution.

Third, student involvement must be more than the usual token indulgence. I suppose we ought to be realistic in recognizing that a minority of students today will never be satisfied with whatever role

[1] Henry May, "The Student Movement," *American Scholar*, Summer 1965, p. 398.

they play. But the presence of this minority should not dissuade us from attempting to achieve a genuine interchange among faculty, students, and administrators. Let us also be realistic in recognizing that the teaching faculty will be least anxious to involve students in educational policy making. And so:

Any steps must be a reflection of deep educational commitment and certainly not mere response to pressure. Merely raising the question of student involvement on most American campuses is a good exercise these days if only to straighten out campus thought regarding the effective role of the student. If the rationale proves to include "education for leadership," then our campuses can serve as splendid laboratories involving something more than the presidency of the Chess Club. We can begin to capitalize on the new student interest in educational matters against the old student concern for trivia. For years, we have wanted a fire to burn; let's not throw water on the first flames.

Finally, valuable student involvement won't just happen. Most of us do not expect the younger, new faculty members to serve on key policy committees. We give them at least a year to get to know what is expected and to gain a perspective which experience alone can bring. If, therefore, we want genuine student involvement, we must provide a system which encourages them to acquire both experience and perspective. We must not make the mistake of blaming students for being transients on a college campus. The perspective gained should include what Charles Frankel urged when he wrote: "[The college] must find a way to communicate to [the student] that learning has its own imperative standards and demands, and its own schedules and routines, and that these cannot be modified for reasons of personal self-expression or convenience." Give one student one year of apprentice observation on one faculty committee and he'll know that lesson for years to come!

The result of student involvement in the formation of educational policy may well be the emergence of a new sense of academic community, possibly something quite different from what we have known before. For years we have been thirsty for student responsibility; we pontificated and then seeded the clouds in despair. The resulting hurricane has brought us wind and fury. Out of it can still come a new and brighter day.

The presence of students on every major committee surely could help us also to overcome a prevailing tendency to belittle undergraduate teaching. We are going to have to learn to accept and welcome criticism, to go on working under its severe eye, to maintain our sense of humor, and to be even prouder of the results because they were achieved as a community undertaking.

Involvement means caring. Students today *do* care and care deeply. Involving them in the total work of the academic community is one important way for the American college to prove its faith in a generation in which, frankly, we had damn well better believe.

Organizing
an
Effective
Student-Faculty
Dialogue

CHARLES E. ODEGAARD

By its very nature the act of teaching requires that the instructor teach something to the student. We all admit that the teacher should be a master of his subject. Recent debates over teacher education have highlighted again the need for the teacher to be thoroughly grounded in his subject, and I need say no more on this point.

But it is also the function of the teacher, as the trustee of a disciplined tradition of learning in the modern university, to evaluate through some form of examination the proficiency developed by the student, whether the latter is pursuing the disciplines of the academy or the arts of the professions. We are now entering another era of debate, this time over student control of the curriculum. Some student rebels will be hard to convince that their competence in the practice of many high-level disciplines and professions can be better determined by the aristocratic judgment, if you will, of previously established masters of the guild than by the so-called democratic vote of younger apprentices—however much those apprentices claim that they should be given responsibilities for the management of the educational process.

To assert continued commitment to the idea of a university as a community of scholars in which the younger scholars are apprentices under the tutelage of the older scholars is not, however, to suggest that students should not be involved in significant discussions about educational policy and the instructional process to which they are exposed. We have not—so it seems to me—explored as fully as we might ways of detecting student response to the teaching situations presented to them and to the learning process itself, even though their attitudes may increase or decrease the proficiency attained by them. Students may not yet be experts about the subject, but they are informed about their own reactions to the teaching they receive.

173

Students can help the faculty to improve the planning of courses and curriculum and thereby to improve their teaching as well.

My predecessor at the University of Michigan as dean of the College of Literature, Science, and the Arts, Hayward Keniston, had a lively interest in curricular matters and stimulated much faculty discussion of objectives and methods. Finding a group of undergraduates interested in talking about their educational objectives, courses, and classroom experiences, he proposed that they conduct a series of Literary College Conferences devoted to conversation about these matters. The leadership group established a steering committee which perpetuated itself from year to year by co-opting successors. The college had had a year or two of experience with these conferences when I arrived as dean, and they were continued. Several times a year one or another aspect of the undergraduate program—freshman English, beginning science courses, foreign languages, distribution requirements in social sciences, and the like—were announced as the topic for a conference. Appropriate members of the faculty were invited to attend along with all interested students. Free-for-all discussions ensued. Inevitably each student presented one man's view; there was a tendency, however, for the individual student to generalize from his own experience and his own reaction, attributing his conclusions to all his colleagues. Though intriguing lights were cast on our instructional operations, it was difficult to know what conclusions should be drawn; faculty members were on their own when it came to evaluating the criticisms. As one might expect, complaints tended to be expressed more dramatically than praise. Understandably it was difficult to convince many faculty members that the student opinions reported in such conferences were valid and significant generalizations deserving of their serious consideration in evaluating their own teaching efforts and courses.

Accordingly, it was decided to supplement this opinion-gathering device with a more statistically reliable one. Faculty members competent in scientific polling techniques were asked to develop questionnaires and interview schedules to be administered to controlled samples of the student population. The particular areas to which attention was directed were often chosen as a result of the conference discussions. The results were then made known to the conferees, and discussion of them served to keep alive student interest in the educational processes. At the same time faculty members of departmental and college curriculum committees reviewed their own efforts in the light of these findings. Numerous small changes were brought about by the faculty response; and occasionally a department put itself through a considerable change. I recall one case where the survey indicated that a particular department was avoided even by good students whom it would have liked to enroll. Consequently, the department altered its personnel policy, giving recognition to types of faculty performance which it had previously overlooked and even recruiting appointees with skills previously ignored. Involving students in such discussions had in my judgment a salutary effect on our teaching.

I have the same reaction to similar efforts at the University of Washington. Our students, operating through their student government organization, have shown increasing interest in educational matters. A student-appointed educational commission has invited faculty members to serve with them in sponsoring discussions on particular topics. These discussions have led to a few reports on selected instructional activities. In certain instances, students have been given advice and assistance in polling student attitudes through scientific surveys whose findings have been considered in reaching decisions on educational matters.

Our students were intrigued enough by these matters that in 1964-65 their president approached our University Senate with the proposal that student members be placed on key educational committees. Such requests have so far met with a stony reception, but there has been some suggestion that the student organization might appoint a companion committee to a Senate committee with a similar area of concern and that the two committees might meet jointly to discuss educational issues.

Meanwhile, the leaders of our student government have moved ahead on their own to a plan for student evaluation of teachers. In the spring of 1965, they arranged for the distributing of questionnaires to students enrolled in about 175 heavily populated courses, mostly lower division. The resulting harvest of student opinion is being turned into a publication, *Course Critique*, which will grade the professor and his course on a scale from A to E and will include a brief essay on the faculty member. I understand that at one point a suggested subtitle for this *Course Critique* was *The Swine Return the Pearls*. In any case this publication will probably be read with avidity. It will obviously still be largely a one-way communication device but it may evoke rebuttals from the faculty. Under the prod of this student initiative, perhaps a more enlightening and useful form of dialogue between faculty and students will come about.

I hope that we will develop better procedures than we now have for discussing educational policy with students. The faculty must continue to be the guardians of academic disciplines and of professional competences, and this means that they must make the decisions about the curriculum and the academic staff. But their effectiveness in transmitting the traditions of the disciplines and professions to the next generation can be increased by greater sensitivity to student reactions to instruction and greater interest in obtaining reliable information about student response.

With more students of greater maturity appearing in our universities, it is imperative that faculties bestir themselves to establish improved communication with students. If they are to respond more fully to the opportunities of the university, students themselves need to have a wider awareness of the characteristics of the educational process through which they are passing and of the reasons for the requirements they are asked to meet. Above all they must be given an opportunity to develop some appreciation of the relevance of their educational experience to their future responsibilities and opportunities. Students are asking questions about the significance of the educational enterprise. Should faculties in response not seek ways to organize an effective dialogue?

The Liberal
Curriculum
in a Scientific
and Technological
Age

MELVIN KRANZBERG

OURS HAS BEEN CALLED a scientific and technological age. This, I take it, means that we are *aware*, but far from understanding, that science and technology have become major creative as well as disruptive forces in the twentieth century. Our students are probably more aware of these forces than we, for they know they will have to live with them. I suspect, too, that we who are charged with the liberal higher learning in America are actually unprepared to lead students toward the historical, social, aesthetic, and philosophic understanding of science and technology. This kind of ignorance runs to one of the fundamental problems of liberal education: the nature of reality. I shall argue that, judging by our curricula and our writings, most of us have failed to understand the scientific and technological aspects of reality not only in our own time, but also in the past.

I begin the argument by asking two questions: (1) Is there any evidence, aside from notable exceptions, that the faculties of our educational institutions understand the scientific and technological forces which have produced our society? (2) Does the curriculum reflect the significance of science in the past, present, and future? I am afraid the answer to both questions is "No." It seems quite likely that the situation will be rectified—and soon. The question is whether by faculty or by students. Frederick Rudolph demonstrates elsewhere in this volume that students established the extracurriculum—football, fraternities, and fun—as educational process. Students helped lead the nineteenth century revolt against classicism, and they created the pressures which established the elective system, the major-minor system, and vocationalism. None of these academic institutions seems to inspire confidence that student leadership is better than faculty leadership. It is only better than no leadership at all. I therefore argue, indeed plead for, *faculty* leadership toward a decent

177

respect for the understanding of science and technology in the liberal curriculum. I plead for a decent respect for reality.

The Nature of Western Civilization

The students we are preparing for life, usefulness, change, and happiness in the latter half of the twentieth century are drinking from a stagnant pond of doctrine asserting that Western civilization is based upon the Judaeo-Christian-Greek tradition. The fact is that technology and its precocious sibling, science, are the distinctive hallmarks of Western civilization. The Scientific Revolution of the seventeenth century and the Industrial Revolution of the eighteenth and nineteenth centuries—not the Renaissance or the Age of Reason —brought essentials to our civilization unknown to Greece or Rome, India or China. The importance of science and technology is that they differentiate our society from all others. The roots of our religious, ethical, and political heritage unquestionably sink deep in the Christian, the Greek, and the Hebraic traditions. Yet contemporary Western culture takes much more sustenance from science and technology than from those older roots.

One test of this assertion is to consider what "westernization" means for non-Western societies. All our experience suggests it means the acquisition of the techniques of Western science and technology, not—and usually explicitly not—the political institutions, religious faiths, and moral attitudes of the West. This holds for Japan, China, India, and the African states except as we imposed our institutions and attitudes by force, fraud, and that species of persuasion sometimes called education. The brutal facts about how we brought in our ideological baggage as well as our hardware stand as monuments to those who believe that these impedimenta are truly the essential element of our culture. Our practice is something else, and it is arguable that Western culture is up against problems created by science and technology to which the Judaeo-Christian-Greek religious, political, and moral principles have no satisfactory answers.

Sore issues about the nature, behavior, and future of man and society have come up within the past half-century. Some old, inherited considerations in dealing with the problems are state sovereignty in politics, free enterprise in economics, precedent in law, salvation in religion, and the centrality of the West in history. These ideas, however elaborated, strike nearly everybody having man *qua* man in mind as at least provincial, possibly reactionary, and certainly dated. The theologians have lately come up with ecumenism, but that merely reduces quarrels without actually confronting the real challenges in religion.

So far as our curriculum responds to the Christian-Greek-Hebraic traditions and omits the understanding of science and technology in their worldwide significance and historical perspective, that curriculum is also provincial, reactionary, and dated. Conceding, for the moment, that this is the case, how do we account for it, if science and technology are actually so important to our culture? Why is the study of their development and social impact neglected by reputable historians, political scientists, sociologists, humanists—indeed, by the scientists and engineers themselves? Well, I am glad you ask me. I am caught, not in a contradiction but in an abyss of *lacunae.*

My explanation points to a snobbery at least as ancient as Plato's notion that formal knowledge is virtue, whereas manual labor lacks dignity and is confined to lesser individuals of inferior capacity. Science and technology do, indeed, dirty the hands. The abhorrence of dirty hands, understandable in a social system involving slavery, persists to this day. Lately the slaves—the scientists and engineers— have been remaking the world around us. Some of them, pardonably, adopted slavish attitudes of active scorn for the wit, the wisdom, and the lore of the past; for the discussion and criticism of ideas; for the arguments of ethics, politics, law, and aesthetics. Their ignorance was and is monumental, and I do not excuse them. Among most scientists and engineers, indeed, there has been little concern with the history, sociology, and human impact of even their own fields. Why bother with the past, they ask, why investigate what has been superseded? These are ignorant questions.

Improving the Curriculum

The neglect of the study of the development of science and technology in relation to society and culture has distorted our education insofar as education must keep in touch with reality. The sciences, engineering, and medicine are difficult mountains of learning, yet we must climb them because they are there. How can we effectively bring them into our curriculum for students who must work, live, and deal with issues of learning, change, and happiness in the later twentieth century? I do not know, but I have some suggestions.

Even under the older study of military and political history, we historians should have recognized the significance of technology. The switch to iron weapons toppled those ancient empires whose military forces were still armed with bronze or copper weapons. Lynn White, in his *Medieval Technology and Social Change*,[1] has shown how the small innovation of the stirrup changed the nature of warfare and brought about changes in the political and social structure. W. H. McNeill's *Rise of the West* [2] is the first general history which takes account of technological factors in acculturation processes throughout the human ecumene. Its date is 1964, a time when the dependence of warfare, politics, economics, history, literature, and the arts upon technology is so plain that it is a work of supererogation to enumerate particulars, but enumerate a few is precisely what I propose to do.

Only a dozen universities offer graduate programs in the history of science, and there is only one in history of technology. Only some fifty universities offer undergraduate courses in the history of science, and fewer than a dozen in the history of technology.

Political scientists still analyze, without conscious mention of science or technology, the rise and fall of states, the pressure and power groups within nations, the development of new political procedures, forms, and institutions. At a time when science and technology are actually being institutionalized in our national political process, few political science departments offer courses dealing with science and public policy. Students of constitutional law deal with recent Supreme Court decisions on state legislative reapportionment, but how many of them recognize that those decisions are incorporating into the political structure the social fact of urbanization? If they do, how many trace the urbanization phenomena meaningfully to technology? Of what value are courses in metropolitan and regional planning which deal with traffic congestion, air and water pollution, and slum blight without understanding the technological forces which not only created, but also could solve or palliate the problems? How many political scientists in the field of international relations treat science and technology as the basic elements they are in international prestige and power? Yet all diplomats, soldiers, and heads of state deal with these matters every day.

Investigations of economic processes take account, perforce, of the technological transformations which have been major factors in economic change. Yet how many economists go below the surface to analyze the specific nature of the technological changes on which given economic changes are based? I am sure that when they come to it, they will be in for some surprises.

---

[1] Oxford: Clarendon Press, 1962.
[2] Chicago: University of Chicago Press, 1963.

The sociologists too frequently do little more than pay lip service to technology in their courses on marriage and the family, criminology, and urban sociology. The crucial detail is missing. Exactly how does a particular technological complex affect marriage and the family, and how is that technology affected in the interaction? Again, there are going to be surprises. Superficial mention of science and technology is worse than omission altogether. The lack of intellectual and scholarly rigor is less appalling than the lack of curiosity to get closer to the heart of the matter.

The Misuse of "Humanism"

The humanists present a more offensive case. From some scholars, we hear that science and technology are subverting human values. This salute to the influence of scientists and engineers is curious. During most of the history of man, the term "humanistic" was used to distinguish what was human from what was brutal. Today we find that "humanism" is contrasted with "science and technology," and "humanistic" is used to distinguish everything else. The humanities are claimed as home by a few antirationalists who deny that rational attempts to understand the workings of the physical universe and to deal with human material wants have any bearing upon man's pursuit of the good life. Even Aristotle is against them on that point.

Humanism, meaning "spiritual" in contrast to "material" goals, is a heady draught from which India, once a leader among civilizations, is slowly recovering. Yet some of our philosophers are burying themselves in a kind of nirvana of semantics and grammar. The philosophy of science is often mere logic and methodology. We seem to have a philosophy of antitechnology but no philosophy of technology. If there are any modern philosophers dealing with the great moral issues of the times, as did the systematic philosophers of the past, I have not heard of them. Yet science and technology have brought us face to face with ethical problems which have no counterparts in the past, and we badly need philosophers. Barnaby Keeney has pointed out in connection with automation:

> The real problem is not the utilization of leisure, important as it may be, but rather the development of an ethic and an outlook appropriate to new circumstances. We have now an ethic in which work is equated with virtue. Before long, we shall have to develop one where not to work very long for a living and to be content is as virtuous as labor itself. This will require hard work by some well-

trained philosophers who have competence outside the area of symbolic logic. We are going to need those philosophers very badly.[3]

There have been some investigations of the impact of science on literature. The Modern Language Association has a section devoted to "Science and Literature," but its attention seems wholly devoted to the counting of scientific references in authors' works. Marjorie Nicholson did some pioneer work on the impact of science on literature. Only recently, in the writings of Henry Nash Smith, Leo Marx, and Allan Trachtenberg, has there been an attempt to measure the impact of technology on the American novel. The many courses on the Victorian novel mention, but hardly analyze, the literary manifestations of the great industrial transformations and the Darwinian evolutionary concepts from which the authors drew their preconceptions, their attitudes, and frequently their subject matter. Yet the new literary form of the novel was born at about the same time as the Industrial Revolution, and poetry enjoyed the greatest audience it ever had during the height of England's industrial supremacy. I suppose both are mere coincidences in the minds of the "intellectual Luddites" teaching our literature courses.

The creative artist of the nineteenth and twentieth centuries is supposed—by a curious quirk of pedagogy—in art history to be revolting against the dominant trends of his time based on science and technology. The documentation of this potent cultural influence of science and technology is, I am sure, unintentional.

A really heartless critic might say that our present curriculum is misinforming our students about the past, adding to their ignorance of the present, and denying them decent preparation in fundamentals for the future. The liberal curriculum, I hasten to add, is no worse than the scientific and engineering ones. There are plenty of cookbook-style laboratories, unimaginative classroom exercises, and mathematical pomposity, all on a nuts-and-bolts level, without any genuine insight into the significance of science and technology. Can it really be that our entire educational system, in most fields and at most levels, tends most of the time to disregard two major determinative forces—technology and science—in the uneven human story? I confess that such exaggerations of my position have frequently been attributed to me, and I further confess that these extreme arguments have sometimes tempted me.

[3] "A Proposed National Foundation for the Humanities," *Key Reporter*, Autumn 1964, p. 4.

Yet the major thrust of my argument is to show that existing courses need scientific and technological parameters if they are to provide a meaningful education for young people of the latter twentieth century. Too many important subjects in the traditional corpus of learning are still treated in traditional ways not meaningful in the context of mid-twentieth century. I do not mean to throw out the entire tradition; I think it wholly salvageable.

The problem is not so much what is taught as how it is taught. We should always study the Middle Ages, for example, but I question that those studies should concentrate upon the question of whether feudalism is better explained by German or Latin precedents. Yet because that question was a major bone of contention among nineteenth-century French and German medievalists, imbued with nationalistic fervor, it still is emphasized today. We have more to learn from and about the Middle Ages. That pious, active era was not at all concerned with whether or not feudalism possessed more Roman elements than Teutonic, or vice versa; people were faced with problems of making a living, having some measure of social and political security, and achieving personal fulfillment, even as they are today. And the problems were closely related, then as now, to the technology of the times.

Educating the Faculty

It may be that our curriculum is irrelevant because our faculties are uneducated. Yet we have seen how a whole generation of mathematics teachers has been retrained at the secondary and primary school levels. Is it too much to assume that the faculties engaged in the higher learning cannot also explore, learn, and start afresh? Their positions of defense which I have reconnoitered range from half-hearted to weak.

We still find, for instance, those who glorify the study of the classics in the present by pointing out that nearly every man in the British Parliament in the early nineteenth century could read and speak Greek. The point has two inferences, both of which, it seems to me, are false. One is that the British Parliament dealt successfully with the sore nineteenth-century problems of scientific, technological, and industrial change. Certainly Bentham and Marx did not think so, and this negative verdict is reached by most historians, on different and additional grounds. The second inference is that *how* able men are educated doesn't matter so long as they learn *something*. We do think that subject matter counts and that education, particularly of the able, matters a great deal. Are there any serious proposals today that we should turn our students back to learning Greek?

Yet our present curriculum still has commitments that are nearly as irrelevant as Greek; at the same time we omit scientific and technological materials that are as relevant as the speaking and writing of English. Let us change all this. Let not posterity say that our generation failed to educate them meaningfully for a world in which science and technology are the founts of the fundamental changes they will have to deal with. It is probably our fate as professors to be first loved, then understood, and finally despised by our students. Let us not help them document that final position.

A
Student
Looks at
the
Curriculum

JOSEPH D. McCLATCHY

A CURRICULUM THAT IS RELEVANT is one by which and in which a student can best develop himself intellectually. Theoretically, therefore, there should be as many different curricula as there are students. Most colleges, however, follow a similar curricular pattern: a foreign language requirement, at least one year of a laboratory science, some sort of general humanities course, and so forth. Those colleges with a particular sectarian or vocational bias will also include their own special courses, consistent with their institutional goals. These are all time-tested educational procedures, of which most students would probably approve (at least, if you asked them *after* they had taken the courses). Also, these courses are almost entirely concentrated within a student's first two years, supposedly allowing him elective freedom during his junior and senior years. However, the course load now demanded by his major department usually limits the student severely in his choice of electives and, for the most part, keeps him confined to his own area of specialization. So the result of this type of curriculum—and it seems to be the type found almost everywhere —is that the student comes to college with everything already planned for him, or at least "predestined."

Such a situation is probably unavoidable. The college administration seeks to give the student a "liberal" background, and the departmental chairmen call for more work in his major. The humanist faculty demand the traditional general courses and re-emphasize their importance in a technological culture; the scientific faculty, on the other hand, argue that you can't fix a fracture with Shakespeare, and want their students to take even more science courses. Academic restrictions due to the programed course of studies plus the increasing demands for specialization are indeed a major problem, and one that is seemingly insoluble.

And this, in turn, brings up the larger and inevitable question of the college's role in the student's development. To what extent should or *can* the college impose its own programed course of studies on the student? How much say should or can the student himself have in the matter? Who, in fact, is most responsible for the composition of the curriculum: the administration, the faculty, the students, a combination of two, or of three?

When the average freshman comes to college, the administration presupposes—perhaps rightly, perhaps not—that he is not sure of what he wants to do with the next four years. And consequently, they tell the student to follow, as it were, their bouncing ball to intellectual maturity and academic success. Curricular regimentation is especially heavy in the freshman year, although most often combined with an effort to introduce the student to the "adventure of ideas."

But what about the next three years? Or what about that type of student, seen in increasing numbers, who is already determined in his plans before he comes to college? It seems that only recently have those in responsible positions awakened to the needs of these students. Briefly put, what seems to be desperately needed in American higher education is a more creative role for the student. If his development is ideally to be a self-development, then it is imperative that he be intimately involved in the process of his own education. To truly encourage a discipline of intellectual responsibility and a sense of the importance of his education, the college must account for the individual student in his individual education.

In this instance, what is needed is a more extensive system of sympathetic, knowledgeable, and responsive counseling, in order to help the student plan his own education. Just as important is an updated curriculum. Given the opportunity, almost every student will take the courses he *wants* to take. And courses should be popular, as well as academically demanding.

But regardless of what courses the student is taking, they will be of little value to him unless they are properly taught. I would hesitate to rehash this well-worn point except for its increasing importance. It is not just a question of having two thousand people facing a televised teacher. At times, one hundred, fifty, even twenty students are too many for a class. The personal exchange of ideas and feelings that is the essence of the classroom is becoming more important and more infrequent.

No less important in any discussion of this sort is the importance of the so-called secondary curriculum. Naturally, those colleges and universities which are located near large urban centers with their cultural complexes have a great advantage. But this does not excuse the smaller college for not providing its students with a stimulating and valuable "secondary curriculum." First of all, there are the extra-curricular activities—glee club, newspaper, athletics, political societies, and so forth. These should all be as closely integrated with student life as possible, not only as a source of recreation and participation, but also as an outlet for creative energy and imaginative effort. Any and all of these activities can be an important factor in a student's development—positively and negatively. And by encouraging and even financing them, the college is dramatically demonstrating its interest in and concern for the student body.

Also, to accommodate the legendary collegiate individualism, or rather perhaps to encourage it, why not some imaginative planning on the part of the administration? The poet- or artist-in-residence has been proved to have a far-reaching and beneficial effect on the students, if only by stimulating their interest in unexplored areas of the cultural spectrum. The new 4-1-4 plan at Cornell is a marvelous example of students' being allowed to pursue their own special interests under the auspices of the college. Most institutions boast of the lecturers they have had speak to their assembled masses, but how many can say that they gave their students an opportunity to talk with the lecturer—as an individual, or in small groups? If the college is the meeting place of questioning minds, why not give the students a chance to ask a few questions?

And again, are there sufficient outlets on the campus for the students to make use of their own particular talents? Most colleges have an adequate athletic outlay, but do they have facilities for a student string quartet, or for a group to produce an avant-garde play, or to sculpture, or to debate Viet Nam? If not, there most certainly should be. In many cases, this side of a student's life is more important than the strictly academic, if only because it is often the more personal.

The current attitude of graduate and professional schools would seem to be most encouraging. The emphasis they are placing on a broad liberal arts background cannot help but enlarge their students' outlook on the past and perspectives for the future. I only wish that many of their fellow educators would follow their lead and recognize the increasing importance of the humanistic studies in higher education. Today's world, as modern as it is, is but the present significance of an ageless tradition and heritage, the realization and appreciation of which is so essential in facing the problems of tomorrow.

The problems I have mentioned—restrictive curricula, inadequate counseling, unimaginative administrative planning, and failure to tap the creative resources of the students—are only a very, very few of the difficulties to be found today in American colleges. They have all been noted and debated for a long time now, and are still far from easy solutions. I am convinced that today's student is as deeply concerned about his education as are those actually in charge of it. He realizes that his future depends upon and derives from his four or more years of higher education. He must be given every opportunity to enjoy freely the benefits that the really best education can offer.

Effective Teaching: The Relevance of the Curriculum

WILBERT J. McKEACHIE *

As AN ADVOCATE OF MEASURES to improve college teaching, I have sometimes argued that the curriculum—which occupies countless faculty committees for hours and hours of heated discussion—is far less important to the quality of a student's education than the teaching he receives—an icon which we piously bow to but seldom get excited about. I'd like to argue that our major error in curriculum planning is to plan the curriculum solely in terms of the structure of the subject matter without taking into consideration the faculty who are to implement it. Curricula should be designed, like golf courses or bars, for pleasure—faculty pleasure. I am quite serious in asserting that a primary determinant of the effectiveness of a curriculum is its effect upon the attitudes of the teachers who are to put it into operation.

What can good curriculum planning do for the professor?

First, it can provide him with stimulating students. One of the major joys in teaching is the unexpected question, the sturdy challenge to accepted dogma, the "illumining" insight of a student with a lively curiosity and a solid background. Sometimes our curriculum is so neatly ordered, so rigidly constructed, that students arrive as if on an assembly line nicely ready for the operations we perform, but completely predictable in their responses to our teaching. A curriculum in a department with a consistent theoretical point of view and a rationalized set of prerequisites is prone to this weakness.

Equally often our curriculum is so loosely ordered, so open to prostitution to any professed need, that student backgrounds are too divergent to permit meaningful colloquy and we are reduced to a review of the most elementary concepts of our field. The ideal curriculum would be one which brings students with enough divergencies in personality, enough naïveté about the problems, and enough *com-*

* My colleague, Stephen Kaplan, has given me helpful suggestions for this essay.

189

monality in language concepts and knowledge to permit new ideas to be born and communicated.

A second contribution of good curriculum planning can be opportunities for the continuing education of the professor. As research has become more and more dominant in the life of the university professor, his teaching has become more and more specialized. Instead of being able to teach any course in his discipline, he began to teach only courses in his own specialization, and from this the trend continued until now he may teach only his own research. Even this may contribute to his learning and development, but I would argue that not only teaching but research itself suffers when a professor is no longer required to keep up with, and integrate, new developments in areas related to but not directly involved in his own research.

Some evidence to support this proposition comes from the work of Donald Pelz, Frank Andrews, and Leo Meltzer of the University of Michigan Institute of Social Research. In studies of Ph.D. scientists in universities and governmental laboratories they found that researchers spending more than three-fourths time on research were less productive as scientists than those spending less time on research and more time teaching or in *administration!* This was true both for junior and senior scientists.

A third contribution of the curriculum to good teaching is its effect upon the professor's enthusiasm. Anyone who has been on the academic scene for any length of time has seen the sparks of inspiration kindled when a group of faculty members have battled through the conflicts and compromises of a new curriculum and finally have a chance to put their ideas into practice. As the new curriculum becomes routine, the original planners move on to other new projects; staff brought in to carry on the courses have not shared in the excitement of planning a new approach, and the stage is set for a revolution. As an administrator I see one of my functions as that of fomenting curricular revolution in order to restore the fun to teaching. Fun for the teacher not only is a worthy goal in itself but also is related to effectiveness with students. Some of our Michigan studies of teaching effectiveness suggest that enthusiasm and buoyancy tend to characterize effective teachers. To maintain this enthusiasm, the curriculum should be subject to revision. When curricula become so ossified and college organization so rigid that curricular change seems doomed in advance, teaching effectiveness almost inevitably deteriorates.

Finally, a good curriculum can provide the teacher with one of the greatest satisfactions in teaching and the most important element for growth as a teacher—the opportunity to see students learn and grow.

All too often we assume that we can deal with the problems of curriculum, teaching methods, and class size independently. This is simply unrealistic. My reviews of the research on college teaching have convinced me that achievement of certain curricular objectives, such as skills in critical thinking, are seriously affected by class size and teaching method. A curriculum in which teachers' contacts with students are distant or transitory is doomed to failure no matter what the logic of its arrangement of sequences of content. Teachers learn how to be more effective teachers by observing the effects of their teaching and by having opportunities to try varied teaching methods. This implies that the teacher will have classes where choice of method is not restricted by size or by a curricular format which demands lecture, laboratory, or some other limited range of methods. It also implies opportunities to know the student as an individual and to observe and guide his development at more than one point in his academic career. While we may often delude ourselves about the degree to which we have contributed to a student's increasing maturity as a scholar, even an inflated estimate of our impact is better than none at all. This implies a curriculum in which an instructor has some small classes and some classes at both the lower and upper levels.

The development of student independence may seem antithetical to the sort of personal relationships which I have just described. To some extent the teacher may sacrifice some of his own satisfactions when his students are no longer dependent upon him, but the satisfactions of engaging in dialogue with students who can read for themselves may well equal those of having a passive, attentive audience. From my standpoint a major goal of curricular planning should be to develop independent learners. Planning for this objective implies that the basic courses should provide opportunities to set standards for reading investigation and writing and to give students practice and feedbacks in scholarly activities. In the more advanced portions of the curriculum students would need less frequent and detailed guidance. For many teachers the opportunity to meet students as budding scholars would enhance both teaching effectiveness and teaching satisfaction.

My theme is simple. No curriculum is better than the teachers who implement it; and quality of teaching depends not only upon the skill and dedication the teacher brings to it but also on the effect of the curriculum on the teacher's development. Thus if one plans a curriculum for the ultimate objective of student learning, he must perforce plan it for the faculty as well.

The Two-Year College's Contribution to Curriculum Development

JOSEPH P. COSAND

CURRICULUM DEVELOPMENT AND TEACHING TECHNIQUES lag far behind the needs of the student and of society in general. It is the rare institution which provides a creative climate for exploration in curriculum development and teaching methods. Monetary support for such research is almost always the first budget item to be cut.

Business and industry have produced a complex world which requires people who can appreciate—culturally, economically, occupationally, and socially—the problems to be solved today, not those of yesterday. Continued adherence to the traditional curriculum and to the sanctified lecture method cannot foster respect for the college, the faculty, or the administration. The curriculum must be something more than a group of courses built around teacher preference and taught from the same notes year after year. We must accept the challenges placed before us and examine with utmost severity our curriculum and the manner in which our classes are taught.

The rapid growth in college enrollment intensifies the problem. Today, high school graduates, and in some states anyone who is 18 years of age, are eligible for admission to college. Mass higher education has become a fact of life. Are we prepared to provide these young people and adults who have equal access to higher education with a realistically developed program of courses, thus giving them an opportunity to achieve? We must, as educators, become just as concerned about the college dropout as about the high school dropout. Both are losses to society. I am convinced that thousands of college dropouts occur because the curriculum is obsolete or the teaching is ineffective. Either condition creates boredom and discouragement.

Liberal arts colleges and community junior colleges are dedicated to teaching, and they should also be dedicated to research and curriculum development. As president of a community junior college in a large urban area, I am faced with large enrollments and with students who are unbelievably heterogeneous in their abilities, educational backgrounds, and socioeconomic environments. We in two-year institutions need especially to consider curriculum development (1) for the student who will eventually transfer to a four-year program, (2) for the nonachiever in high school, (3) for the student who wants vocational training, and (4) for the adult.

Our institution, an open-door college, is concerned with a curriculum for the student who plans to complete a four-year collegiate program. Although the lower-division curriculum is the foundation for upper-division work and graduate school, it is too often neglected at our large universities. Such a curriculum should be broad in scope, challenging, and concerned with values as well as subject matter. There must be honors courses at the freshman and the sophomore levels, just as in the upper division. Staff members must evaluate the content constantly, for the rate of change in certain disciplines—particularly the sciences and social sciences—is so rapid that a course may be rendered obsolete in a very few years.

Lower-division colleges, such as ours, also must develop a curriculum for the student who, though he has potential for achievement, did not do well in high school. The hostility of these underachievers must be understood by the curriculum developers and teachers. It isn't feasible simply to repeat the same high school courses over in college and call the curriculum "remedial" or "developmental." There must be new content, new teaching methodologies, new approaches to the students, many of whom came from homes which, because of environmental deficiencies, have fostered all kinds of insecurities and anxieties. The development of a curriculum for these students must have the best creative thinking of all staff members, especially counselors. And, before the curriculum is imposed upon the students, they should have an opportunity to react through experiences in experimental courses. Once researched and developed, the curriculum will be ineffective unless taught by teachers with exceptional abilities and insight. To salvage these thousands of underachievers requires the best teachers we have, not the least experienced or least able.

Programs in technical education are an essential part of our present collegiate society, and will become even more so as scientific advances in business and industry continue. The community junior colleges, and some four-year colleges such as Southern Illinois University and California State Polytechnic College, are responsible for developing technical curricula which will make the student employable after one or two years of college. If these colleges were doing their job, they would be enrolling half of their students in quality technical programs. However, vocational curriculum development has too often been neglected, with the result that teaching has been ineffective and the student has been deprived of a real educational opportunity. Parents, high school teachers and counselors, and college teachers and counselors have tended to sanctify the A.B. degree and to look down on the technical curricula as below college level. The results have been low enrollments in the technical programs, high enrollments in the respectable "academic" curriculum, and dropouts and failures by the hundreds of thousands.

The technical programs, to be effective, demand careful consideration by all staff members and counselors and by representatives of business and industry. These groups are responsible for seeing that the technical programs prepare the students for citizenship as well as for employment, for cultural appreciation as well as for occupational success.

As our society has developed more complex modes of living, we have become increasingly aware of the great needs for continuing education. The day of the "hobby" course is over. The adult must be provided with a rich curriculum. Adults, if consulted, will surprise the professional adult educator by requesting courses in psychology, anthropology, sociology, philosophy, religion, astronomy, political science, literature, and so on. It is time we looked at the whole picture of adult or continuing education and questioned the validity of present practices. How important is credit? Shouldn't we provide a curriculum which encourages adults to enroll in courses simply for the joy of learning? Who knows—they may already have their Ph.D.'s.

In addition to developing these curricula, we must examine and develop new teaching methods. The two, curriculum and teaching, are forever joined; and one, if weak, can render the other impotent.

Finally, curriculum and teaching methods must be evaluated by all participants—teachers, students, and administrators—and by all disciplines. Isolation within a discipline is a luxury no college can afford. Interdisciplinary participation often results in interdisciplinary courses which become cornerstones of the entire lower-division program.

To be effective, the curriculum must be altered to reflect changing technological developments, cultural values, and student attitudes. It must be nourished in a climate which permits and encourages research. Research in industry, business, the sciences, in college and university laboratories, involves billions of dollars. Perhaps research in curriculum development and teaching methodologies and provision of funds to help teachers learn new techniques of instruction are more important than all other types of research. Perhaps we might then educate our citizens to realize their potential, occupationally, culturally, socially. Perhaps we might then see develop a revolution of ideas which could lead to the creation of a society free from vested interest power structures. Perhaps we might then be well on our way to a Great Society.

And
Sadly
Teach

FREDERICK L. GWYNN

WHAT ROLE HAS TEACHING PLAYED in the present crisis in higher education, and how can it help us to avoid future crises? My thesis-answer is simple but sad: The ineffectiveness of much college teaching may well be the major *cause* of the crisis, and it may spawn many more crises.

Ineffective teaching may be identified by certain methodological symptoms: the professor's misuse of lecture and discussion, his failure to establish goals for individual student contacts, and his comparative absence of feeling. Behind these weaknesses lie more general academic vices of disorganized student feedback, inadequate training of college teachers, and lack of teaching theory. Individual conversion and mass action for good teaching are needed to help prevent future conflict.

The 1964-65 campus revolts seemed to be directed against the tendency for most colleges and universities to be oriented toward an image compounded of their traditions, administrations, faculties, curricula, and plants—rather than of their students. Even if the revolts were provoked partly by nonstudents, by concurrent civil rights protest, and even by the old college predilection for swallowing gold-fish, the orientation issue was and is most serious.

The Vacuum in College Teaching Today

My guess is that underneath the current activism, as underneath the more familiar academic apathy of students back through the Silent, Progressive, and Lost Generations, is an expanding vacuum, the result of a half-century of weak teaching that insults students by not paying enough attention to them. Details of this history are hard to come by, since few analysts penetrate classrooms, since (as Riley and his collaborators note) professors have to think well of their own abilities in order to survive,[1] and since the increase of dormitories, degrees, and salaries has lulled much suspicion.

But those persistent scattered reports of dissatisfaction continue, and clouds larger than a student editor's hand have formed periodi-

---

[1] John W. Riley, Jr., Bryce F. Ryan, and Marcia Lifshitz, *The Student Looks at His Teacher* (New Brunswick, N.J.: Rutgers University Press, 1950), p. 14.

cally. A visitor to a number of varied campuses like the late David Boroff can say, "retrograde teaching plods on. Talk to students and you compile a bleak anthology of boredom, inertia, and ineptness among teachers." [2] One recent document indicates that even the graduate experience is "a discouraging encounter with intradepartmental personal rivalries, seminars that go nowhere, dogmatic faculty, and social isolation." [3]

I would not retail these views if my own did not corroborate them; of the eighty-four college-university teachers I have observed in the classroom during the past thirty-two years, about half as my mentors and half as colleagues in English to be evaluated on my own and other campuses, only about one-quarter seemed to me during my visits to be actively achieving their teaching potential. James Michener may have given an unfortunately realistic proportion when, in praising one of his teachers, he said recently, "In his lifetime a man lives under 15 or 16 Presidents, but a good teacher comes into his life but rarely." [4]

Let me specify the major weaknesses of in-class and out-of-class teaching in higher education. I draw partly on responses to and inferences from an informal survey I made of the attitudes and habits of about two dozen college and university teachers of high repute, but my most authoritative information comes from my visits, from informed student comments, and from the failures of the one teacher I know best.

Inefficient teaching probably cannot be traced to the professor's lack of knowledge or of preparation: the student's complaint has often been "He knows his stuff but he can't get it across," and most teachers may even overprepare their information.

The real weakness, in my opinion, lies in the polarities of class hours given over completely to lectures—multiple, hard-boiled monologues put into one semester's basket with the excuse that the students number more than twenty—or to so-called discussion—softboiled dialogues with classes under twenty in which the professor depends on the automatic epiphanies of one or two extroverted students. Although the little research I have seen on the subject concludes that lectures are for information and discussions for producing

[2] Boroff, *Campus U.S.A.: Portraits of American Colleges in Action* (New York: Harper & Bros., 1960), p. 193.
[3] R. P. Cuzzort, "The Superior Student in Graduate School," *The Superior Student*, May-June 1965, p. 3.
[4] *Time*, June 18, 1965, p. 36.

thought,[5] I infer from the same statistics that some students respond best to being talked at and some to being talked with, and I have a corollary impression that some professors talk-at better and some talk-with better. If this is true, the only reasonable class program is, as in opera or in marriage, a mixture of aria and recitative on the one hand, and ensemble work on the other, no matter what the class size. Professors, by definition, must talk to profess, but if they also want to be teachers, they cannot profess too much or too little. Yet this is the kind of methodological consideration that rarely comes to the professor's attention.

Teaching outside of class presents problems of analysis because visiting is impossible, but one feels that if Socrates is rare in the classroom, he must be rarer in the agora of the coffee shop or the sanctuary of the office. Yet students and faculty all know what John Ciardi meant when he praised the "go-to-class, hang-around, talk-to-students" professors,[6] probably because the vision is so often shattered by the realities of the magnetic faculty club, the comfortable home, and the out-of-town consultation or convention.

My survey respondents say quietly that it is very important for faculty to maintain contact with students outside of class, and that their own growth in college was strongly influenced by such contact. But just how much real teaching goes on outside of classroom, laboratory, or formal tutorial? Not much, one suspects, in most conferences or *klatsches*, unless the professor engages in active diagnosis and organized discussion instead of merely friendly conversation or monologue. Most students don't know the right questions to ask in conference or table talk, and this lack demands the preplanning scorned by many professors operating beyond the classroom.

In any kind of teaching—either lecture-discussion or conference-conversation—most teachers are chiefly interested in subject matter. Yet one of the most vital features of Lewis Mayhew's background paper on the learning environment is its emphasis on the part that personal feeling must play in collegiate instruction: "the university should be a place in which both cognition and affection are viewed as effective and valuable forces." For too many of us, the stifling of feeling is supposed to confer rationality. We avoid demonstration and autobiography on principle, and we forget that a purely cognitive contact can be only brief and incomplete, encompassing a small portion of the very subject matter of the humanities and social sciences.

    [5] B. S. Bloom, "Thought-Processes in Lectures and Discussions," *Journal of General Psychology*, April 1953, pp. 157–69.
    [6] Ciardi, "Manner of Speaking," *Saturday Review*, March 27, 1965, p. 13.

The great Brooklyn College survey of fifteen years ago showed that "in courses where value judgments and matters of conviction are most likely to arise, the student body in the main wishes no Olympian objectivity," [7] and recent existentialist complaints about distant and uncommitted professors are even more emphatic. The projection of personal feeling will not, of course, compensate students for absent-minded professors, but its lack may account for the absence of students from a professor's classroom.

Yet these failures during contact hours are weaknesses of awareness and technique, which the individual teacher can remedy. We must now isolate the more profound and more impersonal forces causing weak teaching: the disorganization of student feedback, the lack of teacher training and supervision in graduate school and department, and the inadequacy of theoretical teaching and learning models.

Allowing for Student Feedback

There may be only two ways of normalizing college teaching—the controlled student rating, and the controlled department rating.[8] Uncorrelated and unweighted rumor accounts for most classroom enrollments and reputations, and surely a lack of organization in such feedback contributes heavily to crisis. Although Riley *et al.* say that course ratings have existed since 1922,[9] their use is mostly sporadic and inefficient, depending on the whim of individual teachers or student groups who often operate with highly unprofessional questionnaires and sometimes spill the beans to the wrong people for the wrong reasons. But the widespread use of student responses to teaching, fed back to the professor instead of to some informal student guide to courses, could painlessly alert many a professor to his shortcomings and at the same time act as a safety valve for students. An appropriate concern with actual teaching as well as with subject matter would be manifested if a professor issued sample opinion sheets with syllabi on the first day of classes, consulted them periodically as pedagogical guidelines, and administered them at midterm as well as term's end to allow this class rather than the next to benefit from its own opinion. Surely, this kind of motivated and systematized cooperation between instructor and student would stimulate the teaching-learning process and establish a personal link of mutual respect. No student could claim that he had no voice in contributing

[7] Riley *et al.*, *The Student Looks at his Teacher*, pp. 73–74.
[8] See Charles Fenton, "Publish or Perish Revisited," *College English*, May 1960, pp. 454–55.
[9] Riley *et al.*, *The Student Looks at His Teacher*, p. 23.

to his own education, and no teacher would be forced to puzzle over those enrollment figures, too small or too large, the next time around the course.

Training the College Teacher

Next, the failure to give adequate training and supervision to potential college teachers doubtless lies behind much ineffective teaching. To quote Robert Benchley, I am aware that this point has been made before, and I can only say that I am making it again. Undergraduates may or may not be aware that their mentors are trained in graduate school chiefly to find books in the library stacks and to write papers—not to teach students—but they are certainly aware of the results. Some professors apparently still think that academic freedom includes having no visitors over the age of twenty-two in the classroom and that any advice about their teaching function beyond what Northrop Frye calls "oracular harrumph" is selling out to the charm schools. As a result, if we have any body of theory and practice for teaching in higher education, it rarely reaches the professor, and until recently pedagogical instruction and supervision in graduate school may have consisted chiefly of keeping graduate assistants from getting out of calendar phase with one another. Things are improving (see reports by John Diekhoff[10] and Russell Cooper[11] over the years) but, in my opinion, supervised practice teaching for prospective professors should begin in college, as it does for schoolteachers, and all graduate programs should include courses in the history and theory of the discipline itself, together with further practice teaching. The notion of internship borrowed from medical education[12] may spread, but we might also borrow the public practices of moot courts from the law school and demonstration homiletics from the seminary to substantiate the supervision. Apprenticeship in full-time teaching should be supervised by master teachers, and promotion and tenure should be offered chiefly on the basis of periodic visitation and conference by people within the department.

Finally, lying behind the lack of pedagogical instruction is the unhappy fact that higher education seems to have no received theory of teaching, no informing set of modes against which professors can

[10] For example, Diekhoff, *The Domain of the Faculty in Our Expanding Colleges* (New York: Harper & Bros., 1956) and *Tomorrow's Professors* (New York: Fund for the Advancement of Education, 1960).

[11] For example, Cooper, "Improving College Teaching and Administration," in *Higher Education: Some Newer Developments*, ed. Samuel Baskin (New York: McGraw-Hill Book Co., 1965), pp. 196–222.

[12] Bernard Berelson, *Graduate Education in the United States* (New York: McGraw-Hill Book Co., 1960), p. 68.

measure themselves and their students. We need more prologomena (and we need them disseminated to more teachers rather than to administrators and educationists) like Israel Scheffler's recent description of the three elemental "Philosophical Models of Teaching," the Lockean ideal emphasizing the "transfer of information," the Platonic-Augustinian "development of insight," and the Kantian "inculcation of principled judgment and conduct." [13] Too often a college teacher merely imitates concrete models from his graduate school without considering the abstract theoretical models, their comparative assumptions and consequences. The greatest teachers have probably been those who have all three of Scheffler's patterns well in mind—purveying some solid knowledge, triggering some insight, and instilling the great principle of acting by principle—becoming themselves what Mayhew calls "appropriate role models" for their students. We also need more studies like Roy Heath's of student types in college, so that teachers can identify and mold the Non-Committers, Hustlers, and Plungers into the Reasonable Adventurers of his title, thereby proving Heath's theorem that "A college or university that does not generate Reasonable Adventurers is not engaged in higher education." [14]

To strengthen college teaching by improving its theory, methodology, training, and feedback, two miracles are required. The first is to give the matter as much publicity in the faculty world as the 1964–65 "student revolt" got in the public press. The American Council on Education might well abandon its debating society aspect in this matter and send a few blasts to teachers instead of more pamphlets to administrators. The second miracle might occur after the blasts. It involves individual professorial conversion from an overwhelming love of subject matter to an understanding of the complementary demands implied by one of Heath's Princeton students, who called his biology professor "the perfect university teacher" because "he's interested in students' learning; not in just presenting things that he knows." [15] Riley and his associates express the positive doctrine in an epigram: "*What the student hears is more important than what the professor says....*" [16] Today, the college-university faculty member who would gladly talk but only sadly teach may be mildly resented. Tomorrow, the student in higher education may not tolerate the professor because he cannot hear him at all.

[13] *Harvard Educational Review*, Spring 1965, pp. 131–43.
[14] *The Reasonable Adventurer* (Pittsburgh: University of Pittsburgh Press, 1964), p. 84.
[15] *Ibid.*, p. 147.
[16] Riley *et al.*, *The Student Looks at His Teacher*, p. 33.

The Art
of Getting
Students
into
Trouble

NICHOLAS HOBBS

CONFRONTED WITH THE TASK of preparing this paper on the professor and the student, and being a proper psychologist, I went to the literature to see what wisdom I could find on the topic. What I found was appalling. It would seem that professors are not necessary at all. A television screen will do as well. Class size doesn't matter: like a cipher, a professor is divisible by a number of any magnitude, with quotient zero. When asked to list important influences in their college years, one group of students mentioned many things, including the cafeteria, and forgot to mention the faculty. The clincher was a study showing that students who were simply assigned the text learned more than students who had benefit of both text and instructor.

But professors must mean something to the students. Too many students have praised too many teachers for us to believe they are dispensable. Besides, the idea that professors are consequential is much more appealing, at least to a professor, than the notion they are not. I therefore resolved to present a few hypotheses, grown from some twenty-five years at the craft, that seek to define what it is about the professor-student relationship that makes a difference in the lives of both. The charming thing about these hypotheses is that they are absolutely unsupported by data.

The first notion is that the good professor conveys to his students something not now measured by achievement tests, and that is *style* in the use of the mind. The professor, in his immediate presence and with not too large a group of students, is required to demonstrate repeatedly and in various contexts the style of an informed and disciplined mind at work on a complex problem. The range of cognitive styles among scholars is immense, and individual differences in student responsiveness to various styles is to be expected. Thus the college should seek to have on its faculty professors representing many different approaches to the mastery of knowledge and should arrange circumstances so that students can respond to cognitive styles attractive to them.

A second notion about professors and students is that the professor must be concerned and committed to what he is doing and teaching. Research shows that ego development in young children proceeds most satisfactorily when parents and children are involved together in activities about which the parents are enthusiastic. Simply putting in time with children, with no zest for the enterprise at hand, is not demonstrably better than neglect. A professor should never be guilty of teaching something that bores him; all he will succeed in doing is making his students dislike the subject. Whatever highlands his heart is in, he should take his students there. It is not important for students to know everything; it *is* important for them to care about what they know. And if the professor has no intellectual uplands to take a student to, he has but one honorable course, and that is—to get out of the classroom.

The third hypothesis notes that to be a scholar is to walk a lonesome road. The scholar/professor (it's a shame the tautology is necessary) must have apartness for himself and seek it for his students. While the faculty committee on parking is oft inveighed against, it nonetheless will endure as a sociable refuge from the demands of disciplined study and thought. Perhaps the greatest single reform that could be effected in higher education in America would be to remove telephones from faculty offices. But we professors would never permit it; their ring is such a solace. The problem is one of the prepotency of immediate rewards over delayed ones, a fact established by many experiments. Colleges are organized around innumerable activities providing immediate reinforcement for faculty and, even more, for students. Scholarship requires the ability to delay gratification, at least at first, until the scholarly process itself becomes intrinsically and immediately rewarding. The good professor, cherishing aloneness for himself, will nurture the capacity for aloneness in his students, until the grip of scholarship is firmly upon them, protecting them from collegiate activities and rewarding them richly in each moment of their pursuit.

In the graduate program in psychology at Peabody College we encourage students to take what we call "a quarter at Woolsthorpe," a period free of all classes and assignments, with faculty and family conspiring to support the student for three months of sustained study guided solely by his own needs for knowing. There are no reading lists, no required papers, no grades; the aspirant scholar is simply given what will always be, in our frenzied world, a most precious commodity: uninterrupted time. The origin of the name is significant. In 1665 a great plague swept England, and the universities were closed. An undistinguished Cambridge student went home to his mother's cottage at Woolsthorpe and there, with no professors to bother him, invented the calculus and started his great experiments on optics. In sanguine moments, I let myself believe that American colleges and universities can find ways of promoting the private enterprise of the mind, short of having a plague.

A fourth idea is that the professor serves as mediator in a required process of self-reorganization in those exciting times when a student commits himself wholly, with passion and discrimination, not just to studying a subject but to *being* a scholar or a scientist or a teacher himself. These exciting times of self-redefinition generate anxiety in the student, an inevitable consequence of abandoning familiar and comfortable patterns of personality organization and seeking new ways of construing himself and his world. The professor serves as a model to be emulated, giving silent assurance that the role aspired to by the student is indeed achievable. More than that, the professor at such times of confrontation can turn anxiety into zest for problem solving by his empathic responsiveness to the doubts and fears, hopes and dreams, that the student experiences in seeking a new and total self-commitment. The professor is midwife to a new self. The tragedy of the crowded class is that many students may approach the experience of self-redefinition as scholar, scientist, poet, engineer, novelist, politician, or teacher, but back off from it to reduce anxiety generated by the prospect of change. Lacking a mature adult to help him through a period of self-discovery, he retreats to good grades and graduation, with a lingering sense of loss, of invitation unaccepted.

Thus far I have talked about the relationship between professor and student as though the student were the sole beneficiary—a severely truncated view of the situation. The professor who is a great teacher must have responsive students, else his role lacks meaningfulness and satisfaction. The debate on how to reward good teaching is too often limited to promotions and increases in salary. While I would be the last to discount these negotiable evidences of appreciation, I would also argue that the good teacher needs most of all an opportunity to work closely with a few students and the reward of knowing that he has quickened their lives through a shared encounter with knowing.

The final notion protests the incompleteness of predominant theories of human motivation and learning that stress the role of drive reduction, of homeostatic tendencies, of the reward value of right responses. The joys of learning transcend those generated by the click of a teaching machine, or by an A racked up at quarter's end. As many experiments indicate, man does indeed seek tension reduction, equilibrium, knowledge that he is on the right track. But this is only part of the story, the part that yields to experimentation. It is equally clear, though elusive to experimental demonstration, that man seeks tension, delights in upsetting equilibria, and loves to get himself lost, just for the fun of setting things right again. Order itself is ultimately boring; the *achieving* of order is man's dish. It is the process of mastery, of expression of competence, not the product thereof, that brings cognitive and aesthetic satisfaction. Scientist and poet alike work to bring order from disarray, to achieve elegance and simplicity in formula or metaphor, but each achieved simplicity reveals new and intricate confusions. Every peak in Darien shows worrisome terrain yet to be worked that men of competence attack with zest. Man the Problem Solver, is even more Man the Problem Maker. So I say that it is the task of the professor, by example and by design, to get his students into trouble, good trouble, intellectual and affective trouble. Let this be his goal: *to teach his students the art of precipitating themselves into just manageable difficulties of their own choosing.* And he should teach them, again by example as well as precept, to choose with taste those areas of life where the ordering of disarray brings most enduring satisfactions.

There are two kinds of questions in higher education today, applicable to two kinds of institutions—the small number in ferment and the large number in dreadful tranquility. For the first the question is: Who is going to make trouble for whom, students or faculty? For the second it is, alas: Is anybody going to make trouble for anybody?

It is clear that students in some universities have precipitated faculty and administration into a considerable amount of difficulty that we hope will be manageable. In other universities there is only collegiate excitement. While some mutuality of trouble making between faculty and students is to be desired and expected, and even encouraged when lacking, the professor must re-establish—or establish—his pre-eminence as trouble maker, as disturber of intellectual equilibria, as advocate when advocacy is required, and as detached observer when cool heads are needed. He will do this through authority gained by competence, by a passionate commitment to scholarship and to the social significance of learning, and by responsible and responsive concern for students.

The
Changing
Role
of the
Professor

FREDERICK H. BURKHARDT

A RECENT REPORT by a congressional committee reviewing the appropriations for Defense Department science research stated that "a retrenchment might, so far as colleges and universities are concerned, have a corollary benefit of making the best faculty more available for the purpose of teaching students." [1]

This statement is characteristic of some of the oversimplified thinking that goes on about the problem which has been called "the flight from teaching." Even if one grants the very dubious assumption that the best faculty are now engaged in government research, it would seem fallacious to suppose that a retrenchment would release the best rather than the poorest. It also seems to me dangerous to scholarship and learning to take a wholesale position that teaching would automatically improve if support for research were reduced. Moreover, it is not true, if one considers all fields and the entire higher education establishment, that research is so well supported as to undermine teaching. In the humanities at least, there is evidence that teaching loads, committee responsibilities, inadequate sabbaticals, and the need to augment salaries by summer teaching all combine to make it difficult to get research done. Almost all the research in the humanities in this country is being done in conjunction with, or on time eked out of, a full day's teaching, counseling, and committee and other semiadministrative work.

This is not to say that there is no problem of effective teaching, but only to deny that it can be solved by the simple method of making it impossible for the professor to do anything but teach. The other demands upon a professor that compete with teaching are not simply attractive escapes from drudgery for lazy men. They are for the most part important activities that need to be done. It is in

[1] Quoted in "News and Comment," *Science*, July 16, 1965, p. 280.

206

the context of all of these competing demands that we must try to solve the problem of effective teaching.

Not very long ago a professor could be described fairly simply as a scholar engaged in teaching. In those days the student was at the center of the conception of a professor's vocation, and the psychological and physical conditions for communicating with students were relatively good.

In the past forty years, however, as a result of changes in knowledge and its organization, and as a result of developments in education and its relation to society and world affairs, our conception of the role of the professor has altered greatly. In addition to increasing the complexity of that role, these changes have worked as centrifugal forces drawing the professor away from the student and weakening the ties between them.

Centrifugal Forces in Higher Education

I should like to discuss briefly three of these forces or trends which have made for increasing the "distance" between professor and student: (1) the increase in specialization, (2) the success of the ideal of service, and (3) the increase in the complexity of our educational institutions.

Perhaps the most powerful force has been the great increase in the specialization of knowledge, one consequence of which is that the professor has come to identify himself more and more with his discipline and his professional peer group. His college or university competes with his professional community for his time and energy and loyalty. Communication with his students now competes with communication with his peers.

Greater specialization has also increased the significance of research. The judgment of his peers about a scholar's position is now as important as the judgment of his college administration. Professional recognition is a powerful force which I suspect operates just as strongly in stimulating research as the alleged "publish or perish" pressures of university administrations and departments.

A second trend which has changed the role of the professor is the success of the ideal of service to the larger community—an ideal energetically fostered by the great public universities and now generally accepted by all. The professor is now not only a learned man who transmits his knowledge to students, he is also an expert sought after by industry and government. Moreover, since the war it has been considered a major responsibility of our universities to help the emerging nations with their educational development. So long as service of this kind remains an academic ideal—and it is hard to imagine its decreasing—and so long as the teaching profession continues to increase at its present rate, it will obviously act as an important cause of absenteeism and division of energies and loyalties.

A third change in role is attributable to the growing complexity of academic administration: the professor has become more and more involved in committee work and a multitude of administrative functions which were unheard of forty years ago. Although these duties are often remote from his teaching and scholarly concerns, they are nonetheless important in creating the conditions in which his teaching will go on, and they often have a direct bearing on whether or not it will be effective. This increased administrative role of the professor, it should be noted, is not only the result of bigness in our institutions but also of greater sophistication about the relationship between the curriculum and all the other activities of the community which make up an institution of learning. Even in small institutions dedicated to teaching the individual student, the members of the faculty spend a surprisingly large amount of time in committee work.

I do not think it can be denied that the above developments have made the role of the professor more complex and the effective performance of his function as a teacher more difficult. Nor is it possible to deny that these new functions are important to knowledge and society; in the abstract they are no less important to get done well than is teaching.

On the whole this change in conception has nothing to do with the size of our educational institutions—in greater or less degree the new role of the professor is the same for the faculty at Bennington or Berkeley or Harvard. The young assistant professor at all three sees his vocation as primarily that of a specialist who will succeed as he wins the recognition of his professional peers through his publications; he regards service on committees of his professional society to be equally as important as service on college or university committees; and he considers a consultantship to industry or government not only an adjunct to his salary but a mark of recognition that scholarship can perform a service for society. The possibility that in the near future he may be teaching in Lagos or Buenos Aires, or working on an AID project in Thailand does not surprise him, and he looks forward to it as a professionally desirable as well as an interesting experience.

In the large universities the problem of effective teaching is aggravated by larger numbers and by depersonalization. The competing centrifugal forces also tend to be stronger at the large institutions because they have greater research establishments, more complex administrative machinery, more contracts and other relationships with government and industry, and more ties with the larger community in the nation and overseas. But the basic problem is the same in both large and small institutions: the complexity of the modern world produces a great demand for specialized knowledge and the pool of scholars at our universities is an essential resource in responding to the demand.

Restoring the Tradition of the Scholar-Teacher

In the context of these competing pressures and demands, teaching has suffered. Some very considerable countervailing forces will have to be generated to restore teaching to its former status in the vocation of the professor. The tradition of excellence in teaching that went with the ideal of the scholar-teacher must be revived at every stage and level of the long preparatory and training process that produces the faculty of our colleges and universities.

Among the things that need to be done, the following seem to me to be especially important:

1. Excellence in teaching must be recognized and rewarded more than it is at present. It is no doubt more difficult to obtain a dependable and objective evaluation of a professor's teaching capacities than of his research and publications, but it is not impossible. In fact some of our liberal arts colleges that prize the quality of teaching have worked out quite reliable measures of assessment. These involve to an important extent the participation of students, which is no doubt why there has been a reluctance to adopt them, but the fact is that students are capable of intelligent and responsible judgments about teaching and can be of enormous assistance to a teacher in improving the effectiveness of his instruction.

2. In encouraging and recruiting potential scholars, more emphasis must be placed upon the motivations and other psychological, social, and moral characteristics that make for good teaching as well as good research. The Woodrow Wilson Fellowship Program has made an excellent start in recruiting scholars who will make good teachers. Its policies and practices could be applied in recruitment in general.

3. Our graduate schools are not entirely immune from the charge that they turn out young specialists who have scarcely thought of teaching as a vocation. More must be done to stimulate a consideration of teaching in the training of scholars. Effective teaching does

not follow naturally from competence in scholarship, nor is it simply an endowment which one either has or hasn't. Something can be done about it and more will have to be done about it if teaching is to be restored to a central place in the vocation of the professor.

4. Finally, teaching and learning must become a much more vigorously prosecuted field of research than it has been up to to now. Although psychology has made enormous progress as a science, educational psychology has been relatively unsuccessful in attracting the interest of the more talented research men in that field.

What the foregoing points boil down to is the action that would follow upon the clear recognition that effective teaching is still the responsibility of the scholarly profession. If this recognition is achieved, we shall be well on the way to restoring the vitality of the ideal of the scholar-teacher.

Institutional
Factors
and the
Learning
Environment

LEWIS B. MAYHEW

FROM THE STANDPOINT of logic, size of student body and faculty ought to be determining elements in learning in higher education. The University of California at Berkeley is one kind of institution; Goddard College in Plainfield, Vermont, is quite another. Although the evidence about the effects of class size is inconclusive and even under certain conditions seems to favor large classes, it would seem logical to assume that the impact of a place in which a student knows all other students should contrast sharply with a situation in which an individual undergraduate or graduate student will never even see the vast majority of his peers. And, of course, size of the campus itself is, with such exceptions as Brooklyn College (18,000 students on 14 acres) and Stanford (10,000 students on 9,000 acres), related to numbers. A large institution, such as Michigan State University, where some students may come but rarely to the central campus during the freshman and sophomore years, might be expected to exert an influence on learning that differs markedly from that on a campus such as Earlham, where all student trails cross daily.

Further, the educational philosophy and, when relevant, the religious stance of an institution is presumed to influence learning both directly and indirectly. Harold Taylor once classified educational philosophies as rational, exemplified by some Roman Catholic institutions and possibly by St. John's College; neohumanist, a position favored by the majority of liberal arts colleges; and instrumentalist, suggested by the General College of the University of Minnesota, Sarah Lawrence College, and certainly by Goddard College. One must believe that an institution seeking to place Dewey's pragmatism into educational effect must have an impact on students different from one which seeks to make manifest the postulational truths of medieval Scholastics. Again, one feels that a liturgical campus, stressing daily mass and surrounding students with visual representation of religious faith, leaves an educational imprint that contrasts with that left by an institution in which even prayer at ceremonials is eliminated. And a college stressing a vigorously specified set of standards of personal conduct is surely a different sort of place than one which has from its inception allowed students adult latitude in setting personal dimensions to their conduct.

Although the evidence about the effectiveness of college faculty can at times shake professorial egos (in one study, teachers were not even mentioned by students in response to an open-ended query about educational influences), nonetheless, feeling and logic suggest that kind and quality of faculty are somehow involved. Faculty members who place institutional loyalty above disciplinary loyalty could be expected to feel one way about students, while their colleagues whose satisfactions come chiefly from national professional recognition certainly feel another.

Similarly, administrative structure and professional-administrative-social structure may be involved in the educational outcomes an institution typically achieves. If the president, vice-president, and deans are preoccupied with off-campus relations, fund raising, and the details of managing a complex establishment, such a place differs from one where the president's door is always open to faculty and students. The fact that a president lives on campus and opens the door of his home to students or faculty several times each week says one important thing. A president who lives in a different part of a large city away from his campus and who each night joins the commuting rush says something else. A campus that is pervaded by a sense of community, where central administration, clerical and grounds workers, faculty and students are on first name basis, should contrast with an institution where friendships and social life are organized hierarchically.

Since college students experience a range of problems, from routine academic ones to those of a deeply disturbing personal nature, one would also assume that colleges which differ from one another in how they help students solve problems should differ in their impact. Stephens College insists that each student see her adviser at least six times during the academic year. At Sarah Lawrence each student will see her don at least once a week. In contrast, there are other colleges in which advising is limited to registration time and the dean of students handles counseling cases in his spare time. Or, just as colleges differ from one another in staffing residence halls, so should they differ in influencing student attainment of educational outcomes. The college that views most student problems as being rooted in theological concerns and issues obviously approaches the resolution of them differently from the college whose large counseling staff is oriented in the psychoanalytical tradition. Presumably such differences will be reflected in how and what learning takes place.

On the basis of admissions policies, institutions can currently be classified as open-door, selective, very selective, or highly selective. Further, they can be classified as community, regional, state, or national in their appeal to students. Or, obviously, they could be described as nominally integrated, deliberately integrated, or essentially segregated with respect to race, religious involvement, or even social status. Whatever the bias in admissions policy is, one must assume it will affect the learning environment.

To these, other considerations might be added. The City College of New York or New York University, simply by their locations and access to a metropolitan culture, is different than Hiram College or Stanford. The relative affluence of institutions has long been considered important by such agencies as the regional accrediting associations. Funds limit, if not determine, the richness of program which, in turn, is supposed to condition learning. The physical plant of the college may also be operative in learning, and certainly the curricular and extracurricular emphases of colleges ought to make some differences. One has the feeling, for example, that the particular course structure of the College of the University of Chicago during the 1930's and 1940's made that student body different from students in colleges still stressing the free elective system. Although overseas experiences have been variously evaluated, their very existence testifies to a belief that somehow experiencing a different culture is important for some students. A campus sponsoring an elaborate program of cultural events—lectures, concerts, plays, art displays, and artists, and writers in residence—may condition learning differently from a Spartan campus on which the weekly grind of course work is relieved only by the week-end flight from campus. Or a college which assigns no grades to freshmen ought, one theorizes, to affect performance differently from the institution that uses first-semester grades to accomplish a difficult screening task.

These are all *surmises*, however. In order to evaluate such theories or practices, more verifiable information is needed. While no comprehensive body of research exists to explain how institutional factors affect the learning climate, there *are* a number of discrete studies or speculations based on research whose results shed light on the problem.

Curriculum, Professors, Students, Administration, and Facilities

The visibility and even specific nomenclature of curricular programs seem to have some impact on student academic performance. Dressel and Mayhew, after studying test performance of students from nineteen colleges, suggested that the greatest gains in general education took place on campuses that (1) were residential, (2) clearly designated the general education program as a unique and separate part of the college, (3) assigned full-time faculty to teach general education courses as full-time duty, and (4) emphasized a reasonably elaborate, formal evaluation program. [1]

Whereas discreteness of various parts of an academic program appears to be related to the learning climate, the sheer size of the curriculum does not. Earl McGrath and his associates have studied strong, well-established, recognized liberal arts colleges and find an enormous variation in the number of courses offered by departments in different colleges. Yet, the number and range of course offerings appear unrelated to such factors as student enrollment, number of courses required for a major, satisfaction of department chairmen or deans with curricular effectiveness, or student achievement in graduate school. [2]

McGrath believes that curricula in liberal arts colleges could be kept relatively small and still be effective. Indeed, he believes that the undergraduate college may even become less effective if it insists on offering quite specialized courses that are more the province of the graduate school.

The outcomes of education implied by McGrath are roughly those which Stern lists under the heading "intellectual climate" in his studies of various college campuses. In a highly intellectual climate there is a strong motivation for academic achievement, considerable opportunity and desire for self-expression, and high achievement of academic awards such as subsequent graduate degrees and scholarships. Colleges which demonstrate this climate typically are small, residential, independent liberal arts colleges located in the Northeast or Midwest. But more important, a highly intellectual climate seems associated with factors that could be replicated in other types of institutions. Faculty members are personally committed to scholarly

---

[1] Paul L. Dressel and Lewis B. Mayhew, *General Education: Explorations in Evaluation* (Washington: American Council on Education, 1954).

[2] Earl J. McGrath, *Memo to a College Faculty Member* (New York: Bureau of Publications, Teachers College, Columbia University, 1961).

activity and communicate to students an enthusiasm for a subject. They define high standards of performance and provide students with ego support to achieve them. They serve as critics and judges of student mental effort but are more concerned with person than with regulation. These effective colleges also reflect a permissive atmosphere regarding student conduct, an absence of a detailed and rigorously administered code of student behavior, and an absence of suspicion of students on the part of the faculty. The physical plant offers students places to withdraw in privacy, yet provides uncomplicated access to faculty so that interaction may take place informally. And the characteristics of the student body are unique. Even as freshmen, students at these effective institutions demonstrate superior intelligence, breadth of interest, high motivation, and a spirited independence.[3]

This environment, which leads to a refined intellectual climate, possesses many dimensions. The organization of the curriculum of the freshman year seems especially critical. "The first year, indeed the first months, can be a revelation, a grim disillusionment, or just another routine stage to be endured. Some students [speak] of how imagination was kindled at the very beginning—and how that made all the difference. A good many look back on that year with distaste and resentment."[4] Those colleges in which the freshman year is rewarding to students have made a deliberate effort to make the freshman year important. Devices vary from the Harvard Freshman Seminars to the Hofstra course, An Introduction to Science and the Humanities, to the social science sequence at Montieth, to programs designed for the gifted. The important element is that the unique needs of freshmen are recognized.

Another dimension is the size of institution or, rather, the size of the unit within which students function. It appears that only in the context of smallness do students have a true opportunity to establish the relationships with teachers that they believe to be important.[5] Students who are becoming educated do not like or accept the experience of being ignored by teachers. This does not mean they want to associate on terms of complete equality. There is always a distance between the adult teacher and the almost-adult student. But they do want and value working with a professor on an intellectual prob-

---

[3] George S. Stern, "Student Ecology and the College Environment," *Journal of Medical Education*, March 1965.
[4] Esther Raushenbush, *The Student and His Studies* (Middletown, Conn.: Wesleyan University Press, 1964), p. 152.
[5] *Ibid.*, p. 129.

lem to which each can devote himself. Teachers who have a passionate commitment to a subject and to life and who can communicate this to students are the ones students value most. Students quickly distinguish between an impersonal teacher who cares that his students become engaged in their work and the one whose impersonality cuts off communication. What students want and value most are teachers ". . . who not only [give] them knowledge but who [share] the experience of knowledge, who [communicate] their own intellectual vitality, their conviction of the worth of ideas, and the importance of feeling the sense of life." [6]

But students themselves serve as an additional institutional factor contributing to educational outcomes. John Bushnell, drawing on the Vassar studies, makes explicit the significance of the student culture and some of the mechanisms through which it operates. [7] A student body possesses characteristic qualities of personality, modes of interaction, and systems of belief which are passed on from one student generation to the next. This culture is a prime educational force for assimilation into the student society and is a prime concern of new students. This does not mean students are uninterested in the curriculum—for the most part they are dutiful, hard working, and ready to accept the value the college places on courses.

> However, except for a minority, the fundamental philosophy of the College and its academic and intellectual aims do not enter primarily into the formation of the central values and habits of life of the student body, [8]
>
> .   .   .   .
>
> . . . student bodies in our colleges and universities function in a fashion which bears an intriguing similarity to the group behavior of an American colony located in a foreign capital. I call this parallel the "market place analogy" and, while it may have mildly humorous overtones, I think it does underscore one of the basic problems besetting our institutions of higher learning. The U.S. tourist who arrives in a foreign country has, putting it broadly, two directions in which he can go. He can accept the canons of the local enclave of Americans—eat American food, wear American fashions, drink American cocktails—or he can go native to an extent, that is, interact with the urban and rural population, set about to learn the language and to familiarize himself with indigenous customs, dress,

---

[6] *Ibid.*, p. 136.
[7] John Bushnell, "Student Values: A Summary of Research and Future Problems," in *The Larger Learning*, by Marjorie Carpenter (Dubuque, Iowa: W. C. Brown & Co., 1960).
[8] *Ibid.*, p. 56.

food, and the like; try to cull what, for him, is best in the "new" way of life which he now sees on all sides. However, "going native," or even an approximation thereof, is generally frowned upon by the colony membership as something which is antithetical to their identity as Americans. One cannot, at one and the same time, immerse oneself deeply in the foreign experience and maintain active ties with the American colony.[9]

This phenomenon operates not only in liberal arts colleges but also in professional and graduate schools as well. Medical students, for example, quickly form a society which has a culture discrete from that being offered by the faculty. Medical students decide what is important to study. They decide what short cuts are possible and what ideas the faculty have which are worth accepting.[10]

Although there is a tendency currently to minimize the educational significance of college presidents and to consider them merely mediators and fund-raisers, some still consider them to be influential. Dana Farnsworth is one who believes that the president is the single most important influence in building a helpful environment to stimulate student responsibility. A good president is one who thinks first of student welfare, who treats students with fairness and who considers them as individuals. When faced with student behavior having possible public relations implications, such a president would likely take the point of view not to worry about the institution's reputation but rather be concerned about what is best for an individual student. This kind of president would entrust considerable authority to students and would maintain informal contacts so as to know how such authority was being used. A president who is inconsistent in decisions, who responds unwisely to pressures from parents, alumni, or publishers, who interferes with the decisions of subordinates, who is afraid of students, and who keeps to himself will inhibit the development of students.[11] And one can assume that the same general point of view can be applied to other administrators. Deans, department heads, and the like can, by the conduct of their offices, determine the institution's learning environment.

Until recently an overlooked strand of institutional influence was the campus itself and the buildings and space which it comprises.

[9] *Ibid.*, p. 58.
[10] E. C. Hughes, H. S. Becker, and B. Geer, "Student Culture and Academic Effort," in *The American College*, ed. Nevitt Sanford (New York: John Wiley & Sons, 1962).
[11] Dana L. Farnsworth, "Who Really Helps Our Students," *Personality Factors on the College Campus* (Austin: University of Texas, 1962).

Gradually, however, has come an awareness of the idea of Neutra that "The Shapes on a Campus Are Not Extracurricular." [12] He and the faculty of St. John's College in Maryland thought deeply about the modes and purposes of education at that institution. They finally decided that there were two ways of advancing wisdom. One was through dialectic and the other through observation. To accommodate both, he designed a lecture hall and discussion room to reflect the central purpose of that college, and to each laboratory he attached a seminar room to symbolize dialectic and observation. In doing so he was trying to show that the shapes of campus architecture "mean a soul impact on the young people who go here to learn and on the older people who here go through their lives to teach." Harold Gores makes the same point with his remark that "a college is people, ideas, and a place—and in that order. A college aspiring to completeness in all things will somehow find a way to cast up a physical environment that supports and sustains its mission." [13]

Actually, the buildings of a campus tell much of the essential spirit of the institution. Architects shown unnamed photographs of brick buildings at the University of Missouri, Christian College, and Stephens College were able to separate them simply on the basis of knowing the educational philosophy of each.

The single factors of curriculum, professors, students, administration, and facilities do not operate in isolation. Increasingly it is clear that satisfaction or success of a college experience is a resultant of the interaction process between students and the total college environment. Students act on the environment and the environment acts on students and each is affected by the reaction of the other. One can observe this by focusing on students who seek to satisfy certain needs through manipulation of the environment, with satisfaction being fulfillment of those needs. Or, one can observe the same phenomenon by focusing on the environment which poses requirements to which students must adjust. Satisfaction here would be the measure of fit— of how successful students are in meeting the requirements. [14]

From such a conception it is possible to study the degree of student satisfaction as one measure of institutional influence on learning.

[12] Richard B. Neutra in *Current Issues in Higher Education, 1957*, ed. G. Kerry Smith (Washington: Association for Higher Education, N.E.A., 1957), pp. 24–30.

[13] Harold B. Gores, "Bricks and Mortarboards" in *Current Issues in Higher Education, 1963*, ed. G. Kerry Smith (Washington: Association for Higher Education, N.E.A., 1963), p. 38.

[14] Bryant M. Wedge (ed.), *Psychosocial Problems of College Men* (New Haven, Conn.: Yale University Press, 1958).

A study from one institution cannot be generalized to apply to all, but it may suggest leads or hunches of relevance. Four classes at Yale were each asked to fill out a questionnaire during the spring of their senior year. The responses from each class proved to be highly consistent. For the majority of students, the senior year was most enjoyable and the freshman year least so. Junior and senior years were most rewarding, and freshmen and sophomore years least so. The elements of the Yale experience which contributed most to enjoyment of each class, arranged in rank order, were roommates and friends, social activities, junior and senior departmental courses, extracurricular activities, other junior and senior courses, athletics and sports and courses taken during the freshman and sophomore years. The listing of the same factors ranked according to student development revealed a similar ordering but with a few differences. Junior and senior departmental courses led, followed by roommates and friends, other junior and senior courses, social activities, extracurricular activities, courses taken during the freshman and sophomore years, and athletics and sports. When asked about improvements they would like to see at Yale, each class seemed to want more personal contact with faculty, more personal direction in courses and studies, and fewer lectures and more discussions.[15]

Interaction of Student Subcultures and Institutional Objectives

How the student and the collegiate environment interact is still unknown in any precise detail, but current research and theory are beginning to suggest some of the ways. It now seems possible to identify at least four student subcultures, each of which is affected differently by the various other elements of a particular institution. The collegiate culture, which emphasizes fraternities, sororities, social life, football, and campus fun, is not hostile to the college. Indeed it may generate strong loyalties to it. Rather it is resistant to serious academic demands from the faculty. Then there is the vocational subculture that flourishes on many urban campuses. This is a world in which students—many of whom are married—work part time and take courses leading to a degree which will mean a better job. Students have little attachment to the college and also are resistant to the intellectual demands the college might make unless these appear

[15] *Ibid.*, pp. 19–30.

to contribute directly to attainment of the vocational goal. A third subculture is the academic one and is composed of serious students who have accepted the intellectual values of the faculty. Members of this group work hard, earn good grades, talk about their course work, and manifest a strong emotional tie to the institution through identification with the faculty. Products typically aim at graduate and professional school. And lastly can be found the nonconformist subculture. Members are often deeply involved with ideas but use off-campus groups and currents of thought as points of reference. They demonstrate a rather aggressive nonconformism and maintain a critical detachment from the college. This subculture offers to rebellious youth a temporary but genuine alternative, which must reject the other three subcultures.[16]

The collegiate environment interacts with each of these subcultures and affects members along several dimensions. Perhaps the most significant of these dimensions is the institutional ethos, which is derived from present and historical purpose, distinctiveness of character, the interests and orientation of faculty, and administrative concerns and interests. Single-purpose liberal arts colleges have generally been the locale for the collegiate and academic subculture, while tax-supported colleges and universities serving cities or states have encouraged the vocational subculture and tolerated the other three through curricular offerings which would allow members to survive. For example, the curriculum in a large urban institution will consist of a large number of vocational courses but enough liberal arts courses so that a college-oriented student can stay in school. A college which has developed a distinctive character, as has Reed College, will tend to be supportive of the subculture most consistent with that character. One cannot visualize a strong collegiate, nonconformist, or academic subculture on the campus of Pace College, to which students go to receive the specialized training needed for work in the New York financial offices. And, of course, faculty interests are important. One can visualize a range of faculty, from those who are locally oriented and who see their chief role as helping students, through to a cosmopolitan faculty whose chief interests are off campus. With a predominantly local faculty, student subcultures blend and come to be one with the total institutional culture, while cosmopolitan faculty tend to allow student subcultures to develop

[16] Burton R. Clark and Martin Trow, "Determinants of College Student Subculture" (Unpublished MS; Center for the Study of Higher Education, University of California, Berkeley).

and exist independently. Until recently, college administrations have generally tended to favor and to encourage collegiate subcultures over others as being more predictable, routine, and acceptable to important constituencies. A collegiate student government, for example, is not nearly so dangerous as would be the urge of an academic or nonconformist group to assume some measure of student responsibility. Big-time athletics—an important part of the collegiate way of life—has typically received administrative support as being a safety valve for student emotions and a way of marshaling powerful alumni support.

But factors other than ethos are also operative. The authority structure through the support of values and interests does much to determine which student subcultures will flourish. Four-year state colleges are likely to be characterized by strong presidential authority exerted in favor of vocationalism. Private liberal arts colleges having strong academic subcultures are likely to manifest strong faculty control. But in the large universities with a marked bifurcation of faculty and student interest, little or no relationship between control and institutional style exists. In some universities, faculty power predominates and in others presidential or board influence is greater. A second dimension of the authority structure is student involvement. Colleges having a strong academic subculture are likely to have a strong student government, while colleges of strong student vocationalism appear generally at the other extreme.

Then, size and complexity, requirements for admission, and the relative autonomy of the institution also contribute to various student subcultures. Large institutions which have not deliberately broken students into smaller groups, as has Harvard through its houses, seem most supportive of vocational subcultures. Highly selective admissions policies will be inclined, although not absolutely so, to support the dominance of academic subcultures. While there are some notable exceptions, colleges that seem to merge with the larger society and whose students commute are likely to support a vocational subculture, to tolerate nonconformist groups, but to discourage collegiate or academic groups. It is in the autonomous, residential college, located somewhat away from other social influences, that one finds the climate most sympathetic to an academic ethos.[17]

The presence or absence of any of these subcultures on a given campus suggests a chicken-and-egg sort of dilemma. Do the student-composed elements in the learning environment become that way

[17] *Ibid.*

because of other factors in the institution, or are they that way before college? Is Darley correct in his remark that, "Without cynicism, one might state that the merit of certain institutions lies less in what they do to students than it does in the students to whom it does it." [18] The evidence on such questions is mixed, but the tendency seems to support the belief that differential productivity of different institutions is determined by concentration of different types of students. Dressel and Mayhew [19] found that experiments involving highly authoritarian and highly nonauthoritarian students could not be conducted on some campuses because authoritarian students tended either not to attend or to leave early in the freshman year. Holland compared National Merit Scholarship winners and near-winners who attended high- and low-productivity colleges and found differences in academic motivation and differences in parental values placed on study. [20] More recently the Center for the Study of Higher Education at the University of California, Berkeley, has studied the colleges selected by scholarship winners and near-winners with substantially the same results. "In general . . . it was concluded that high ability students attending highly productive institutions have a pattern of traits, values and attitudes which is more closely related to serious intellectual pursuits than do high-ability students attending less productive institutions." [21]

If such elements of the college do affect the learning environment, it then becomes necessary to discover how they interact and what the dynamics actually are. Currently, one can only speculate, but the experiences of some institutions do provide limited bases for speculation.

One has the impression that certain of the colleges roughly describable as experimental have had a peculiar and lasting impact on the lives of students. Colleges such as Bennington, Bard, Goddard, Sarah Lawrence, Reed, Stephens, and Antioch are among those identified by Jacob, Eddy, Stern, and Newcomb as being influential. It is possible to reason that the one thing all of these institutions possess in common is that each operates from a consistent and pervasive

[18] J. G. Darley, "Diversification in American Higher Education" (Lawrence, Kan.: National Association of Student Personnel Administrators, 1956), pp. 45–66.

[19] *General Education: Explorations in Evaluation.*

[20] J. L. Holland, "Determinants of College Choice," *College and University,* Fall 1959.

[21] Paul Heist, T. R. McConnell, Frank Matsler, and Phoebe Williams, "Personality and Scholarship" (Unpublished MS; Center for the Study of Higher Education, University of California, Berkeley).

educational philosophy. The existence of considerable personal freedom for students, a sense of community, emphasis and respect accorded the performing arts, a fusion of academic and off-campus or
work experience, a preoccupation with individual and small-group
problem solving, and a concern with the personality or character
outcomes of education all appear to be manifestations of a definite
educational point of view. Someone has remarked that these colleges
seem to represent the intellectual confluence of Dewey's educational
point of view and Freudian psychology. But whether this particular
judgment is warranted, a progressivism does seem to operate and do
so effectively. David Boroff sensed this in his remark that "Colleges,
then, have been catching up with Sarah Lawrence, but the latter—
along with Antioch, Bennington, Reed, and a few others—is still way
ahead of the academic procession." [22]

Role Models and Small Groupings

One also has the feeling that the existence of appropriate role
models with whom students can identify is involved in the influence
or lack of influence the collegiate environment seems to have. The
point is made negatively by the lament of the University of California students that the sheer size of the institution denies them the
chance to relate to and identify with mature, professional adults.
Only when the faculty and students made common cause in December 1964 did students feel they belonged. Or, the point can be made
positively through David Riesman's analysis of the effectiveness of
certain Midwestern liberal arts colleges in producing scholars, Ph.D's,
and college teachers. Young people, from relatively unsophisticated
homes in small Midwestern towns, farms, and villages viewed their
college professors as urbane, indeed glamourous figures who represented a life style worthy of emulation. The same phenomenon did
not operate in institutions attracting wealthier students from homes
in the urban East. To these students, men in business, finance, law,
and medicine seemed worthier models. Undoubtedly this condition is
changing, but the dynamics underlying it continue viable. An institution which faces young women with a faculty of older and somewhat disillusioned female teachers attuned to standards prevailing in
an earlier era denies itself the potent educational tool of possible
student identification with faculty. Similarly an institution which encourages its senior faculty to be off campus more than it is on and

[22] David Boroff, *Campus U.S.A.* (New York: Harper & Bros., 1958), p. 161.

which presents students with young instructors or graduate students may also be jeopardizing one strand in its learning environment.

This phenomenon of identification may also be involved in another sort of influence which comes from grouping students, for academic purposes, into units small enough to allow intimacy to develop. Stephens College has developed its House Plan in which 100 students and five faculty pursue a common curriculum while living or having their offices in a single residence hall. Raymond College of the University of the Pacific lodges 250 students in a single complex and provides them with a full-time faculty. The College of Basic Studies of Boston University organizes its student body into groups of 100 students and assigns eight faculty members to guide the students through a two-year prescribed curriculum. And New College of Hofstra University is based on a similar scheme. Each of the efforts has resulted in greater learning, greater longevity in college, more expressed satisfaction with the collegiate experience, and more marked changes in measured values than exhibited in other parts of the same institution. Paul Dressel made the same point when, after studying a number of liberal arts colleges, he remarked that the best liberal education was being provided by a small school of journalism of a large private university. The school was located on the edge of the campus where the small faculty and student body worked at studies in which each had an intense personal and professional interest.

Perhaps one reason these small groupings of students and faculty have been effective is that the total environment is small enough to be operative on each student. Regardless of how many Nobel prize winners a campus boasts, of how many lectures or concerts come to the campus, of how rich are the library holdings, of how many courses are in the college catalogue, they are not educationally effective unless students interact with them. Perhaps there exists a point of diminishing returns beyond which size, variety, and frequency of activities, events, and academic opportunities simply become confusing stimuli to which students cease to respond. Or, perhaps the timing of activities is such that the attraction of other, less intellectual matters is compelling. For example, a commuting college which schedules most of its cultural events in the evening hours very likely deprives those elements of the environment of any lasting educational significance. Or, a large university which spreads its residence halls on the far edges of the campus but concentrates its art displays, library, and offices of counselors and major professors on the central campus may cut most students off from an operative environment.

The Reward System

Then, the prevailing reward system on a college or university campus must be considered as a major influence. Whether faculty members like it or not, students are highly motivated to obtain passing grades. Students seemingly will learn whatever is necessary to get the grades they want. "If teachers base their grades on memorization of details, students will memorize the text. If students believe grades are based upon their ability to integrate and apply principles, they will try to acquire such ability." [23] The power of such motivation can, of course, have favorable or unfavorable effects. Recent evidence suggests that at least half of all college students have engaged in some form of academic dishonesty. Although, typically, students believe cheating to be morally wrong, nonetheless some engage in it in response to the pressures or motivation of the academic system. Those who have difficulty adjusting to the role of students, as evidenced by poor study habits and low grades, are more likely to cheat than are good students. [24]

The reward system may, of course, possess other dimensions. At one graduate school of education, students believe that the only acceptable form of doctoral research is statistical and experimental in nature. Despite disclaimers of the faculty, students believe that the central power figures are those preoccupied with research methodology; hence, they respond to the direction from which rewards flow. An institution which prides itself on the number of its graduates who enter the strongest graduate schools encourages student selection of courses most likely to ensure high grades and adequate preparation. A junior college which emphasizes the success of its transfer students encourages student preoccupation with the transferability of courses elected.

Attributes of Institutions of Higher Education

The elements of the collegiate environment, then, which seem to have special relevance for learning are the visibility, balance, and organization of the curriculum, the total college climate, the size of the unit within which learning takes place, the degree of personal interaction with some faculty, the student subculture and the various

[23] W. J. McKeachie, "Research on Teaching at the College and University Level," in *Handbook of Research on Teaching*, by N. L. Gage (Chicago: Rand McNally & Co., 1963), p. 1119.

[24] William J. Bowers, "Student Dishonesty and Its Control in College," *Educational Digest*, April 5, 1965.

subgroupings within it, the administrative point of view, the campus itself, the interaction on the campus, the self-selection which creates a given student body, the prevailing educational philosophy or lack of it, the presence or absence of role models, the blending of learning and living, the operative environment, and the reward system. It becomes relevant to discover whether these can be so juxtaposed as to have validity for the many different sorts of institutions which American higher education comprises.

In one sense such an effort might be judged to be fruitless. One of the glories of American higher education is its diversity. Thus, there are liberal arts colleges, teachers colleges, state colleges, state universities, private universities, junior colleges, and a variety of technical and professional institutions. There are secular and religious colleges, large ones and small ones, single and multipurpose institutions, and institutions whose faculties represent the full spectrum of philosophic position. Yet, in another sense, all of these institutions are seeking to do approximately the same thing. Only the techniques and approaches seem to be different. One might assume, or at least hope, that all institutions of higher education might seek several attributes, each of which implies transcendent educational objectives.

First among the attributes is a climate in which ideas are believed to be important in and of themselves. Obviously, ideas which will lead to action of some sort are not to be discouraged. A university is an instrument of society which trains people in the skills of a vocation, of citizenship, and of the arts of successful living as determined by that society. The university will, of course, assume that many ideas are of worth simply because of their relevance for their practical purposes. However, a university should also foster another attitude toward ideas. It should be a place where the abstract refinement of a concept is accepted to be of as great worth as building a house or auditing a set of books. Further, the university should possess a tone in which students and faculty feel a desire to invent, explore, and discuss ideas. Nor should the source of ideas be primarily verbal. Ideas first expressed in sound, color, or in line are to be valued as well as those exposed through verbal or quantitative symbols. In addition, ideas need not all be of "high seriousness." The campus should not make people ashamed of the pursuit of the light and fanciful any more than it should discourage pondering of questions on the nature of man and of the significance of justice. The notions from a Steinberg cartoon may have as appropriate a place in the collegiate environment as the massive interpretations of God by a Buber or a Maritain.

Second, the campus should provide conditions and should sponsor a spirit in which leisure is enjoyed and respected. It is not the goal of a university to keep its students and faculty at assigned work all of the available time. For that matter, to attempt to do so would be foolishly impossible. Rather, the university should accept leisure as an essential in the lives of men and should provide ways for its creative use. One can contrast a desirable use of leisure with simple time-killing or with filling leisure hours with activities which anesthetize people to the reality of experience. The university would not reject television, nor consumption of food and drink, nor complete idleness. Indeed, these can each be used appropriately as leisure-time activities. It would, however, seek to have its students and faculty select wisely from the many leisure-time activities and enjoy them as complete and worthwhile experiences. This is a difficult concept to express and even more difficult to achieve. One can contrast the person who spends hours before the television screen simply to pass the time before some other scheduled activity and the one who watches a comedy hour because he enjoys humor. Similarly, the use of alcohol as a means of dulling one's response to reality can be contrasted with the consumption of beer because beer tastes good and doubly so when shared with someone else who also likes the flavor of the drink. Participation in sports simply to expend enough energy to allow one to sleep can be contrasted with participation in games for the sheer joy of feeling one's body respond to the challenges of the game.

Third, the university should create a climate in which academic work is viewed as of essential value rather than as a tedious means to some pragmatic end. Again the university does not reject its purpose to prepare its students to do the many things which they and society need. The university should help students keep in mind the need to become effective teachers, skilled draftsmen, or accurate accountants. However, if such ends are the chief motivating forces in the academic program, the university may be successful but will not be a great or a vibrant institution. In some way the sheer aesthetic pleasure of working a statistical problem or the complete personal involvement in preparing a research paper should be cultivated. Again this abstract perhaps can be clarified by examples. The course in Functional English which is generally regarded as chiefly a hurdle to overcome on the road to a degree or as preparation in skills needed in other courses would be less consistent with the ideal than the same course viewed as a tough, demanding but nevertheless pleasurable experience in itself. Perhaps "pleasure" is the wrong word. Courses may prove vexing to students, but if accomplishment of long, hard assignments is viewed as a worthy purpose, the ideal will have been in part realized.

Fourth, the university should be pervaded by a spirit which encourages people to accept the uncertainties of not knowing how things will come out. The spirit of the frontier, where there are many difficulties, where the possibility of failure always is present, and where the human emotions are always taxed, is the one which is sought. Human beings are always faced with uncertainties, which are never comfortable. They can respond by seeking to find some more clearly understood way, or they can develop a toughness of character which allows them to live with not knowing how the story will end. It is the latter, almost stoical ideal which should characterize the university. To make this concept more specific, the university should be a place in which students and faculty can see their most vital beliefs scrutinized and still not flinch. It should be a place in which change of vocational plans is regarded as simply one other uncertainty with which people must live. It should be a place in which theory can be pushed to the furthest limits of human comprehension without driving students to infantile compensations for the tension of not knowing. The university should be a place in which teacher or student can ask "Why?" until it forces the other to the basic presupposition upon which all belief rests.

Fifth, the university should be a place in which intellectual and creative effort is valued for itself. It should foster the belief that the artist should be more than tolerated—he should be encouraged to pursue his efforts even though the resultant abstractions seem to distort traditional concepts of beauty and even though his effort seems to profit no one, not even himself. It should encourage students to investigate the most esoteric subjects if those subjects seem to have genuine appeal for the student. In short, the university should encourage students to value the experience of creative effort and to value a similar quest by others. This, obviously, is no easy prescription. To accept the endless theorizing about personality structure when it has little relevance to how people seem actually to behave is difficult. To encourage a college sophomore to delve into religious questions which have perplexed centuries of theologians may seem a waste of time. To allow students to proceed down alleys the professor has already learned were blind calls for a high faith in creative effort. Yet all of these must obtain if the goal of a vigorously alive collegiate enterprise is to be even approximated.

Sixth, the university should be a place in which both cognition and affection are viewed as effective and valuable forces. It should not be preoccupied with conscious reason alone. It should accept and teach its students to respect feeling as a worthy means of human response as well as rationality. It should be possible—and judged as normal—for students and teachers to become angry with each other. It should accept as good the expressions of sheer joy which can come from a pleasant afternoon at a football game. It should accept the feelings of uncertainty with which students see basic religious beliefs challenged by the findings of science even when this involves tears. The university should be acceptant of emotional responses to modern poetry, whether those are of like or bitter dislike. However, it should also encourage its students to use reason and feeling as tests for their respective validities.

Last, the university should be a place which makes a significant difference in the lives of its members. Whether one likes or dislikes the particular outcomes of the institution is relatively unimportant in this regard. What is significant is that students and the community should be distinctively different simply because the university exists. By this we do not mean solely the increased purchasing power which a university education brings, nor the increase in numbers of persons from the region listed in *Who's Who in America*. We do not even mean that students should more uniformly accept the beliefs of their professors nor that the larger community should be a macrocosmic version of the university. We do mean that both students and the community should be more willing to consider ideation, to enjoy leisure, to accept academic effort, to encourage creativity, to communicate with each other more freely, and to accept the uncertainties of not knowing.

Guidelines for Creating an Environment Conducive to Learning

To achieve such an environment with the tested techniques and practices currently at the disposal of higher education would seem to require adherence to several principles.

1. The curriculum, the extracurriculum, the direct contacts with students, and the interaction with faculty should all be on sufficiently limited scale that the educational impact can be realized. Whether the device be a house plan, a cluster, college, a team arrangement of teachers and students, or emphasis on the social cohesiveness of major professors and their students, it appears necessary to keep groups relatively small and to allow them to work on things which are of real significance to them.

2. Further, although pluralism is an essential in American society and in its supporting institutions, there does seem need for an ethos, philosophy, or theory which can assign meaning and establish priorities to the educational activities a college or university conducts. It is out of such a back-drop of philosophy that the total institutional climate, which seems so potent in attracting students and in modifying them, can derive. This is to argue that an institution which manifests a prevailing philosophy, whether it be Roman Catholic, military, instrumentalist, or service to agriculture, is likely to be a more effective agent than an institution which reflects, as an institution, all points of view. Since a unifying force seems central, one other matter should be clarified. An institution may reflect a common philosophy in its educational practices, yet welcome a variety of personal viewpoints on the part of its students and faculty.

3. The institution should make clear and explicit the expectations it holds for its students. Simply the act of designating a general education program as a unique requirement seems to make it more effective than a collection of similar but undesignated courses. The fact that institutions have recently made public the profiles of their student bodies and are increasingly suggesting the criteria by which students are selected helps fashion the learning environment. Similarly, the attitudes and behavior of administration seem to be effective and probably should be made even clearer. Students, one must suppose, like to know the rules of the game. Once they are known, students probably adhere to them if they are not too far-fetched in the light of their own understanding of society.

4. Last, an institution should recognize the existence of several student subcultures even on a campus on which one seems to predominate. From what little is known, it seems evident that each of these groups searches for, and to a certain extent finds, educational values consistent with its own orientation. Unless an institution wishes to place itself in the difficult-to-defend position of drifting toward a homogeneous student body, it should provide all such groups with activities and outlets which can be harmonized with the main educational thrust. The existence of an articulate nonconformist or bohemian subculture can be a threat to institutional stability or it can enrich the entire institutional fabric.

PART 4   College
          Students,
          Freedom,
          and
          the Law

Rights and Responsibilities in the Student-College Relationship

CHARLES FRANKEL

A YEAR OR SO AGO, the dean of one of the best-known liberal arts colleges for men made a speech to alumni in which he tried to explain why students behave as they do. It was a sensible and sensitive explanation. Students, he pointed out, are going through a period in their lives of intellectual challenge and a physical and emotional change. The world in which they find themselves is not the world in which they grew up; nor is it the world, they suspect, that exists outside the college walls. Under the circumstances, they cannot help but have basic feelings of uncertainty and insecurity. Many of them, therefore, engage in moral or political experiments which may seem capricious to members of other generations, but which have to be understood and borne. They are efforts by the students to find their way, and to show the world that they are full-fledged individuals with minds of their own. And it is helpful to students, the dean went on to suggest, to know that in their college, despite everything, rules are rules and regulations are regulations. This gives them a sense of safety in an otherwise bewildering world.

A week or two later, the undergraduate humor magazine in the same college appeared. It contained a speech allegedly delivered by a student leader to other students, explaining why deans behave as they do. Deans, the speaker pointed out, are going through a period in their lives of intellectual challenge and of physical and emotional change. The world in which they find themselves is not the world in which they grew up; nor is it the world, they suspect, that exists outside the college walls. Under the circumstances, they cannot help but have basic feelings of uncertainty and insecurity. Many of them, therefore, engage in moral or political experiments which may seem capricious to members of other generations, but which have to be understood and borne. They are efforts by deans to find their way, and to show the world that they are full-fledged individuals with

232

minds of their own. And it is helpful to deans, the student suggested, to know that in their college, despite everything, rules are rules and regulations are regulations. This gives them a sense of safety in an otherwise bewildering world.

I hope this story will suggest the spirit in which I think it is wise to approach the subject of this paper. It reminds us, if we need to be reminded, that students are often too smart for our good. It supports a hypothesis, long entertained by professors, that there would be no problem at all in running a college if only students and deans would go away. And it suggests two fairly obvious but easily forgotten facts. The first is that administrators, teachers, and students, despite the tribal prejudices that exist in each group, in fact share certain common human traits and troubles. The second is that they occupy a common environment in which each places limits on what the others can get away with.

The subject of this paper is the rights and responsibilities that should properly be assigned to undergraduate students in American colleges, and the cognate rights and responsibilities of faculties and administrations with regard to these students. It is a subject that has occasioned some jitteriness during the past year. Undoubtedly, the disorders that have upset many college campuses have usually been the work of small minorities. Many of these protests, furthermore, have been motivated by discontent with social conditions or governmental policies for which college faculties and administrations can hardly be held responsible, and have been inflated by the attention which the press and the other mass media have given them. But liberty, as Tocqueville observed, is perfected by civil disorders. The widespread concern which these protests have aroused suggests that they are symptoms of changes in American colleges, and in American society at large, that are important, that have been taking place for some time, and that call for a review and clarification of fundamental principles. For these changes have altered the relation of the college to society. They have transformed the character of the professor's work and his relation to the college. They have altered the administrator's role. And it is natural that they should also affect the relation of the college student to the educational process, and to the world he is preparing to enter.

It is against this background that the issue of student rights and responsibilities has emerged to trouble us and that it demands reconsideration. And the issue, it is equally important to see, is also embedded in certain persisting peculiarities of American colleges and the American scene. It has a distinctive cultural setting and institutional context. The few remarks about this setting and context which I propose to make will, of necessity, be brief remarks, and, perhaps, all too obvious. They may help us, however, to see our subject steadily and to see it whole.

The Cultural Setting

The relation between the generations in a modern society. In any modern society a certain measure of confusion and concern about the condition of the rising generation is bound to be one of the normal penalties of life. No community that is undergoing rapid change, and that offers its members any considerable range of choices, can expect to be free from a sense of distance and tension between the old, who remember what once existed, and the young, who live at the moving edge of change.

The educational function of the young. Colleges are places where this contest between the generations acquires a structured and formalized character. A college, of course, is not simply a place for conflict between the generations. It cannot function unless there is a fundamental spirit of cooperation and sympathy between teacher and student. Nevertheless, if one function of a college is to transmit to the young a cultural heritage that will allow them to see some continuity between their own situation and that of those who have gone before them, a second function of a college is to provide an environment in which students can react to this heritage, and, in reacting, help to make it fresh and relevant. We neglect a fundamental aspect of the higher educational process in modern society if we fail to see that students in college are testing their elders as well as themselves, and that, in the process of acquiring an education, they contribute to the re-education of their society. In discussing questions of student rights and responsibilities, it is essential to bear in mind that this re-education process is an important social value and that students are indispensable to it. We need students not only so that our intellectual heritage will endure. We need them if this heritage, and its carriers, the professors, are to be saved from stuffiness.

The American experiment in social authority. Although tension between the generations is inevitable in a modern society, American society has certain special characteristics that aggravate this tension. The country is populated by a large number of people who believe that it is every man's natural right to have children who are smarter and more successful than he. It should not be surprising that their children, responding to this expectation, are less than wholly deferential to their elders. American culture is engaged in a tricky experiment in social authority. By stressing change and progress to the extent that it does, it encourages the young to think that it is they rather than their elders who know the score, and it undermines the position of the parent or teacher who would assert his authority on a priori grounds. Whatever one's abstract views about the educational process, it is not easy, therefore, to maintain a system of rigid deference in an American college.

The "in-between" status of youth. The encounter between the generations that takes place in an American college has other curious features as well. In a modern society, "youth" may be culturally defined as the period between arrival at biological maturity and attainment of full status as an independent citizen. It has been characteristic of modern society, and particularly of American society, to extend the length of this waiting period further and further. A fundamental fact of life, setting the context for many of the problems that a college faces, is that it serves as a custodial institution for people in this difficult period of life. It provides a setting within which they rehearse for adulthood, taking on and putting off roles, trying themselves out, and, in general, experimenting under protected conditions with an assortment of ideas and commitments.

The activist orientation of American education. The student's impatience to grow up and to be engaged in the great causes of society has often been reinforced, furthermore, by the attitudes of many professors and administrators. Intellectuals in many countries have pleaded for a closer relation between the life of the mind and the life of action, but this plea has been particularly strong in the United States, where a student's indifference to the outside scene is likely to be taken, not as a sign of single-minded commitment to scholarship, but as a failure on the part of the college to do its educational job.

The extension of educational opportunity. A variety of new conditions has also arisen that affects the relationship of students to their collegiate experience. As a consequence of the expansion of most American colleges, impersonal administrative processes have become more prominent, teaching more mechanical and impersonal, and the physical arrangements for study, recreation, and dormitory life more crowded. Students, inevitably, have tended to feel themselves more and more in the presence of a "system" rather than a personal community. Although this state of affairs is one to which students on the European continent have long been accustomed, it collides with the kind of higher education which most Americans have been taught to regard as normal and desirable.

The college and a technical society. Students themselves have brought new attitudes to college which conflict with their desire for a personal form of education. They have come through a long series of competitive examinations. They are aware of the competition for admission to graduate and professional schools. They know that good jobs in industry are waiting for them, provided their college transcripts are presentable. All this has led many of them to take a more competitive and vocational approach to their education. Thus, the growing role of the university as a service station for industry and government is reflected in the orientation and motivations of students, as well as in the new tasks to which administrators and teachers are turning. This is one of the reasons, perhaps, the minority of students who do not want to play the game have adopted the fashionable slogan of "alienation," and are receptive to the doctrine that colleges and universities have become locked into "the establishment."

Civil rights, civil disobedience, and the politicization of the college. More immediate events in the outside world have also had repercussions on college campuses. The civil rights movement, which is inherently attractive to idealistic young people, has received moral endorsement from the leaders of most American colleges, and has provided a stimulant and outlet for student activism. And the technique of civil disobedience, which has gallantry and drama, has acquired a kind of extended legitimacy from its association with the civil rights movement. Many students have seen in it an escape from political powerlessness, a method of social action by which a committed minority can accomplish major changes. And more important than these attitudes, which are the attitudes of the more militant, is a change in atmosphere and tone that affects large sections of the student body. It was possible thirty years ago to think of a college or university campus as a retreat. The college and university campus today is obviously a part of the world, and at work for it. The dependence of society on the university system—the spread of the university's power in society—is now reflected in what colleges look like physically, in their pace and system of organization, and in the everyday activities of teachers and students. And it is in consequence of this, perhaps, that students themselves have raised with renewed urgency the question of their rights and responsibilities. If society depends for its survival on the world of learning, they are asking, should not learning be used to criticize and change society, and not only to pander to its needs, no matter what these needs may be? The social power of learning and of the college, an increasing number of students appear to be saying, should be used with moral and political purpose, and not merely sold to the highest bidder.

The Institutional Context

The conditions under which students, faculties, and administrations must determine the rights and responsibilities of students are also peculiarly complicated. The college is a meeting ground on which three powerful sets of social institutions converge—the family, the economy and polity, and the community of scholarship. And each of them imposes obligations on the college that are not always compatible with the obligations imposed by the others.

The family. The family of a student normally regards the college as its surrogate, responsible not only for the student's education, but for his or her physical and moral security. A large part of what the American college does is unintelligible unless we recognize that it serves, and is expected to serve, *in loco parentis*. Its religious and psychological counseling services, its fraternity and sorority system, its provision for dances and other social affairs, and its regulation of dormitory and extracurricular life are all, in whole or in part, aspects of this function. The demand that exists on most campuses for professors to provide something more than book-learning—to be mentors, personal advisers, and models of the good life—is also a reflection of the familial function of the American college. And because the college is an extension of the family, it is also expected that college administrations will place their own authority between their students and the authority of civil society. The college's obligation to the student, when approached from the family's point of view, is an obligation to an individual enjoying special protection; and, insofar as this protection is to be effective, the student cannot have all the rights of a free and unprotected adult.

The economy and the polity. If this were the college's only obligation, it would have no problem except the perennial one of inducing young people in their late teens and early twenties to accept parental authority. This, in itself, is becoming more difficult as a result of such changes in our national life as early marriages and eligibility for conscription at the age of eighteen. But it is further complicated by the fact that the college is not only an extension of the family, but of the economy and polity. It is an essential part of the process by which American citizens are recruited, trained, and tested for places in industry and government. Ticklish problems of academic ethics are the consequence. The college's obligation to the student, when approached from the familial point of view, is to his personal development and success. Its obligation, when approached from the community's point of view, is to train the student in socially needed skills and attitudes, and to report his qualifications or lack of qualifications honestly.

The learned community. Finally, the college is itself a distinctive social institution with its own objectives. It is devoted to the advancement and transmission of knowledge and of the traditions of responsible human discourse and criticism. So far as students are concerned, it exists to initiate them into this community of scholars, and to seduce at least some of them into becoming permanent members of it. Accordingly, its interests do not run entirely parallel to those of either the larger community or of the family. On one side, it must resist pressures from the larger society to tailor its offerings to the immediate, practical objectives of a specialized economy and system of government. On the other side, it must expose the student to the dangers of free inquiry, and take a chance on his resilience and maturity—a chance that a fair number of parents are not happy to take. Not less important, it must resist the impression, which many American students have and many of their parents have, that the college exists simply as an instrument for the student's self-discovery. It must find a way to communicate to him that learning has its own imperative standards and demands, and its own schedules and routines, and that these cannot be modified for reasons of personal self-expression or convenience. A central error in Paul Goodman's approach to "the community of scholars" is his confusion of the role of the college as a parent with its role as an institution of learning.

These remarks, which may be obvious, nevertheless have important consequences with regard to the question of student rights and reponsibilities. Learning is a hierarchical affair, as the elementary symbolism of "degrees" attests. It is not possible to make sense of the idea of learning unless the elementary truism is recognized that some people know more than other people, and ought, in consequence, to have more power with regard to the government of the affairs of the learned community. Accordingly, whatever rights the student may possess as a member of society, he cannot have the same authority in the classroom, or in the planning and conduct of his education, that is possessed by full-fledged members of the community of scholars.

A second characteristic of learning has equally significant implications for the question of student rights and responsibilities. Learning is not only hierarchical; it is an activity which requires a measure of disengagement, impartiality, and indifference to the immediate practical significance of the ideas or skills under examination. Learning, and a college devoted to learning, requires a protected environment in which individuals can concentrate on the business at hand, and in which other enterprises must be judged according to their bearing on the central intellectual business of the community. There should be a primary and omnipresent test of the activities that go on in colleges. Do these activities aid or impede free inquiry, disinterested criticism, and the acquisition of learning? Are they conducted in accordance with the rules of fair intellectual give-and-take that should prevail in a voluntary association of students and scholars?

The Formal Rights and Responsibilities of Students

Against this background, let us turn to an examination of the rights and responsibilities of students in their relation to the college. In doing so, we must make a fundamental distinction. There are formal rights and responsibilities in any community, large or small, which can be incorporated into the laws of the community and to which definite sanctions can be attached. But in most communities, and particularly in colleges, there are rights and responsibilities that cannot be formally legislated and enforced. They depend for their implementation on individual self-discipline. Let us first consider some of the formal rights and responsibilities that may reasonably be ascribed to students.

Academic freedom

Many confusions in the discussion of student rights and responsibilities have arisen from a failure to define the concept of academic freedom exactly. It is a puzzling concept partly in consequence of its historical origins. Academic freedom is a legacy from the German universities of the nineteenth century. In the circumstances in which it originated, it represented a special grant of freedom by a monarch to a limited group of his subjects. Professors were promised that they would remain free from external interference or coercion in the pursuit of their scholarly inquiries and in the discharge of their duties as teachers. Students, similarly, were granted *Lernfreiheit*. In its most important aspects, "academic freedom," in a word, was a grant to a selected few of a kind of freedom now possessed by all citizens of a liberal democracy. It was *academic* freedom because it was a freedom limited to academics, a peculiar freedom conceived to be necessary to professors and students if they were to perform their special social role.

The import of this concept is fundamentally changed when it is transported to an age and society in which citizens in general enjoy intellectual liberty. Under these circumstances, it is not because a professor has academic freedom, but because he has the same civil liberties any other citizen has, that he may inquire into any subject he wishes and announce the results of his inquiries without asking anyone's permission. And a student's right to ask questions, to protest against social conditions or government policies, or to associate with others to promote his legitimate interests are, similarly, civil liberties, and not special privileges.

Under these circumstances, what special meaning does the concept of academic freedom have? In the case of professors, where the situation is clearest, the concept has two principal elements. The first is suggested, though not entirely embraced, by the principle of academic tenure. All citizens in a liberal democracy have guarantees of freedom of speech and thought; but no citizen of a democracy, simply in his status as a citizen, is guaranteed access to the materials necessary to conduct inquiries, or to audiences through whom he can make his conclusions public. This, however, is precisely what a college or university undertakes to do with regard to a professor. Moreover, once he has attained tenure, it guarantees that, within the very broadest limits, these perquisites will not be taken away from him. The college or university, indeed, does more than this. By guaranteeing the professor financial security and established membership in an intellectual community, it throws its cloak around him, giving him a form of protection against the informal pressures and persecutions of the surrounding culture which ordinary citizens who ask the wrong questions or who talk out of turn are not likely to have.

The second element in the idea of academic freedom is the principle of academic self-government. Professors, in accordance with their own lights, determine who shall be a member of their club. They lay down the basic rules governing the granting of the degrees, licenses, and other marks of attainment which the academic community controls. They determine among themselves, and without outside interference, what shall be taught and what shall not be taught, what shall be regarded as within the corpus of warranted knowledge or significant opinion and what shall not be. "Academic freedom," in short, entails the recognition that scholarship is not simply an individual practice, but a social enterprise, and that this enterprise shall be controlled by an autonomous community which lays down its own laws for the conduct of its business.

Certain consequences follow from this conception of academic freedom. It is not the case, for example, that a college or university, in the name of academic freedom, has an obligation to present *all* ideas or points of view. It has no obligation, for example, to see to it that its department of economics contains representatives of every school of economic thought that exists in the larger community. The ideas or opinions represented in a collegiate program of education must be simply the ideas and points of view presented by persons who, in the judgment of their colleagues, are competent practitioners of their disciplines. The right of any opinion to be heard, which is a right outside the campus, does not apply to the classroom. And this is not because the college does not practice free inquiry. It is because free scholarly inquiry is inquiry controlled and governed by scholars in accordance with their own standards. The claim made by some students that they should be entitled to present, in the classroom, spokesmen for points of view opposed to those put forward by their professors cannot be sustained. It demands that the academic freedom of their teachers be abridged.

Do students have academic freedom?

There are two extreme views on this matter. One view is that students, once admitted to a college, possess academic freedom just as professors do. However, if what has been said about academic freedom is valid, this view cannot be sustained. Students cannot be granted tenure; and they cannot, without parodying the idea of learning, be given equal rights with their teachers to determine who shall be a member of the teaching staff or what shall be taught. They are not, in this sense, full citizens of the learned community.

Nevertheless, the reverse position—that academic freedom is exclusively a freedom for professors—also overstates the case. It is sometimes argued that grants of freedom to students—for example, to invite speakers of their choice to the campus—should be construed as matters of pedagogical policy rather than as the recognition of basic student rights. A faculty and administration, according to this view, may decide that granting students such a freedom is educationally desirable or administratively prudent. But it is under no fixed obligation to grant this freedom. This position is mistaken, I believe, for at least two reasons.

The first is that faculties and administrations are not unfailingly right, and students are not unfailingly wrong, about the ideas that should be put before students for their serious consideration. The right of students to present and to consider points of view of their own choice outside the classroom, and the right to do so as an intrinsic part of their collegiate experience, is a necessary condition for students' own free inquiries. The granting of this right cannot be construed as a matter of pedagogical policy, subject simply to the determination of the faculty. It is properly regarded as the recognition of a constitutional right of students, a right they require as a protection against pedagogical domination.[1]

The second reason the view is mistaken that students have no academic freedom in their own right is implicit in what has just been said. Students are part of the educational process, contributors to it and not merely beneficiaries of it. They do as much to educate one another as teachers do, and sometimes they educate teachers. The freedom of the academic community, therefore, rightly includes the freedom of students to continue inquiry and debate outside the classroom, and to examine both their teachers' views and alternatives to these views. The college has an obligation, insofar as its resources permit, to make its facilities available to students for such inquiries. In doing so, the college does not grant students a privilege. It responds to their legitimate claim, as members of an academic community, to contribute to its activities. The students' right to such facilities is limited only by reasonable requirements for the orderly maintenance of the college's primary educational program.

Another right illustrative of the special academic freedom of students is their right to be protected, as professors are protected, from the penalties that might otherwise fall on them in consequence of their free pursuit of an education. The educational process is basically compromised if students have reason to believe that the questions they ask or the opinions they express while in college will

---

[1] Obviously, special questions are raised with regard to this principle in the case of sectarian colleges committed to the propagation of definite creeds. Students who voluntarily attend such colleges accept special disciplines. They may regard limitations on their right to inquire as imprudent, but their complaints against such limitations cannot be be expressed as a demand for rights.

be held against them in later life. The college, as an extension of the economy and the polity, has a responsibility to provide government or industry with information about the student's qualities and capacities. As an educational institution, however, it must draw the line when it is asked to provide information about the content of the student's questions or opinions, or about his activities as a member of the college.

Due process and civil liberties

A fertile source of error in the discussion of student rights comes from the failure to remember that, whether or not it is right to say that students have special academic freedoms, they unquestionably have civil liberties. This means, to begin with, that as citizens, and not simply as students, they have the right to be treated with due process.

In the case of colleges and universities, the courts have increasingly taken the position recently that the admission of a student to a college is a form of contract and, as such, is subject to the requirements for fair dealing that surround all contracts. Setting legal issues aside, the reasons are overwhelming, it seems to me, for asserting the right of all college students to the protections of due process. The extension of due process to the relations of individual citizens with the private organizations to which they belong is one of the major characteristics of the contemporary movement of law in liberal societies. This extension of the idea of due process to the behavior of private governments realistically reflects the fact that the individual's destiny, in a modern society, is increasingly at the mercy of the organizations on which he depends. And this is true not only of the individual's relation to a corporation or a union, but to a college as well.

The regulations to which students are expected to conform should be known to them, therefore, and should not be subject to arbitrary interpretation or unmeasured sanctions. When students are being considered for disciplinary action, they should have the right to present evidence in their defense, and their cases should be considered with deliberation and in accordance with well-settled procedures. I do not believe, however, that it is necessary or desirable to copy mechanically all the characteristics of due process that belong to civil society. The primary function of the administration of discipline in an undergraduate college, and of the judicial processes that surround it, is educational, not punitive. Ideally, the relationship between the student and his judges should be personal, not impersonal;

and the deans or others who do the judging, as educators, require more room for discretion than officers of a court. If procedures such as an adversary system have any place at all, it is only in the very largest and most impersonal institutions.

Students, as citizens, are quite properly assigned other rights which all members of communities in a free society normally possess. These include the right to petition, to picket, and to organize associations to promote legally permitted interests. On the college campus, it also includes the right of students to affiliate with national student organizations, the right to choose their own leaders, subject only to such reasonable restrictions as acceptable academic standing, and the right to choose their own advisers from the faculty. These are not properly construed as privileges granted to students but as aspects of their rights as citizens. Colleges and universities are, among other things, systems of power and status. That the various interests present in them should be represented is a reasonable inference from democratic principles.

The most troublesome question that can be raised about this position has to do with the rights of students to use the campus as a place to take actions directed at conditions outside the campus. One may grant, it can be argued, that students have the right to meet and discuss such issues as civil rights or Viet Nam. It would be fruitless to try to prevent them from doing so in any case. But one need not grant, it may be said, that they have a right to use the facilities of an institution devoted to the pursuit of learning to organize and act for political causes extraneous to that institution's business. And their right to do so, it may be added, is all the more questionable since such activities are at least sometimes directed and guided by people outside the campus whose interest in using students has nothing to do with the advancement of their formal education. Particularly in the case of a private college, which controls its own territory, can a case not be made for the college's right to restrict students' political activities on the campus to purely intramural issues?

The practical considerations that lend weight to this position are fairly obvious. A college campus can come to resemble a carnival if even a small minority of students refuse to exercise self-discipline in the expression of their political views. The dignity, the concentration, the discipline, appropriate to a community engaged in study can be destroyed. And students who are naïve in the ways of the world can be exploited. Nevertheless, this position seems to me to fall down for both practical and theoretical reasons. It is impractical and imprudent, in most cases, to demand that students take their political activities to places where the college's authority does not extend. They will simply go across the street, and will have an extra slogan to put on their placards. And, in theory, this position is vulnerable so long as the college administration itself, as part of its regular activities, invites spokesmen for conventional political positions to the campus, or gives honorary degrees to public figures, or permits recruiting officers from corporations and government agencies on its premises. Moreover, rather a large number of nonpolitical activities permitted or encouraged by college administrations, from football rallies to fraternity house parties, also bring a certain carnival atmosphere to campuses. When the activities in which students are engaged are otherwise legal, their right to engage in them on the campus is appropriately recognized as part of their civil and political liberties. The question whether these activities are extramural or intramural in objective is not to the point.

However, the right of students to engage in such activities on the campus obviously stops at the point at which its exercise interferes with the right of other members of the scholarly community to pursue their regular educational, administrative, or ceremonial activities. I am also inclined to believe that special restrictions on the manner of exercising one's rights apply to a college campus which do not apply elsewhere. Picketing a professor's classroom to express disapproval of the views he expounds, for example, falls outside permissible bounds. A college is a community of students and scholars. Personal harassment, innuendo and insult, and physical pressure, explicit or implicit, have no place in it. And it is appropriate to demand that all the members of a scholarly community, in their relations to one another, conform to standards of good taste and decorum more stringent than those that can be imposed on the community at large.

Does the college's authority extend to the student's extramural activities?

Finally, the question may be raised about the college's authority with regard to the extramural activities of students. Generally established principles, I believe, apply to this problem. When the student's actions have been found by due process to be illegal, and when these acts involve moral turpitude on his part, the college has the right to take such action as it deems proper. The imposition of its authority over the student's extramural conduct under other conditions than these, however, constitutes an infringement of his rights. This is not to say that the college may not offer its counsel and advice. That is a matter to be left to its judgment—let us hope, its good judgment.[2]

The Informal Rights and Responsibilities of Students

There are no social codes that can be enforced exclusively by external formal sanctions. All require, if they are to be effective, individual self-discipline and judgment. This applies particularly to codes that reserve extensive areas of free choice and action to individuals, and it applies with greater force still to the codes of an academic community. More than formal student rights and responsibilities, it is the informal principles and understandings appropriate to conduct in a college that probably need re-examination and re-formulation. Formal sanctions cannot be attached to these principles and understandings. But no college can be governed effectively unless administrators, teachers, and students in general are aware that they exist, and generally abide by them.

The government of the college

The student is an apprentice in the academic community and does not have the credentials to justify his exercise of equal authority with the faculty or the administration in the government of that community's affairs. He is, furthermore, a member of a transient population, while his teachers, deans, and president presumably are not. The model of full political democracy, therefore, simply does not apply to the campus. Neither does the model of collective bargaining, for the relation between the student and those in charge of his education is not a bargaining relationship. From a purely formal point of view, all that can be said is that students have the right to bring their interests and opinions to the attention of the college.

But there is a profound difference between a situation in which students have a formal right to petition and protest, and one in which there are regular procedures for close and continuing consultation with them. An effort to draw a blueprint for student government applicable to all situations would be foolhardy. However, in their

[2] The differences between public and private institutions raise questions relevant to this entire analysis that I do not have space to explore. I believe, however, that the principles outlined above are basically applicable to both categories of institution, especially because the line between the two is becoming increasingly fuzzy.

capacity as educators, administrators and faculty members have an unmistakable, though not formally codifiable, responsibility to consult with students honestly and actively. Prudence as well as academic etiquette recommends this principle. Colleges and universities might not have experienced many of the difficulties which they have experienced during the last year if this principle had been more generally observed during the years preceding.[3]

Responsibilities of students in pressing their case

If we can assume the existence of a setting in which consultation is a regular and effective procedure, there are, it seems to me, reasonable restraints which students should impose on themselves in pressing their case. Articles in student journals, forums, debates, and discussions with teachers and administrators are techniques for promoting an idea or a cause that are appropriate to an academic community. They are consistent with the manner in which a community devoted to the life of the mind should conduct its business. Picketing, demonstrations, chanting, and similar actions are inappropriate unless these other alternatives are unavailable, or have been shown to be inadequate as techniques for getting an administration's or a faculty's attention. Students have a responsibility to bear these considerations in mind when they choose a method for presenting their case. They also have an obligation to distinguish between their right to have an administration or a faculty hear their case, and the right always to have that case approved.

The rights of students with regard to their teachers

The growing demands that are being made by students for closer and more personal relations to their teachers have been treated with a solemnity they do not entirely deserve. Some teachers are good teachers although they do not have close personal relations with their students; some are good precisely because they shun such relations. Some teachers, again, are at their best before large classes.

[3] I cannot help but add that closer and more constant consultation between administrations and faculties than now takes place in many institutions would also be desirable. Administrations today complain, with some justice, that professors are "discipline-oriented" rather than "institution-oriented." There are a number of reasons for this state of affairs, but one reason may be that many administrations do not invite faculties to play more than a peripheral role in the making of major institutional decisions. When faculties are treated as outsiders looking in, they are not likely to become institution-oriented.

And a reasonable number of teachers who are quite presentable members of college faculties are not people with whom I would wish my own children to have close, personal contact. The growing impersonality of our colleges has led to a kind of fetishistic adoration of the Mark Hopkins model of education. I do not believe that students themselves invariably wish this sort of relationship. A fair number of them are as reluctant to come close to professors as professors are to come close to them.

Moreover, it is not the case that "teaching" and "research" are, in actual practice, separable tests of a faculty member's competence. Unless senior professors adopt a policy of periodic visitation to the classrooms of younger faculty members, the evidence which is at their disposal for judging a younger man's competence as a teacher is often inadequate unless it is supplemented by other evidence attesting to his competence as an expositor and contributor to his discipline. Nor is the assumption warranted that "research" generally interferes with "teaching." It can; more generally, however, it means that the teacher may have something interesting or important to say in the classroom. Even when a professor's activities take him away from the campus frequently, this is not to be taken as a sign that his performance of his responsibilities as a teacher automatically suffers. He may bring excitement and greater worldly experience back to the classroom.

Having said all this, it remains the case that students in American colleges have a residual right to be taught by people who are paying attention to their task as teachers, and who are ready to regard this task as a central responsibility. Regrettably, it must be admitted that a large number of students are today being shortchanged. Professors who accept the protections and privileges of tenure or who want those protections and privileges surely have a personal moral responsibility to measure and balance their commitments to research and to teaching, and to undertake only those outside activities that are likely to enhance their capacities and performance as teachers and scholars. It should also be said that administrations have a responsibility to provide the salaries and amenities that would make it easier for teachers to concentrate on their tasks and to be aware of their students as individuals.

The government of residence halls and extracurricular activities

The responsibility of administrations to consult and the right of students to be consulted apply to the regulation of dormitory life and of nonpolitical extracurricular activities as well as to the government of the central educational activities of the college. There is, however, a controlling principle that should be taken for granted in such consultations. The college maintains residence halls and supports extracurricular activities because these are necessary or desirable for the accomplishment of its educational purposes. On the one hand, the college has an obligation to prohibit activities which interfere with these purposes. On the other hand, the regulations it adopts with regard to dormitory life and to extracurricular activities must be justified either because they contribute to these purposes or because the college may reasonably assert its authority *in loco parentis*.

Civil disobedience

No discussion of student rights and responsibilities would be complete at the present time if it omitted the question of civil disobedience, a question about which there is growing confusion. The attractiveness of this technique of social action to many students is great. Some clarification of the principles that may properly be thought to govern its use is desirable. There is room here only for a schematic statement. In the first place, many actions conventionally designated as cases of civil disobedience are not properly designated as such. They are actions taken to test the constitutionality of specific ordinances, and are taken in the belief that it is the ordinances that are illegal rather than the actions they prohibit. In the second place, it is axiomatic that genuine civil disobedience is not a civil liberty, and cannot be granted legal status. If and when it is justified, that justification must proceed by appeal to moral principles held to be above the law.

The conditions under which, in a democracy, such principles may be invoked with any claim to moral legitimacy are severely restricted. Specifically, five limitations apply. (1) The evil being opposed must be a grave and urgent evil. (2) Legal alternatives for combatting this evil have to have been tried and found wanting. (3) The acts that are undertaken must be nonviolent. (4) They must not be random in character, but must be *directly* related to the evil being combatted, and aimed at persons directly responsible for its perpetuation. (5) An act of civil disobedience must be a measured action, respectful of the general structure of law, and reasonably calculated to avoid undesirable consequences disproportionate to the desirability of the goals being sought. Otherwise, it moves toward the area of insurrection, which raises quite different moral issues. A defensible moral claim to engage in acts of civil disobedience therefore carries with it, normally, an obligation to submit, if only passively, to the processes of the law when they are invoked against one.

Given these severe limitations on the right to civil disobedience, it is difficult to imagine the circumstances under which it would be a morally justifiable method of action on most college campuses. One cannot lay down an ironclad rule that it will never be justified. But such actions as student sit-down protests intended to prevent R.O.T.C. parades, which have taken place on some campuses, have no standing in the area either of academic freedom or recognized civil liberties. And neither do they have standing as cases of morally justifiable civil disobedience.

The social obligations of students and teachers

A final word should be said about the obligations of scholars and students to be active participants in the affairs of their society. It is surely a function of undergraduate colleges to provide their students with the opportunity to acquaint themselves with facts and issues relevant to their subsequent activities as adult citizens of their society. Beyond this, however, colleges differ, and, I believe, may be permitted to differ. Some take it to be an institutional responsibility to arouse their students' sense of social obligation and commitment; others leave the issue of social and political engagement to the judgment of the individual student and teacher. Fortunately, students may choose what kind of institution they wish to attend. So far as I can see, once they have made such a choice, they have a right to ask, but they cannot demand as a right, that their college be different from what it is. Whatever one's private educational ideals, no one can argue, consistently with fundamental principles of individual liberty, that one has a *right* to be a member of a college that encourages or requires its students to be political actors. And the reverse is also true. No categorical case can be made for the proposition that students or teachers should refrain from political activity.

There is a case to be made, however, for the exercise by teachers of a certain kind of self-restraint with regard to their students. The advocacy of a social cause is the teacher's right, so long as he meets standards of fair teaching and competent scholarship. But the relation between a teacher and a student is one that can give a teacher great influence over a student; and the closer the relationship, the more this is likely to be so. It is improper, it seems to me, for teachers to exploit such a relationship by actively attempting to recruit their students for social causes. The line between enthusiasm for a cause and active recruitment for it, admittedly, is not easy to draw in practice. But it is not different from the line which is drawn by the courts between abstract advocacy of a doctrine and positive action on its behalf. To be sure, the obligation to exercise such self-restraint cannot be codified or given official standing. It can take effect only if individuals accept it. And it is possible, of course, that a number of my colleagues will not agree with me about its validity.

Institutional Policies

Like all abstract discussions of morality, however, abstract discussions of the rights and responsibilities of teachers, students, and administrators are of limited value unless attention is paid to the character and tone of the environment in which these rights and responsibilities operate. This paper is already overly long, though each of its sections, I fear, is brief to the point of dogmatism. I shall pile one more sin upon these others, and add one final remark. Formal sermons on rights and responsibilities tend to mount in number and shrillness, I suspect, in direct proportion to the absence of close consultation and cooperation between students, faculty, and administration. There is no reason, indeed, why the code of rights and responsibilities that govern a college, and the system of sanctions that enforce it, should not themselves be the product of cooperative study and effort by members of these three groups. In the process, they might rediscover one another as persons, rather than as abstract types. The expansion of American colleges cannot be arrested. But administrative rigidity and remoteness, and cold and impersonal teaching, are not inevitable consequences of this process. They are consequences of institutional drift.

Academic Freedom for Students: Issues and Guidelines

E. G. WILLIAMSON and JOHN L. COWAN

WHAT FREEDOMS DO STUDENTS actually enjoy today? On nearly every campus the issue of freedom is a most controversial one, and several concepts of freedom compete for the loyal commitment of students, with resultant agitation and unrest among students today.

The present paper* reports a summary of findings of an objective research about some of the contemporary issues of students' academic freedom. In the final pages of the report the authors suggest some guidelines for the orderly and formal enactment of students' freedoms.

History of the Study

In 1961, the executive committee of the National Association of Student Personnel Administrators appointed a special commission, under the chairmanship of the senior author, to study "The Student and Social Issues." It was the purpose of the commission to draft a proposal for the discussion of students' expression of viewpoints and advocacies, especially concerning controversial and divisive societal issues. At one of its early meetings, the commission decided that both a discussion and a statement of principles would be premature and, therefore, proposed a research study of the facts: what freedoms do students currently enjoy, on what kinds of campuses? The commission found that although many members of the academic community are committed to strong views about students' freedoms, and although this is one of the most important issues currently confronting the university, no comprehensive study had been made in which objective relevant facts were delineated about current policies

* The interpretations and opinions expressed in this paper are those of the writers. They do not speak for Commission VIII of the National Association of Student Personnel Administrators or for the Edward W. Hazen Foundation, which supported the research.

and practices. Thus, much information on which sound views and decisions could be based was lacking. The commission therefore recommended the present study partially to fill this deficiency.

In contrast with such a research approach to the problem of identifying students' freedoms, several groups have issued *pronunciamentos* delineating what they think are desirable freedoms for students. None, however, has sought to base statements on observations of existing freedoms, but rather, some advocates seem, implicitly, to assume the absence of freedom for students. For example, the United States National Student Association made such a statement as early as 1947. Later, the American Civil Liberties Union, through a special committee, issued a formulation of rights of privacy, free discussion, and due process involving student discipline. Currently, Committee S of the American Association of University Professors is preparing a similar statement. Clearly, these three statements contain many appropriate and desirable proposals. Nevertheless, in discussing and evaluating these and other proposals and advocacies, all interested groups should benefit from the knowledge of current practices and viewpoints that the present study has been designed to obtain. It is hoped, thus, that everywhere discussions can proceed on an effective scholarly level, rather than producing visceral tensions and unproductive arguments based on limited understandings of the present state of freedom.

Research Design

With the generous support of the Edward W. Hazen Foundation, the NASPA commission added student, faculty, and presidential representatives to its membership, and then undertook a national research project in 1963. The research design in outline was fairly simple.

Respondents: Key decision makers and student leaders were asked to assess their state of freedom and to express their views of desirable changes. The president and the dean of students (by whatever titles) were the administrative representatives. As the most responsible decision maker, indeed as the agent of regential or charter authority, the president is conscious of many strong and conflicting pressures from the academic and nonacademic community as he guides university policy and action. His appraisal of these pressures and his own judgment of what is "best" for the institution and its students are clearly very important data in studying the nature of the present situation, the forces and traditions which have determined it, and the prospects for desired change. Although they lack the perspective of the president's position, the deans of students contributed experiences with students and student problems, and thus their views of their campuses are also well informed. The chairman of any standing faculty committee concerned with student affairs, expected most frequently to be a member of the faculty, was also represented. To encourage students to speak for themselves, the president of the student body and the student newspaper editor were also asked to evaluate their campuses. It was hypothesized that differences among the perceptions of these respondents concerning the actual freedom enjoyed by students would be enlightening in determining both gaps in communication and differences in desired goals.

Nature of questions: All respondents were requested to evaluate their campuses during the period fall 1961 to spring 1964, when the questionnaires were mailed. The questions were designed to identify changes in campus climate, issues, and topics students would be permitted to discuss, acceptability of certain forms or methods of student expression, and the acceptability of certain off-campus speakers. Open-ended questions were also asked, to induce description of problems the respondent might feel were inadequately covered in the questionnaire.

Obstacles: Since decision making does not, and sometimes indeed cannot, take place in public discussion, we hypothesized a possible reluctance to full disclosure. Also, we wanted to make clear that this was not a study designed to advocate some special form of freedom, but rather an objective identification and analysis of facts and perceptions regarding current student freedoms. Finally, the "nuisance" reaction produced by innumerable questionnaires crossing the president's desk had to be alleviated. To help achieve full and frank response, the then-president of the National Association of Student Personnel Administrators requested that each dean of students act as a research agent for us on his own campus. Moreover, the identity of each respondent—individual and institution—was to remain confidential.

Response: Because of the willingness of the deans to act as our facilitators, the response was extraordinary. At least one questionnaire was obtained from 850 of 1,000 regionally accredited, four-year colleges and universities across the country. Complete response (five questionnaires) was received from 695 institutions. Usable questionnaires were returned from 757 presidents, 813 deans of students, 807 student body presidents, and 785 student editors. Of the 800 student affairs committee chairmen's questionnaires returned, 149

(19 percent) indicated there was no such committee at the institution. This in itself may prove to be a significant finding. Chairmanship of existing committees was held by faculty members in 444 (55 percent) institutions and by deans of students in 207 (26 percent) colleges.

Sample quality: Our analyses revealed that the questionnaires from each respondent group—presidents, deans of students, chairmen of committees on student affairs, student body presidents, student editors, and institutions returning all five questionnaires—came from institutions which are statistically representative in every respect of the approximately 1,000 four-year, regionally accredited, degree-granting colleges and universities. Thus, responses are proportionately representative of all institutions in terms of the following classifications: sex of students—men's, women's, and coeducational institutions; predominant racial characteristics of students—Negro and white; size of enrollment; curricular emphasis—universities, liberal arts, technical, and teachers colleges; type of control—public, private nonsectarian, Protestant, and Catholic; and geographical accrediting region.

Reliability determination: Naturally, the validity and reliability of the questionnaires are of crucial importance to the interpretation of the assembled data. These are technical matters, and will not be dealt with here, except to report that the high internal consistency of response, high coefficients of reliability for derived scales of freedom, and the apparent openness and sincerity of response to our open-ended questions indicate satisfaction of these criteria.

Some Preliminary Results

Role and views of the president

The president is under pressure from many, often conflicting sources, each of which seeks to dominate decision making concerning the appearance of Communist speakers, nonviolent civil disobedience of students, picketing, and demonstrations. In any specific decision-making situation, the president must maintain the integrity of the institution and his staff associates. He must, at the same time, adhere to fundamental principles of good educational practice and seek to strengthen his role as educational leader and as visionary in the academic community and in the surrounding community. Moreover, the president must weigh the merits of various advocacies and opinions clamoring for attention.

Concerning decision making in the area of student affairs, for example, the president must seek to achieve a balance of working relationship with the dean of students. Sufficient autonomy and authority must be given to the dean of students so that his professional integrity is not compromised. For, if the dean of students is perceived merely as the agent of the president, his educational relationships with students will be seriously impaired, and he will be unable to serve the valuable function of shielding the president from unnecessary and sometimes destructive controversy. Likewise, the president must, through consultation, seek relevant counsel and advice of informed faculty members and students.

Through each decision, the president must seek also to provide relevant information to all persons in the college and to interested persons in the surrounding community. He must provide for them that measure of educational leadership which delineates the aims and purposes of the institution and transmutes hostility into support. Moreover, he must explicate his basic principles of education and administration which serve as rationale for his actions. Furthermore, the president must evaluate the legitimacy of the advocacies of various individuals and groups concerned with university affairs—whether these advocates seek to restrict or extend the freedom of students.

In complex decision making, then, the president is not merely a computer which, according to some simplistic and rigid formula, manipulates external vector forces acting upon him to present the resultant vector as his output policy. Nor is the president free, as an educational leader, to resolve complex problems, at all times and in all ways, solely on the basis of any one, overriding principle. In fact, the president operates with a series of principles of different levels of importance, each of which enters his decision-making evaluations. Thus, in this delicate and supremely human task, the president is not entirely a free agent; rather, like Aristotle's statesman, he must practice the "art of the possible." But, like Aristotle's politician exercising "practical wisdom," the college president must act so as to aim toward the "good" of the social system. Therefore, practicing the "art of the possible" cannot be the excuse for an expedient decision.

The nexus of the decision-making problem is probably best understood in terms of the "price" to be paid for any given choice. Samuel P. Capen, when president of the University of Buffalo, asserted that the president should act on the basis of his own reason and judgment to implement what he believed to be the "right." Specifically, he believed in academic freedom and contended that to compromise freedom was to compromise the aims of the university. Speaking at the Conference of Trustees of Colleges and Universities in 1935, he asked, "Is it [academic freedom] worth the price?" He continued:

> This is not the place—nor do I have the time—to argue that question. I venture therefore, rather briefly and dogmatically, to state my own opinion. Yes, it is worth the price, any price. Higher institutions are by definition committed to the search for truth and to the dissemination of the results of that search. The quest is nearly always futile if the inquiry is circumscribed in advance.[1]

Through our questionnaires we sought to determine whether presidents and deans adhere to this inflexible principle today.

Seventy-one percent of the presidents and 80 percent of the deans of students agreed *without reservation or qualification* that "an *essential part* of the education of *each student* is the freedom to hear, critically examine, and *express viewpoints* on *a range* of positions held and advocated regarding issues that divide our society." (Italics used in questionnaire.) Here are responses of four individual presidents, who remain unidentified in accord with our commitment to allow only the research staff to see the answered questionnaires.

We believe that this statement is a fair and proper summary of the institutional philosophy of this college. It is one of the obligations of an institution of higher learning to create an environment in which each student is free to hear and to express his viewpoints on controversial contemporary issues as it is his same privilege to hear and to express views about past issues in human society. The college is not an intellectual morgue, devoted only to post-mortems.

· · · · · ·

This statement of the necessity of freedom is important, although translating it into practice does not contribute to the administrator's ease.

· · · · · ·

Students should be challenged beyond conformity: the college forum is necessary for truly liberal education.

· · · · · ·

. . . speakers must be approved but any controversy is allowed on this campus.

Deans of students also advocated the concept of academic freedom:

This is an underlying part of our educational philosophy. Discussion of campus issues and all views thereon is encouraged in student government

---

[1] Samuel P. Capen, *The Management of Universities*, ed. Oscar A. Silverman for the Council of the University of Buffalo (Buffalo, N.Y.: Foster & Steward Publishing Corp., 1953), p. 28.

bodies and the college newspaper. Community, national, and international issues are presented from all points of view in classrooms, innumerable campus-wide lectures, and in student organizations.

.   .   .   .   .   .

The above statement reflects the philosophy, if not practice, of our institution. In fact, as a college of science and engineering, it is often difficult to find a good hearing on political issues because a need for such hearings is not always strongly felt.

.   .   .   .   .   .

We encourage our students to study controversial issues and then speak their thoughts freely.

In addition to the 71 percent of presidents and 80 percent of deans who supported this statement of policy without reservation, 14 percent of the college presidents and 13 percent of the deans agreed with it *in general* but added the qualification that student freedom had to be exercised "responsibly and critically." The statements of two presidents illustrating these qualifications follow:

We believe at [our university] that a central concern of education is the preparation of an enlightened, a thinking people who will make for a better government and a better society. This can best be accomplished in an atmosphere of academic freedom, permitting individuals to understand controversial issues as well as those which conform to accepted tenets of our society. Only in this way, we believe, will young people learn to make wise choices; to tolerate the rights of others; and to reason and come to logical conclusions on personal, community, national, and world problems.

At the same time we believe that some vigilance must be exercised by administration and faculty to the end that the wishes of a small group of students will not undermine the major purposes of the college education nor mar the responsible and constructive image of the institution. We have found it possible to harmonize these concerns within a dynamic institutional setting to the general satisfaction of faculty, students, and trustees, although there are no firm or fixed answers in any of these situations.

.   .   .   .   .   .

Free inquiry is essential even if politically sensitive issues and people are involved. Some judgment by "advisers" is occasionally required, but students want to know and should feel free to know. Sensation seeking is not always to be confused with free inquiry. This line is a delicate one sometimes with students, but a discussion of the purposes of any meeting usually can arrive at an agreed-upon goal in the few cases where there may be a question. Freedom of inquiry should be supported. Freedom of expression should be coupled with responsibility to get the facts. This is the weakest point of student performance. They have to learn the difference between opinion, rumor, prejudice, and fact, and they must learn to prefer fact to their opinions.

Ten percent of the presidents and 6 percent of the deans of students expressed *some agreement* with the statement but set clearly defined limits, usually for political or religious reasons. Some examples of responses in this category of "restricted agreement" are the following:

Some controversial figures are too hot for this campus to handle.

. . . . . .

We agree but freedom is questionable for Communists, subversives, advocates of the overthrow of the government.

. . . . . .

In general the above statement is part of the philosophy of this college, however, as a Catholic college there are fundamental concepts of natural law, dogma, and morals which would prevent this statement from being accepted in an absolute manner. In some matters it would be permissive to "express viewpoints," but not to advocate them.

Only 30 presidents (4.5 percent of those responding to the question) and only 1 percent of the deans disagreed with the idea that students should be free to hear, critically examine, and express viewpoints on a range of issues. Their disagreement was usually on the grounds that this freedom was incompatible with their understanding of the mission of their institution or that it might cause intellectual damage to "immature" students. One dean said:

A student by his position is learning. To put obstacles in his way in the form of falsehood inhibits or retards the learning process unless a mature and experienced person aids the process of delineating chaff from wheat, truth from falsehood. A philosophy of education based on absolutes provides the student with a sound foundation as a starting point and as a point of comparison. A student who is allowed to hear, examine, and express viewpoints indiscriminately benefits neither himself nor his peers.

Thus, the great majority of presidents and deans advocated the principle of students' freedom. Such advocacy was especially strong in the New England, Middle Atlantic, and North Central states, in private nonsectarian universities and liberal arts colleges, and in public universities. The minority qualifications, restrictions, and disagreements were found slightly more frequently in the Southern, Northwestern, and Western regions, and in technical institutions, teachers colleges, and Catholic universities and liberal arts colleges.

Measures of freedom

It would be naïve to think that freedom is a bipolar, either-or phenomenon, that campuses are either "wide open" or "completely closed." It would even be unrealistic to rank colleges or respondents from colleges on some hypothetical scale between wide open and completely closed. How do you weigh freedom to invite any speaker on one campus against freedom to attack the administration in the student newspaper on another campus? Nonetheless, this kind of problem does, in fact, arise in any simplistic attempt to analyze our data. For example, no college president considered his campus completely closed, and only 3 percent responded in the most permissive response category to forty specific questions. This would suggest that these campuses are very permissive, but the specific wording of questions does not allow the interpretation that these campuses are completely open. Moreover, analysis of answers of the other respondents from the same campuses reveals that there is no campus which all five respondents perceive to be completely open.

Rather than attempt to construct a single scale and include in it a variety of incommensurable elements, we concluded that a more accurate assessment of the freedom on our campuses would emerge by ranking the respondents of all institutions on several scales, each measuring one aspect of freedom. Although the relative importance of each scale, or dimension of freedom, is not yet clear, and although these scales may be somewhat altered in our final report, analysis of the data by the technique of factor analysis suggests six separate but related scales for the objective measurement of academic freedom for students on the campus.

These six scales can be divided, for ease of presentation, into four groups. One is freedom of topic discussion, another is freedom in inviting off-campus speakers, the third is freedom of mode of expression, and the fourth is a freedom to engage in civil rights activities.

Freedom of topic discussion is a grouping which contains two scales. The first is freedom to discuss political-social issues; the second is the freedom to discuss religious-moral issues.

Freedom for inviting off-campus speakers must be treated with two scales, one for "acceptable speakers" and the other for "controversial speakers," since these two categories are treated in different ways administratively and freedom in one category does not necessarily imply the same degree of freedom in the other.

Freedom of mode of student expression can be treated with one scale running from highly demonstrative and potentially inflammatory passive resistance sit-ins on the one extreme, to passage of a resolution by student government after it has been approved by an all-campus referendum on the other.

Freedom to engage in civil rights activities is encompassed within one complex scale. This one includes discussion of specific topics, mode of expression by demonstrative technique, and invitation of specific speakers who are identified with the current civil rights movements.

Preliminary analysis reveals that the "controversial speakers," modes of student expression, freedom to discuss religious-moral issues, and the civil rights scales are the most reliable and most discriminative among the many different types of institutions. For example, great differences between the average scores, for each respondent group, are found on the civil rights scale for Southern Negro colleges and Southern institutions with predominantly white enrollment. Although our research may not have identified all the relevant factors, it has made it clear that freedom for students is much too complex to be considered an either-or phenomenon. To present a fair and accurate assessment of the campus, several scales must be used for measuring the several dimensions of students' freedom.

Respondents' appraisals of the extent of existing freedoms

Rather than describe here in detail the extent of existing freedom as measured by the six scales described above, we will present these data in a later publication, and we offer here only a few findings concerning the general areas of freedom of topic discussion, of mode of student expression, and of inviting off-campus speakers.

FREEDOM OF TOPIC DISCUSSION

Our questionnaire listed fourteen controversial political, social, economic, and religious issues, and each respondent was asked to assess the freedom enjoyed by students in his institution to discuss and make public, "unpopular" viewpoints regarding these issues. A certain small amount of perceptual dissonance was observed here— deans perceived their institutions to be less restrictive than did student body presidents. The perceptions of presidents seemed to supply a relatively good measure for consideration in this paper.

More than 75 percent of the presidents reported that student groups could discuss and publicize unpopular positions concerning thirteen of the fourteen topics. The fourteenth topic was abolition of laws prohibiting interracial marriage, but almost 70 percent of the presidents said that even this issue could be discussed on their campuses. The only other topic which produced a restrictive response of any consequence was: "U.S. dissemination of birth control information to underdeveloped countries." But only 14 percent questioned the advisability of discussing this topic. Most of the objections to the discussion of interracial marriage came from presidents of Southern institutions, but even here almost half of the presidents reported no restrictions in operation. Four out of ten Catholic college and university presidents reported restrictions on the birth control topic, thus providing the bulk of the objections to that subject. In contrast, 94 percent of the presidents of large public universities and 90 percent of the presidents of private liberal arts colleges reported that students could publicize unpopular opinions on this topic.

Among the other topics which students were almost uniformly free to discuss were issues such as "total military disarmament," "abolition of the House Un-American Activities Committee," "local fair housing legislation," "abolition of prayers in public schools," and "Federal aid to Yugoslavia." Thus, although certain issues are restricted on some campuses, the numerical extent of these restrictions is small, and the overwhelming consensus of all respondents —administrators, faculty, and students—is that the freedom to discuss controversial issues of local, regional, national, or international significance is clearly established on "most" campuses. To be sure, this freedom is most firmly established in large and small public universities and in private nonsectarian universities and liberal arts colleges. It is less firmly established in teachers colleges and in Catholic colleges, especially concerning certain doctrinal issues.

FREEDOM OF MODE OF STUDENT EXPRESSION

Exploration of yet another area of student expression produced rather clear delineation of what measures students are permitted to take to advocate and influence social or political reform. Respondents were presented with nine situations, such as: "student organization pickets a public meeting," and were asked whether the university had a written policy which would apply, and in any case whether the university's response to this student action would be "quite permissive, fairly permissive, or not permissive." As with the other questions, there was a "cannot say" category. In general, responses to these nine situations indicated considerable student freedom. Five important aspects of this type of freedom are political campaigning, petitioning public officials, student council resolutions, student demonstrations, and newspaper editorializing.

On-campus support of a national election candidate is the most widely held of these freedoms. Eighty-six percent of the presidents and a high proportion of the other respondents reported that their institutions were "quite" or "fairly" permissive in dealing with this kind of activity. In the analysis of this information we discovered that the types of institution which are most free in other respects are least free in tolerating partisan political activity on the campus. Thus, the most restricted in this regard are the large public universities, especially on the West Coast—the same institutions which were found to be relatively permissive in other matters.

The right to petition government agencies or officials for redress of grievances is almost as well established as the right of political campaigning. Eighty-two percent of the presidents report that they would permit such petitioning, and this opinion is shared by students, deans, and faculty. The same institutions which restrict political campaigning on campus also restrict petitioning—namely, the public colleges and universities. The unusual restrictiveness of these institutions in political matters, in contrast with their tendency to permissiveness in other areas, is possibly the result of their dependency on the legislature as a source of funds and controlling authority. This does not mean that there is no political freedom for public university students: indeed 70 percent of the public university presidents assert that their students may circulate petitions. But in the cases where, in public universities, political freedoms are restricted and other freedoms may be enjoyed, a disparity exists which could understandably be a source of student unrest.

The publication of student council resolutions advocating a viewpoint is a widely practiced freedom. The student council is authorized to speak for the student body, following a referendum, on 90 percent of the campuses according to the deans, 89 percent according to student body presidents, and 86 percent according to the presidents. Although, in general, students perceive their campuses as more restricted than administrators perceive them, students actually reported freedom to publish resolutions more often than did deans or presidents. Student body presidents reported that they enjoyed "very much" freedom, while student editors reported that they were slightly more restricted. The greatest difference among respondents appeared in perceptions of freedom to publish student council resolutions without first submitting them to referenda. Here, student body presidents perceive considerably more freedom than do the presidents of their institutions.

Even the differences in response to these two situations among presidents present a major problem of interpretation. Forty-four percent of the presidents perceived permissiveness for publication of a resolution *without* referendum, whereas 86 percent would be permissive following a referendum. This difference may suggest that many presidents do not think student government is truly representative of the student body. If this were the basis for deciding that a referendum is necessary, we reasoned that classifying responses by size of enrollment would reveal the smaller schools (where it is perhaps more likely that student government is representative of and responsive to student opinion) not requiring the referendum and the largest institutions considering the referendum a necessity. Our data, however, indicate that the opposite is true. Large public universities and private universities are the only categories of institutions in which more than half the presidents indicated permissiveness for publication of a resolution without prior referendum. The ease of determining the consensus of the student body by means of a referendum may, therefore, be a more important consideration to presidents than is the question of representativeness of the student government. A more meaningful interpretation of these discrepancies of response must await further analysis.

The freedom to employ certain techniques of demonstration, such as picketing a public meeting or "sitting-in" at a local lunch counter, is probably not widely practiced, and there is considerable disagreement among respondents about how much freedom students really do enjoy in this regard. Concerning the picketing issue, only 30 percent of the presidents reported their institutions as "quite permissive," and another 29 percent reported as "fairly permissive." Twenty percent said they were not permissive, and a similar number declined to comment. Among the student respondents, one-third did not comment, 20 percent said their institutions were not permissive, 25 percent found fair permissiveness, and only 16 percent reported their universities to be "quite permissive." Results for the sit-in question were substantially the same, but with more "cannot say" responses. These responses indicate that certain techniques of demonstration are not widely accepted, and the extensive perceptual dissonance between students and administrators may indicate that this is a very serious matter awaiting resolution. The greatest freedom on this issue is currently found in the large, nonsectarian universities, both public and private.

It is sometimes or even generally contended that editorial freedom is highly restricted in our campus newspapers, but our research results indicate considerable—though far from complete—freedom in this regard. Students and administrators alike asserted that their institutions were "quite permissive" regarding editorial freedom on controversial issues at half of the schools, and that a "fairly permissive" situation obtained at an additional 35 percent. We asked student editors to report about direct censorship, and to elaborate on the more subtle ways in which the censor might exert his influence. Fifteen percent of the editors reported censorship during the two and one-half year time period of the study, but none of the editors in Protestant universities or large public universities reported censorship. In 10 percent of the smaller public universities and in private Protestant liberal arts colleges, editors reported censorship. But one-quarter of the teachers colleges and one-third of the Catholic colleges reported censorship. Further, 40 percent of the editors must submit editorial copy before publication. Although the very fact of this requirement may influence them to moderate their stands, administrators, faculty, students, and outside groups call the editor to account for published material. One-third of all editors had been privately reprimanded or censured for their "extreme" stand on controversial issues. In 20 percent of the schools, someone had proposed that a student editor be removed from office during the two and one-half years of the study. In 6 percent of the schools editors were actually removed. Perhaps the other 14 percent "fell into line." Editors need not always be disciplined from without— half of the editors reported that they had voluntarily refrained from printing inflammatory editorials because information supplied by the administration or discovered through their own efforts indicated the untimeliness of some editorials.

FREEDOM TO INVITE OFF-CAMPUS SPEAKERS

The question concerning campus speakers was the most specific of all our questionnaire items, listing the names and identities of seventeen persons, all of whom had been the source of some controversy on some campuses. Respondents were asked whether these men had spoken or could speak on the campus, or whether, in their estimation, the administration would strongly question the advisability of an appearance of the speaker. It was clear at the time the questionnaires were designed that data were confounded in the list of speakers; that is, we would be unable to make positive inferences regarding some factors that bear on the acceptability of the speaker.

We assumed that such matters as the speaker's public stature, the position he advocated, his moral position, and his reputation for disrupting campus life would be important. They seem to be. We will consider the answers given regarding three groups of speakers.

Earl Warren, Barry Goldwater, Augustin Cardinal Bea, Martin Luther King, and John P. Humphrey are all of high stature and are considered controversial in a nonpejorative sense. They would be permitted, probably even welcomed, on over 80 percent of our campuses. Student responders tended to view their campuses as more permissive with regard to these speakers than did the presidents or deans of students, but the perceptual dissonance was very small. There is, of course, a major difference in regional response to Martin Luther King.

The number of presidents questioning the advisability of any of these five speakers is very small, but worth noting. The number questioning the advisability of Chief Justice Earl Warren was four; of the director of the United Nations Human Rights Division, John Humphrey, 13; of Roman Catholic prelate Augustin Cardinal Bea, 18; of Senator Barry Goldwater, 20; and of Martin Luther King, 61. Differences classified by region or by type of institution were not significant, with the exception of a slightly more frequent restrictive response from Southern institutions.

A second group, categorized as the "controversial speakers," was comprised of eight persons who had spoken or could speak at 44 to 60 percent of the institutions, according to the presidents. They were James R. Hoffa, Robert Welch, Governor George C. Wallace, Barry Sheppard, Frank Wilkinson, Brewster Kneen, Robert P. Moses, and Fred Schwarz. A great many of the vital issues confronting Americans today are represented by these eight speakers — segregation, integration, socialism, the power of congressional investigating committees, anticommunism, pacifism, and morality in trade-union leadership. These speakers, because they constitute a middle group of controversiality, provide a more sensitive index of campus freedom than do the others. The analysis of the determinants of freedom in this area and of the differences among campuses has too many facets for a brief presentation. Nevertheless, at the risk of oversimplifying a presentation of such complexity, we shall briefly indicate a few extreme differences.

For presidents of large public and private universities, these eight speakers generally are considered within the range of persons that students may freely invite to their campuses. With the exception of James Hoffa, each of the controversial speakers could address students at 80 percent or more of the private universities and at more than 70 percent of the large public universities. It should be kept in mind, however, that these two categories of institutions constitute only 13 percent of all the institutions studied.

In contrast, many presidents of Catholic liberal arts colleges seemed to view many of the eight "controversial" speakers as representing positions clearly in conflict with the mission of their institutions. Twelve percent of these presidents would permit Alabama's Governor Wallace or Socialist Barry Sheppard to speak on their campuses; 19 percent would allow James Hoffa to speak; and 23 percent reported that Robert Welch could appear. Robert Moses, about whom 37 percent of the presidents of Catholic liberal arts colleges responded "could speak," was the most acceptable of the eight speakers for institutions of that category. Analysis by geographical region revealed a clear tendency for the Southern schools to be more restrictive concerning these eight speakers, while New England institutions were the most permissive.

Four of the listed speakers—George Lincoln Rockwell, Sir Oswald Mosley, Daniel Rubin, and Malcolm X (assassinated February 21, 1965)—represent the extremes that are generally considered beyond the limits of acceptable student academic freedom. These "highly controversial" speakers are individuals whose proposed solutions to social and political problems directly contradict many established forms of thought and action in the United States. An invitation to any of them to address campus audiences is almost certain to involve the institution in a storm of protest, and we may safely say that students who invite any of these speakers are testing the limits of their freedom, on even the most open campuses. Yet students do sometimes invite them to speak, and 17 percent of the institutions would grant permission for all of them to speak, according to the presidents. But our data indicate that student responders perceive their institutions as much less permissive regarding these speakers than do administrators.

According to the presidents, Oswald Mosley and Malcolm X could speak at 32 percent of the institutions and Daniel Rubin at 28 percent. George Lincoln Rockwell, least acceptable of all 17 listed speakers, had spoken at 17 of the 757 colleges from which presidents responded, and an additional 171 presidents indicated that he could speak, if invited.

Those colleges and universities that are most permissive for our other speakers, both in regional analysis and by category of institution, remain the most permissive, but not as permissive for "highly controversial" speakers as for those classified as "controversial." Thus, the New England region is the most open for these four individuals. Three of them—Malcolm X, Daniel Rubin, and Oswald Mosley— could speak at approximately half of the New England colleges and universities, but George Lincoln Rockwell would be permitted at no more than 37 percent of these institutions. Southern institutions would be the most restrictive for the highly controversial speakers, with no more than 17 percent of the presidents reporting that any of the four could speak.

Institutions with strong religious ties are the most restrictive regarding this group of speakers. We found, for example, that Malcolm X could have spoken at 68 percent of the private universities, 61 percent of the large public universities, and 56 percent of the private liberal arts colleges. Only 7 percent of the Catholic university presidents would have offered him a platform, as would have only 21 percent of the Protestant liberal arts college presidents. Communist Daniel Rubin could speak at 65 percent of the private universities as contrasted to only 3 percent of the Catholic liberal arts colleges.

A small number of presidents, typically from the very permissive institutions, noted that Rockwell could speak, but that they would question the advisability of inviting him. These presidents seem to be saying that their institutional policies or traditions permit students to invite *any* speaker, but, as educators, they want students to use their freedom with responsible discretion—by *not inviting* certain speakers. Apparently in the judgment of these presidents what Rockwell has been known to say or do is not considered relevant to the higher learning. Or the presidents may be saying that the "price" for having Rockwell on the campus is greater than they would like to pay. No doubt, sometimes students confuse the president's judgment that it would be "inadvisable" to invite some speaker with the lack of freedom to invite the speaker.

Operational bases for presidential decision making

Through a series of free response questions, we sought the presidents' reflections on detailed aspects of institutional procedures for handling situations involving controversial speakers. A very brief résumé of the significant findings can be presented here.

PREVALENCE OF GUIDELINES FOR DECISION MAKING

At the outset of our research we realized that there would be many patterns of administrative operation, yet we assumed that the existence of codified policies specifying the institutional position concerning most aspects of student academic freedom, particularly the various modes of student expression, would guide presidential decision making in crisis situations. We were startled to discover that, with the exception of policies regarding off-campus speakers, only 6 percent of the responding presidents reported the existence of written policies for any mode of student expression. Usually a few presidents of each category of institutions—whether by size of enrollment, type of control, or curricular emphasis—reported having a written policy covering student expressive methods. Most of the very few presidents reporting the existence of written policies, however, were from public institutions, especially large universities.

A more extensive series of questions revealed that one-third of the presidents reported their institutions to have written policies governing invitations of nonuniversity speakers by organized student groups. Forty-two percent of the presidents reported no written speakers policy but claimed to be guided in decisions by clear traditions and established precedents. One-fourth of the presidents indicated that they had neither written policy nor clear traditions to guide their decisions regarding the appearance of off-campus speakers. The largest percentage of the presidents reporting the existence of written policy (77 percent) were in large public universities. Slightly more than half of the presidents of the smaller public universities and the private nonsectarian universities also reported written policies. More than half of the presidents of Catholic universities and liberal arts colleges indicated that they relied on traditions or precedents as guidelines for determining speakers policy for specific occasions.

THE VALUE OF ENACTED POLICY

Are presidents in institutions having written policies more likely to make decisions congruent with the stated level of institutional permissiveness than presidents in colleges operating without clearly delineated policies? Presidents were asked to describe the most recent situation, arising during the period of the fall of 1961 to the spring of 1964, involving the invitation of an off-campus speaker, which matter had become critical enough to be brought to them for prior review in the decision-making process. Of the 320 presidents answering this section of the questionnaire 27 percent did not permit the invitation or the appearance of the proposed speaker. The most frequently given reason for not permitting the speaker was that he was known to advocate action contrary to local, state, or national law. The fact that the speaker was known to hold a viewpoint which would be unacceptable or extremely unpopular in the community in which the institution was located was also frequently given as a reason for denying the speaker the use of the college platform. With equal frequency those presidents not permitting the speaker to appear on campus claimed that his discussion of the issue would have served no significant educational purpose.

Of the 320 presidents commenting on their review of decisions concerning the invitation of off-campus speakers, presidents having permissive written speakers policies were more likely to have reported receiving "considerable criticism" from sources internal and external to the university than those who were guided by tradition or who reported no apparent guidelines for decision making. In making their decision regarding the invited speaker, presidents in institutions having a written speakers policy—no matter what the stated level of permissiveness of the institutional position—were much more likely to have permitted the invitation than were those without a codified policy. Moreover, the data revealed that presidents in those institutions having clear tradition were more likely to have accepted the proposed speaker than were presidents in those institutions operating without policy guidelines. These findings are of great significance.

We also asked presidents to indicate whether they had "interpreted" the educational philosophy of their institution to the public prior to the critical speaker decision. There was significant statistical evidence showing that those presidents who had interpreted their speakers policy publicly prior to the controversial situation were more likely to have accepted the proposed speaker than were those who had made no previous public explanation of their institution's position concerning this mode or form of students' freedom. These findings were obtained at each stated degree of permissiveness of the institutional position regarding off-campus speakers.

These findings indicate that clarity of purpose and goals, expressed in terms of codified policy, are significant means to the achievement of purpose. Moreover, these findings demonstrate that the communication and explanation of the aims and purposes of educational policies to the institution's several publics buttress the president in his decision-making task. Many of the presidents, commenting on the interpretation of policy to the public, indicated the fact that this communication must be a continuous process.

Processes of policy determination

It is evident that our study, when completely analyzed, will only partly describe some elements of the many institutional approaches to policy formation. Our questionnaires were designed to seek information regarding certain institutional procedures in order to assess the degree to which students significantly participate in the policy-making process. This freedom to participate in self-government and to have a significant voice in the determination of institutional goals, rules, and procedures seems to us to be the most crucial of all student freedoms because of its effect on the uses of other freedoms. In this connection we discovered that students are not now entirely without this freedom: indeed, they hold membership in policy-making committees in about 60 percent of the institutions we studied, and they have a full vote in 84 percent of the committees on which they hold membership. Voting membership ranged from 89 percent of the large public universities to 21 percent of the Catholic liberal arts colleges. In 40 percent of all institutions, students are able to review policy changes governing students prior to adoption by the university. *In those institutions where students have these powers, there is also more freedom in topic discussion, in speaker selection, and in permitted mode of expression.*

It is not clear whether student participation causes greater campus freedom, or whether it is an effect of greater permissiveness by the administration. Probably administrative permissiveness and student participation reinforce each other, but, in any case, the presidents reportedly find such participation useful. Seventy-seven percent said it was helpful, if only in gaining student support for acceptance of university policies. But many presidents admitted that there was much to be desired in the level of competence displayed by students in policy-making meetings: undergraduates were often seen but not heard; their presence was often of a ceremonial nature. Nevertheless, *the greater the voice of the students in policy making, the more enthusiastic the presidents were about the benefit of this participation to the institution.* As one president succinctly expressed the opinion of many, "An hour of talks beforehand is worth twenty afterward."

This nearly completes the brief summary of our findings for this report; yet one question begs an answer:

Is More Freedom Desired and Desirable?

To answer this question, one needs to know two things: how much of what types of freedom are currently enjoyed, and how much of what types of freedom are desirable and, indeed, necessary to the fulfillment of the mission of the institution. In preparing this report, we have gathered data from presidents, and from others, which describe, in bare outline, the extent to which certain freedoms are practiced currently. For example, the freedom of a group of students to take an extreme stand on a controversial issue, to sit-in at a local lunch counter, or to picket a public meeting is much less widely established than is the freedom to petition, to campaign on campus for a political candidate, or to vote a student council resolution after a student referendum. Likewise, "highly controversial" speakers such as Malcolm X, George Lincoln Rockwell, or Daniel Rubin are more likely to be banned from campuses than are "reputable" speakers such as Chief Justice Earl Warren, Augustin Cardinal Bea, or Barry Goldwater. These results are not surprising in themselves, but our empirical study provides statistics that show just how widely practiced are these various freedoms, and where they are practiced geographically and by college type and size. More importantly, our data show where there are surprising gaps and inconsistencies in the practice of freedom, which possibly are causing some degree of student unrest.

We recognize that both this presentation of our study and, indeed, the completed study have serious limitations as means of assisting the practical administrator to apply in day-to-day decisions his principles of freedom. Even in description, in this report, it has been necessary to look only at the extreme groupings of institutions to highlight the major differences. Likewise, the precise classifications we have employed are subject to some question. In other words, we would not want any reader to assume that there are no differences, for example, among individual Catholic liberal arts colleges in their practices of freedom. Indeed, there are wide institutional differences, and some preliminary analyses suggest that these differences are attributable, in part, to the sponsorship by different religious orders, the nature of the curriculum, the faculty, the interests and abilities of students, the administrative organization, procedures and practices employed, and the community in which the school is located. Nor would we want our readers to assume that there are no differences among other institutions concerning different forms of freedom. This presentation has not permitted description of the analysis showing subtle, but often important, nuances affecting the contemporary exercise of student freedom.

Our report does not, indeed it cannot, fully answer the second half of the question. Deciding how much of what types of freedom are desirable in fulfilling the institution's mission is a matter which must be, in our view, dealt with by a college in the context of its own particular situation. But we can provide some information to suggest that more degrees of freedom are desirable. There appears in our data a serious discrepancy between the ideology of freedom for students and the practice of that freedom. The first section of our data presentation showed an overwhelming assent to the concept that an essential part of the education of each student is the freedom to hear, critically examine, and express viewpoints on a range (we might have said the widest possible range) of issues facing our society. Later sections of the report show that there are many restrictions on freedom even among those who agree, without qualification, with the ideal of academic freedom. It would seem, then, that within those institutions where there is a major discrepancy between ideal and practice, there is an implied need for more freedom. Moreover, we are convinced that our data provide information which points to need for change in policy-making and decision-making processes. We show the viewpoints of our respondents—presidents, deans, faculty, and student leaders—and, to some extent, what they think should be done. Thus, potential areas of conflict are indicated, and perhaps through communication these conflicts can be fairly and rationally resolved before they take a serious and unacademic form.

Aside from the question of whether there ought to be change, there is the fact of change in contemporary stresses within American higher education.

The academic year 1964–65 erupted an abundance of evidence that the climate of student opinion and action was in a state of unrest. The incidents, studies, reports, comments, and interpretations were before the academic community throughout the year, from the opening day of classes (in Berkeley) to the last day of classes (in Ohio State and the University of Minnesota, not dramatic enough to be covered by news media as was the Berkeley phenomenon). The year brought forth at least one innovation in student academic freedom— the "teach-in." In view of the dynamic quality of the current climate of change, many of our findings may already be out of date! Nonetheless, for some evidence concerning the changing climate of student expression we return to a résumé of data.

The changing climate of student expression

While many outward indications point to the emergence of a new generation of politically active and cause-committed students, our data tend to qualify any such broad generalization. In 57 percent of the institutions, one-tenth or fewer of the students were estimated to be active participants in matters involving controversial political or social issues, and in half of these fewer than 5 percent are active. Twenty-three percent of the 757 responding presidents reported that 10 to 25 percent of their students participate in activities designed to express their viewpoints on controversial issues. Only 55 of the presidents (7 percent) said that one-fourth or more of their students participated in such activities.

In attempting to locate the existence of political activism, we discovered that a larger percentage of the student bodies of private nonsectarian institutions are politically involved than are students within public colleges and universities. The highest ratios of active students were reported by presidents of liberal arts colleges, both sectarian and nonsectarian, and by the presidents of Catholic universities. The lowest estimates of politically active students came from presidents of large public universities. More than half reported that fewer than one in twenty of their students demonstrate an active concern with public affairs, and only one in ten reported that more than 10 percent of their students demonstrated such concern.

Although the percentages are relatively small, they do represent an increase in the number of students who have been moved to action in recent years. Estimating changes during the two and one-half years following the fall of 1961, 80 presidents, 11 percent of the 757 responding, reported a large increase in the number of students on their campuses taking part in some activity designed to express student viewpoints on controversial issues. Another 320 (42 percent) perceived some increase but did not consider it to be large; 357 presidents (47 percent) either did not estimate or reported there had been no increase.

Besides the increase in the numbers of students actively expressing viewpoints on controversial issues, our data point to other changes in the campus climate. A majority of the presidents reported that students are currently addressing themselves more to controversial issues and are using more demonstrative techniques. Most presidents, however, did not consider that their students were advocating more extreme positions.

Changes in the campus climate are dramatic and startling when analyzed according to form of institutional control. Changes on Catholic campuses can be described as no less than phenomenal! Ninety percent of the presidents of Catholic colleges and universities report the emergence of a new social and political awareness among their students. More than three-fourths of the presidents of private universities also noted this change, and more than half of the presidents of all other types of institutions.

Much of the awakened interest of students is observable in classroom and group discussions, but some of it is appearing in a more activistic manner. Seventy percent of the presidents of Catholic institutions and almost three-fourths of the presidents of private universities stated that their students are becoming more openly demonstrative. Slightly more than half of the presidents of public universities reported that their students are seeking to make known viewpoints by *more demonstrative* techniques. An increase in political activism was also reported by slightly less than half of the presidents of Protestant institutions, private liberal arts colleges, and teachers colleges. From technical institutions the fewest presidents reported that students are becoming more openly demonstrative.

The presidents' replies to questions which sought to identify "climate" of discussion and demonstration, tend to be consistent among the various categories of institutions. However, the relationships among the various categories of institutions, in terms of climate, are very different from the other relationships we have previously examined. In previous discussion, with few exceptions, we found that the large public universities and the private liberal arts colleges and universities were designated as "permissive or open," and the Catholic liberal arts colleges and universities and the teachers colleges were considered "restrictive." More presidents in categories of schools at both ends of the permissive-restrictive dimension, however, report changes in climate than do presidents of institutions ranked in the middle of the scale. In other words, presidents of the most permissive and the most restrictive institutions are, at once, reporting the largest incidents of ferment and unrest.

We do not as yet know what specific meaning to attach to these findings. But one of the most striking findings is the changing climate, possibly leading to considerable disruption, in Roman Catholic institutions.

Changing practices in judicial review

Although we do not intend, in this paper, to deal extensively with a summary of court actions in recent years to see how they affect the form and practice of academic freedom for students, we would be remiss if we did not point to some of the current trends. In the past half-decade, in particular, there has emerged a growing body of legal literature which analyzes, predicts trends of court action, and advocates the establishment and protection of the rights of students by judicial action. Because of the changing importance of educational opportunity, the changing character of students, and change in the courts' willingness to review certain appeals from students, one author [2] builds a case for the protection of student rights in publicly supported universities on the basis of the "equal protection" clause of the Fourteenth Amendment. Moreover, there is an emerging argument [3] which contends that private colleges serve "public functions" and, thus, should operate under the same rules as public institutions. We would not pretend to predict the future actions of the courts; yet there is evidence to suggest that past court actions extended and expanded in the future could lead to a much greater participation of the courts in concerns of higher education, traditionally left to the discretion of the institution.

Clearly, there are other major movements which indicate consideration of change in higher educational institutions. For the most part, these concerns are pressing hard on the imagination of educational leaders to find means to deal effectively with them. The matter of extending student freedom is only one of the problems with which busy administrators must grapple; yet we feel that evidence is sufficient to suggest that it must be rationally studied. Furthermore, it is our contention that the problem of student academic freedom is of utmost importance because it strikes at the heart of the educational enterprise—fundamental aims and purposes. If change in the form and substance of student freedoms is, indeed, upon us, then it behooves us to examine the nature of the change and what the future might portend.

Alternative Methods of Establishing Student Rights and Freedoms

Current discussions of student freedoms and rights are seldom appraised with regard to the appropriateness of the means of establishing rights in association with the nature of the rights themselves. Especially on university campuses, student demands for rights are often so emotionalized, and even sanctified, that the end goals desired seem often to justify the means employed.

The observed means of establishment, of course, range from the declaration of the inalienability of rights, to the assumption that they were always there in the same way as a covered Grecian urn to be dug out, or marble to be carved in the image of the model employed.

[2] William W. Van Alstyne, "Student Academic Freedom and the Rule Making Powers of Public Universities: Some Constitutional Considerations," *Law in Transition Quarterly*, Winter 1965, pp. 1–34.

[3] For a discussion of this point, see Clark Byse, "Procedures in Student Dismissal Proceeding: Law and Policy," *Journal of College Student Personnel*, March 1963, pp. 141–42.

Other advocates of some freedoms and rights act in such a way as to indicate that their very act of demanding a right was an acceptable means employed to establish it and, in effect, that the demand did establish the right desired.

We seek here to delineate the appropriateness of means employed to establish desirable rights, proceeding from an assumption that the collegiate institution does possess authority to enact whatever rights and freedoms are relevant and necessary for achievement of its institutional mission, as defined and redefined over the years. We shall, therefore, take for granted the authority to grant or enact rights within the institution's governing body.

A number of means exist for establishing freedoms and rights for students in the academic community. There is the popular method of rioting and demonstrating in the manner of Latin American and Oriental universities. Many a dean of students in foreign countries has been barricaded in his office until he "gave in" to demands. In many countries scarcely any academic year adjourns without at least one large-scale demonstration or even actual rioting with some destruction of property.

We would classify this means to an end as more appropriate in the market place than in the community we call academic. But we must give attention to the reality of the psychology of the collegiate adolescent, who is revolting against authority symbols. Sometimes this form of revolt results from an overgeneralization of his resentment of parents, or sometimes it originates in riot "just for the hell of it," or even because it is springtime, and "we have been confined and restricted unduly during the long winter months." This form of action does not seem to be appropriate or relevant to the academic mission or to the academic style of living. And when rioting and demonstrations of a violent character occur, some of the alternative forms of enactment have failed to win acceptance.

A second widely utilized procedure for establishing rights and freedoms stems from the source of authority of the institutions' governing boards and administration. In America we have long chartered academic institutions by locating the source of legal authority and fiscal responsibility in the governing board. Sometimes students and faculty alike misunderstand this form of academic corporation and confuse it with the citizenship privileges and status of the political jurisdictions.

Legally the institution *is* its governing board. And, in a very real sense, and sometimes in a tragic sense, the governing board has determined whether or not the students would have certain rights and freedoms. There are many unexamined aspects of this particular line of thinking and, no doubt, some day there will be court review of the relevancy of trustees' actions with regard to means of establishing freedoms and rights. In fact, there has already been some indication that courts will require trustees to exercise their authority over students with due regard to the nature of the collegiate mission and the relevancy of their actions to that mission, *as well* as to the citizenship rights of students.

The same points may be made with regard to the use of presidential and faculty authority, a form of delegation of the trustees' charter authority. Parenthetically, we must recognize that trustees, faculty, and presidents can become very authoritarian and very restrictive in the exercise of the authority and no doubt sometimes extreme demonstration or even rioting results from students having seemingly exhausted other means to desired ends.

A third complex means may be characterized as emerging from the pressure of observed innovations imported from other campuses. One need not experience the national August phenomenon of the National Student Association convention more than once without observing that this is, indeed, and usually in a highly constructive way, a mechanism of communication among student bodies with respect to desired student freedoms and rights. And indeed, the importations of practices, restrictions, and rights from other campuses are sometimes employed by students because of the resistance to change, accommodation, or even review on the part of the agents of institutional authority. Sometimes these two conflicting forces trigger demonstrations and pressuring as a means to the enactment of rights.

A fourth means of establishing rights and freedoms is illustrated by three current documents. This is the method of resolving or adoption of standards of desirable rights for students. The documents of the Association of American University Professors, the American Civil Liberties Union, and the National Student Association are instances of national organizations calling attention to desirable practices and policies and, in effect, serving as a means of advocating local consideration and adoption. These three documents have had, in many instances, desirable effects in calling attention to neglected areas of freedoms appropriate in an academic institution.

But again, sometimes, it is not clearly evident to those who advocate a resolution, or a standard, that they do not possess authority to establish the rights desired but must rather "persuade" agents of authority to take such legal action. In other instances, the advocacies, sometimes calm and sometimes riotous, of such desirable rights may come to have the force of traditions even though there is no official action on the part of the institutional authority. But students feel more secure about rights and freedoms when there is some policy statement adopted by the proper institutional body, which then at least precludes some of the confusion and controversy over what is or is not an acceptable practice according to unwritten tradition.

A fifth alternative means to desirable ends is our favorite. This we characterize as "continuous" or "periodic" informal conversations or consultations between those who possess authority and those who wish to influence the use of that authority in enacting rights and freedoms. This means calls for a quality of human relationships more in keeping with the character of institutions of higher learning.

Such a means permits the kind of academic controversy appropriate to the higher learning: that is, the confrontation of competing *ideas*, not persons, which takes place in a more relaxed atmosphere, one in which cerebration replaces hatred and abuse of opponents. To be sure, this continuous conversation sometimes interferes with getting on with the business of the institution, the mission that, with regard to the nature of man's struggle for freedom in the political community, is sometimes segregated to classroom learning.

This means to the desired goals of freedom has been called a "continuing seminar," because in a seminar there is fluidity, flexibility, informality, and the search for as much relevant information as can be found. In seminar consultations there is a continuing examination of all relevant data, with the goals being appraisal of alternative interpretations and advocacy, including those diversities of conclusions so characteristic of the academic community.

It is our hypothesis that establishing desired changes in student freedom should take place within the context of inquiry and action as employed by educational institutions traditionally. For the higher educational institution to retain integrity of purpose and action, methods of establishing desirable student freedoms should be congruent with the educational mission of each institution. This implies that the most appropriate approach to change is one which is thoughtful, orderly, and respectful of constituted authority. Transformation should be based on the consideration of relevant facts, if available, and on the reasoned expression of opinions in an honest and open confrontation of opposing positions, whether they be from trustees, administrators, faculty, or students. Moreover, we suggest that, to obtain maximum benefit for the institution and for students, representatives of all constituents of the academic community should participate in formulating changes. This would, of course, mean that students themselves should participate fully and thoughtfully in such efforts. Finally, we advocate strongly that the process of orderly change be initiated by the president of each college and university. We turn now to a simple listing of some guidelines for consideration of desirable changes in students' academic freedom.

Guidelines for Orderly Change

Diversity rather than uniformity is characteristic in American higher education, for the concept of free men functioning in free institutions is our basic heritage. Likewise, one conclusion is very clear from our study: there is diversity among institutions regarding the forms and extent to which student freedoms are practiced. For these reasons we posit that the most important actions, which must be taken to instrument orderly change in the establishment of student freedoms, should be initiated locally in each college and university in the nation. We will, first, emphasize guidelines for action at the local level. A further rationale for this emphasis arises because local and regional conditions appear to be important partial determinants of the extent to which certain forms of student freedoms are exercised.

Guidelines for local action

At the outset, our appraisal suggests that presidents and deans of students should review, evaluate, and upgrade student personnel staff and services to the end of developing the extracurriculum as a sound program focussing on the education of students. Such an evaluation implies, in some instances, that a reorientation and rethinking of the philosophy of student personnel services will be necessary. It seems no longer feasible, if it ever was, to assume that the major function of the dean of students is to remove a "troublesome" burden from the president's shoulders. Nor is it appropriate to think that student personnel services are solely designed to focus on the pleasure, entertainment, or "welfare" of students during their out-of-the-classroom hours. Rather, the student personnel dean is to be viewed as an educator, as is any other member of the faculty. To be sure, he functions in much different ways, but in the main he should work imaginatively to create programs and opportunities which will make the institutional environment more conducive to educational experiences for students. A major role for the dean of students, we feel, should be one of developing those opportunities which will produce maturing experiences regarding the nature and use of freedom. In this function, as Thorndike suggested, "Should we not, first of all, make sure that . . . controversy is made the occasion to learn, to renew, or apply, fundamental facts and principles?" [4]

Second, we feel that presidents and deans of students should employ the organization of committees of administrative, faculty, and student groups by encouraging discussion of the issues of student academic freedom. In some cases such discussions could easily take place within the curriculum. In this we are suggesting that academic freedom—its conceptualization, history, and meaning—is a legitimate subject for academic discussion. We would also suggest that the reasoned discussion of this subject in formal meetings would yield much needed understanding preparatory to thoughtful enactment of policies.

In the organization of various task-oriented educational policy-making groups, changes should be made. We feel very strongly that appropriate revisions of organizational structure are necessary to establish student representation and active participation on important faculty committees. Moreover, it would seem that the responsible performance of student government groups could be encouraged by the referral of important issues and problems to them for consideration and action. Further, it would seem that the dignity and worth of students would be enhanced if procedures were established and used for formal and informal consultation prior to the enactment of any regulations affecting them.

A most important guideline—one which is partially substantiated by our data—is the establishment of formal organization, if such does not already exist, for the formal enactment of policies governing student freedoms. We suggest that the organizational structure make provision for *periodic* formulation, review, and reformulation of these policies and practices. It has been our experience that regularizing the review process permits a much more rational discussion of the issues involved when crises do arise. A point of reference, with a history of understanding, emerging from sometimes long and arduous conversations, clears the air for discussion of the real issues, with less venom motivating the disputants. This formal process can and should be coupled with imaginative programing of continuous informal conversations among students, administrators, and faculty. We have concluded that "planned" informal seminars, symposia, and retreats are valuable tools to bring about some degree of mutual understanding and agreement on the points of disagreement. We suggest that

[4] Edward L. Thorndike, *The Teaching of Controversial Subjects* (Cambridge, Mass.: Harvard University Press, 1937), p. 16.

such conversations should be characterized by flexibility, fluidity, and the search for as much relevant information as can be found. Attempts should be made to open conversation with as many students as possible at every level of student leadership. Special attention should be focused on the so-called politically apathetic students, and as well those who are "discontent" or "trouble makers."

Finally, we suggest that concerted efforts be made by the president and the student personnel staff to interpret the desirability and even necessity of student academic freedom to the many publics concerned with the affairs of the institution. Our data support our contention that the public statement and explanation of policies encouraging student freedom buttress the president in his decision-making duties. We think that the strength of the statements of principle by presidents and deans of students augurs well for future development in the complicated task of educating the public about the legitimate aims and purposes of higher education. It would seem at this juncture, although we have no research data to support us, that boards of trustees and regents can be of inestimable value in making clear the firm institutional commitment to the necessity of responsible exercise of freedom by students—and, indeed, by all scholars. By virtue of their position, trustees are often the most appropriate persons in the academic community to take a firm public stand to assist in communicating the needs of the institution to the nonacademic world.

Guidelines for national action

Two lines of action seem, to us, to be more appropriately attacked at the national level of educational organization—the establishment of statements of desirable academic freedom for students and the further delineation of the problems and issues of student academic freedom by research methods.

On the basis of our research findings and as a result of conversations with students, faculty, and other administrators, we suggest that there is need for a cooperative joint statement of desirable student freedom to be issued by national educational and professional organizations. We would not, at this time, wish to define either the substance of, or method for obtaining, such a statement; yet it would seem appropriate for it to arise out of the cooperative efforts of such organizations as the American Council on Education's Commission on Academic Affairs, Committee S of the American Association of University Professors, the United States National Student Association, the National Association of Student Personnel Administrators, the National Association of Women Deans and Counselors, and the American College Personnel Association. These organizations would not be representative of interested persons of all institutions; thus, the conversations leading to the writing of a statement might well be open to representatives of many other organizations—if not as participants, then as consultants. Indeed, the prime benefit of the effort, it appears to us, would be the thoughtful *conversations* leading to some formulation.

In conclusion, we have discovered that our research leaves us with more questions than answers. To be sure, further analyses will reveal valuable information; yet many puzzling aspects of the concern for student freedom and for ways of effective administration of educational institutions beg for answers. Consequently, we strongly encourage national professional and research organizations to undertake studies and experiments to delineate and illuminate these issues. For example, we feel that a research project similar to the study we have undertaken for the National Association of Student Personnel Administrators should be undertaken for junior and community colleges and eventually among high schools. We reason that the profound understanding of responsible exercise of academic freedom must begin early in adolescence if mature learning is to be assured.

Further delineation and assessment of various methods of policy formation and decision making at all educational levels is needed. Evaluation of the effectiveness of various methods of consultation and communication with students and definition of the role of governing boards of trustees in the establishment of student academic freedom are matters justifying major research efforts. Although there are many other topics that need research, two more strike us as being of great importance to the subject of our report: examination of the nature and prevalence of procedures for due process in disciplinary actions, and study of the roles of nonuniversity groups in the formulation and implementation of policies governing student academic freedom.

Some
Concepts
of Student
Academic
Freedom

LAURENCE V. BRITT, S.J.

IF I WERE TO FOLLOW standard procedure in starting a discussion on student academic freedom, I suppose I would begin by citing the glaring headlines over articles reporting student unrest, student demonstrations, student riots, student revolt, and so on. It would then be in order to suggest that somehow or other students of today are different from all earlier students and that, although they may be somewhat unreasonable, they have gained so much momentum that, for practical reasons, we will all probably have to accede to their demands, if only to keep the peace and get on with our work. Some might consider this a practical approach, but I would hate to see any group of educators or students wasting time on attempts to resolve any problem on the basis of simple expediency.

At the risk of seeming to start from out in left field, I would like to begin with moral philosophy or theology. Almost any elementary moral treatise, whether philosophical or theological, will begin with a consideration of *human* acts, as distinguished from "acts of man" (indeliberate acts such as respiration, digestion, and the like), and of the conditions required for any act to be truly human. It seems to be generally agreed that for an act to be a truly human act, imputable for praise or blame, it must, among other things, be free not only from external necessity or compulsion but also from internal necessity. In short, strictly human acts are those and only those that proceed from man's deliberate, free will.

This may seem to be rather remote from the present topic, but it must be remembered that we are talking about students—about human beings engaged in the process of acquiring an education. Howsoever education be defined, it is basically a matter of personal growth and development; and if it be education worthy of the name, as opposed to rote learning, conditioning, indoctrination, or training, it must be classified as a human activity. Consequently, freedom is presupposed, for this is by definition a prerequisite for any kind of human activity. In short, if one is to be truly educated, he must enjoy that freedom which is indispensable for the achievement of that personal growth and development which is education. We could probably presume general agreement on this basic point, but I think it may be important to make it explicit, if only to indicate that the student freedom we are here talking about stems directly from the nature of man and the nature of the learning process; it does not depend on positive law or privilege. Each individual student, by the very nature of things, has the right to freedom in searching for truth, in expressing and communicating his opinions in his search for truth, in exploring the thousand different facets of truth, in following his own conscience, and in deciding his own destiny freely and in accordance with his own conscience.

The Misinterpretation of "Student Academic Freedom"

The difficulty, of course, arises from "student academic freedom" being used all too often in a context that has little relation to anything academic. Or it is considered as an end in itself, as a kind of *summum bonum*, to which, in some mysterious fashion, everything else must be subordinated. It would be helpful, I think, if terms could be more precisely defined, and if student academic freedom could be limited to the academic context and considered not as an end but as a means to important ends, or more properly as a condition necessary for the achievement of a great purpose. Pope John XXIII had something like this in mind, I think, when he spoke of peace among nations as requiring truth as its foundation, justice as its rule, love as its driving force, *liberty as its atmosphere*.[1]

If we make the mistake of assuming that freedom is an end in itself, something good in itself, to be achieved at almost any cost, we will probably make the further mistake of assuming that such freedom must be without any limitation or restriction whatsoever. If, however, we accept it as a means to an end, or as a condition prerequisite for the achievement of an end, we will more easily understand that, in practice, this freedom may in fact be restricted and that it should be used only to the extent that it is actually helpful in striving for the end desired.

It will be more readily understood that, good though they be, freedom and individual rights do not exist *in abstracto*, but are enjoyed by and exercised by individual human beings who, in turn,

[1] See the encyclical *Pacem in Terris*, April 11, 1963, Part V, Paragraph 5.

exist not *in abstracto*, but in a real world in which they are but individual members of various societies which happen to have other members with similar rights and privileges. This point was emphasized recently in the story told of an enthusiastic fight fan who was giving a vivid and animated description of a prize fight to his companions on a crowded subway. At one point, in an effort to exemplify a wild punch that had been thrown in the ring, he swung one arm around in a wide arc and unintentionally punched a bystander in the nose. A slight altercation promptly developed. After a somewhat heated exchange of words, the boxing enthusiast insisted: "I have a right to swing my arm around if I want!" To which his victim responded: "Yes, you have a right to swing your arm around, but your right ends where my nose begins!" It's a simple story, but it may illustrate that rights can have their limitations.

Any discussion of this topic should include practical consideration of the restrictions or limitations that might legitimately and even necessarily be imposed on academic freedom and student freedom in general, because of the requirements of the common good, or because certain institutional regulations or controls are required for the attainment of the institution's purpose, or because of the rights of others, or because some individuals are not sufficiently mature and responsible to use freedom wisely. We may shrink from the thought of any restriction of freedom at all, especially if it is termed "academic" freedom, but it seems to me that we take it for granted that in other areas individual freedom will often be restricted.

For example, an individual (student or otherwise) is presumably free to attend or not attend the Metropolitan Opera. If he elects to attend, however, he must first fulfill certain conditions: he must purchase a ticket, arrange to attend at a prescribed time, appear in what is normally accepted as conventional attire, conduct himself in acceptable fashion. It is expected that he will not interfere with other patrons' enjoyment of the opera. If he elects to come in shorts, he may be refused admission. His ticket of admission entitles him to be a member of the audience, not a member of the cast, so he is not free to join in the singing of his favorite aria. In many ways, then, by making his original choice to attend the performance, he has agreed to having certain restrictions imposed on his conduct and behavior. At home he may sing to his heart's content, but this would scarcely be tolerated at the opera.

This might suggest that, although freedom is a necessary condition for the process of education, it is not something absolute. One's decision to enter a particular college or university will normally entail some surrender of personal freedom that might otherwise be enjoyed. This would seem to follow logically from the fact that a college or university is a community or society made up of many members, united together and using common means for the pursuit of some common good. The institution is not founded for the exclusive benefit of an individual student, but is for the good of society and its many members. Generally speaking, the courts have sustained this view, ruling that the right to attend a specific college or university is not a natural right, but a civil right or privilege, and that university authorities may make all necessary and proper regulations for the orderly conduct of their institutions and preservation of discipline therein, so long as such regulations are reasonable, necessary, and for the common good.

Clarifying the Meaning

It seems to me that the whole question of student academic freedom would be clarified considerably if we kept in mind not merely freedom, but freedom with responsibility in a society made up of many members, working together and, in large measure, using common means for the attainment of a common good. Second, I think it would be helpful to distinguish *academic* freedom, which is related to an individual's unhampered pursuit of truth, from other forms of freedom which may relate to overt action, participation in popular or unpopular demonstrations, use of university facilities for personal purposes not directly related to academic goals, use of an institution's name, or conduct that may be unconventional, immoral, or illegal. Freedom, unfortunately, is not an univocal term, but has many connotations.

The academic community, then, must, first of all, clarify the precise significance of "student academic freedom." Once that has been done, it may be easier to address ourselves to other forms of freedom and to explore ways and means of ensuring maximum freedom for all without running the danger of having an individual's exercise of freedom interfere with the common good. If we try to remember that true Christian freedom does not consist in an anarchic conception of freedom or in rejection of all legislative disposition, and that freedom is not some sacrosanct ultimate but a means or an instrument to help discover the true, the good, and the beautiful, it seems to me that it should be possible for us to work out practical policies that would ensure the maximum good of all concerned.

A Student
Looks
at
Academic
Freedom

GREG LIPSCOMB

It is interesting that the Library of Congress catalogues student academic freedom under the caption "Teaching—freedom of." This is a holdover from a time in American educational history when student academic freedom was thought of as an adjunct of, and secondary to, teacher academic freedom. This pattern of thought originated in the wardship attitude of colonial colleges, "when colleges were hardly more than high schools and students were still pupils," [1] and was left untampered by the selective importation from German universities of the freedom to teach and not of *Lernfreiheit*, the freedom to learn.

I say *holdover* because for the last twenty years, student academic freedom has been recognized as a distinct concern of the educational community. It has been a time of definition and clarification. The result is a fairly clear concept of the rights of the individual student in the world of ideas. And there has been a tolerable consensus among educators about what those rights should be.[2] *Should* is the proper word because, as with civil rights, the pragmatics of implementation, the how and the when of the process, not the vocal recognition of the right, have presented problems to officials. The students should be able to hear any speaker they wish, but the arduous task of giving the final nod, or relinquishing the power of the nod altogether, somehow a painful process. Suffice it to say that the administrator

---

[1] Robert M. MacIver, *Academic Freedom in Our Time* (New York: Columbia University Press, 1955), p. 205.

[2] Generally, the pronouncements of professional organizations such as the A.A.U.P. and treatises on the topic of academic freedom phrase their definitions in absolutist terms. MacIver's definition is typical: "the freedom to question and to differ, without authoritative repression and without scholastic penalization . . ." (p. 189). This freedom entails freedom of speakers, editorials, and discussions.

288

should have the stamina and the firm commitment to ideas that would enable him, indeed compel him, to match practice with theory.

But the sixties pose a different problem. It is, perhaps, time for redefinition. The American concept of student academic freedom has been confined to the relationship among ideas, the individual student, and his surrounding society, educational and otherwise. Thus the issue has been the same whether the incident in question occurs in a class of four or four hundred. The European and Latin concept of student academic freedom, on the other hand, deals more with *mass* academic freedom—the relationship among ideas, the mass of students, and their surrounding society. This approach necessarily encompasses a broader scope of ideas than its American counterpart, as well as a different problem of implementation. Hence there is frequent confrontation in foreign universities of opinions about, for instance, how the institution should be run and how much the ideas of students, as a group, on running the institution should be registered and recognized. These are essentially mass student academic freedom problems as opposed to individual ones. An analogy might be drawn to the labor movement. Somehow the problems of management are different when a single worker requests special consideration on the grounds of personal budgetary difficulties, than when four thousand workers are pounding the president's desk for rights stretching from coffee breaks to actually sharing in company management.

To extend the analogy, we are now in the John L. Lewis days of student academic freedom. This is so whether one believes the American definition is gravitating toward that of the Europeans and Latins, or simply that the American definition still holds true, but is now acquiring connotations peculiar to mass education. Regardless of the approach, I think Berkeley cannot be written off solely as an issue in democratic government. It is an issue of student academic freedom. Indeed, perhaps democratic government in this instance is a question within the purview of academic freedom, and Berkeley is but the Los Angeles of the issue: a black eye, but nevertheless significant. Blending the approaches, one could say that contemporary issues have come to define student academic freedom as student freedom in the academic community—not just freedom to explore ideas and express them within that community—for though this latter element is perhaps the end goal of the academic process, the multitudinous other factors bearing on its realization are certainly more than merely incidental, and indeed at times—Berkeley—become the focal point of concern.

What are some of these "other factors"? Primarily they are the freedoms to participate in defining academic freedom. Student academic freedom has been defined as the freedom to learn. Among the best modes of learning is doing. One does not receive an education; he acquires it. "Freedom is not inherited . . . as property rights [are]. . . . Freedom can only be inherited in the sense that every succeeding generation has the opportunity to hammer it out for itself on the anvil of experience." [3] Friedrich Paulsen defines academic freedom as the freedom to learn to govern oneself. With respect to the issue at hand, this entails *real* responsibility in students—participation, not just consultation, functionally, not just formally. "Genuine responsibility is the child of the freedom to act." [4] And genuine responsibility in this instance must include a decisionary voice in all elements having an effect on students, including academics. (It goes without saying that extracurricular activities should be entirely student-directed.) Academic freedom is inexorably intertwined with academic responsibility. Administrators and faculty will deny that such a student right exists with respect to academic policy, but they would not if they subscribed to the community concept of the academic institution, "the set of common standards developed by interaction of its members," as Phillip Monypenny states, "developed out of shared experiences rather than imposed by authority, . . . products of consensus," not of edict.[5] It matters to the student whether a class is four students and a professor or four hundred students and a teaching assistant. It matters whether the "publish or perish" rule minimizes time spent with students. It is an aspect of mass academic freedom to allow students to voice this concern, and it is an issue of implementation of that freedom to have their voices heard. The right to speak, to be complete, must include the right to speak effectively. What other city would tolerate closed doors to its citizenry on issues of governmental substance? Or viewing the university as a business, if we must, the students, simply stated, have consumer rights, the right to an academic profit-sharing plan in the business of cooperative intellectualism. In terms of the traditional American definition, how can there be a free flow of ideas when the specified channels of educational experience are charted by computers? An

[3] Harry D. Gideonse, "Academic Freedom: A Decade of Challenge and Clarification," in *Academic Freedom*, comp. by Neal Johnston (Philadelphia, Pa.: U.S. National Student Association), p. 1.

[4] MacIver, *Academic Freedom*.

[5] "Toward a Standard for Student Academic Freedom," in *Problems in Student Rights and Freedoms* (Philadelphia, Pa.: U.S. National Student Association, July 1964), p. 105.

environment of mass student academic freedom can be brought about only by the participation of the mass in creating that environment.

It will be argued that students are yet too immature to take part in the academic governing process. But college is primarily a place for maturing, and people mature best by doing. By and large, the student citizens of academic communities are higher in intelligence than the general citizenry of the standard American community. And in the latter, though the citizens may not know as much about governing as does the mayor, this does not preclude them from bearing on his decisions. The academic community, like any community, needs a system of checks and balances, else there is academic taxation without representation. "A democracy encourages to the highest degree possible the participation of the governed in the governing process." [6] Students certainly should not have control; but they should have academic due process. No one holds a monopoly on truth; and though we may not be able to define truth, the process of attempting to is essential. Recognition by administrators of student participation in this process will enable administrators to do more than just plow the field. They will also plant the seed.

In the specifics, how can the solutions to problems of mass academic freedom be implemented? Permanent channels of communication should be established. Berkeley found itself floundering under *ad hoc* committees during its several crises. These channels should be designed to cater to mass modes of student expression, be it through student newspapers, popularly elected student government (often, actually, not so popular), or peaceful demonstrations (often more popular). The channels may be formal, as with student votes on administrative and faculty policy committees or frequent news releases from the president's office published in the student newspaper; or informal, as with occasional commingling of top administrators and students over coffee or meals. The air about these channels should be one of consent and permissiveness, an encouragement to the free flow of ideas, regardless of their nature, a condition so essential to our traditional concept of academic freedom. And to erase any flavor of suspicion, *in loco parentis*, that practice which encourages the will not to be curious, which feeds our youth intravenously with noncontroversial pabulum, and which engenders the wrong type of *alma mater*, should be abolished.

As a sidenote, administrators have the special duty to convey to the general public, often the other side of the academic freedom

[6] American Civil Liberties Union, *Academic Freedom and Academic Responsibility* (New York: A.C.L.U., 1956).

forces, these concepts of student participation and the creation of an open market of ideas. This can be done through alumni journals, speeches to citizen groups, and testimony before the legislature. In times of crisis, the head administrator should be the first to defend the students. If he does not, perhaps he can escape temporarily by compromising policies; but in the long run he cannot find victory, for he will be compromising principles.

I will concede that my approach to the question of student academic freedom, stressing the means instead of the end, is perhaps tangential, if not semantical. But it is only relatively so. I contend that the future is tantalizing us with more than old problems under new guises. It evinces new problems whose predominant characteristic is size. The projected college enrollment and the estimate that by 1970 one-half of our population will be under age twenty-five affirm this. Hence, all our prior problems and solutions, including those of student academic freedom, must be viewed from a new perspective.

A Teacher
Looks
at Student
Academic
Freedom

PHILLIP MONYPENNY

THE GREAT GROWTH of our educational institutions and the increasing importance of higher education, both in society as a whole and in the careers of individuals, pose threats to the character of freedom in our society not generally recognized by either faculties or administrators. The closely intermeshed requirements for degrees at any educational institution already impose controls on individual development and initiative which may very well repress creativity and individuality of response and which reward the person who is able to adapt to externally imposed standards of behavior rather than the person who is "inner directed," to use Riesman's phrase. The force of these controls is greatly enhanced by the emergence of the "total institution"—to take a phrase from Erving Goffman—which provides all things: housing, food, recreation, medical care, personal and psychiatric counseling, even public spectacles; an institution in which the student is submerged for nine months or even twelve months of the year to such a degree that it takes unusual initiative to leave the extended campus.

Today's institution has added the powers of landlord, maitre d'hotel, family counselor, priest, athletic coach, and general law enforcement officer to the inherent powers it has to set intellectual tasks for students and to judge their performance. It watches the students in their dormitories and it controls their social life not only by regulating hours, the consumption of liquor, and the right to leave the campus, but also by organizing activities for them to take part in. The university student unions with their professional staffs are an independent world into which students are inducted, organized, and rewarded for participating in institutionally sponsored affairs, the blueprints for which lurk in the filing drawers of the central offices. Student publications are sponsored and censored, and student organizations are regulated in matters of finances, constitutions, times of meeting, and spheres of activity, in the name of coordination and responsibility.

This total institution is defended—like its counterparts, the monastery, the mental hospital, the reformatory, and the military services —on the grounds that it is necessary to shape all student experiences to the undefined goals of the institution. The education mission is now found to extend to disciplinary procedures and the control of student activities. Like members of some religious sects, our students are asked to love their lashes and those who lay them on. The educational community, like the therapeutic community, has indeed become total.

Not only are these educational communities total institutions, but also they are interlinked by the fantastic efficiency of communication. A student entering a dormitory in Florida is investigated by inquiries made to his dormitory counselor at Illinois not with respect to whether he paid his bills or damaged the furniture but with respect to those vague behavioral categories by which psychiatrically oriented (but not trained) housing staffs determine whether their fellow human beings are "adjusted" or "unadjusted," are desirable influences in "wholesome" living units, or are possible sources of infection.

Under these conditions the place of students in the educational institution—a matter which has always been left to the discretion of university and college administrators without much outside interference, even by the courts—needs some attention. The basis upon which I and the other members of Committee S on Student Academic Freedom of the A.A.U.P. have approached this question has been that of the educational community. However, it is the educational community not as a total institution, but as a community which embraces two structurally distinct areas—the area of formal instruction and the area of informal learning—that has concerned us. The faculty and the administrators thoroughly dominate the area of formal learning. They, and the process of the discussion of educational matters among the general public, have thrown the students into an enormous insecurity in which they must continuously prove themselves by strenuous and often self-defeating efforts. We have increased assignments, raised the standards of admission not only to graduate and professional schools but to special curricula in the undergraduate colleges, revised courses and curricula to stress the abstract elements in the several disciplinary areas, and often reminded our students of the panting hordes who wait outside the gate, ready to step into any vacancies which their inadequacy may create.

It would seem that there ought to be some areas of calm outside this storm where students can follow their own volition, can make their self-discoveries unseen by the intrusive eye of their adult associates in the community, and can develop skills—whether at courtship or politics—which are not in the formal curriculum.

It is necessary to keep some areas open for student initiative because the educational institution is sure to be bound by orthodoxies no longer universally current, however much its faculty and some of its bolder administrators may think of themselves as unconventional innovators, challenging the cherished certainties of their age. If the faculty and the administration are very intrusive in the area of nonclassroom life, they risk being irrelevant and destructive as well, whether through effective repression of all initiative or by the stimulation of open conflict.

The explorations and self-discoveries with which Committee S has been concerned in its effort to frame a protective statement have been largely those of the intellect. We have therefore discussed in some detail freedom to hear speakers, to discuss, to propagandize, to organize, and to advocate. We have discussed the control of the student press and the independence from faculty and administrative control of student government. However, limitations on intellectual pursuits arise in other ways as well. They arise from the students' feeling that their expressions of belief and their organizing efforts may result in adverse recommendations for employment, for admittance to graduate and professional schools, and for financial assistance. They arise in the question of whether the legitimate disciplinary powers of the institution may be used to restrain students from expressions of opinion and from actions which are uncomfortable for the institution rather than essentially illegitimate. They arise in the area where institutional powers may be used to provide additional sanctions to those already imposed by the general civil authorities.

The question of the relation of the institution to propaganda, agitation, and protest is a particularly important one in the present day, and nowhere may institutional powers be more destructive than here. With our heritage of revolution and internal conflict, we cannot believe that the normal process for resolving social issues is reasoned discussion among good men. Change normally brings conflict, especially when the use of governmental powers is part of change and the resistance to it and the forces of change require and will get contentious leadership. That leadership, whether it is Frances Willard, Eugene Debs, or Robert Welch, is performing a necessary social function. The leadership of all movements, whether the cause is the protection of slavery in the territories, the annexation of Texas, or the abolition of nuclear weapons, comes from the most educated and privileged stratum of the population. Our college and university population *are* that stratum and they are at an age when their commitments to careers, modes of thought, and modes of social participation are being determined.

It is absurd to expect them to stay aloof from the great causes of their day, whether they register for ambulance duty with the Allies in World War I, go to jail as pacifists and draft resisters in World War II, or demonstrate for or against U.S. policy in Viet Nam at the present time. The university and the college are negating the social and educational purposes they exist to serve when they attempt to obstruct or penalize participation in such movements beyond the point at which the processes of ordinary law penalize it and beyond the self-imposed penalties which stem from inadequate academic performance, caused by want of regularity and energy in meeting academic commitments. In exercising tolerance and forbearance in dealing with civil rights demonstrators and objectors to national policy, the university administrators and faculty are not being generous and charitable toward erring souls. They are only acting consistently with the educational mission of their institution, which exists rather to find knowledge and standards of conduct than to transmit them unimpaired and unchanged.

Because the university and the college have such an overwhelming influence on careers, even the pettier areas of its control over the student body can be destructive of individual opportunities and can dampen the disposition to intellectual exploration. The intellectual confidence to examine old positions and set an independent standard for both knowledge and belief may not be independent of the emotional confidence that accrues from having a secure area of independent personal decision. Restrictions on hours, travel, visiting in rooms, and liquor; insistence that students cooperate with local law enforcement officers in exposing youthful departures from established convention—all have an implication of adult tyranny and repression for young people, though they may not have such an implication to those of us who impose them. As a minimum, student participation in the determination of policies with respect to out-of-classroom conduct is rather an administrative device for avoiding unnecessary conflict than a matter of essential rights, but it should also promote an atmosphere of mutual confidence in which learning can take place.

In these areas also heavy penalties may follow from rather minor infractions, and the usual problems of proof and due process are inescapable.

In other words, student academic freedom presents the familiar problem of finding, in educational institutions as for the general society, appropriate restraints on power, power which has great potentiality for creativeness and good, but which, like all power, may be diverted to repression.

Demonstrations, Freedom, and the Law

NICHOLAS deB. KATZENBACH

I WOULD LIKE TO DISCUSS a concern which educators and law enforcement officers have very much in common—that of demonstrations. That there is a relationship between civil rights demonstrations, which are often the concern of the Department of Justice, and student demonstrations, with which educators sometimes have to cope, is obvious. Both are conceived as a form of protest. To a degree, the same techniques are used. Indeed, in some instances, the same young people have carried the heat of civil rights passions from a summer in the South onto the campus in the fall. But too often this heat, generated by decades of injustice and oppression against the Negro, has dissipated into a mere fever when it has reached the campus. The similarities are only surface and there is a world of difference.

The Negro and Civil Disobedience

For a century the Constitution has guaranteed the Negro American the formal legal rights of citizenship and full participation in our society. For a century these constitutional guarantees have, until recently, been without real meaning for most Negroes. I think that future generations will look back upon these times with little understanding and less sympathy and will wonder why it took so long. And I confess that I myself wonder.

Initially the vindication of Negro rights was in the courts. Participation in other areas of our political life was, in many parts of the country, simply not available to the disenfranchised. And so it was by the slow, tedious, and expensive process of litigation that legal barriers, clearly unconstitutional, were all too gradually broken down. The technique of substituting mass protest and demonstration for court process is relatively recent. With it has come a rather fuzzy and somewhat inarticulate doctrine of civil disobedience. I say "inar-

298

ticulate" because it seems to me that every theoretical justification for civil disobedience carries its exponent too far.

By and large, the nation has viewed the protest movement from the view of the underlying moral issue rather than in terms of legal niceties. And I think that this has been the right and sound response. The "fires of frustration and discord," in President Kennedy's phrase, were burning in every city where legal and political remedies for just grievances were simply not available. The people sought redress in the streets in demonstrations, parades, and protests. That these demonstrations have been peaceful, orderly, and dignified is a tribute to Negro leadership and to the faith Negroes have had that countless injustices could and would be remedied by the process of political change. That these demonstrations occurred also offers a lesson.

The value of a demonstration can be gauged in part by what it seeks to *demonstrate*. The civil rights demonstrations in the South have in fact demonstrated a profound truth—a truth which could be evidenced in perhaps no other way: the unrest and dissatisfaction of the Southern Negro. Such a statement may sound palpably obvious, until it is compared with the soothing assurances which had so often been voiced by Southern white leaders—that the Southern Negro in fact accepted the caste structure of the region not only with complaisance, but with gratitude. As these protests showed, the Negro was not only *not* complaisant, but held such passion for full citizenship that he was, and is, willing to risk intimidation of the worst sort in his effort to achieve it.

We may accept or approve of disobedience in a different form of government, where there are no effective public forums for change and redress. It was such protest that gave this nation birth. It was such protest that was imported here from Gandhi's India, where it was the sole means of expression for Indians at a time when they did not have self-government. But when, as in most parts of this democracy—for most people on most issues—the power to bring about change lies in the hands of the voter, we would anticipate rather different conduct. Put plainly, we may seek redress and change through political processes but we are expected, while we are seeking, *to obey the law*.

The built-in outlet for grievances in our society is political: the squeakier the wheel, the faster the response, normally, of appropriate elected officials. And yet, in the South, there was no response to Negro needs by local officials, for there has been no Negro vote to help elect or defeat them. The Negro not only has been the bottom layer in an economic and social caste system, but also he has been systematically excluded from any expressive, participating membership in the political structure.

The civil rights demonstrations of the South have thus furnished us a second lesson: that the Southern Negro has had no alternative method of expressing grievances; that his citizenship in a democracy has been largely irrelevant to him because he could not exercise the rights of citizenship. I hardly need review the devices used to discourage Negroes from trying to vote, or the church burnings and bombings designed to discourage him from trying to assemble. The futility of seeking public expression for the Negro can be epitomized by a single, insignificant incident. A Negro boy walked down the street of his Southern town and was arrested. Why? Because his teeshirt bore the legend "Freedom Now." On what charge? Parading without a permit.

The nation largely accepted, understood, and sympathized with Negro demonstrations in the South, I think, because we recognized both that the Negro was oppressed and that he was so completely oppressed he had no other way to seek his freedom. With the enactment of the Civil Rights Act of 1964 and the Voting Rights Act of 1965, and with President Johnson's unyielding commitment to civil rights, the avenues of political participation are now being opened to the Negro in the South. It is our firmest resolve to make that opportunity meaningful by the next election. What such opportunity for political expression will mean to the future course and purpose of protest demonstrations will require extensive soul-searching and responsible analysis. For as Bayard Rustin has shrewdly observed, the relationship of the protest to the ends to be achieved will be more tenuous in the future than it has been in the past.

Confusions in the Student Protest Movement

When I said at the outset that I regard civil rights demonstrations and student demonstrations as only superficially similar, I did not mean to suggest a blanket impatience with or disapproval of student dissent. Let me make it plain that I believe the social commitment of many students, as sometimes evidenced by protest demonstrations, to be not only protected by the Constitution but also fortunate. Their concern with the ills of society can do much to remedy those ills— if it is in fact a commitment and not merely a fleeting excitement. But some student demonstrations do raise questions that cannot lightly go unanswered by those who would protest.

The first question is not whether they should demonstrate but *what* it is they seek to demonstrate.

Often, their aim has been the defense of individualism in a society of mass and machine. The validity of their cause is beyond question. There is perhaps no more telling evidence of how widespread is our concern than the speed with which our vocabulary of modern individualism has become cliché. Society is at the mercy of a "technocratic juggernaut." Industrialization has polluted the spiritual climate with "depersonalization, urbanization, and centralization." The individual, increasingly, is "psychologically dispossessed," "alienated," and "anonymized."

However trite the terms, each of them is a valid concern. What strikes me is the extent to which student rebels treat them all synonymously; for that is the same extent to which they obscure and perhaps even exaggerate the very real, specific underlying concerns. By railing so hard against the deadening effect of the mass generality, they dissipate the insight and energy which ought better be devoted to opposing the corrupting specifics.

Just how diffuse the generality has become may be gauged from the credo of the Free Speech Movement in Berkeley: "We must now begin the demand of the right to know; to know the realities of the present world-in-revolution, and to have an opportunity to think clearly in an extended manner about the world. It is ours to demand meaning; we must insist upon meaning!"

I would suggest that the beginning of meaning is not to synonymize all our concerns about the problems of modernity and technology, but the contrary: to isolate and analyze to determine what is in fact deadening and what is not. Should we not, for example, sort out the impacts of size and technology on the university? For there are clear benefits for students to reap from the larger school. The larger the academic community, the more opportunity there is for the very diversity we prize.

If there are six professors of history whose views a student may reject, the more likely, in a large institution, that there will be twelve others with whom he feels comfortable. If there is a Greek letter emphasis in student social life, the more likely, in a large institution, that the individual will be able to find a circle of independents who prize scholarship, or beards, or music.

Further, in a mechanical sense, what, after all, is inherently objectionable about having a computer collate grades, or class schedules, or tuition bills—if the result is faster and surer than that of a clerk on a high stool with a quill pen? What is the injury to soul or spirit if five hundred rather than fifty other students are exposed to Hegel at the same time? Fact and truth do not exist in finite amounts, like a pot of mashed potatoes in the dining hall, to be prorated according to the number of students. Economies of scale need not mean parsimonies of spirit.

By rebelling with such prodigality against so diffuse a target, the students miss the target. Indeed, too often all a demonstration may prove is that students have become polished in the techniques of demonstration. As A. H. Raskin observed in a notable discussion of the Berkeley disorders, student "activists obviously have developed a vested interest in finding things to fight about." [1]

This is not to say that the submergence of the individual is not a valid mark. This is not to say that students should submit to the herd. It *is* to say that students, like all of us troubled by the fact of dilution of the individual's role, need to sharpen and clarify their aims. It is not record-keeping by punch card that we should fear, but the absence of animate attention to what is on them. It is not an elephantine lecture class that depersonalizes education, but a shortage of able section instructors with whom to discuss the lectures. It is not identical automobiles or toasters that we should guard against, but the passivity that can permit mass-produced forms to mold our higher tastes.

Student Protest and the Ethics of Civil Disobedience

But even if student targets could be so narrowed, it remains fair to ask whether demonstrations are either an appropriate or even an effective weapon. The comparison—indeed, the contrast—with the civil rights movement is instructive. However valid these campus concerns may be, do they even approach the duration, the directness, and the depth of the injustices inflicted on the Southern Negro?

On the contrary. It should not be supposed that because students use many of the same techniques as Negroes in the South that their dissatisfactions are as profound. However deeply felt, such vaguely expressed grievances are so pallid by comparison with those of the Negro that to demonstrate over them can be to dilute and debase the moral significance of demonstrations for civil rights.

Put simply, the freedom to eat, to vote, to learn—indeed, to live—justifies far more than the freedom to exclaim four-letter words. Dif-

[1] "The Berkeley Affair," *New York Times Sunday Magazine*, Feb. 14, 1965, pp. 24–25 +.

fusion of goals is one peril the student dissenter must acknowledge, but there is also a second peril, that a demonstration becomes an instrument not of persuasion but of coercion.

The distinction between persuasion and coercion can perhaps best be stated once more in terms of the Negro revolution: The goal of the Negro must be to seek to change an entire political system. The goal of the student is to seek to influence a specific decision or policy. The Negro, without access to any of the democratic forms of expression, has had little choice but to demonstrate. The student, whether he objects to conformity or to government policy in Viet Nam, has a range of alternatives.

It is not as though students are foreclosed from effective communication with faculty or administration. It is not as though students are denied expression through campus organizations or newspapers. Or, *if* they are, it is not as though they were denied recourse to their parents or the community at large. Their dissent, no matter how bitter or extreme, is welcome. It may contribute to their goal of influencing decisions. But at the point that it becomes coercive—when students lie down on the tracks to block a troop train—protest changes from essential ingredient to something alien to the liberal tradition. Efforts to coerce are wrong in principle and ineffective in practice.

Positive Outcomes of Student Protest

Whatever else may be said, the pressures for expression and for individuality are, and should be, greater in the university than perhaps anywhere else in society. The underpinnings of this rebelliousness surely grow from what we would teach our youth. Where else could students have developed so passionate a regard for individual dignity but in college classrooms? How else could they have found inspiration, if not for their attentiveness to their lessons in Socrates, learning that he spoke for individual worth and freedom; of the teaching of Immanuel Kant, who said, "Treat other human beings as subjects, not as objects"; or of Martin Buber, who taught that we should regard our fellow man as "thou," not as "it."

Such lessons reach to the core of liberal education. Small wonder that they are seized on by students, anxious as ever to search out the naked emperors of our society. It is perhaps inevitable that, so impelled, the rebelliousness of young people may go out of focus. The question for higher education thus may be not how to quell demonstrations but rather how to communicate to students the need to set their faces against truly deadening conformity; how to resist the pressure of that inert hand most meaningfully; how to demonstrate, in short, both the individuality and the respect for law that underlie our society.

Procedural Due Process and the College Student: Law and Policy *

CLARK BYSE

THE POLAR JUDICIAL DECISIONS concerning the law's procedural requirements in student dismissal proceedings are *Hill v. McCauley*,[1] an 1887 case involving Dickinson College, and *Anthony v. Syracuse University*,[2] decided in 1928. The most important judicial contribution is *Dixon v. Alabama State Board of Education*,[3] decided in 1961. After outlining the facts and holdings in these three cases, I propose, first, to indicate what courts may be expected to do in the future when student dismissal or suspension procedures are challenged as contrary to law and, second, to suggest the rudiments of the procedures that colleges and universities should observe when suspending or dismissing students.

The Three Decisions

Hill v. McCauley

On the evening of November 9, 1886, as the faculty of Dickinson College, Carlisle, Pennsylvania, was meeting, a disturbance occurred in the vicinity of the meeting room. In the words of President McCauley, the disturbance consisted of "hooting, singing, making noises, throwing small stones against the front window, and a large one thrown through the back window with great force which passed through both rooms, and in close proximity to some of the faculty, and out the front one."

A week later, John M. Hill, a second-year student, was summoned before the faculty and was informed by President McCauley, "Mr. Hill, the faculty are satisfied that you were connected with the riotous

---

* This paper is a condensed version of a previous discussion of the same subject; see Byse, "Procedure in Student Dismissal Proceedings: Law and Policy," *Journal of College Student Personnel*, March 1963, pp. 130–43.

[1] Commonwealth *ex rel.* Hill v. McCauley, 3 Pa. C.C. Rep. 77 (C.P. Cumberland Cy. 1887).

[2] 224 App. Div. 487, 231 N.Y. Supp. 435 (1928).

[3] 294 F.2d 150, *cert. denied*, 368 U.S. 930 (1961).

conduct of Tuesday night,[4] the 9th of November, and they have asked you to come in that you might make any statement in regard to the matter that you may wish, if any." Hill asked what was meant by riotous conduct and was told that it was "singing, hooting and throwing stones." Hill denied throwing any stones. He also said that he had been studying in his room when he heard the noise and had come down to where it was. Hill later stated that he had left the faculty meeting thinking that he "was clear of the matter."

After Hill left the faculty meeting, the faculty voted to dismiss him. Hill then brought an action for a writ of mandamus to compel the College officials to readmit him. President Judge Sadler of the Court of Common Pleas of Cumberland County was sharply critical of the faculty's action. "Investigations such as this," said the Judge, "ought to be carried on in such a way as . . . is most conducive to a just determination of the guilt or innocence of the party charged," that is, "in accordance with the principles of natural justice and the laws of the land." Specifically, (1) Hill should have been notified of the charge of misconduct made against him in such detail that he would realize its gravity and the harm which might come to him if the charge were sustained; (2) the testimony against him should have been given in his presence; (3) he should have been afforded a full opportunity to question adverse witnesses; and (4) he was entitled to call other witnesses to explain or contradict the testimony of the accusing witnesses.

The Judge also held that the proceeding was defective in that when Hill was brought before the faculty, he was informed that the faculty was satisfied, persuaded, or convinced of his connection with the riotous disturbance of the week before. This deprived Hill of the "legal presumption in favor of innocence" and violated the rule that the burden of proof is on those who assert the accused's guilt.

---

[4] The evidence in support of this conclusion was as follows: Before Hill was brought into the meeting room, President McCauley stated to the faculty that two days after the disturbance he had been informed by Robert Young, a janitor, that Mr. Hill "was there in great excitement brandishing his arms, making a noise and running up into the college and out." A member of the faculty, Professor Rittenhouse, reported that he had learned from a student that the student "had observed Hill at the disturbance and that he, the student, was surprised and disgusted." The name of the student was not disclosed to the faculty. Another member of the faculty, Professor Morgan, stated that on the evening of November 9 during the disturbance he "went to the hall door and saw someone on the stairway leading to the story above, who appeared to be coming down, but who turned about when he observed . . . Morgan, and hastened up again, making a noise in his haste to get away" and that when Morgan asked Robert Young, the janitor, who the person was, he received the reply that it was Hill. So far as can be ascertained from the opinion of Judge Sadler, this was the sum total of the evidence against Hill.

The Judge noted that although it was undoubtedly true that "the faculties of colleges are usually composed of exceptionally wise and good persons . . . , the experience of mankind has long demonstrated the unwisdom of conferring absolute and irresponsible power upon any body of men, however estimable, except in extraordinary and unavoidable cases." He also rejected the argument of the college—which he said was advanced with "great earnestness and warmth"—that the relation between student and professor is similar to that existing between parent and child, and that there would be as much justification for interference by the courts with the discipline of the one as of the other.

It is perhaps anticlimactic to state that Judge Sadler concluded that since Hill was not given "such a trial as he was entitled to under the laws" of the state, his dismissal from the college was invalid.[5]

Anthony v. Syracuse University

At the other extreme from Judge Sadler's decision and reasoning in the Dickinson College case is the opinion of Justice Sears of the Appellate Division of the Supreme Court of the State of New York in *Anthony v. Syracuse University*. Miss Beatrice O. Anthony, then seventeen or eighteen years old, was enrolled in the home economics course at Syracuse in September 1923. At that time and in September of 1924, 1925, and 1926 when she registered for her second, third, and fourth years, Miss Anthony signed a registration card which contained these words: "I agree in honor to comply with the regulations and requirements of Syracuse University and to cooperate with the University authorities and my fellow students in maintaining high standards of conduct and scholarship and in promoting the general welfare of the University. It is understood that I accept registration as a student in Syracuse University subject to the rule as to continuance therein found . . . [on a specified page] of the University Catalogue." The rule referred to in the registration card and printed

---

[5] Hill never was reinstated. He had applied for and was refunded a proportionate share of the fees he had paid for the fall semester. The college argued that this amounted to a voluntary severance of his connection with the college. Judge Sadler reserved the point for later decision. But Hill apparently never pressed the point. See J. M. Morgan, *Dickinson College: The History of One Hundred and Fifty Years, 1783–1933* (Carlisle, Pa.: Dickinson College, 1933), pp. 353–54 for a discussion of the Hill case. Professor Morgan (who was a member of the faculty at the time of the Hill affair) reports: "[Since Hill] had accepted the return of part of his college fee . . ., the Court . . . [held] under advisement the question of his reinstatement. So the case continued to stand, and stands to this day. This, of course, made appeal to the higher courts impossible, as there was no final decision." I am indebted to Gilbert Malcolm, provost of Dickinson College, for this reference.

in the university catalogue was amended slightly in 1924 and from that time read as follows: "Attendance at the University is a privilege and not a right. In order to safeguard those ideals of scholarship and that moral atmosphere which are the very purpose of its founding and maintenance, the University reserves the right and the student concedes to the University the right to require the withdrawal of any student at any time for any reason deemed sufficient to it, and no reason for requiring such withdrawal need be given."

On October 6, 1926, Miss Anthony was dismissed from the university. Although Miss Anthony demanded to be informed of the reasons for her dismissal and an opportunity to be heard, she was told only that the university officials had heard rumors about her, that the officials had talked with several girls in her sorority house and had found that although she had done nothing lately she had caused considerable trouble in the past, and that the officials did not think she was "a typical Syracuse girl."

Miss Anthony then brought an action to compel the university to reinstate her. The university defended on the ground that because of the statement in the registration card and the rule printed in the catalogue, the contract between the university and Miss Anthony authorized the university to dismiss her at any time for any cause whatever. The trial judge rejected this argument, discussed the right to notice and hearing in language similar to that used by Judge Sadler forty years before, held that the rule which purported to empower the university to dismiss a student without stating any reason was invalid because it was contrary to public policy, and ordered reinstatement.[6]

The university appealed, and the judgment of the trial judge was

[6] Anthony v. Syracuse University, 130 Misc. 249, 259, 223 N.Y. Supp. 796, 808–809 (Sup. Ct. Onondaga Cy. 1927): "[When] as in this instance, a student demands to know the reason why [he is to be dismissed], thereby challenging the existence of any grounds for the claim that he has failed to safeguard 'ideals of scholarship' and 'moral atmosphere' of the institution, and asks to be given an opportunity to state his side of the case, if there be a case against him, before he is deprived of valuable rights, that student is entitled to the elementary right of notice and opportunity to be heard. This element of notice lies at the very basis of the condemnation of property; and much more inherently does it lie at the basis of what is tantamount to an impairment of reputation. Given that opportunity, in the presence of admitted or established facts, the court would hesitate long before it would interfere with the discretion of the University; but here we have no facts, nothing but a dismissal 'in order to safeguard those ideals of scholarship and that moral atmosphere which are the very purpose' of the founding of the University. The position taken by the defendant is fraught with such obvious perils that it seems unnecessary to recite them; but what a field for rumor, for malice, for prejudice, for falsehood to roam in leading to conduct on the part of the University which might be entirely honest but at the same time based upon a total lack or misapprehension of facts!"

reversed. Justice Sears, who wrote the appellate court's opinion, reasoned as follows. The parties voluntarily entered into a contract. A student is not required to enter the university and could, in fact, after entry withdraw without reason at any time. A university need not accept as a student one desiring to become such. "It may, therefore, limit the effect of such acceptance by express agreement and thus retain the position of contractual freedom in which it stood before the student's course was entered upon." There is no reason why a student cannot agree that the institution may terminate the relations between them. "The contract between an institution and a student does not differ in this respect from contracts of employment." Therefore the only significant question in the case is what are the terms of the contract. This requires an interpretation of the rule. Properly construed the rule does not give the university "an absolute right to dismiss . . . for any reason whatever." It may only dismiss for reasons which relate to safeguarding the university's "ideals of scholarship" and "moral atmosphere." But although the university must have a reason for dismissal which relates either to scholarship or moral atmosphere, it need not state the reason. The student has the burden of proving that the reason for her dismissal was not within the terms of the regulation. Miss Anthony did not sustain that burden and therefore the judgment of the court below is reversed.

Dixon v. Alabama State Board of Education

After a sit-in at a publicly owned grill located in the county courthouse at Montgomery, Alabama, and other demonstrations in Montgomery and elsewhere, six Negro students at the Alabama State College in Montgomery were expelled from the college. The students were not notified of any charges against them and they were not given any opportunity to be heard. Instead, each student received a letter from the president of the college notifying him that he had been expelled. The letter did not state the grounds for the recipient's expulsion; but it did refer to reports of "the various news media," and it is likely that the students knew their expulsion was related to their alleged participation in the sit-in and other demonstrations.[7]

---

[7] The letter contained a copy of a regulation of the State Board of Education which stated four general grounds for expelling students. One of the grounds, which was printed in capitals in the copy of the regulation received by the students, reads as follows: "for conduct prejudicial to the school and for conduct unbecoming a student or future teacher in schools of Alabama, for insubordination and insurrection, or for inciting other students to like conduct." It should be noted that the Court of Appeals found that the "misconduct for which the students were expelled has never been definitely specified." 294 F.2d at 151.

The students brought an action against the board, the college, and the president to restrain them from interfering with the students' attendance at the college. The Federal district court dismissed the action.[8]

The decision was reversed by the Court of Appeals in an opinion by Judge Rives, a highly respected and able member of the Federal judiciary.[9] Judge Rives took as his text the proposition that whenever "a government body acts so as to injure an individual, the Constitution requires that the act be consonant with due process of law." Judge Rives found the requisite injury in the facts that, first, "without sufficient education the plaintiffs would not be able to earn an adequate livelihood, to enjoy life to the fullest, or to fulfill as completely as possible the duties and responsibilities of good citizens," and, second, "expulsion may well prejudice the student from completing his education at any other institution."

The court rejected the argument advanced by the defendants and apparently based on the reasoning of Justice Sears's opinion in *Anthony v. Syracuse University*, that the students had waived their right to notice and hearing, because a regulation of the State Board of Education published in the college catalogue provided, "Just as a student may choose to withdraw from a particular college at any time for any personally-determined reason, the college may also at any time decline to continue to accept responsibility for the supervision and service to any student with whom the relationship becomes unpleasant and difficult." First, said the court, this provision does not clearly indicate an intent on the part of the student to waive notice and hearing, and, second, a state "cannot condition the granting of even a privilege upon the renunciation of the constitutional right to procedural due process."

The question that remained was: What does procedural due process demand? The court's answer was that this depends upon the circumstances and interests of the parties involved. The interest of the students in remaining in the college of their choice is of "extremely great value." Also, in student dismissal cases "there are no considerations of immediate danger to the public, or of peril to the national security, which should prevent the Board from giving the accused students notice of the charge and an opportunity to be heard in their own defense." The court concluded its opinion by stating its

[8] Dixon v. Alabama State Board of Education, 186 F. Supp. 945 (M.D. Ala. N.D. 1960).
[9] Judge Wisdom concurred with Judge Rives. Judge Cameron dissented. The Supreme Court later denied certiorari, 368 U.S. 930 (1961).

views concerning the nature of the notice and hearing required by due process. The intrinsic importance of the statement and the fact that it will be widely quoted and relied upon by other courts which may have similar cases in the future [10] justifies this rather lengthy quotation:

> The notice should contain a statement of the specific charges and grounds which, if proven, would justify expulsion under the regulations of the Board of Education. The nature of the hearing should vary depending upon the circumstances of the particular case. The case before us requires something more than an informal interview with an administrative authority of the college. By its nature, a charge of misconduct, as opposed to a failure to meet the scholastic standards of the college, depends upon a collection of the facts concerning the charged misconduct, easily colored by the point of view of the witnesses. In such circumstances, a hearing which gives the Board or the administrative authorities of the college an opportunity to hear both sides in considerable detail is best suited to protect the rights of all involved. This is not to imply that a full-dress judicial hearing, with the right to cross-examine witnesses, is required. Such a hearing, with the attending publicity and disturbance of college activities, might be detrimental to the college's educational atmosphere and impractical to carry out. Nevertheless, the rudiments of an adversary proceeding may be preserved without encroaching upon the interests of the college. In the instant case, the student should be given the names of the witnesses against him and an oral or written report on the facts to which each witness testifies. He should also be given the opportunity to present to the Board, or at least to an administrative official of the college, his own defense against the charges and to produce either oral testimony or written affidavits of witnesses in his behalf. If the hearing is not before the Board directly, the results and findings of the hearing should be presented in a report open to the student's inspection. If these rudimentary elements of fair play are followed in a case of misconduct of this particular type, we feel that the requirements of due process of law will have been fulfilled.[11]

Summary

Judge Sadler's early clarion call has been muffled by a cacophony of opposing voices. Although no court seems to have followed the literal approach of *Anthony v. Syracuse University*, the case has not been overruled, nor has its reasoning been explicitly rejected by any

[10] See, for example, Knight v. State Board of Education, 200 F. Supp. 174, 182 (M.D. Tenn. N.D. 1961).
[11] 294 F.2d at 158–59.

court. Those courts which have ruled that the student should be given notice and opportunity to defend himself have not agreed with Judge Sadler concerning the nature of the hearing. Not even Judge Rives, whose opinion in the Dixon case is clearly the most able and impressive of all those written in this century, would require an opportunity for confrontation and cross-examination; in addition, Judge Rives was most explicit in confining his holding and opinion to "public" institutions which are subject to the constraints of the Fourteenth Amendment that "No state . . . shall deprive any person of life, liberty or property, without due process of law. . . ."

I turn now to the more difficult task of stating what I think courts will do in the future when dismissal or suspension procedures are challenged as contrary to law.

What Courts May Be Expected To Do in the Future

Although one may strive to be objective, there is danger that in defining a broad concept like "due process of law" or "fair hearing" one will be influenced by his own convictions. It is only fair, therefore, that you know my views or, if you will, my predilections. I believe that when vital personal interests are at stake, the official who is to act should be fully informed concerning the factual bases of his proposed action; that the person whose interests are directly involved is uniquely qualified to assist in the development and verification of the needed data; and that when the decision hinges on controverted facts relating to past events, the methods of a trial—principally notice of the charges, cross-examination, rebuttal testimony, and decision on the record by an unbiased tribunal—will be a superior means for discovering falsehood and correcting unwarranted inferences. I would also underscore Mr. Justice Robert Jackson's admonition that "due process of law is not for the sole benefit of the accused. It is the best insurance for the Government against those blunders which leave lasting stains on a system of justice which are bound to occur in an *ex parte* consideration." [12]

Having thus expressed my faith in the adversary system as a means of achieving fair and enlightening decisions, let me add two important qualifications. First, the methods of a trial are not appropriate for resolving some issues. Thus, if an institutional regulation provides for suspension whenever a student is indicted for a felony, insistence that the fact of indictment be ascertained only after opportunity

[12] Dissenting in Shaugnessy v. United States *ex rel.* Mezei, 354 U.S. 206, 224–225 (1953).

for confrontation, cross-examination, and rebuttal testimony would be doctrinaire in the extreme. Similarly, the methods of a trial would be a wasteful and inefficient means for ascertaining whether a student has achieved the grade average required for continuing in the institution. Second, due process is a flexible conception whose content will vary in light of the circumstances and interests of the parties involved. Also, due process imposes procedural minima; it does not demand the best possible procedure. Extreme care must be exercised, therefore, not to fall into the trap of equating the requirements of the Fourteenth Amendment with one's personal views of desirable procedure.

The concepts of due process and fair hearing are shaped in significant part by tradition, usage, and stare decisis. But as one of our ablest contemporary jurists, Justice Roger J. Traynor of the California Supreme Court, reminds us in terms reminiscent of Cardozo, "Courts have a creative job to do when they find that a rule has lost touch with reality and should be abandoned or reformulated to meet new conditions and new moral values." [13]

Recognizing, then, my own general preference for Judge Sadler's approach and bearing in mind both the flexibility of due process and the competing demands of creativity and continuity in the development of law, I venture the following predictions.

1. Courts may be expected to become more sensitive to the demands of procedural regularity in student dismissal proceedings, because: (*a*) As a higher percentage of the population attends colleges and universities and as the nation's economy calls for more and more specialization, the value and significance of higher education to the individual becomes increasingly greater. (*b*) It is becoming harder and harder to secure admission to the institution of one's choice and therefore dismissal involves a harsher sanction than in the assertedly good old days when one could get his education by being "thrown out of the best colleges in the country." (*c*) In other areas of the law in recent years, courts have been particularly sensitive to the importance of fair procedure when vital interests, particularly reputation, have been at stake, and this procedural concern undoubtedly will in time have an effect on the manner in which the judiciary decides student dismissal cases.

2. The courts will insist that state-financed institutions give the student notice of the charges and an opportunity to defend himself.

[13] Traynor, "Law and Social Change in a Democratic Society," *Illinois Law Forum,* Summer 1956, pp. 230, 232.

The Dixon case will become a leading case in the field, and Judge Rives's prescription of the kind of notice and hearing to be given will, in general, be followed. Although Judge Rives specifically stated that a full-dress, judicial hearing, with the right to cross-examine witnesses was not required, because such a hearing, "with the attending publicity and disturbance of college activities, might be detrimental to the college's educational atmosphere and impractical to carry out," I do not believe that this will prevent courts from holding that confrontation and cross-examination are required in certain circumstances. If, for example, in a dismissal proceeding involving alleged cheating, it develops that the decision will depend upon whether the tribunal believes the accused or his accusers, cross-examination should be required, because this is the method which long experience has shown is the best assurance of fair and enlightened action. Please note the circumscribed character of this proposal. It is only when cross-examination is the condition of enlightened action that it should be required by the judiciary. Lawyers who represent dismissed students would do well to accept this approach. For in the present state of the law, judges—even a judge as perceptive as Judge Rives— will not be impressed with a broadside argument that a student must be given a trial-type hearing before he is dismissed. Indeed, in every case, counsel for the student should endeavor to convince the court that the procedural safeguards he demands are needed not because of some abstract right to due process or to a fair hearing but because his client has been prejudiced by their denial.

3. Regulations or bylaws of state-financed institutions that purport to authorize summary dismissal either will be interpreted not to confer such an authority or will be held to be unconstitutional or ultra vires.

4. Judges may for a time continue to distinguish between "public" and "private" colleges and universities. But I believe that they will come to recognize that from the standpoint of procedural fairness there is no sound reason for distinguishing between the student who attends, say, Stanford rather than California, Northwestern rather than Illinois, Duke rather than North Carolina, or Harvard rather than Massachusetts.[14] It is true, of course, that the Fourteenth

---

[14] Professor Chafee has pointed out that the "pecuniary consequences of dismissal from a private school or college are less severe than those of dismissal from a public school or state university." Chafee, "The Internal Affairs of Associations Not for Profit," *Harvard Law Review*, May 1930, pp. 993, 1022. Although the extent of the pecuniary harm will be different in the two situations, I do not believe that this difference is sufficiently significant to justify different kinds of dismissal procedures in the two types of institutions.

Amendment provision that "No State . . . shall deprive any person of life, liberty or property without due process of law" limits "state" rather than "private" action. Although the concept of "state" action is in the process of a development that eventually may make the due process limitations of the Fourteenth Amendment applicable to dismissal proceedings conducted by so-called private colleges and universities, that development has not yet come to fruition. But the Federal Constitution is not the only, or even the principal, source of law. State courts have ample power both to require procedural fairness in dismissal proceedings and to limit or, if necessary, to invalidate regulations or bylaws of "private" institutions that purport to authorize summary dismissal or otherwise restrict the student's right to a fair hearing.[15] This is an area in which, in the long run, creative judges like Cardozo, Traynor, and Rives will cautiously but surely develop the law to the end that students in "private" colleges and universities will be accorded the same safeguards as their counterparts in "public" institutions.[16]

5. Finally, there should be a mention of the problem of waiver. What will courts do if the student does not request the opportunity to confront or question his accusers or to examine the information they have provided? Will they rule that a failure to request or object constitutes a waiver of the error, or will they hold that it is the responsibility of the tribunal to see to it that the student is given the type of hearing that fairness demands?[17] Although I cannot state with any confidence that the courts would so hold, it is clear to me that if the student is not represented by counsel, the burden of assuring a fair hearing should be placed on the institution.[18]

[15] See *ibid.*; Seavey, "Dismissal of Students: 'Due Process,'" *Harvard Law Review*, June 1957, pp. 1406–10; Summers, "The Law of Union Discipline: What the Courts Do in Fact," *Yale Law Journal*, December 1960, pp. 175–224.

[16] I include Judge Rives in this group with full recognition that in his Dixon opinion he distinguished *Anthony v. Syracuse University* on the ground that it involved a private university and followed "the well-settled rule that the relations between a student and a private university are a matter of contract." 294 F.2d at 157. But this statement was neither necessary to his opinion nor essential to the holding in the case. It is what we lawyers call "obiter dictum" which I am confident Judge Rives would disclaim in an appropriate case.

[17] See, for example, University of Ceylon v. Fernando (1960) All E.R. 631, 642, in which Judicial Committee of the Privy Council held that the institution's failure to suggest to the student that he might wish to question the accusing witness was not sufficient to invalidate the proceedings. This part of the opinion of the Judicial Committee is criticized by S. A. de Smith in "University Discipline and Natural Justice," *Modern Law Review*, July 1960, pp. 428, 430–31.

[18] See Gellhorn and Byse, *Administrative Law: Cases and Comments* (Brooklyn: Foundation Press, 1954), pp. 302, 306–8, 313.

What Colleges and Universities Should Do

My lack of experience in affairs of student discipline bespeaks circumspection in suggesting procedures that colleges and universities might observe when suspending or dismissing students. I shall not, therefore, propose a detailed procedural code for adoption by interested institutions. Instead, I shall make one categorical assertion, advance several general suggestions concerning desirable procedures, and conclude by listing a few problems which I believe deserve brief mention.

The categorical statement is taken from the dissenting opinion of Justice Galen in the Montana suspension case of *Ingersoll v. Clapp*, "A case of this character (i.e., one in which the student was suspended without a fair hearing) should never be before the courts and would not therein be given serious consideration were administrative officers disposed to perform their simple duty in the premises." [19] My conception of the proper performance of "their simple duty in the premises" is as follows:

1. The student should be given written notice of the specific charges and grounds which, if proved, would justify suspension or dismissal.

2. The notice should state that if the student so requests he will be given a hearing at which he may be represented by a person of his choice.

3. The nature of the hearing should depend upon the circumstances of the case. The procedure should be such as to enlighten the tribunal concerning the facts at issue. In some instances it would be sufficient to permit the student to submit evidence or argument challenging the charges and grounds stated in the notice. In other instances the names and statements of accusing witnesses should be furnished, and, in still others, there should be cross-examination. There should be an opportunity to submit oral and written argument. A record of the hearing should be kept by a stenographer furnished by the institution.

4. A decision should be reached on the basis of the statement of charges and grounds and evidence adduced at the hearing. The student should be given written notice of the decision and reasons thereof.

5. If possible, there should be an unbiased appellate tribunal to which the student could appeal.

If colleges and universities will comply with these rather simple requirements, courts will not intervene. But mere avoidance of

[19] 81 Mont. at 220, 263 P. at 439 *supra* note 16.

judicial intervention is not a very lofty aspiration for institutions of higher learning in a society which rightly emphasizes the dignity of the individual. The question that remains, then, is whether there are safeguards—in addition to those that the law requires—which should be provided by the institution. Let me close these already too extended remarks by listing some possibly relevant queries.

How should the prehearing investigation and interviews be conducted? Should the suspected student be fully informed concerning the information the institution has assembled, or should he be told in general terms that he is suspected and be asked to make a statement? Should he be permitted to have a friend or representative present at the prehearing interview? If the student fails or refuses to answer questions, what inferences may be drawn? Should the institution inform the student concerning his procedural rights and, if so, in how much detail? Should the institution recommend or, in some cases, provide counsel? May the official who conducted the initial investigation participate in the ultimate decision? To what extent should representatives of the student body participate in disciplinary proceedings? Should there be a procedure for disqualifying allegedly prejudiced decisional officials? Under what circumstances will summary suspension pending a hearing be justified? To what extent should "voluntary" resignations be encouraged? Should reports of psychiatrists or social workers be utilized and, if so, should copies be furnished the student? What should be done if the hearing officials become convinced that the student has lied: should he be summarily dismissed for lying or should there be an additional hearing to determine whether in fact he did lie and if so what sanction should be imposed? And, finally, although it may not be directly related to procedure, what about the vital and difficult problem of sanctions? What purposes—deterrence, retribution, rehabilitation, maintenance of the integrity of the educational process—are served by expulsion, suspension, rustication, reprimand, or other sanction?

The answers to these questions will be found neither in law reports nor in statute books but in the minds and in the hearts of the men and women who are responsible for administering student discipline in American institutions of higher learning. Theirs is a heavy responsibility. In discharging it they should heed the advice of that most distinguished student of American freedoms, the late Zechariah Chafee, Jr., "[An] institution which professes to prepare youth for life in a democracy might wisely give them an example of fair play when it is conducting its own affairs." [20]

[20] Chafee, "Internal Affairs of Associations," p. 1027,

Campus Life in a Litigious Age

DONALD C. MUNDINGER

Due process is inherent in the rule of law. Historically, in the Western world "due process" was developed as a protection for subjects against an arbitrary and irresponsible government. It was not a device which justified insurrection and rebellion; rather, its purpose was to nurture order by guaranteeing to the people substantively just laws and procedurally just administration of the law.

The task of this paper is to indicate areas in which both substantive and procedural due process are applicable in the relationship of the college to its student body.

The issue is a significant one in higher education. In a democratic society, colleges exist for the enrichment of society and for the promulgation of human ideals. It would be a betrayal of their mission if colleges were to ignore the elementary canons of justice. Furthermore, they are aware of this fact. Paul Woodring, writing in the *Saturday Review*, quotes Lipset and Seabury as follows: "Universities are probably more vulnerable to the civil disobedience tactics than any other institution in the country precisely because those in authority, whether administration or faculty, are liberal." [1]

Student Rights and College Authority

Due process in college is vital because as educators we are dedicated, by temperament and profession, to the ideal of justice. A second reason for its importance today is that due process is normally invoked by a small number of students: that is, a minority within the student body which is frequently critical of our society. It is essential that individuals or small groups be protected and their rights not disregarded or ignored because they are unpopular, critical, or "abrasive." I repeat: justice is an ideal that is prerequisite to

[1] Sept. 11, 1965, p. 77.

318

democracy, and the free universities in a free society must jealously defend and extend its existence.

Colleges, like other contemporary social agencies, have become progressively more organized and institutionalized as they have attempted to serve an increasingly larger number of students and to extend their range of services. As a consequence, there has been a drift away from the warmth and intimacy which have traditionally been associated with the university community. The nature of the college is changing, and the traditional concept of the faculty is also undergoing redefinition. As a result, problems of administration have become complex. The situation is complicated by contemporary students' zeal for direct involvement in educational, political, and social policy. This has raised questions concerning the students' rights, not only on campus and in academic affairs, but also in extramural affairs, especially the civil and political rights areas. The contemporary college is wrestling with this problem.

The traditional areas in which the college has exercised authority over student life include the following:

1. *Student conduct:* the relationship between college and student, especially freedom of expression and protection against unjust grades and evaluation. Procedures and regulations involving attendance, graduation requirements, conduct on campus, and the use of university facilities are further examples.
2. *Students' extramural organizations:* the right to organize and use college facilities for activities which are related to the educational purpose.
3. *Student government:* the establishment and operation of a student government and the delegation of authority to deal with significant questions of student life.
4. *Student publications:* freedom to exchange information and ideas.
5. *Student discipline:* the student's right to a fair procedure in alleged social offenses.
6. *Honor system:* a student-enforced alternative to the faculty proctor examination system.
7. *Academic records:* protection against the abuse and improper or harmful disclosure of a student's academic record or his personal or disciplinary history.

These are important areas of life for the college student. At this moment, popular student opinion questions the authority of the university in many or all of these areas. University involvement in the social, extramural life of its students is a logical extension of the principle of *in loco parentis*. A sizable segment of university people and students seriously question the viability of the *in loco parentis* principle. There is some belief that since parents are not even *in loco parentis*, it is unreasonable to expect universities to assume this responsibility.

Students' Rights to Due Process

In the areas listed above, the minimum requirements for due process on the American campus include the following:

1. Students should participate in the establishment of rules and regulations which govern student life on the campus.

2. Rules governing students' extramural and social life, as well as academic regulations, should be published, circulated, and made available to the entire academic community.

3. The student who commits an offense should be apprehended in a fair and reasonable fashion.

4. The accused student should have fair judicial procedures. This frequently involves some student participation in the judicial mechanism.

5. There should be some appeal mechanism: the "convicted" student should have some recourse other than the dean of students or a vice-president for personnel, and he may appeal to the president and ultimately to the board of control.

Of special concern to students who are active in civil rights movements or in foreign policy protest demonstrations is what is commonly called "double jeopardy." I think that technically this is a misuse of the constitutional expression. However, it is in current usage among students. The basic complaint is that the offending student is penalized by two authorities, civil and academic, for the commission of a single offense. Campus opinion holds that a student should not be penalized by his college for his off-campus political activities. The college community generally accepts this position. The American Civil Liberties Union in a brochure entitled *Academic Freedom and Civil Liberties of Students in Colleges and Universities* makes the following statement:

> In their non-academic life, private or public students should be free from college control. On the other hand, the college should not be held responsible for the non-academic activities of its individual students.
> . . . No disciplinary action should be taken by the college against a student for engaging in such off-campus activities as political

campaigns, picketing, or participating in public demonstrations, provided the student does not claim without authorization to speak or act in the name of the college or one of its student organizations.[2]

Arrest and conviction for offenses which involve moral turpitude or which are of a criminal nature is, of course, another matter and may result in the disqualification of a student for college.

Striking a Balance

Contradictory forces are present. On the one hand, the overzealous attention to procedural due process in an academic institution can be an impediment and obstruction to the realization of the true mission of the university: transmission of learning, research, and service. And yet when a student's academic career is at stake, elementary fairness demands careful respect for and protection of the student's procedural and substantive rights. Perhaps the following paragraph by Nathan Glazer, which appeared in the *New York Review of Books*, expresses one faculty point of view on this question:

> The faculty is not interested in exercising student discipline over liquor, sex, cheating, and other things that they are happy to leave in the hands of the administration. Nor do they relish devoting endless time to hearings in which students and administration are represented by lawyers, and in which any normal lay intelligence finds itself overwhelmed by legal technicalities and political infighting. . . . Faculty discipline would become the pro forma activity of faculty dragooned into it, or willing to waste their time at it. It will become another cog in the committee system that uses up faculty time and helps prevent student-faculty contact.[3]

Cumbersome and complex disciplinary machinery is distasteful to many of us because it infringes on the time we normally dedicate to teaching and research. But as attendance at college becomes more and more the accepted pattern of American youth, the importance of due process on the campus can only increase. The danger is always present that people in authority, faculty and administration, may act in an arbitrary and discriminatory fashion. Procedures must be present to require those who are in authority to be held responsible.

It is refreshing, however, that in the main the college will function because of the mutual respect and tolerance that exist among students, faculty, and administration, and because mature, responsible, and reasonable people have dedicated themselves to the task of learn-

[2] New York: American Civil Liberties Union, 1963. P. 11.
[3] Feb. 11, 1965, p. 22.

ing and study. The academic community is and must remain personal. Rules and regulations must not interfere with the educational objectives and students must always have the guarantee that they will have the right and opportunity to be treated as individuals.

In conclusion, I feel we must recognize that we are now living in a litigious age. I think that it is a litigious age for primarily two reasons:

First, the interest of our civil society in the preservation of civil rights and the extension of civil rights logically leads to a student awareness of the necessity of individual rights and their extension and application in the university community, and

Second, as the university attracts a more intellectually oriented student with a higher academic capability and a keener awareness of social questions, the logical result of this new breed of student is a demand for a greater amount of freedom and involvement not only in his social life on campus, but also in academic policy. It is safe to say that university paternalism is dead and that the student will demand procedural safeguards and expand his influence in university policy decisions.

Due process on the campus will be in a stage of continuing definition and must be extended to all parties in the educational process, including those who are called "irresponsible rebels."

Due
Process:
A
Student's
Viewpoint

DENNIS SHAUL

EXPRESSING A STUDENT'S VIEW on due process is a dangerous task; I wish to put forward a few disclaimers at the outset. First, there is no single opinion or even a representative opinion among students on what due process in the university ought to be. More importantly, this question is one which, for reasons later examined, is not widely discussed even among the most activist students.

Second, one of the major reasons that student discussion of this subject (where it has occurred) has not always been fruitful is that the language and terminology employed have often been fuzzy. This reflects, partly, the fact that students are not legally trained, but more importantly it demonstrates, perhaps, that students are not particularly interested in carefully devised codes which guarantee and spell out due process. Rather they cherish the hope that the vague feeling they have about what constitutes fair dealing will be in some way honored by the administration too.

Most students would take as settled questions many of the points encompassed within the concept of due process. Whether or not their institution agreed, they would take it as a desirable practice that regulations binding on them should be made known in advance; that when accused, they should have the right to make a defense and should be subject to no form of prejudgment; that the punishment should fit the crime and should be designed to foster the over-all purposes of the university and the student's own education.

Most students would see these principles as more than just desirable; they would be the prerequisites of a fair system. It must be said that they are seldom articulated except when some campus controversy has already, for one student or another, called into question the basic fairness of the system he sees about him. At that point, he is likely to go much further in his attack and his proposals. In fact, what usually occurs is that the student critic attempts to borrow

323

wholesale from the only other system he knows—the civil society itself. He is then likely to recommend that the student should have benefit of counsel, should be tried only by a jury of his peers, and should be able to assert his right to refuse to answer and his guarantee against unreasonable search and seizure.

Whether this attempt to import the methods of one society into the environment of another has merit depends entirely on the nature of the institution involved. For example, the college with an enrollment of one thousand or less will find an adversary system a wholly foreign element. In the more intimate environment which one may presume exists in such a small institution, it will be impossible to pretend that justice can be totally impersonal. It is probably also wrong to think that in such an institution the student's best defense will be assured by providing him with counsel.

This very example does underscore one of the shortcomings of the present student discussion on due process; not enough differentiation is made among different types of institutions. Student critics, using the pattern of a single civil society, all too often seek to impose it on institutions which have a variety of environments and goals. The difficulty is made more acute since the discussion usually follows a particular incident at a particular institution. This often means that the proposed solution is geared less to the real needs of the campus than to ensuring there will be no repetition of the incident.

It is not likely that the due process issue will receive a better discussion in the near future. In schools where the student is most content (where procedures conform closely to his notions of fairness), the system is often informal, flexible, and personal. In any case, students who are nearly content are not likely to publish their views. Often where students are very discontented with due process, they are also discontented about more explosive issues, and these receive their attention. Due process in itself is unlikely to inspire this kind of excitement.

Much attention has centered lately on what might be regarded as a secondary layer of due process issues—those issues encompassed within the question of how far the student may go in using the university as a staging ground from which to attack problems beyond the campus itself. The answer most often given is that the student's right to picket, his right to free speech, and the like extend to the point where these rights begin to interfere with the institution's mission. But that answer, correct as far it goes, also leaves itself open to the most arbitrary type of administration. Written guidelines arrived at through student-administration discussion, and subject to regular review, may offer hope of a solution.

Written guidelines setting out the essentials of due process for disciplinary cases in general often do not exist or are not sufficiently detailed at our colleges and universities. Students, especially in larger universities, are beginning to press for them. That pressure can be particularly healthy if it stimulates a dialogue between students and administration on how to deal with some of the more frequently recurring incidents. Such discussion can help prevent the outbreak of bitterness and frustration which has manifested itself at several institutions during the last year or so.

But even large universities will probably continue to rely on a set of due process guidelines that are basically informal principles, understandings, and traditions. Involving students in a periodic review and reformulation of these is a more difficult but more important task than merely drafting guidelines. Since these unwritten guides are used more often and are more likely to seem arbitrary, they provide—potentially—the material for acrimonious disputes. A formal right to protest or an individual student's right to a hearing won't substitute for a spirit of cooperation, and that, in turn, most often requires procedures for continuing consultation between students and administration.

Much of what a student thinks of his institution depends on how well it conforms to his vague and seldom articulated idea of what fair treatment is. Both university and student would benefit if more systematic and frequent attempts were made to explore what—for a given institution—does constitute a course of fair dealing. For often a student's view of how the university operates colors his view of how society itself operates. In this area, too, the university carries the responsibility of being the model teacher.

Due
Process
and the
"Private"
Institution

EDMUND McILHENNY

HISTORICALLY, THE COURTS have been extremely reluctant to enter into the area of college discipline, so long as the university has acted in response to sufficient reasons and not arbitrarily or capriciously.[1] Originally, the relationship between student and tutor was *in loco parentis*, the institution having the rights, duties, and responsibilities of the parent.

The earliest instance I have been able to find of the overturning of an administrative decision involved Cambridge in 1732.[2] Here, a master was deprived of his academic degrees without notice or hearing, and the court condemned the procedure as being contrary to natural justice.

The University of Minnesota was ordered to reinstate a student in 1908 because of abuse of discretion by administrative officials under similar circumstances.[3] In 1928, a suit was brought against Syracuse University by a student seeking readmission after dismissal. The plaintiff urged that her right was based upon a contract between her and the university. The court went along with this theory and said that she could not recover except upon the contract. It was pointed out that the contract, however, embodied regulations of the university permitting the university to terminate the relationship without giving any reason for doing so, in order to protect the ideals of scholarship and moral atmosphere.[4]

It is at this point, I believe, that we can see clearly for the first time the beginning of the sublimation of the *in loco parentis* concept and the emergence of the theory that the student-institution

[1] Frank v. Marquette University, 209 Wis. 372, 245 N.W. 125 (1932).
[2] The King v. Chancellor of the University of Cambridge, 2 Ld. Raym 1334, 92 Eng. Rep. 370, K.B. (1732).
[3] Gleason v. University of Minnesota, 104 Minn. 359, 116 N.W. 650 (1908).
[4] Anthony v. Syracuse University, 224 App. Div. 487, 231 N.Y. Supp. 435 (1928).

relationship is *ex contractu*, at least insofar as private institutions are concerned.

As this theory was emerging, a number of decisions over a period of many years had enunciated the thesis that a student involved in a disciplinary proceeding was, according to the terms of the contract of admission, entitled to a notice of the charges against him and a hearing to determine the facts, as essential procedural requirements to a valid expulsion.[5] However, the substance of the procedural requirements was not further delineated.

A distinction must be made between state and private institutions. The public university is amenable to the Fourteenth Amendment prohibiting any state from making or enforcing any law which shall abridge the privileges or immunities of citizens of the United States; or deprive any person of life, liberty, or property without due process of law; or deny any person within its jurisdiction the equal protection of the laws.

The general rule has been stated in the following encyclopedic summary:

> Since public universities and colleges are subject to the control of the legislature, the right of that body to legislate for their welfare, to enact measures for their discipline, and to impose upon the trustees thereof the duty of enforcing these requirements is undoubted. However, where the power is delegated to them to do so, university and college authorities may make all necessary and proper rules and regulations for the orderly management of the institution and the preservation of discipline therein, and rules enacted in the exercise of a power so delegated by statute are of the same force as would be a like enactment of the legislature, and their official interpretation by the university authorities is part thereof . . .

For both public and private colleges, the question of

> . . . whether the rules or regulations are wise or expedient or their aims worthy is a matter left solely to the discretion of the authorities, and with the exercise of such discretion the courts will not interfere, in the absence of a clear showing that the authorities have acted arbitrarily or have abused the authority vested in them. Every student on his admission impliedly promises to submit to and be governed by all the necessary and proper rules and regulations which have been or may be adopted for the government of the institution, although rules and regulations may be annulled by the courts when

[5] See Stetson University v. Hunt, 88 Fla. 510, 102 So. 637 (1924); Koblitz v. Western Reserve University, 21 Ohio C.C.R. 144, 11 Ohio C.C. Dec. 515 (1901); and Baltimore University v. Colten, 98 Md. 623, 57 Atl. 14 (1904).

found to be unauthorized, against common right, or palpably unreasonable.[6]

In 1961, in the landmark decision of *Dixon v. Alabama State Board of Education*,[7] the court clearly distinguishes between the procedural responsibilities of public and private institutions, and holds that it is the Fourteenth Amendment constitutional due process that the public institution is required to fulfill, and contractual due process that the private school must fulfill.

The court outlined its views on the nature of the proceeding that was due a public-institution student charged with disciplinary violations. The court also indicated that a private institution had the right to adopt a regulation waiving the procedural formalities, provided they did so in a clear and explicit manner, but that a public institution could not. The court indicated that the required notice should specify the charges which, if proved, would justify the penalty. It said the nature of the hearing depended upon the circumstances of the case but should include the rudiments of an adversary proceeding, such as the names of witnesses, the substance of the witnesses' testimony, and an opportunity to defend and produce witnesses; the results of the hearing should be reported.

No one can argue with the reasonableness of the foregoing, but it seems equally clear that any stereotyped procedural rules will not necessarily guarantee that the best result will come of such a hearing.

In the first place, it would seem that disciplinary proceedings are neither criminal nor legal in structure, but are rather adjudicatory. This term has been defined by the Supreme Court as a procedure by which an agency takes "any affirmative action which will affect an individual's legal rights." [8]

The constitutional approach raises the question of right to counsel; to cross-examination of witnesses; to the privilege against unreasonable search and seizure; to the exclusion of evidence obtained in a nonsanctioned way; and to the right against compulsory self-incrimination.[9] These are novel concepts in the field of university discipline, and have never been considered applicable to the private institution.

This does not mean, in my view, that any less justice will be done by a private institution than by a public one, but rather that the private institution may go about its disciplinary business according

---

[6] 55 *American Jurisprudence*, verbo Universities and Colleges. §19, pp. 13–14.

[7] 294 F.2d 150 (1961), C.A. 5, *cert. denied*, 368 U.S. 930, 7 L. Ed. 2d 193, 82 S.Ct. 87.

[8] Hannah v. Larche, 363 U.S. 420 (1960).

[9] *Texas Law Review*, XLII, 350.

to its own conscience as current circumstances seem to make advisable, rather than according to the stereotyped rules of procedure—provided of course that in doing so, it does not act arbitrarily or abusively.

Until fairly recently, no one has had any difficulty in determining which was a private and which a public institution. However, it is becoming increasingly difficult to distinguish between them from a constitutional due process basis.

In 1961, in the *Burton v. Wilmington Parking Authority* case,[10] the Supreme Court enunciated the doctrine that private conduct does not violate the Fourteenth Amendment "unless to some *significant* extent the state in any of its manifestations has become involved in it."

Under this sort of aegis, while Girard College was administered by public officials there was state action, but when the method of appointing the trustees was changed, there was not sufficient state action to involve the Fourteenth Amendment.[11] But the Pratt Library in Baltimore was found subject to the Fourteenth Amendment because the public fisc was the major contributor.[12] On the other hand, the Walker Hospital in North Carolina was found to be private although about 5 percent of its property came from the state.[13]

The latest case in this line is *Hammond v. University of Tampa.*[14] In this case, the court said that, although the University of Tampa is not a city or a state institution in the usual sense, its establishment was largely made possible by the use of a surplus city building and the use of other city land leased for the university's purposes. This city "involvement" was held to constitute state action under the Fourteenth Amendment.

There is no formula for determining what is *significant* state action. The courts have indicated that each case must be examined on its own facts, but the tendency seems to be toward a doctrine that any action of this sort, if important, is significant.

One distinguished jurist indicated in an opinion (later recalled) that:

[10] 365 U.S. 715, 6 L. Ed. 2d 45, 81 S.Ct. 856 (1961).

[11] Pennsylvania v. Board of Directors of City Trusts of the City of Philadelphia, 353 U.S. 230 (1957), *reversing* 386 Pa. 548 *which affirmed* 4 Pa. D. & C.2d 671; *appeal dismissed* 357 U.S. 570 (1958).

[12] Kerr v. Enoch Pratt Free Library of Baltimore, C.A. 4, 149 F.2d 212 (1945).

[13] Eaton v. Board of Managers of James Walker Memorial Hospital, 164 F. Supp. 191, D N.C. (1958), *affirmed* 261 F.2d 521, C.A. 4 (1958), *cert. denied*, 329 U.S. 984, 3 L. Ed. 2d 934.

[14] C.A. 5 (May 1965), 344 F.2d 951, No. 21512.

At the outset, one may question whether any school or college can ever be so "private" as to escape the reach of the Fourteenth Amendment. In a country dedicated to the creed that education is the only "sure foundation . . . . of freedom," "without which no republic can maintain itself in strength," institutions of learning are not things of purely private concern. The Supreme Court of the United States has noted that "in these days, it is doubtful that any child may reasonably be expected to succeed in life if he is denied the opportunity of an education." Brown v. Board of Education of Topeka, *supra*, 347 U.S. 493, 74 S.Ct. 691, 98 L. Ed. 873. . . . No one any longer doubts that education is a matter affected with the greatest public interest. And this is true whether it is offered by a public or private institution. . . . Clearly, the administrators of a private college are performing a public function. They do the work of the state, often in the place of the state. Does it not follow that they stand in the state's shoes? [15]

Although the foregoing statement has no present judicial effect, it demonstrates the point to which some jurists are prepared to go. The error of the logic expressed in this opinion lies, I believe, in the presumption that, because there is a great public interest in education, the private college is performing the work of the state. This, I believe, is palpably incorrect. Historically, the development was the other way around.

It should be observed, however, that each of the foregoing cases involved matters concerning racial discrimination, and that there is no comparable jurisprudence involving the issue of state action in student due process cases. But it also must be said that the same tests are theoretically equally applicable to due process of law as are applicable to racial discrimination, and that the traditionally private institution is becoming ever more dependent upon government support through the increasing flow of state and Federal funds to undernourished budget and building programs, so that a position of nonsignificant state action in the private institutions may be completely untenable in many instances. I hope that this is not true, but I can give no assurance.

During the past year, we have seen the issue of an unlimited right to free speech temporarily disrupt the academic atmosphere and administrative control on one campus, and we have heard the thesis expounded that criminal charges by the civil authority prohibit university administrative discipline of the student on the grounds that

[15] Guillory v. Administrators of Tulane Educational Fund, 203 F. Supp. 855; *vacated* 212 F. Supp. 674 (1962).

it would constitute prohibited double jeopardy. I do not believe that either question is legally supportable on the basis of any existing jurisprudence. But these matters have not yet been finally determined judicially.

It may be that "due process of law" as applied by the courts is being overemphasized with regard to student discipline. No one can seriously dispute that in student disciplinary action a procedure should be followed that will strive for the determination of truth and the application of justice tempered with wisdom. But it should also be remembered that the university and the student are equally concerned that this procedural end should be attained.

I do not believe that the disciplinary case should be categorized as an adversary proceeding. The student and the administration are not on opposing sides; their interests and their goals should be the same. Accordingly, the rules of procedure that are appropriate to criminal proceedings, or even to civil proceedings in the courts, are not necessarily compatible to the academic forum.

The application of the "state action" concept to the traditionally private institution does not seem to be relevant in determining what sort of hearing should be accorded a student who is alleged to have violated university regulations. It seems somewhat absurd to think that the issues of what sort of defense an erring student has the right to present in a disciplinary hearing may be determined by the amount of state support the institution receives; but that is the basis upon which the theory of state action has been applied to the traditionally private institution.

Due process of law does not provide for the wisdom of guidance and counseling; it does not make allowance for the benefits of student self-government and the inevitable technical errors of procedure that occur. It does not take into consideration the academic environment of the institution or the adolescence of the student. It is not concerned with motivation. At the student level, these factors may be more important than the technicalities of constitutional due process.

Dixon v. Alabama State Board of Education has laid down general guidelines applicable primarily to state institutions in disciplinary proceedings. Except for the reference in this decision to "an adversary proceeding," I believe that the rules are fundamentally sound, particularly in view of the court's implication that its role of review is to be procedural rather than substantive. It may be that the institution, which is a direct agency of the state and acting directly for the state, should be encumbered by constitutional due process;

but I would hope that the historically private institution would remain unfettered by these rules, so that it can continue to make its own way according to the dictates of its conscience in good faith, in an atmosphere that defines the interests, aims, and ambitions of the faculty and student body to be the same rather than adversary in nature.

Freedom and Responsibility in Higher Education

LOGAN WILSON

MY MAIN PURPOSE HERE IS neither to delineate the uses of intellectual controversy nor to defend the necessity for academic freedom. I am a strong believer in the need of freedom for each segment of the academic community, but what I want to emphasize at this time is the corollary obligation for all who share in it to act responsibly—a notion that in some circles is apparently not very popular these days.

The governance of higher education, like the conduct of foreign policy or the handling of civil rights, is a public policy issue and one which brings forth arguments from a good many self-appointed authorities. Some persons within academic circles, for example, like to talk about a Golden Age when universities went their ways without interference from administrators, trustees, or outside busybodies. Those who hold this view do not necessarily stage sit-ins or teach-ins to protest the *status quo*, but they do express a mythical view of the past as well as an unrealistic attitude toward the present. There have never been any universities which ran themselves! The oldest of all universities, the University of Bologna, was governed by the students. They hired and fired the rector and the teaching staff until control gradually shifted to the civil government. A few students at some U.S. colleges seem to advocate return to the Bologna scheme, but as yet I have not heard any expressions of enthusiasm for the idea from trustees, administrators, or professors. However this may be, current student unrest and the apparent desires of some students to become activists in all manner of affairs, both on their own campuses and away from them, is so manifest that the public at large is becoming confused about who is supposed to do what in the realm of higher education.

Really meaningful higher education is today a complex and expensive undertaking. Establishing a small junior college may call for a

333

capital investment of several million dollars, and a new medical school may necessitate a minimum outlay of at least $25 million. Few individuals or private groups can command funds of this magnitude, and it is not surprising that higher education has been moving steadily into the public domain. Furthermore, the support and operation of viable colleges and universities are by no means the simplified operations some of their critics would have us believe. The cooperation and coordination of many diverse interests are preconditions for successful enterprise, and there must be some basic understanding about a reasonable division of labor in the achievement of common objectives. It is no wonder, then, that self-constituted experts on shortcomings in university governance would rather attack existing institutions than go out on their own and establish new ones.

To begin with, a modern university must have a sizable constituency. It was once possible for a handful of teachers and learners to band together and maintain any kind of academic community that the surrounding society was willing to tolerate, but few students today and even fewer faculty members would be willing to take the vows of poverty required to maintain such an enclave. Moreover, they would not be able to marshal the financial support necessary to maintain adequate libraries, laboratories, and other essentials for contemporary teaching and research. Not only is the university an indispensable institution for contemporary society, but also broad-based support is essential for the university.

Components of the Academic Institution

Although it is a truism to say that state universities were created to serve the educational needs of their states, it is a mistake to regard them as state agencies differing in no significant way from highway departments, welfare bureaus, and other governmental operations. Legislatures have the authority to provide or withhold funds for teaching, research, and public service, but the advancement of learning is impeded rather than aided when legislatures try to determine what should be taught, how research should be conducted, or how the public must be served. Whether publicly supported, or privately endowed, or church-related, colleges and universities can serve their constituents best when they are assured the academic freedom necessary to their missions as sponsors of unrestricted inquiry. In short, although centers of learning may decay from being too isolated from the surrounding society, they also may deteriorate from being insufficiently insulated against its direct pressures.

Standing as a buffer and conduit between the outside world and universities are those appointive or elective groups of laymen variously termed "trustees," "regents," or "governing boards." They have the privilege and responsibility of representing the interests of the public at large to the academic community, and vice versa. They possess the legal prerogative to run our universities, but most of them have the good sense not to attempt it. The most effective governing boards confine their efforts largely to basic policy questions and other areas where their influence can be most useful in maintaining and improving their institutions, and do very little direct governing.

Even though boards are not invariably clear about their basic functions, by and large it seems to me that lay trustees are a greatly underappreciated source of strength in the progress as well as the stability of American institutions of higher education. Most of them give unstintingly of their time and energy, and not a few contribute substantially from their personal means to the institutions they serve without compensation.

Of the many decisions a governing board may make from time to time, the most crucial, in my judgment, is choosing its chief executive officer. Not only must the president be a capable executive for the trustees, but also he must be an understanding spokesman and leader for his colleagues in administration, for the faculty, for the students, and, on occasion, for the alumni and other groups. To paraphrase one of Harry Truman's utterances, the president or chancellor of an educational institution occupies the desk where the passed buck finally stops. If he is to be an effective administrator, he must delegate large measures of authority and responsibility to the deans and to the faculty; if he is to be a courageous leader, however, there are on some occasions no substitutes for his own firm decisions and actions.

It is paradoxical that while many faculty members complain of complex universities being overadministered by professionals, they seem to want to minimize their own participation in administrative tasks. With many professors unwilling to administer and students incapable of doing so, it seems to me that everybody would fare better on some campuses if there were less grousing about *the* administration (always referred to as "they" when things are not going well) and more acknowledgment that administrative officers are more useful than the academic anarchists would have us believe.

Since other kinds of organizations may have trustees, administrators, and even students, the professor is really the unique genus in the groves of academe. Students come and go annually, department chairmen are often rotated every few years, and even presidents seldom last out a decade, but the tenured members of the faculty usually remain as long as they choose to do so. They have the main jurisdiction over what will be taught and how. Not only do they preside over the curriculum, but also they exercise individual judgments about which persons may become teachers, accountants, doctors, lawyers, scientists, and what not. In addition to passing critical judgments on students, they initiate appraisals of one another to help determine which of their colleagues will be promoted, held back, or dismissed. In brief, professors have a good deal to do with making and implementing university policy—despite their professed distaste for administration.

During the last decade or two, many university professors have likewise become heavily involved in research and public service. In response to pressures from business, industry, and government, they are more frequently secluded in their laboratories or their offices, and even away from the campus altogether for considerable amounts of time. Thus, one hears complaints about the faculty's neglect of undergraduate teaching and the division of their loyalties between local duties and outside assignments.

Defining Rights and Responsibilities

In view of the rapidly enlarged size and greatly increased complexity of many universities, disjunctions are to be expected. Gone forever, I suspect, are the halcyon days when campuses were retreats for those who wanted merely a quiet life. Institutions of higher education in general and universities in particular are now deeply involved in the most basic problems of our era. Classrooms, libraries, and laboratories are now occupied from early morning until well into the night, and the long summer vacation when operations ceased altogether has become a memory.

Reflecting many of the conditions of modern life, the university is inevitably a locus of keen and sometimes fierce competition. What the Germans term *Gemeinschaft* has been displaced by *Gesellschaft*, as the spirit of a homogeneous community gives way to the depersonalization of a heterogeneous society. Although correlations between the size of an academic community and the satisfactions or dissatisfactions of its members remain to be demonstrated, the wave of student disquiet all over the country is undoubtedly related to these environmental changes.

The issues which provoke current episodes of unrest have ranged from freedom of speech and political action to complaints about library hours and dormitory rules; they have been economic, social, ethical, legal, philosophical, administrative, and occasionally educational. Some of the protests have been deeply felt, responsible attempts to express legitimate points of view. Others have been unruly expressions of ill-defined dissatisfaction and general antagonisms regarding matters having little, if anything, to do with the campus itself.

Looking back at the history of the student's role in American higher education, it should be noted that until fairly recently our colleges and universities acted *in loco parentis*—a relationship usually demanded by parents, often disliked by the faculty, and frequently rejected by the undergraduates. Protests customarily took the form of simply breaking the rules. As rules became more and more unenforceable, policies changed, and many institutions relaxed their strict supervision. By the late nineteenth century students gained three major areas of freedom: self-government, the honor system, and programs of independent work.

In the mid-1950's the American Council on Education conducted a study of student participation in institutional administration and policy making. It reported that student participation "in the making of college and university policy is an accepted fact on some campuses, an unrealistic proposition on others, but on many others a subject of serious study and discussion." [1]

It seems to me that in colleges and universities all over the nation we need to re-examine the rights and responsibilities of trustees, administrative officers, faculty, and students. During recent years faculties almost everywhere have gained immensely in their rights and privileges, and justly so, but perhaps the time is overdue for some of our institutional faculties to codify the responsibilities they should assume to go along with their freedom and influence. Also, we need to get a dialogue under way about the freedom being claimed by and in some instances extended to students. What are their corollary responsibilities? Should they, for example, have the same rights and obligations as citizens outside the university?

Even if one assumes the narrow view that the only right a student is entitled to is the freedom to learn as much as he can while enrolled, this alone would appear to entitle him to express himself

---

[1] Harry H. Lunn, Jr., *The Student's Role in College Policy-Making* (Washington: American Council on Education, 1957), p. vi.

regarding the learning and living opportunities provided by the institution of his choice. Let me illustrate: Professors grade student learning; I see no really valid reason for denying students the right to grade faculty teaching. If done in a careful way, I think that such evaluations might have very beneficial effects on both learners and teachers. I believe that students also are entitled to be heard about the rules and regulations pertaining to their behavior, but not to be the final arbiters—as some collegians are now demanding—in such matters. I have little sympathy, for example, with those students who feel their freedom encroached upon because university dormitories are operated differently from commercial hotels or motels.

A *Bulletin* of the International Association of Universities, issued in 1965, has the title, "Some Basic Problems that Confront Universities in All Parts of the World." One of the fourteen basic problems raised by F. Cyril James, the author, is "The Place of the Student in University Life," which is stated as follows:

> What is the place of the student in the corporate life of a university? Is he raw material to be fitted into the conveyor belt of the academic curriculum and, when satisfactorily educated, to be given a degree, although during all his years at the university he has played no lively and active part either in its government or in association with the members of the teaching staff? Is he a colleague of the faculty, to be considered as an equal, if younger, member of the community, as used to be the pattern in the colleges of Oxford and Cambridge? Is he, in fact, the boss of the institution (as sometimes happens in South American universities) where the students, constitutionally or unconstitutionally, exercise a veto upon the appointment of rectors and senior university officials, not infrequently dis-organize the operations of the whole institution, and sometimes embroil the university in politics by their demonstrations and strikes?[2]

As James has pointed out, there are no simple or easy answers to these questions. Between the extremes of the student as the product of an assembly line and the student as the arbiter of academic enterprise, there may be many workable forms of relationship between the individual and the institution. Existing forms are often very imperfect, of course, and many of our procedures undoubtedly need restructuring to improve communication and participation.

Where reform is needed, I hope that we can proceed through dialogue rather than negotiation and that all parties concerned will view themselves as partners rather than adversaries. I believe that

*Pp. 9–10.

change can be accomplished more effectively through due process than through explosive demonstrations and other extremes of action and reaction. In my judgment, the quality of university education in the United States will be undermined and the public benefits of our institutions diminished if we permit our campuses to become centers of dissension and continuous embroilment.

To be sure, one of the university's basic functions is to be a testing ground for ideas. It is not an authoritarian institution where behavior is expected to take the form of command and obedience. The competition of ideas on the campus necessarily produces tensions and countervailing forces: this is a sign of intellectual vitality as contrasted to the placidity of stagnation. But competition must not be allowed to degenerate into the kind of conflict which destroys academic freedom itself.

In addition to needing freedom, so as to nourish criticism of society, the university also must have discipline and order, so as to foster respect for law. For the students, it is intended to be neither a country club nor a perpetual debating society, but a place where they can learn to be happier and more useful members of the larger community. This would seem to me to imply the observance of good manners and social decencies, together with the development of a well-trained mind. Some of today's students with their "dirty sneakers, unkempt hair, dreary folk songs of the social struggle, and semi-barbarian speech and manners" (as one critic has characterized them) convey just as false an image of the university, in my judgment, as did yesterday's stereotyped generation of contented playboys. The typical university student today is represented by neither of these images.

Fortunately for our nation as well as for higher education, the public has a very favorable image of the modern American university. It is rightly regarded, I believe, as one of the main engines of our civilization. We can keep it this way if responsibilities are kept in balance with privileges, and if everybody concerned will think about duties as well as rights. Educators and students must all remember, furthermore, that today every university is much more in the public view than it once was. Its traditional immunity from undue outside interference implies a capacity for self-regulation and self-renewal, and to protect this autonomy all of us who really care must see that its integrity is preserved, for what happens *in* our colleges and universities may be of most immediate import for trustees, administrators, teachers, and students, but what happens *to* them is an outcome in which every member of our society has a stake.

PART 5 **Stress
in
the
College
Experience**

Before the Doctor Comes: Conditions of Stress on the Campus

PHILIP SHERBURNE

THERE WAS A TIME when educators hardly concerned themselves with problems of student mental health. When they did, they handed the problems over to the psychiatrist or the dean. In most cases, they dismissed—and still dismiss—the issue by hiding the problems and their solutions within the mysteries of the student health center. The casualties, to the extent that they can be identified, are sent there to be treated as people who have problems, while the rest of the university goes about its business. The health centers and clinics are distinct little solution boxes, almost totally unrelated to those big solution boxes that encompass the rest of the college. They treat emotional disorders, but they do not make these disorders less likely in the future.

Other problems of student mental health are handled by the dean of students on the grounds that they are merely the problems of adolescents growing up and adjusting to responsibility. Again, the treatment is geared largely to the casualty student and to disorders on the campus. Mysterious theories concerning social responsibility and growing up are developed for use in the student personnel office. This solution box is integrated with the noncurricular fabric of the campus (minus the health center), but, again, it is separate from and often contradictory to the academic life of students.

From this traditional clinical and disciplinary treatment of emotional disorders, we suddenly come upon today's strange new approach of considering problems as the result of "student stress in the college experience." "Student stress" is neither a clinical term nor an evaluative one defining a disciplinary role. When we examine student stress in the college experience, we are looking for those factors which are inherent in the total college experience—academic, emotional, social—and which may cause either positive or pathological stress.

Within this more general framework, we hope to find ways to encourage "good stress" and to eliminate or to help students cope with "bad stress." To do this, we need to know something about the student's environment and what it does to him, and we need to direct ourselves toward improving that environment. In short, we need now to find ways to treat the causes as well as the resulting disorders.

Fortunately, stress is not a loaded word, so we can apply trusted values to discern "good stress" from "bad stress." Generally, I find that the least profitable stress—that which hinders development and creates emotional paralysis and destructive activity—is the kind that is sublimated or repressed. Conditions of open conflict are generally healthy, I feel, if the conflict can be approached, considered, and resolved. The same problem, if repressed, camouflaged, ignored, or otherwise mistreated, is what I would call a condition of unhealthy stress.

If this and subsequent sessions are to have any major impact, then, they ought to *open up discussion* of problems of student stress, thereby eliminating many of their ill effects. The technique of talking about problems is older than psychotherapy, but ever since the development of psychotherapy we have apparently professionalized that technique for use in remote little solution boxes. Such a pattern, if continued in our clinics and deans' offices, will, to be sure, make our sick people saner; but it will not prevent our sane people from getting sicker.

The Major Causes of Stress

When the National Conference on Student Stress was discussed in a special workshop at the National Student Association Congress in August 1965 there seemed to be overwhelming approval of this kind of open discussion and of the possible changes in campus environments that might result from such discussion. As the delegates identified the major stress points in their college experiences, the discussion, even on such short notice, proved quite informative and useful. Three wide areas of stress were defined by this student group. Primarily, they emphasized the contradiction between the standards of excellence and the actual practices of colleges and universities. Second, they were bothered by the intensity and rigidity of the academic program. And finally, there were problems of relating both to academic life and to the more impressively relevant social world around them.

The pressure for excellence has apparently been taken seriously by most students. It may well provide a partial explanation for the disappearance of Joe College. A proper appreciation of excellence assures us that its characteristics are not the sort that can be computerized. Yet the whole method of student evaluation is carried out by crude, divisible digits and the IBM machine. Although this evaluation has become increasingly crucial, the student is unwilling to respect and trust it. Among friends who know better, the whole affair is a superfluous game. I know someone who dropped out of school *because he was succeeding* and suddenly realized that he didn't believe in what he was doing. Compensation in the form of deeper, more individual evaluation is lacking, for personal contacts with faculty are minimal to nonexistent. Having to choose between the pressures for excellence and the reality of the college experience too often produces a good many emotional and academic casualties.

This gap is a strange one. Students seem willing to accept the professed values of the college, its demand for excellence, and its commitment to the search for truth. It is the practiced values that cause the problems. The student sooner or later realizes that the college is in a sense a business, that efficiency is more important than excellence, and that the search for truth must be directed by other forces. The very values that the college attempts to teach and inculcate, it undermines daily in its own operations. Further, the values of one area, the academic sphere, may clash with the practices in another, the noncurricular; for the standards of inquiry, fairness, and personal integrity are hardly uniform. There is suddenly a premium on cynicism and gamesmanship. As Erik Erikson asked in *Childhood and Society*,[1] what can one become but a cynical little game player or a neurotic character, unbending in spiteful misdirection.

Although students have apparently accepted the standards of excellence, they are nevertheless disturbed by the intensity and rigidity of their academic program. This is no contradiction; as one student said to me, "They don't give us enough time to think. The whole four years is one tense panic after another." The program allows little time for pursuing an idea to its ends, for independent study, for integrating course topics, for using knowledge. At the end of it, we can expect nervous graduates, operating *ad hoc* through each crisis, overwhelmed by a formless life, and committed to the security of mediocrity.

If the conflicts over excellence and intensity are relatively new bases for stress points in the student's college experience, the old

[1] New York: W. W. Norton & Co., 1950.

problem of adjustment must also take on new ramifications. Freshman adjustment is complicated by the continuing breakdown of the family as a social instrument and the consequent early sophistication, in one form or another, of many of our younger people. Partly for this reason, some older pressures are more demanding today.

On the one hand, the freshman is motivated by the intense social demand, once a mere family heritage, to get his degree—or to regard himself as a failure for life. Inevitably, some flunk. The social myth declares the college dropout a life-long failure. We have allowed college to become a social panacea without which there is nothing, and we calmly sit by as students break down under the pressure and forever withdraw. The student's estimate of the real value of success in college seems not to be one of our major concerns, although it is most certainly his. On the other hand, the freshman is motivated by a greater need for people and responsibility with which he can test ideas and actions. His contact with social institutions is extensive, so he is sophisticated; but it is not profitable, so he is frustrated. His distance from faculty and responsibility complicates his task and prolongs his confusion. We supply him with graduate assistants, freshman roommates, and handbooks, while he strikes out for greater contact with adults—faculty, administrators—responsibility, the real world. The student's estimate of the reality and meaning of the college experience seems also not to be one of our major concerns, although it too is central to him.

It's not only the underclassmen who face this problem of relating to both the college and real life: it may most crucially affect seniors. A striking change comes over seniors, I have found, when they face the prospect of applying their college experience to future life. Friendships alter, personalities change, loyalties dissolve: it is as if college has become a forgotten vacation. In this final test of the meaning and relevancy of the curriculum, it is suddenly obvious that the college experience has been a game with frustrating consequences.

Throughout these comments, I have referred repeatedly to the college world as against the real world, to preparation as against experience. Many have commented on the impatience of our generation, our desire to get out and act now, our need to assist in social leadership. It seems equally true that these opportunities once existed, not in college, but in jobs and in apprenticeship roles. With recent affluence and the rise in youth unemployment, formal education has been prolonged. The coincidental privileges have increased and responsibilities decreased. It may be, then, that the pressures from students for social responsibility have increased only because other avenues for this role have been disappearing. It is harder now to strike out for a responsible social role, and the difficulties have driven many to extremes. In most cases, we have relied solely upon fellow students for support. Here, then, is a set of factors resulting in stress: a true aspiration for responsibility, an increased blocking of channels, and the resulting tension-ridden development of alienated (though purposeful) student movements. This desire to be social actors has not been understood by the college, so the college experience is seldom relevant to what students want to do. If students continue to leave the campus to find for themselves some meaningful relation between their development and what they are doing, then the college will, by contrast, continue to grow less and less relevant, more and more an isolated experience.

Lessening Harmful Stress

The alienated student is likely to be the one who is sensitive to this situation. This student has one major outlet, the community, where his response to the remoteness of his environment is to bridge the gap. This individual, on the whole, can be a creative and helpful person, if only educators and leaders would accept him as such. The alienated student who withdraws and who builds his own little world away from the pervading one is our most shameful loss. His voice now, and maybe forever unless we open up to him, is reduced to a poem that howls behind closed bedroom doors.

There are other areas where students, if assisted, might reduce harmful stress. For instance, they are already doing some small bit to close the gap between practiced and professed values, but alone they only create new problems. The collegiate cocoon of Class Day, Homecoming, water fights, and similar social adhesives is disintegrating through student neglect. Excellence and serious academic commitment demand more intellectually fertile bonds. To replace the collegiate culture, however, we have little to offer. Learning is more lonely today than ever before for want of methods of making excellence a community endeavor. College presidents are to be praised for recognizing that *in loco parentis* is no longer the basis for a college community, for we are finally in agreement that such a theory assumes not the maturity but the frivolity of students. Now, students and educators must get together and build a new college community.

To lessen the stress created by the rigidity and intensity of the academic program, we might consider loosening up some structural and attitudinal limitations. Can we not, for instance, be less demanding about the four-year curriculum and minimum credit loads, more liberal about independent study and withdrawal opportunities? There is no automatic input/output ratio for excellence. Besides increasing alternatives *in* college, we might also reduce some of the pressure by providing socially acceptable alternatives *to* college. Work-study programs, leaves of absence for a year or more, and an administrative office that assists students in finding community opportunities would immensely reduce the artificial stress of a frantic, lock-step academic program.

The problem of improving social adjustment, whether for lower- or upper-classmen, relates very closely to the relationship between students and their faculty, the community, and those socially responsible roles that will help students make realistic assessments of college and of their own potentialities. Opportunities and ideals must be tested with educational and community leaders. By encouraging and providing cooperative projects and more extensive communication, the burdens of the freshman and senior years, as well as the frustrations in between, can be reduced and placed in a more critical and "copeable" perspective.

These recommendations, whatever their value, must be secondary to one general and more immediate consideration. We will always have demands and pressures in college, and we will always strive for excellence, or we would stop having colleges. But if the stresses that result must be accepted quietly, then withdrawal or conformity are our only alternatives. It is of enormous importance, then, that colleges and universities open up avenues for considering stress problems—and with that small beginning we will already have reduced their ill effects. Through planning, housing, and curriculum, we need to develop campuses that replace lonely crowds with groups of friends. We need example and partnership from faculty and administrators. If students sense that everything in the college can be understood only by professionals, then the discussion stops and you will have problems because our problems will remain. Questions of college goals and operations should be open to analysis by members of the college community, and students should be encouraged to report critically on their college experience. Finally, of course, the student health center should also be opened up to the college, so that it can point out unprofitable stress points in the campus organization. What specific improvements are to be made from these opened-up opportunities, only reason should dictate.

As a student, I would be remiss to omit students from my list of those responsible for dealing with stress. Most important is the necessity for the students to take up a perceptive self-analytical role, and to provide more helpful friendship to classmates. Educators may be under pressure to withhold us from too active an involvement, but the pressures behind us will be no less demanding. I hope, however, that students and educators can agree on at least one thing: That students face a weighty responsibility for understanding the stresses that affect them, for talking about them with others, and for seeking the ways in which academic performance and emotional growth can be productive. Such a search is in keeping with our ideals of what the college experience should be.

The
Invisible
Curriculum

BENSON R. SNYDER, M.D.

MOST DISCUSSIONS OF STRESS in the college environment center on several recurring questions. Is the stress too great? Are we causing illness in our students? Is the rebellion or the alienation neurotic? Since the decompensations that we call neurosis have their origins in the period before college, discussion between educators and psychiatrists usually move in one of two directions. One is the suggestion that increasingly rigorous selection may reduce the present incidence of illness on campus. The other approach involves an examination of the factors in the college experience precipitating breakdown and dropout. There is some risk, inherent in both lines of inquiry, that discussion will focus on those illnesses of students that interfere with their making use of the educational experience provided for them. Failure to adjust and inability to become engaged may then be seen as primarily a reflection of some emotional or cognitive disturbance in the student. The campus is regarded as the stage, not as one of the central actors in the drama.

My own clinical and research experience suggests a third, and to me compelling, alternative: the public and private drama of the interaction between the student and the college.

Let us begin by considering the nonneurotic stresses inherent in higher education today. The sum of these stresses has been described by Dean Speer at M.I.T. as making up the "invisible curriculum." Though the students perceive this "curriculum," they seldom talk about it in explicit terms with faculty or deans. On most campuses this invisible curriculum remains a private matter, talked about with roommates, alluded to in conversations at home or with the faculty. The stresses are not described in a catalogue nor openly acknowledged on the campus, though faculty and administrators often have some sensitivity to their presence. The question, then, about stress in the college experience can be recast. Does this invisible curriculum significantly influence the range of a student's response to his higher education?

The child, as he grows up, learns to distinguish between the *public*, "unclassified" information which he has about his family and that information which is restricted, private, only for the hearing of those he trusts. He may set personal limits on what he says to others about the family, because, for example, of an inner sense of shame, a fear, which even trust cannot easily overcome. He comes to know the information about his family which is public: the picture of his family that is spoken of in school and the community. Family myths, or perhaps better, shared conceptions of causality, may be challenged by his experience or by confrontation with other families or other institutions. Our concern here need not be with the fact of such dissonance between a private and a more public body of information, between a formal and an informal curriculum. It is the manner in which the individual comes to terms with, integrates, resolves, or lives with these separate views that is most crucial to our discussion of stress in the college experience.

The student comes to college with a catalogue knowledge of the campus amplified or corrected, as the case may be, by other inputs from guidance counselors, from alumni, from visits to the scene. A relevant and interesting study done recently by George Stern strongly suggests that the admitted freshmen and the trustees held an essentially similar view on at least one campus and that this view diverged significantly from the view of campus life held by the students and faculty already there. The administration's view was somewhere between the views of these two groups.

The freshman arrives and within the first week his expectations are challenged by a considerable input of less public, more informal, if not private, information. For example, not only does he find out which fraternities exclude Negro students, but also he becomes aware that very fine discriminations are made on the basis of the shoes that one wears, the cut of one's clothes and hair, the tone of one's voice. The student gets a great deal of semiprivate information on the social and psychological climate into which he has moved. There are strong pressures on the student to "swallow it," as one freshman put it. The stress here is social and psychological and it impinges on the student's inner sense of self; whether or not he puts on the external signs of a particular identity, like ready-made clothes, obviously depends on many factors. This choice represents a stress for most students; and the stresses—pressures operating toward such conformity—lie as much in the invisible as in the formal curriculum, probably even more in the former than in the latter. The unique solutions that students develop have consequences that may extend far beyond the freshman week. The quizzes and the grading in the informal, invisible curriculum are covert but compelling. The student, with all these questions unresolved, then goes to class and hears still other voices challenging him to look at his preconceptions. The cognitive stress of the classroom can and probably often should be profound, but we need to be more specific. Let me try to illustrate the range, subtlety, and complexity of stresses on the student. I ask you to look at these examples against the background of the invisible curriculum.

Item 1. The student goes to lecture and hears from his professor that the course in question is exciting. Much independent thought will be demanded. He is urged to think about the subject, reflect on what he reads, and develop the habit of skepticism. The first quiz, in the student's eyes, calls for the playback of a large number of discrete facts. The message that some students hear is that reflection or original thought is for the birds, and memorization will get the A. Some possible student responses to such dissonance include alienation, cynicism about the academic enterprise, a determination to play the academic game with shrewdness, or conformity to the task of getting grades.

Item 2. A student, who smilingly but correctly described himself as disadvantaged, went through one and one-half years at an elite university in a fog. Though highly able, he spent almost all of his time keeping, in his words, "afloat." He was terrified that his inadequacies would drown him. The courses were challenging, and his professors did genuinely encourage reflection. But he had no time, or at least felt he had no time, to do more than prepare the work for the coming day. Coming from hill country in the South, he "stole time to take in the art galleries," was excited by the symphony, hungry for all he could get of urban life. Literally, these were only small hours out of days and weeks and months devoted to schoolwork. After losing his scholarship because of a drop in grades, he went to a "third-rate school" which was, he felt, only interested in his getting a working knowledge of the field, in getting a degree. There was no request to think about the subject matter, to derive first principles. In his view, the informal curriculum demanded only attendance and cognitive servitude: he did very well academically with ease. Most important, he had time to take a job in a lab to compensate for the boredom which he felt in class. I underline the marginal time that was freed by the change in schools. It permitted him to explore a field in a manner that had not been possible before.

As an outgrowth of his job the student eventually made a change in major field. His work had involved developing a small but highly imaginative workable piece of hardware with important research implications. This experience gave him a sense of competence as well as excitement that he had not known before and freed him further from both the latent and overt curricula at his school. The moral of this account is not to plead for mediocrity or third-rate schools but to suggest that stress and pressure come in unexpected places and must be taken into account in the curriculum and in the planning of the courses, in the understanding of the impact of the total educational experience. The student did indeed feel constrained and bored in the initial period at the third-rate school, but he had the freedom which was not formally intended by the system to pursue a question and become involved. There was excitement and there were challenging questions at the first school, but there was no time to pursue them.

Students develop a variety of strategies to deal with the almost inevitable dissonance between expected present, actual present, and hoped-for future. Certain strategies, certain solutions used by students have much higher survival value in one academic setting than in another, in one academic field than in another. The institution, more than the student, sets the odds on the various strategies and coping patterns that will win. Further, the invisible curriculum may play as important a role as the formal curriculum in determining which strategies, which solutions, are maximally adaptive. It is this central observation which underlies and gives substance to my comments concerning nonneurotic stress in higher education. Those strategies having survival value for the present do not automatically serve the student well in mastering his field or developing his heart and mind. It is precisely this that challenges educators to consider the consequences of both curricula for their students.

Students who resolve the stress of dissonance by denying its existence, adjusting, fitting in with the public view of reality, may have a far more comfortable passage through college than those who hear the dissonance and try to understand it. There are a variety of paths through educational institutions. Which path is followed and with what distress or dissonance depend in part on the student's knowledge of the formal and visible as well as the invisible curriculum.

In order to judge whether a particular educational environment is stressful for a particular student, we must understand the obvious as well as the covert factors which operate on the campus to make certain information public. Certain views are shared by the whole community and certain information is held to be private or secret. I emphasize the importance of the kinds of information available in an educational institution and the factors influencing its flow because of the impact of these conditions on the student. The information characteristics of the environment are bound to have an effect on the student's cognitive horizons, on his perception of his experience, and on the actions that he considers possible for him in the face of stress. One of the aims, then, of higher education can be described as an effort to increase the student's ability to deal with dissonance, not by innocence or denial, but by honest attention to how he comes to terms with the dissonance. It is essential, however, that this be managed without the student becoming a manipulator, a cynical gamesman who scoffs at genuine commitment. His own unique and special voice must be preserved while he learns to listen to the dissonance around him.

How can an educational institution assess the stresses that we have been talking about? How is it to understand the impact of its students, its faculty, its administration on one another? I pose these questions rather than attempting to answer them.

Different colleges have different working models of what they consider students to be. On one campus they are spoken of as plants to be tended by the gardener dean. On another campus they are sometimes spoken of as a product produced by the academic machine. The image of the IBM card, to be treated gently, neither mutilated nor spindled, does not come only from students. I have said perhaps no more than that the student is an integral part of a dynamic system. His failure, his distress, his stress, is, in some measure, *our* failure, *our* distress, *our* stress.

In order that educators not deceive themselves, the role of the invisible curriculum must be acknowledged. The separation of the two curricula is arbitrary and fallacious. A dialogue between the two is overdue.

Patterns
of
Student
Stress

ALAN FRANK, M.D.

THE VIEW OF THE COLLEGE WORLD from one campus or region is likely to be not only quite distorted but also quite provincial. Rather than pretend to a knowledge of other schools, I would like to discuss what I see on my own campus, digress from there, and trust that at least some of what I say will generalize to other colleges. And rather than attempt to review the many kinds and sources of stress among students, faculty, and staff, I would like to move upstream a bit from where I usually watch the bodies float by, to scout some of the places where at least a few of them may be falling in.

One of the things that distresses students most seems to be the problem of size and its attendant patterns of management. The impersonality implicit in the need for dealing with the sheer numbers of students and our very high regard as a culture for efficiency have led to an uncomfortably close analogy between educational processes and industrial processes. There is quality testing of raw materials; punch card production control; machines to teach; quality control by examination; even a manufacturer's warranty which goes along with the finished product guaranteeing certain qualities.

In a culture which is basically "thing"-oriented, it should not be too surprising that we adopt patterns which have been successful in dealing with large numbers of items on the industrial assembly line. Social invention, after all, is a very difficult business. But I question whether our verbal emphasis on educating the individual is enough to counteract the behavioral impression that may be left that we really do expect a uniform product.

Another aspect that students frequently emphasize indirectly is the difference in values expressed by various segments of the campus and the larger community. On the one hand, there is the staff, which by and large try to emphasize the individual and his development as a human being; and on the other hand, there is the IBM registration and records system; there is the faculty adviser who, ideally, helps the student plan an individualized program; and there is the course requirement system. Additionally, there are residence hall counselors and advisers; and there are parietal rules.

The college today appears to be caught between a number of demands which conflict with each other. The tradition of education, with all that it implies of the search for truth and knowledge in a community of scholars, conflicts with demands for technical training and cultural learning requiring a somewhat different kind of community; and the increasing awareness of students' needs for assistance in growing up calls for still another community focus. The time when those who went to college either come from backgrounds with similar values and aspirations or were working hard to acquire them is past. Increasing numbers of students seem to view the college as some kind of maturational ritual, or an initiation rite leading automatically to a good job and the Good Life.

It is easy enough to dismiss this problem, as I have heard faculty do, by stating that students with such attitudes should not be in college in the first place. But they are, in increasing numbers, and supported by a culture that sees a college education in rather unscholarly, pragmatic terms. The Community of Scholars did not confer the M.R.S. or P.H.T. degrees, nor is it my impression that their educated man was expected to "work," as we understand the term. Instead, he had a profession in the traditional meaning of the word.

A number of students seem to envy those who are registered in engineering, education, medicine, nursing, or law. They feel that some students in these schools have settled the question of who and what they are going to be when they grow up without having to work for it. They recognize that some students have traded in the identity their families tried to give them for a more or less ready-made professional identity. We could make such students work harder and longer on personal maturation by adding course content which relates their subject matter to the social world in which they will practice, or we could make it a little easier on some of the other "undecided" students by removing the question about anticipated major from the college application form.

There are, in other words, many ways in which the patterns of higher education could be reviewed and revised with an eye to reducing the number of factory seconds—the human wreckage—we now turn out. Not that I am against stress, for it does seem to be an inevitable component of the human condition. Students, like people, do need to learn to cope with it, too. But some of the stresses in college, as in our culture, are not functional any longer, and may do more to hinder than to help. This is one place where the increasing knowledge of what it means to be a human being could probably be of considerable benefit.

There is another level at which one can view not only our colleges but our culture; it emphasizes a somewhat different kind of stress. I will introduce this by adding to the long list of definitions of man the somewhat overelegant one that the human organism is a data-processing machine designed to perceive and create patterns. What gets programed into this machine throughout life is handled at the organized level of patterns rather than as discrete bits of data such as historical dates and chemical melting points. From this point of view there are a number of interesting questions one can ask about what goes on in education generally. That students have always invented mnemonics may be a partial answer to the question of what happens when information is fed into a machine which is coded in a somewhat different way from the information.

The concept of pattern versus discrete data shows up clearly in another way. The student—an organized if shifting pattern, we hope —is exposed to an adviser, a residence hall director, some teachers, and, depending on his initiative, to deans, counselors, and possibly even a psychiatrist. It has been said that sometimes the best opportunity the student has for an encounter with an older "whole" person is in his contact with the dormitory maid or the night watchman—everyone else is functioning in a role, which is only a fraction of a person. It is dangerous to be a whole person because it means being vulnerable, and I rather doubt that in the students' eyes many of us are good models for what we hope they will become.

One of the more optimistic and interesting signs that has shown up in recent years is the developing interest in the patterns of what goes on between people. It cuts across the fractional lines of anthropology, psychiatry, psychology, and sociology and has relevance to them all. At the moment, I suppose the most popular concept is that described in Eric Berne's book, *Games People Play*,[1] which is a distant cousin of Stephen Potter's concept of Oneupmanship. The concept of "games" on campus appears to be potentially fruitful. Take, for instance, the game students play with administrators. It requires three players: a student, an outraged member of the community at large, and an administrator. The moves consist of an ill-timed or otherwise provocative article in the campus newspaper, an

[1] New York: Grove Press, 1964.

indignant question to the administrator in response to the article, and the administrator's attempts to get off the hook. I speak of this sequence as a game because it does seem to consist of a series of more or less stereotyped moves which are quite predictable. There are undoubtedly extensive series of games played by members of the campus community: the chances are that if we could identify some of them we might not feel quite so vulnerable as whole people. And we might be able to invent some constructive games, too.

Another interesting concept related to stress is the "double-bind." The principle involved is that in the question "When did you stop beating your wife?" and it was first elaborated in Jurgen Ruesch and Gregory Bateson's *Communication: The Social Matrix of Psychiatry*,[2] and later by Jay Haley in *Strategies of Psychotherapy*.[3] To move the principle onto the campus, I was talking to a group of high school honor students recently, and found myself needling them for being docile sheep without the creativity or initiative to do other than that which they were told and expected to do. Of course we expect them to be innovators in our eyes—they are the natives in the contemporary world whereas we are immigrants—but we usually punish them for it. Too often a student entering college is encouraged to begin to think for himself and then given poor or failing grades when his thinking doesn't match the teacher's.

Double-binds seem to be one of the previously unrecognized talents of human beings generally. One aspect of them is their relative inescapability once one is caught in them, something like the predicament of the man who has just taken a large mouthful of too hot coffee at a party: whatever he does next will be wrong. The student is told he must assume responsibility for his own behavior, but then is faced with a set of parietal rules and required attendance at classes. He is expected, and subtly told, to revolt against control as part of the process of assuming what has been described as the "burden of liberty"—but he may be suspended or expelled if he does.

One of the more enduring double-binds for students is to be found in sex. Our culture states unequivocally that sexual intercourse before or outside of marriage is forbidden. Equally unequivocally it states that sex is an instinct that cannot be controlled, especially among youth, as Kinsey's researches demonstrated. Interestingly, our Victorian grandfathers resolved the conflict by placing sex behavior outside polite society: our children insist that it is part of living and

---

[2] New York: W. W. Norton & Co., 1951.
[3] New York: Grune & Stratton, 1963.

in addition avoid some of the conflict by petting, a social invention our culture hasn't learned to deal with yet.

Faculty, staff, and administration are also caught in many such double-binds. Take the teacher who is hired to teach but is advanced for his publications. Or the administrator who would like to reward good teaching as well as publication. Then there is the dean or counselor who has been taught that discipline is incompatible with helping a student because one must be nonjudgmental to help.

I'm not going to attempt to resolve the problems I have been discussing. I'm not sure that they should or can be resolved in the usual sense of being eliminated. Some of them may be important growth experiences for students. More probably they can only be mitigated and eventually supplanted by other problems arising out of new perspectives and new understandings. Perhaps, as one social philosopher put it, we can only hope to do for our generation what our fathers did for theirs. With the increase in the rate of change which we are experiencing, this can be a formidable task in itself without our trying to reach an ideal.

It seems to me that in such perspectives on human behavior as games and double-binds, we begin to approach the human condition in terms of patterns rather than entities, and to add a new dimension. I suspect that not only will our understanding of stress and distress be improved by awareness of such pattern concepts, but that we may then be able to ameliorate some of the stress we build into adolescence and into social institutions including education, and some of the distress usually accompanying rapid social change.

Student
Ambivalence
and
Behavior

RALPH F. BERDIE

ALMOST ONE-HALF OF THE STUDENTS who enter college obtain no degree. Some obtain prior to graduation what they wish from college —knowledge, vocational skills, or a mate. Many leave college because of extrinsic conditions related to finances, health, or inadequate collegiate instruction and examination. Many more, however, leave or have trouble in college because of conditions more intrinsic to the personality, intrapsychic or interpersonal conditions influencing student behavior. These students have difficulties which both result from and engender stress.

My thesis is that the concept of stress is useful in considering the behavior of the college student and that it can influence conditions that affect his behavior provided it is employed systematically by persons in higher education professionally and scientifically prepared to deal with student behavior.

The concept, or rather the word, *stress*, can be used in the word games we all play as we find new terminology to restate our old ideas and biases. Our graveyard of outworn words in higher education is no smaller than that in any other part of our lexicon—workshop, excellence, creativity, dialogue, group dynamics, underachievement. The word "stress" as we are using it may join these other words, but while it has some viability let us examine it.

What Is "Stress"?

An engineer might discuss stress as if he were talking about something that existed. He observes an elastic body when external forces are applied to it and he infers the presence of stress on the basis of his observations of the body and the forces. Often he does not realize he is talking about a concept that helps explain the relationship between the force and the object. In the social sciences, and quite recently in education, we also have begun to reify stress. The concepts of stress and pressure, when applied to students, are useful, particu-

359

larly for purposes of communication and sometimes for purposes of delusion, but we must be careful to remember that we are talking about students reacting to and behaving in an environment consisting of other students, professors, families, newspapers, television, and computers.

Our reason for discussing stress and students is to learn more about how we can change student behavior. When we attribute student discomfort and destruction to the inevitable size of universities, the imminent authoritarianism of parents and professors, and the increasing complexity of society, we have explanations of little value. We need theoretical models that will help us understand stress and find ways to deal with it.

The model I have selected is based on the psychological phenomenon of ambivalence. Ambivalence here refers to coexisting and contrasting needs, values, attitudes, feelings, emotions, and desires. Equally effective models could be based on reinforcement theory, role theory, psychoanalytic theory, field theory, decision theory, or phenomenology; it is to be hoped that other persons will attempt to structure such models.

Ambivalence and the College Student

No human motive is pure and direct. Every desire reflects its antithesis. Every action is slowed slightly by the anchor of its opposing wish. Ambivalence is a psychological, physiological, and most necessary aspect of human life. Many ambivalences are easily tolerated and in no way disrupt behavior. Some ambivalence results in learning, creation, and invention. Other ambivalences result in indecision, discomfort, unhappiness, faulty logic, and riotous behavior. We can say that ambivalence results in stress and stress is inferred when these positive or negative behaviors are observed.

The student comes to college a bundle of ambivalences and the college does much to increase these. Many of the ambivalences which the student has are reflections of opposing, or apparently opposing, values to which he has been exposed. Our culture is one that encourages diversity of behavior and values and one that tolerates, and even stimulates, a multitude of attitudes and points of view, often in opposition. Students from earliest childhood are taught many things that in no easy sense can be reconciled to one another, and students intelligent enough to go to college frequently are the ones most bothered by these discrepancies.

What are some of the contrasting values that result in ambivalence?

Material possessions are most important, but at the same time materialism is evil.

One must respect authority, but it is quite all right to ridicule leaders.

Work is unpleasant, but at the same time one should enjoy one's job.

Society exists to advance the welfare of the individual, but the individual must sacrifice his welfare for society.

Plan ahead, but live for today.

Do what is right, but satisfy your peers.

Individuals have a need for privacy and also a need to know of the actions of others.

One must conform to the stereotypes of masculinity or femininity appropriate to one's sex, but women must be strong, independent, and self-sufficient and men must be cultured, sensitive, and affectionate.

One must base his actions on reason and intelligence, but one also must be spontaneous, feeling, and impulsive.

A culture that values decisiveness and contemplation, reason and emotion, the subjective and the objective, dependence and independence, competition and cooperation, respect and skepticism, faith and knowledge, the Puritan ethic and the Freudian ethic, is a culture more difficult to grow into than a culture that defines its values more simply and arbitrarily. Opposing values and contrasting attitudes produce stress in small children, and the years just prior to college accentuate the old stress and produce new.

Everything the college student does and believes is a potential source of stress. Many students join fraternities or sororities in spite of strong feelings that these societies are evil. Many students select one curriculum in spite of the great attractions of others. Students may associate with persons because of certain characteristics and in spite of other characteristics. The universality of ambivalence cannot be denied; the stress produced by such ambivalence during the college years has been given too little attention.

Ambivalence more specific to college stems from:

The authority of the faculty balanced with the responsibility of the student.

The universality of knowledge divided into segments of departments, credits, hours, and courses.

Knowledge for its own value in a setting of pragmatism and vocationalism.

Values of individual excellence assessed through competitive comparisons.

The disinterested scholar in a community calling for informed and impassioned action.

Contemplation and patience balanced against the need for position and decision.

Handling Ambivalence and Stress

One advantage of using the ambivalence model in considering the stress of the college student is that the work of psychologists and psychotherapists has provided suggestions about how ambivalence can be reduced and stress handled.

As a psychologist who deals almost exclusively with people, I feel ambivalent myself in talking about that other favorite subject of the psychologist, the rat. We have learned a great deal, however, about psychological conflict in its simplest form, a type of ambivalence, from research on rats, and much of this research has been modified and done on humans so we have evidence that at least some of the principles we have derived from rats apply to humans.

Producing conflict or ambivalence in rats is not difficult. When placed in the middle of an alley that has water at one end and food at the other, a rat who is both hungry and thirsty is in a state of conflict. Presumably he is ambivalent, although this particular term is not used by the more respectable animal psychologists. However, these psychologists have suggested, on the basis of their research, that simple conflict, or ambivalence, can be reduced in several ways. First, it can be reduced by manipulating needs involved in the conflict, either reducing some or increasing others until the conflict diminishes. Another method of reducing conflict is to increase or reduce incentives. A small boy may choose a soft drink over an ice cream cone, but he may choose an ice cream sundae over a soft drink. Further manipulations to reduce conflict make use of changes in time or space. When goals and needs are equal, the nearest goal usually will be the most potent.

An important means of reducing conflict with humans, and one used frequently by therapists, is dependent on the principle that when a person in a state of conflict or ambivalence understands the nature of his conflict, the stress is, or can be, reduced. The more knowledge a person has about his conflicting attitudes, values, or behaviors, the less stress he will experience. Closely related to this procedure, and perhaps dependent on it, is that of resolving conflict or reducing ambivalence by restructuring situations, values, or attitudes so that they are no longer in conflict. Many persons have resolved their ambivalences toward religion and science in this way. A whole psychology of dissonance has been based on this concept.

The rat in a maze and the college student do not have much in common, but if the phenomenon of stress that we infer in the student in any way resembles the behavioral status of the rat in a state of conflict, then our explanation may help make sense.

Implications of the Ambivalence Model for Higher Education

Accepting as fact that all students come to college under stress and assuming that some, but not all, of this stress can be explained by our ambivalence model, what are the implications for collegiate planning?

Stress resulting from ambivalence can be affected by manipulating the needs or the emotional state in which the ambivalence has its origin. The simpler physiological needs can be manipulated, and some evidence, particularly that of McClelland's studies of the need for achievement, suggests that more complex human needs also can be manipulated. We are not ready yet in higher education, and perhaps in society, for programs designed to affect needs systematically, although the success of Hitler and of modern advertising suggests great potential. In other words, it will be some time before we are able to deal with student stress by increasing or decreasing the basic needs of students.

Stress resulting from ambivalence can more promisingly be affected by manipulating the incentive or reward system related to the needs. By increasing or decreasing the reward and by adjusting the length of time between performance and reward, a conflict system can be changed. At least three types of extrinsic incentives are used in higher education—recognition, expanded privileges, and financial aids. The faculty, the administration, other students, parents, friends, and the community all provide recognition for various kinds of activities involving athletics, dramatics, course work, and student activities. Recognition includes election to honorary groups or offices, letters and medals, course grades, honor lists, financial prizes and awards, and publicity. Privileges include access to special university facilities and resources, such as libraries, seminars, special courses and student retreats, appointment to student and faculty committees, and consultation requests from faculty and administration.

No formula can determine how a college can manipulate its incentive system in order to enforce the values it wishes to predominate or to develop those behaviors most desired. Periodically and frequently each college should examine the incentives it uses and its methods of rewarding certain behaviors, and then decide to what extent the system is doing what it is supposed to do.

The ambivalence model we are using here lends itself to one most promising approach. The college can help students understand and deal with the normal stress of college and community by helping students gain increasing awareness of the conflicting values and attitudes underlying stress. This knowledge alone will not result in students' responding to stress constructively, but without this knowledge we are fairly certain that stress will be mainly destructive. What can the college do to better its information to students regarding the ambivalent world in which we live?

Many courses in a college curriculum deal with these matters. Courses in cultural anthropology, social psychology, history of civilization, comparative culture, and comparative philosophy have as their content the values with which we are concerned. Many of these courses, however, have objectives other than those of increasing students' understanding of conflicting values.

Many other courses have content that lends itself to these objectives. Courses in American history, general psychology, sociology, introductory sciences, foreign languages, English literature, and geography all provide opportunity for sensitive and well-informed instructors to make students aware of the world of ideas and attitudes in which they live.

In achieving the goal of informing students about ambivalence in their world, the content of the course is no more important than is the method of instruction. A course in American history may teach a student much about the events and behaviors of the men who made our history but give them no idea of the evolution of ideas and conflict of attitudes that resulted in our contemporary culture. Perhaps the adjectives "comparative" and "developmental" should be included more explicitly in most of the course titles in our liberal arts program.

The curriculum provides only one means for increasing the awareness of students. Cross-cultural contacts with students and faculty members from other societies provide an additional means. Fortunately, most institutions are well aware of this function; persons from other countries are on our campuses, but unfortunately their presence alone is not sufficient to produce the awareness we are seeking. Many extra-course experiences on a campus can contribute to the student's understanding. Forums accompanied by discussion, musical programs and festivals, opportunities for reading and for travel all provide students with increased understanding of the values and countervalues that pervade our society and that result in personal ambivalence. If these experiences are to serve this purpose, however, they must be designed and conducted appropriately.

Understanding the nature and history of conflicting values is only the first step in helping students deal with stress. To live effectively and with satisfaction in a complex society, a person must continually restructure those situations, values, and attitudes that are or appear to be in contradiction. A student must learn to understand why authority is essential and why authority must be feared. He must learn to understand that the dignity of the individual can be upheld only by the strength of society. He must learn to understand that compassion is not a characteristic of only one of the sexes, that strength and sweetness are not in opposition, and that courage and fear are two sides of the same coin. He must learn that all men feel both humane love and animal hatred.

Courses and extra-course experiences can provide background, information, and knowledge, but in addition the college must see that students have many and repeated opportunities to discuss and review with others their ideas and feelings. The college cannot end its responsibility when it gives to the student the magic box that contains all this information. Rather, it also must stand by the student as he stirs around the contents of the box, as he tries on first one garment and then another, as he examines the fabric of this idea and the texture of that. The college or its representative must observe the student as he reacts to these experiences, ask him questions, indicate hidden aspects, and provide support as he tries on new ideas and attitudes.

The concept of stress as delineated here is not one to be used in higher education by either the timid or the amateur. Just as the professor of history or of physics must know his subject and its methods, and have the skill to teach it, so must those responsible for the important educational task we have been discussing know students and have the skill to influence students.

Responsibility for educating students in a college is shared by many on the staff, and no one function is the monopoly of any one person. Each important function, however, must be the special concern and call for the special skills of specific qualified persons. If student stress is to be a resource in achieving our goals, then deans of students, counselors, psychiatrists, and residence advisers will have to provide leadership, consult with others in the administration and faculty, and learn and teach to others new and appropriate attitudes and methods.

If the sciences of anthropology, social psychology, psychoanalysis, and personality development and the philosophies of existentialism, phenomenology, and behaviorism have meaning, a new kind of education is needed in higher education, not to supplant what we have but rather to attempt to achieve with students the old objectives so long unobtained.

To recapitulate, I have proposed that many college students have difficulty because of intrapsychic stress that can be explained using the model of ambivalence. This ambivalence is a reflection of the diversity, complexity, and contradictions of our social attitudes. The modern college can use a variety of programs, procedures, and personnel to help the student gain understanding of conflicting values, evaluate and restructure them, and comprehend what they mean to him. Accomplishment of this high purpose requires the efforts of many in the college and, most importantly, requires leadership from persons professionally prepared to understand and deal with students and society.

PART 6   Higher
          Education
          and
          the Moral
          Revolution

The

Vanguard

of

the Dysphoric

Generation

BUELL G. GALLAGHER

MOST STUDENT GENERATIONS in American higher education have, in varying degrees of intensity, questioned or rejected the moral codes of their day. But the customary questioning, testing, prodding, exploring, and rejecting have, in this particular moment, reached a point of intensity and of generality which fully justifies the title given to this discussion: We *are* experiencing a revolution in morals on the campuses.

A decade ago, it was proper to speak of a "breakdown" in morality. Today, it is more nearly correct to speak of a "revolution."

My own student generation lived through the decade of the Coolidge prosperity and the Hoover boom, only slightly bothered over the scandals of the Harding administration and Teapot Dome, only mildly uncomfortable over the paternalism endemic on college campuses, only too satisfied with Joe College antics. Campus revolt tended to center around personal privilege rather than social issues. The hip flask was more important than racial discrimination, and the football game was more important than labor's right to organize. To my college generation, things in general looked pretty good. The war was over. The future was bright. Mankind could expect an indefinite extension of progress, upward and onward forever—and each one of us knew that he had an open future in this brave new world. Nobody had heard of Adolf Hitler. The League of Nations was still functioning. There hadn't been a serious break in the stock market since the mild depression right after the war. World peace would come through good will and disarmament. We were euphoric.

At least, we were euphoric in terms of social morality. In matters of personal morality, we were a little less sure about things. We had all the difficulties of late adolescents emerging into adulthood, with sex drives maturing and sex taboos demanding abstinence or sublimation, with campus democracy taking on the characteristics of rotten borough city politics, with honor systems and cheating constantly getting in each other's way. But the generation of the flapper and the Charleston and jazz was having a happy fling, didn't want to be bothered too much over the profundities of faculty old fogies, and delighted in inventing ways to flout or at least to circumvent the rules of the establishment. In our general euphoria, we didn't revolt —we merely enjoyed ourselves.

Then came the crash. In bewilderment, the nation noted that the men who were identified as the scoundrels of the moment—the stock-brokers who had ruined the financial strength of the nation and the speculators whose gambles had carried us all down to bankruptcy as well as the bankers who closed their doors and wiped out the life savings of widows and orphans—these who were selected as the scapegoats by the righteously indignant nation of 1930 were pre-dominantly college men. "Why hadn't college taught them any morals?"

Meanwhile, back on the campuses, a new generation of students emerged. They saw the fall of the Weimar Republic and witnessed the rise of Hitler. They shared in the struggle for the rights of labor and applauded the Wagner Act. They saw Roosevelt's first hundred days bring a nation back from the awful abyss of complete collapse and get it started on the road toward the welfare state. With the Spanish Civil War and the rising cloud of another world war on the threatening horizon, the college generation of the 1930's had a morality quite different from that of the 1920's.

Delight was now taken not so much in *evading* the prissiness and hypocrisy of the old moral codes, as in puncturing the pretensions of the euphoric order. And action, direct action, became for many the *sine qua non* of education: you hadn't been to college unless you'd been on a picket line. Where the generation of the 1920's had been euphoric, the 1930's produced the anti-euphorics. They were not always sure what they were for—but there was pretty general agreement about what they were against. They were against the tinsel and cheapness of euphoria. They were realists. Morality came to mean (*a*) espousing the correct social issues and (*b*) moving in circles of friends who shared one's rejection of old moralities and were ready to experiment with new patterns of personal life. So, the anti-euphoric generation was genuinely in revolt against the social and personal moralities of its predecessors.

Came World War II, during which whatever morality may properly be ascribed to a war situation dominated. Idealists concentrated on winning the peace which was to follow the immoral war; but the war itself tended to blot out, or at least to dwarf, all other matters of morality. All values were subordinated to the overriding dominance of the military struggle. This frame of reference was perpetuated by the Korean War; and the only difference back on the campuses was that the new crop of returning veterans brought to academic life a kind of hardness and down-to-earth practicality which intensified the learning process as veterans drove themselves to make up for lost time. In a sense, the morality of the Fast Buck was again ascendant.

Not until the late 1950's did a new morality begin to assert itself. For twenty years the campuses had been dominated by the ethics hammered out during war and depression. Now came a student generation for whom the Great Depression was something you studied in high school civics class and both world wars were things you had to pass tests about in history classes. But other things—great and vital and exciting—were happening right now. The Supreme Court said that the Constitution meant what it said; some North Carolina freshmen thought that therefore they ought to be able to buy a hamburger at the drugstore which had already sold them toothpaste; and the sit-in was invented. Freedom Riders and Freedom Marchers and lie-ins and wade-ins and sleep-ins followed, right up to the teach-ins. The civil rights struggle burst upon the horizon of the college student like the glorious sun of a great new day. He was confronted with a moral issue in which he believed it was clearly possible to know without hesitation what was right and what was wrong. All the pretentions and compromises and iffy words of the previous generations were rudely thrust aside. He had a Cause, and his morality derived from involvement in that Cause. Not to be involved was immoral.

At the same time, a profound change had come over personal morality. In matters of sex, of the use of alcohol, of academic honesty in examinations and term papers and the like, the new generation did not merely reject all former patterns. It established its own new patterns which tended to be almost the precise opposite of the patterns of the generation with which I began this story. Where the students of the 1920's were euphoric, the present generation tends to be dysphoric. Where the 1920's based a false feeling of well-being on false values and false enjoyments, the 1960's bases its standards on equally false dis-values and equally erroneous sources of displeasure, to achieve an equally false feeling of ill-being. Today we are confronted on our campuses with the vanguard of the dysphoric generation, the provisional climax having been achieved in the new pornopolitics, which has not been limited to Berkeley.

The 1960's would thus appear to have produced a student generation in which social morality is dictated by the necessities of the civil rights struggle, whereas personal morality is what is left after restraints and inhibitions have been swept away. If this curious compound of self-righteousness in social matters and determinedly deliberate experimentation in personal matters appears to pose dilemmas for the individual student who is caught between the compulsions of the new social morality and the license of the new personal immorality, perhaps the dilemmas are as real as they appear to be. Certain it is that Paul Krassner speaks for an increasing number of the present generation when he says, "I believe that existence has no meaning, and I love every minute of it."

Up until this time, most college presidents and faculties and students have accepted the words of G. K. Chesterton: "Art, like morality, consists of drawing the line someplace." The dysphoric generation claims that the acceptance of the aphorism is precisely what is wrong with the whole world. And its dysphoria is expressed in action.

College
Students
and
Moral
Values

GRAHAM B. BLAINE, JR., M.D.

I FEEL A LITTLE LIKE THE WITNESS who was asked to tell the district attorney when he had stopped beating his wife. I have been invited to discuss the college student and the moral revolution when I am not at all sure that I agree with the basic assumption that there is or has been a moral revolution. *Webster's International* defines a revolution as a "total or radical change." In the three areas which I have been asked to comment on—sex, drugs, and extremism—there is no reliable evidence to prove that there has been a total or a radical change in student attitudes or behavior over the past twenty years. Emphasis must be put on the word "reliable," for there is ample *evidence*—based on opinion and on statistics—but it is so contradictory that no reliable conclusions can be drawn.

Individuals, polled or interviewed, seem either to exaggerate what might be considered immoral aspects of their behavior or else to hide them. Their responses depend to some degree on their sex and to a much larger degree on the nature of the interview and the personality of the interviewer. Thus, in a questionnaire survey, Dr. Mervin Freedman [1] found that 22 percent of the female college seniors in his sample had experienced intercourse, whereas an informal personal poll conducted by Gloria Steinem,[2] a writer for *Esquire* magazine, found the percentage to be 58. Other studies and estimates have resulted in still different figures. In the area of sex, as well as in the area of drugs, there are not consistent statistics which determine whether or not there has been a significant behavioral change in recent years. Even if observers of today's patterns of behavior agreed with each other, there is little of value from the past to use as a base

---

[1] Freedman, "The Sexual Behavior of American College Women," *Merrill-Palmer Quarterly*, January 1965, pp. 33–48.

[2] Steinem, "The Moral Disarmament of Betty Co-Ed," *Esquire*, September 1962, p. 97.

line. Personal memory is most unreliable, particularly for those embarrassing adolescent years, and statistical studies done twenty years ago are equally as contradictory as the recent ones.

Even though we cannot prove that there has occurred a total or radical change, we do know that drugs are being used unwisely on the campus, that there are unwanted pregnancies among undergraduate students, and that extremists have been involved in riots and seriously disruptive insurrections. Whether there are more of all of these detrimental occurrences now than formerly really does not matter. We should do all we can to understand the causes of these undesirable events and be ready to use this understanding to prevent or at least to reduce their occurrence. Knowing what leads to the development of a morality which encourages students to take drugs, to be promiscuous, and to involve themselves in riotous behavior means knowing the psychological configuration of the late adolescent and the ways in which it responds to the action and attitudes of authority.

Psychologically, the late adolescent is not prepared for adult sexuality. The average college undergraduate by his nature prefers an emotional and a physical relationship with the opposite sex which is intimate and private but not one which includes intercourse. Dr. Paul Walters [3] in his excellent paper on promiscuity in adolescence puts it this way, "The sexual impulse of the adolescent seems to be . . . diffuse and unfocused and consisting of vague longings for fusion with the loved object." By this he means an emotional fusion or identification rather than a physical one. Later in the same paper he states, "Premature sexual intercourse represents a serious failure in the development of the adolescent ego."

This is not to say that some students of college age are not mature enough to be comfortable in an adult sexual relationship (the many successful undergraduate marriages are proof of this), but it does point up that it is unwise to assume that college students in general are asking for permission and facilities for enjoying sexual intercourse with each other. Two coeducational colleges to my knowledge have given their students free access to bedrooms and in both cases the students themselves have asked for restrictions to be imposed. They sensed a pressure to engage in a type of sexual activity which did not seem appropriate to them.

The deterrents to sexual intercourse which had meaning two decades ago are no longer useful as supports for traditional morality.

[3] Walters, "Promiscuity in Adolescence," *Journal of the American Orthopsychiatric Association*, July 1965.

Venereal disease is still with us, but its cure is quick and painless. Pregnancy can be prevented with certainty provided protective measures are taken. And organized religion has for many become permissive in its attitude so that hell-fire does not threaten impetuous lovers today as it did formerly. Arguing the merits of chastity with a bright modern college student is a difficult and usually a futile task.

The psychiatrist, however, has facts which college administrators and parents do not have, and it is important that these facts be shared with students if they are to face the decisions ahead of them sensibly. In addition to the fact that healthy adolescent sexuality does not usually include intercourse, there is the fact that delaying sexual gratification until marriage does not cause a degree of frustration liable to lead to psychological damage, nor can sexual experimentation before marriage be correlated with greater sexual compatibility after marriage. Psychiatrists also know that the unconscious can contribute to the initiation of an unwanted pregnancy. Without being aware of it consciously, a young man can so strongly need to prove his masculinity or a young woman her fertility that logical precautions can be "forgotten" and unfortunate consequences follow.

Much information of this sort can be transmitted by means of group discussions which include psychological as well as physiological and moral subject matter. College students today do appear to have developed a new kind of sexual morality based primarily upon fidelity rather than chastity, but their desire for straight answers and free debate with elders remains very strong and can be utilized to equip them with important information available only from discussion with professionals in the fields of psychology, medicine, and ethics.

Drugs are becoming more of a worry to administrators and this is probably because the supply is more plentiful and because use of them is less carefully hidden. The appearance of organizations such as the one to legalize marijuana has made students less ashamed of their dependence on this drug, and the publicity about the psychedelic drugs has unfortunately made some users of these substances proud that they have had what they term a "drug experience."

Some researchers have expressed doubt about there being such a thing as a drug-taking personality, but among the college population there seem to be definite characteristics which are clearly identifiable in the student who misuses drugs consistently. Many students do truly experiment only once with drugs such as marijuana or mescaline, simply on a dare; but those who routinely ingest such substances usually fall into a category best described as the inadequate personality. They feel less than whole—as though something had been left out of them when they were first born. Drugs provide a temporary respite from this feeling of relative ineffectiveness. Most of them do not prove themselves adequate by doing anything remarkable when under the influence of a drug, but they *feel* as if they *could*. They often believe that this feeling of strength and confidence will stay with them after the effect of the drug has worn off: this is one reason they continue taking it. Some of these people frantically take up one drug after another, in search of one that will permanently turn the trick, until they end up addicted to one of the narcotics. Rarely does this occur in college, but each case of this kind is a truly tragic one.

Psychological counseling is far more effective than drugs in helping people who unrealistically fear they are inadequate to cope with the social and academic aspects of college. Provision of easily available and competent counseling services helps channel students away from the inappropriate use of drugs, but control of the source of supply and education about the inherent dangers are also an essential part of any drug control program in a college or university. It must be remembered that the one-shot experimenter is not entirely safe, for the ingestion of a single dose of a psychedelic drug, such as LSD or psilocybin, can lead to crippling mental illness even in an apparently healthy student. Particular care should be taken in regard to controlling and circulating accurate information about these drugs. Student attitude toward drugs is usually rather amoral. They look upon them as dangerous—often attractively dangerous—and universities should probably deal pragmatically with their students in this area rather than morally.

Riots have always been part of the burden which students impose upon authorities in colleges, but recently these insurrections seem to have become more violent and more vindictive. It is hard to say whether this is because the civil rights movement has given to civil disobedience some degree of honor which it never had before or because the students have more justifiable causes for complaint. Clearly, however, there are an increasing number of students demonstrating their dissatisfaction in a destructive manner. In a number of cases administrative actions seem to have been responsible for the riots themselves or for increasing the extent and the degree of their violence. Students expect authority to react to their rebellion but to react in a strong and unflustered manner and not to cave in no matter how strong the provocation. Dr. Carl Binger tells a story which epitomizes neatly this ambivalent student attitude. During a riot in

Harvard Square in the early days of this century, an elderly Cantabrigian emerged from the subway on his way home from his office in Boston. He was amazed at the furor he found in the Square and asked a disheveled student who was rushing by what was going on. "We are rioting, Sir," was the reply.

Student riots need a climate, a cause, and a trigger to become matters of serious consequence. In the case of the 1964–65 unpleasantness at Berkeley, the rapidly expanding university with its consequent disproportion between students and competent faculty, counselors and advisers provided an explosive climate while the strong desire on the students' part to cooperate in the civil rights movement served as a cause. The unexpected announcement of an arbitrary administrative change in policy became the trigger. Student reaction was in turn reacted to in a vacillating fashion. People in authority at different levels were at odds with each other. This both delighted and disappointed the students and was largely responsible for increasing the intensity of their rebellion.

A willingness to discuss matters of policy with students, combined with the reservation of the right to make, hold to, and enforce the ultimate decision regardless of student agreement with it, is usually the wisest administrative policy. This was demonstrated at Brandeis in 1963–64 when the students threatened mass resignations over an open-door policy put into effect during women's visiting hours in the men's dormitories. The president of the university, on the one hand, stated that he would accept any and all resignations, and, on the other, agreed to let a representative student group present their views on the policy to the board of trustees. Here, firmness combined with respect for student opinion probably averted a crisis of serious proportions.

Student mores may have changed a little over recent years. Existentialism and the emphasis on science and technology have brought self-centeredness and cold logic into the ethical thinking of today's young adults in place of the more emotional and spiritual absolute values of the Victorian era. But for all their arrogance and defiance, these are the most intelligent and the healthiest group of college students there has ever been. Each young generation seems to need to feel that they are different. They want to forge their own moral values out of their own experience and shaped by their own inherited but unique environment. It is too early to tell whether the present morality is better or worse than previous ones. It is up to the young to prove its worth and up to educators to give them room to do so but also protect them from unnecessary harm. Not an easy task.

Higher
Education
and
Moral
Responsibility

W. CLARKE WESCOE, M.D.

HIGHER EDUCATION AND THE MORAL REVOLUTION is a broad title for discussion. It is essentially noncommittal: It does not imply, certainly, cause and effect (perhaps it should); it implies at the least a reactivity; it implies at best an involvement.

Moral revolution indicates an unsteady state, perhaps more unsteady than I am willing to acknowledge in the area of morals. The unsteady state is different from that with which I, as a biologist and physician, was concerned. My training leads me to a concern for homeostasis, a compensation, a continuing search for balance. If, however, one enlarges, as I choose to, the term "moral" to include spiritual values and idealism, and accepts Max Lerner's second sense of "revolution"—a drastic, highly accelerated pace of change, one is in a position at least to comment on student attitudes and institutional involvement.

The New Idealism

No one, I suspect, would deny that we see today, certainly more than we did a decade ago, the idealism of youth dramatically at work at home and abroad. The Peace Corps volunteers, the Vista volunteers, the participants in various educational programs directed toward the underprivileged, the participants in the movements related to civil rights, all in their own way demonstrate idealism profitably and effectively channeled. There is a spiritual connotation to this involvement, one that may well be called a spiritual awakening. This involvement, this expression of concern, this willingness to work for the betterment of others in an altruistic fashion is praiseworthy. In my relatively brief personal experience of fifteen years as a college administrative officer and in my review of educational history, I can find no other period of such dramatic achievement. One hopes, of course, that institutions, their faculties and staffs, played more than a passive role in this awakening and will continue to do so. This is educational fulfillment at its best—a continual challenge to the intellect and a continual stimulus to the spirit.

My own contacts with students, and they are many and diverse, lead me to the conclusion that the vast majority of them are deeply concerned with moral values and have high standards of personal conduct. Our campus religious organizations are strong, their membership large. I see about me everywhere a concern for moral and spiritual values, a deep concern even if there is a certain skepticism about accepted norms. Unfortunately, these concerns are not nearly as well publicized as are other occurrences which verge on the aberrational. Our communications media tend to deal more with the latter and the public consequently becomes preoccupied with them.

The Aberrational in Student Behavior

In respect to the aberrational, I must speak primarily in my role of physician. I do not wish to simplify a complex situation, but some simplification is necessary. As educational institutions, we are concerned with individuals who wish to be considered mature (and some of them are) but who are still struggling through the period of late adolescence. For the young woman, the sham of maturity can be assumed by sophisticated clothes, haute couture, and a worldly attitude toward social and interpersonal relations. For the young man, the sham of maturity can be assumed by stressing overgrowth of one characteristic of the male—facial hair—and by a casual attitude toward alcohol and sex. (I should add that I cannot simplify the situation relative to the overgrowth of the scalp hair for the issue is quite clear, and here I speak with emphasis, that an abundance of that covering in no way bespeaks either maturity or virility; here there must be involved some Freudian mechanism—and for that I defer to my psychiatrist colleagues.)

No longer children, not quite adult, college students are tempted to experiment with many things. Further, they live in an environment where experimentation is the rule. Who, then, can be surprised if experimentation occurs? And occurs at times with less than adequate controls?

The aberrational aspects are primarily connected with alcohol, relationships with the opposite sex, and, in a minority of circumstances, extremism of various kinds. In this area, I seriously question, although my research is limited and my experience brief, that we are experiencing a revolution. My most convenient visual research source is the college yearbook; my most convenient social science research source is the older staff. I find no real evidence of a dramatic change. There may be more frankness but there is, I believe, no tremendous change in the group with which I have my greatest experience. In this regard, I recall the words of a distinguished Indian physician at the First World Conference on Medical Education: "Gentlemen," he said, approximately, "it occurs to me that what we are discussing is ourselves when young." A recent issue of *American Heritage* contains a great deal on this subject: The campus of the thirties, although less well populated, was not entirely different from the campus of today.

In a simplified scheme of things (and I am annoyed by attempts at oversimplication), higher education and the institutions which represent it have the responsibility to enhance the moral and spiritual values of the student, and to control, and perhaps even to eradicate, the aberrations, after they have been carefully defined. I know of no better way to achieve these ends than that exemplified in medical education. In a very large sense, even today in a highly scientific age, medicine is taught by precept. The teacher is a model for his student, someone to be emulated. The young physician is rare who does not, consciously or otherwise, pattern himself after a preceptor. Perhaps the scheme is too simplified, perhaps the success of medicine is dependent upon its dealings with a more mature individual possessed of a professional commitment, but precept still appears to be an ideal way of teaching values as distinct from facts.

The greatest thrill of the medical educator is the opportunity to work with the idealistic. In medicine, idealism finds expression easily and is universally applauded. In other educational fields idealism finds expression not quite so easily—expressed by some, it is likely to be looked upon by others as corny; to some, it may appear radicalism. In these fields we have a more difficult synthesis to achieve, but just as thrilling an experience.

The Four R's of Higher Education

Let me conclude by enumerating briefly the "four R's" substantive in medical education, applicable as well to every type of educational program involved with moral activity.

The first is *responsibility*. Responsibility, the medical student learns early, is an individual matter. No committee, no group, no number of consultants can accept it. The physician is solely responsible for his patient. The physician individually is responsible for all his own actions. The acceptance of individual responsibility is essential to an ordered society.

Responsibility in itself implies freedom—freedom to act, freedom to choose. Associated with a physician's responsibility is the quest for the steady state—that which we call well-being or health. Physical unrest is damaging. Thus also socially, unrest for the sake of unrest is damaging; progress is not necessarily related to unrest. Ferment is fine, to be expected, even demanded in higher education, but uncontrolled ferment (as any brewmaster or cheese-maker can tell us) is fruitless—even destructive.

The second is *respect*. The respect here is for one's colleagues and their opinions, as well as for the human organism.

The third is *reason*, perhaps better called reasoned judgment. The hallmark of the compleat physician, transcendent of diagnostic skill or manual dexterity, is the possession of reasoned judgment, the ability to know when a problem is within or outside one's own competence.

The fourth is *rectitude*. There is no place in medicine for the morally corrupt, the ethically borderline. The ancient oath—explicit relative to drugs, to continence, to sexual relations—is a constant reminder of the necessity to be not self-righteous but upright in all one's dealings. An institution must be concerned, I believe, with the moral soundness as well as the intellectual roundness of its members. An institution need not be concerned with rigid, fixed moral standards, but it does need be concerned lest established morality be lightly discarded without question or search.

The
Ecumenical
World
of
Search

SISTER JACQUELINE GRENNAN

I HAVE BEEN ASKED TO DISCUSS Higher Education and the Moral Revolution. I am grateful that the title refers to a moral revolution rather than a revolution in morality. I am convinced that the seemingly chaotic state of things dramatized but not contained by the campuses of Berkeley and St. John's may, indeed, say much to those of us with eyes to see and ears to hear and hearts to care.

Today's academics—young or old—have emerged from a culture which often identified morality with moral codes and expected behavior patterns. Each church group, each academic community had its own group-determined grading system for group-determined answers to group-determined exam questions. Morality was largely an expository codification much like a driver's manual in a given state. We had to learn the rules—and how to break them with impunity—in Michigan and Missouri, in New Mexico and New York. We took verbal tests on the manuals in ethics classes and action tests on the manuals under supervision. We violated specific tenets in personal situations, sometimes with guilt, sometimes with rationalization, sometimes with conviction.

But it seldom occurred to us to question the manuals for their inclusions or exclusions. We learned to live within the system or systems. Sometimes we compromised the system here and there, and no one bothered too much if our compromise didn't alter the basic system too much. Sometimes we compromised ourselves by accommodating to the system and its behavior demands. But most of us lived within fairly closed societies and the behavior demands of any one closed society are, I submit, fairly predictable. Mine were the demands of a parochial Roman Catholic environment; others experienced the demands of a parochial Bible Belt fundamentalism, of a Jewish ghettoism, or of a smug atheistic intellectualism. What-

381

ever our closed systems, they provided for us a degree of comforting support. Objective moral codes must be learned and basically adhered to, but they need not—indeed, perhaps must not—be personally made.

I submit that the moral revolution we are witnessing on our campuses today is, indeed, calling the codes into question and rightly so. In my own subsystem students are not only "violating" some of the carefully calibrated norms of morality-behavior with guilt or rationalization, but they are also calling into question the validity of many of the tenets themselves. The present soul-struggle of my Church today in re-examining its stand on birth control is motivated much more, I believe, by the responsible skepticism of the Church's own members than by the pressure of the Rockefeller Foundation concerning overpopulation. I am sure that some of the fundamentalist groups have long been meeting the same responsible skepticism over drinking and dancing and cards. I am sure, too, both from the rush of articles in popular magazines and from common sense, that more sophisticated religious groups and sophisticated student personnel officers are meeting responsible skepticism over any fixed and given propriety in sex relations and in marriage laws that attempt to cover all possible situations with a single prescription or proscription.

At this point, I am obviously vulnerable to the charge that much of skepticism, on both the theoretical and pragmatic levels, may be totally or largely irresponsible, that human beings always have and always will use rationalization to cover their own license and weakness. I accept the charge even before it is made. At the same time, I suggest that our challenge at this moment in time is to accept the skepticism, to encourage it, to nourish it, even to share in it. It is difficult to encourage or demand responsibility for an area of action which we have forbidden or discouraged or ignored. Inasmuch as we as academics, as religious people, as concerned humanists, admit the need for responsible skepticism in every human area and, therefore, in every moral area, we will begin to give our junior colleagues whom we call students the responsibility of freedom. Only if a man is allowed to frame his own question can he be really responsible for his own answer. Only if your students are *encouraged* to frame even more relevant and profound questions can they be really responsible for relevant and profound answers.

I have said that the moral revolution on our campuses today is, indeed, calling the code-prescriptions into question and rightly so. The most encouraging phenomenon of the questioning is its preoccupation with the "sins" of omission rather than the "sins" of commission of the codes. The Puritan-Jansenist codes had much to say about sex and sobriety but precious little to say about the human rights of minorities and the force of passive resistance. The Puritan-Jansenist codes had much to say about responsible behavior but precious little to say about responsible skepticism of the compromise which society has made at any given time on any given social issue. The comparative closure in which we lived even in the pluralistic society that is America made it comparatively easy, I believe, for the codes of each of the closed systems to endure.

Today, however, we in middle age and our students in the blessed and productive naïveté of youth live in what I have been calling the ecumenical world of search. Transportation and communication have potentially at least destroyed the ghettos of nationalism. The open and instant press has potentially at least destroyed the ghettos of religious thought and reopened the channels of religious thinking or contemplation. The system of higher education beginning to open itself to all socioeconomic, national, religious, racial groups will experience with growing intensity the stimulation and disorder of this ecumenical searching. The social and philosophical and religious and moral systems will be subject to the personal pressure and cross-pressure of persons interacting in an open society. Students in such an open society within a college or university are not likely to allow the college or university to remain segregated from the real issues of Viet Nam and Vatican II, of Watts and India. For the world of open communications reaches into the ivory tower and the fraternity house and asks the ivory tower and the fraternity house to respond to the real world.

Teilhard de Chardin, the Jesuit paleontologist who died in 1957, wrote:

> I maintain that it is possible, by following this road, to find substantial reasons for belief in Progress.
>
> The world of human thought today presents a very remarkable spectacle, if we choose to take note of it. Joined in an inexplicable unifying movement men who are utterly opposed in education and in faith find themselves brought together, intermingled, in their common passion for a double truth; namely, that there exists a physical Unity of beings, and that they themselves are living and active parts of it. It is as though a new and formidable mountain chain had arisen in the landscape of the soul, causing ancient categories to be reshuffled and uniting higgledy-piggledy on every slope the friends and enemies of yesterday: on one side the inflexible and sterile vision of a Universe composed of unalterable, juxtaposed

parts, and on the other side the ardour, the faith, the contagion of a living truth emerging from all action and exercise of will. Here we have a group of men joined simply by the weight of the past and their resolve to defend it; there a gathering of neophytes confident of their truth and strong in their mutual understanding, which they feel to be final and complete.[1]

It is "the ardour, the faith, the contagion of a living truth emerging from all actions and exercise of will" that can produce, I believe, the social, moral, intellectual evolutionary breakthrough that modern man needs and must have. Only persons who are responsible skeptics and responsible decision-makers can effect such a breakthrough. Middle-aged academics are part of one culture involved in producing another: part of a culture of two world wars trying to produce world peace; part of a racist, segregated society trying to produce integration; part of a ruggedly individualistic capitalism trying to produce personal responsibility and social concern; part of a moralistic religious society trying to allow the morality of empathy and compassion.

Perhaps the only honest and productive thing we can do is to join with our students in the ecumenical world of search in producing the new worlds of our own academic institutions and of our society at large. I cannot afford to question the institution that is my college without the insights of my students. Neither can I afford to question my world at large without their blessed naïveté. I can encourage them and myself to examine and re-examine every tenet of the present codes lest our skepticism be irresponsible and superficial. If I merit their trust by the honesty of my own scrutiny in its rigor and its freedom, we shall become co-searchers and co-makers of the society which one day you and I must leave to them, that they may continue the search and the making with their children not yet conceived.

[1] Chardin, *The Future of Man*, translated by Norman Denny (New York: Harper & Row, 1964), p. 20.

The Time of the Student: Shall We Overcome?

JOSEPH F. KAUFFMAN

SINCE THE BEGINNING of the so-called Berkeley police action (a term used to describe *de facto* wars that are not formally declared) students everywhere have been inspired to revolt—or as James Reston put it, "instead of chasing girls, the boys are now chasing college presidents." The vigor of the revolt has been such that one can perceive a real fear of students on the part of otherwise strong, confident adults. I am reminded of the neat phrase Dr. Fritz Redl used in a presidential address to the American Orthopsychiatric Association back in 1962—that in America, we have "a love of kids, the neglect of children, and a hatred of youth."

A recent study of the college and university admissions officer conducted by the Bureau of Applied Social Research at Columbia University (and commissioned by the College Entrance Examination Board) showed two findings that guide me in my remarks. The first finding is that "The admissions officer fills a power vacuum that exists between the administration and the faculty."[1] Perhaps of even more relevance is the second finding: "with the numerous responsibilities weighing on him, and with the lack of definition of his role, the admissions officer is nevertheless quite autonomous in his functions and experiences *considerable satisfaction* in his job performance"[2] (emphasis mine).

What is at stake in the growing restlessness and discontent (I would even call it fantastic unrest) evident in our colleges and universities greatly concerns our society and may affect our whole way of life; that issue is the threat to the integrity of higher education itself.

[1] Jane Z. Hauser and Paul F. Lazarsfeld, "The Admissions Officer: Fulcrum for Academic Leadership," *Journal of the Association of College Admissions Counselors,* Fall 1964, p. 4.

[2] *Ibid,* p. 6.

The unrest doesn't start in the university—it is all around us—in our homes, community, nation, and world. And the unrest may turn out to be a powerful force for good, but not unless we respond and join with it to pursue the ultimate values and goals of our institutions of higher education. For we could, by sitting on the sidelines, by remaining aloof, out of touch with it, usher in an era which is best described by W. B. Yeats: "Things fall apart—the center cannot hold/Mere anarchy is loosed upon the world/The blood-dimmed tide is loosed and everywhere/The ceremony of innocence is drowned/The best lack all conviction while the worst/Are full of passionate intensity." [3]

What are the issues with which our restless youth concern themselves (and which some people tend to think are external to the university)? They certainly include world peace, the ethical questions of international involvement, racial justice, conquering poverty, disease, and ignorance, improving our society, and more. (It is my own opinion that John F. Kennedy inspired many of our young people to believe that, as individuals, and as a society, we can do better and a good many are acting upon that belief.)

When you think about it, the messages sent forth by our leaders in higher education are really quite inarticulate and often irrelevant when you compare them to those of a President of the United States of America who can determinedly and publicly declare on national television, "We shall overcome!" Would that we could explain our purposes in higher education and try for a similar response. Or listen to President Johnson's words in an address to students at the University of Kentucky in February 1965: "If you wish a sheltered or uneventful life, then you are living in the wrong generation. No one can promise you calm, or ease, or undisturbed comfort. But we can promise you this. We can promise enormous challenge and arduous struggle, hard labor, and great danger. And with them we can promise you finally, triumph over all the enemies of mankind."

We should know that youth responds to that which is grand and noble in purpose. Aristotle, that great psychologist, tells us that youth "would always rather do noble deeds than useful ones: their lives are regulated more by moral feeling than by reasoning; and whereas reasoning leads us to choose what is useful, moral goodness leads us to choose what is noble."

We know that the social service ethic is increasingly embraced by our best youth, that service in the Peace Corps, tutoring children in

[3] W. B. Yeats, "The Second Coming."

urban ghettoes, volunteer work with migrant workers, the aged, the mentally ill, have evoked responses from students which should fill us with pride. Instead, it seems to confuse us. And, indeed, some do ask, "If more and more young people want to go to college because they know it will increase their lifetime earnings and enhance their employability, how come so many students want to nose into all these extraneous, unprofitable areas?" It is confusing! But while it's confusing it is also understandable.

Erik Erikson, distinguished psychoanalyst, tells us that there is a certain strength in the age of youth which he calls a sense of and capacity for fidelity. He states:

> The evidence in young lives of the search for something and somebody to be true to is seen in a variety of pursuits more or less sanctioned by society. It is often hidden in a bewildering combination of shifting devotion and sudden perversity, sometimes more devotedly perverse, sometimes more perversely devoted. Yet in all youth's seeming shiftiness, a seeking after some durability in change can be detected, whether in the accuracy of scientific and technical method or in the sincerity of conviction; in the veracity of historical and fictional accounts or in the fairness of the rules of the game; in the authenticity of artistic production or in the genuineness of personality and the reliability of commitments. This search is easily misunderstood, and often it is only dimly perceived by the individual himself, because youth, always set to grasp both diversity in principle and principle in diversity, must often test extremes before settling on a considered course.[4]

What are students complaining about and, perhaps even more interesting, what are parents and the mass media reporting as the significant or valid gripes about higher education? A major complaint is that our colleges and universities have become bureaucratic and impersonal. Specialization is carried to an extreme. They are run like industries or corporations. It's difficult to make a personal or human connection. This problem exists in both small and large institutions. Here's a description of Berkeley written for publication by two of its professors:

> At Berkeley, the educational environment of the undergraduate is bleak. He is confronted throughout his entire first two years with the indifferent advising, endless bureaucratic routines, gigantic lecture courses, and a deadening succession of textbook assignments, and bluebook examinations testing his grasp of bits and pieces of knowledge. All too often, the difference between the last two years

[4] Erikson, *Youth: Change and Challenge* (New York: Basic Books, 1963), p. 3.

of a student's education and the first two is chronological rather than qualitative. *It is possible to take a B.A. at Berkeley and never talk with a professor.* To many of the students, the whole system seems *a perversion of an educational* community into a *factory designed* for the mass processing of men into machines.[5]

But listen to this about a smaller institution: The Subcommittee to Study Student Life at Amherst College, said in its Report to the Committee on Educational Policy:

> The false hopes generated by this stereotype [of college as a large, happy family] begin to do their damage as soon as the incoming freshman discovers how little of the intimate small college atmosphere actually exists. Of course he is disappointed and frustrated. He feels cheated, and if he consoles himself with the thought that he and his teachers will become closer friends later on, when he is an upperclassman, he will feel even more cheated as a senior, when he discovers how few (if any) faculty members know him well enough to write a convincing letter of recommendation.[6]

We can list lots of other problems or gripes: poor faculty advising, rigid or irrelevant curriculum, ineffective or reluctant teaching, the impossibility of dealing with some of the burning issues of our day because they don't "belong" in a particular discipline or department, and perhaps most important, a general unresponsiveness of colleges and universities to the "mood" of today's students.

I think students have a right to test us, to probe and size us up. What they are really asking is, "What do you stand for?" and they deserve a response, in our behavior if not in our words. What we have on the campuses of our colleges and universities today is "a crisis of values." For we have, in actuality, an exploitation of the dignity and prestige of higher education for the worst kind of selfish and opportunistic ends. John Gardner has called for the formulation, by faculty, of ethical standards to curb the "crassest opportunism in grantsmanship, job-hopping, and wheeling-dealing." Gardner describes this phenomenon, all too obvious to students, in these words:

> There is a whole generation of able young faculty members who never knew a time when affluence did not prevail. Thus it is hardly surprising that a few of them exhibit an opportunism that startles

[5] S. S. Wolin and J. H. Schaar, Article on Berkeley, *New York Review of Books,* March 11, 1965.
[6] *Amherst Alumni News,* Special Issue, Winter 1965, p. 19. Amherst has plans to expand to 1,200 by 1970.

their elders. Some of these heavily-bid-for young people appear to
have no sense of institutional loyalty whatever and simply follow
the offers where they lead. They regard the agencies that provide
the research grants as their real sources of nourishment. Whether they
correspond with the National Science Foundation from Stanford,
Michigan, or MIT really doesn't matter very much. *In their view,
students are just impediments* in the headlong search for more and
better grants, fatter fees, higher salaries, higher rank. Needless to
say, such faculty members do not provide the healthiest models for
graduate students thinking of teaching as a career.[7] [Emphasis
mine]

I think we need more than a statement of ethical standards to respond to the problems and pressures that beset us. Above all, I think
we need to articulate and demonstrate to our students, as well as ourselves, the honorable and noble purposes for which our colleges and
universities stand. We need to rededicate ourselves to the essential
truth, beauty, and utility which the very idea of a university per-
sonifies. For it is the very fiber of the foundation of higher education
that it will serve to enhance the human spirit, promote individual
dignity, and defend the freedom of human conscience from all its de-
tractors. No social institution created by man has a purpose more
noble than the university.

Yet we live in an era when this noble enterprise is termed the
"knowledge industry," when our greatest institutions are termed
"computerized multiversities," when too many faculty are referred to
as "entrepreneurs," deans as "cops," registrars and admissions officers as "petty bureaucrats"—and I have even noted the reference to
counseling as a "rat fink" operation.[8]

All right—this is unfair, overdrawn and perhaps even ridiculous.
But there's some truth in the implication—enough to make one
angry. And when some student rebellions spill over into attacks on
the very integrity of the concept of the university, then I submit
that we have failed to demonstrate what the idea of a university is
about. In the seller's market that exists in higher education, we
have taken for granted that everyone knew its intrinsic value to the
individual and particularly to society.

We shall overcome only when students perceive that the noble
purposes of the university are believed by us, that we believe them

[7] Gardner, *The Flight From Teaching* (New York: Carnegie Foundation for
the Advancement of Teaching, 1964), p. 12.

[8] See Elton B. McNeil, "Is Counseling a Rat Fink Operation?" *Psychology in
the Schools,* January 1965, p. 24.

worth our commitment, dedication, and involvement. Only then will they get the message.

The search for truth, the promotion of untrammeled inquiry, the protection and cultivation of the human conscience and the human spirit are the real values of the university, noble enough for any emboldened youth and, yes, worth giving one's life for.

All of us in higher education have good reason to be proud of the magnificent response of our colleges and universities to the needs of our government, in research for defense, for the conquering of disease, in overseas services, and in training soldiers or Peace Corps volunteers. Equally impressive has been the response to the need for large-scale expansion of facilities and faculties to meet the tidal wave of students that is upon us. From slightly over 1 million students enrolled in 1940 we reached 5 million in 1965 and expect as many as 10 million within the next decade. No other nation will have made a greater effort for the higher education of its youth.

Now would it not be a great tragedy if, after we have achieved this miracle of accomplishment, we were to discover that a substantial portion of these students didn't even care? That they had gone through the "system" never perceiving its noble purpose; never letting its intrinsic ideals touch their own lives; and never knowing we cared about such things? This is the appalling danger that faces higher education in the time of the student.

AMERICAN COUNCIL ON EDUCATION

LOGAN WILSON, *President*

The American Council on Education, founded in 1918, is a *council* of educational organizations and institutions. Its purpose is to advance education and educational methods through comprehensive voluntary and cooperative action on the part of American educational associations, organizations, and institutions.